THE STREET RODDER'S HANDBOOK

A Step-by-Step Guide On How To Build A Show-Winning Street Rod

Frank Oddo

HPBOOKS

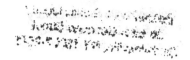

HPBooks
are published by
The Berkley Publishing Group
A division of Penguin Group (US)
375 Hudson Street
New York, New York 10014

First edition: November 2003
ISBN: 1-55788-409-9

AUG 1 2 2005

10 9 8 7 6 5 4 3 2 1

This book has been catalogued with the Library of Congress

Book design and production by Michael Lutfy
Cover photo Frank Oddo
Cover design by Bird Studios
Interior photos and illustrations by the author unless otherwise noted

TABLE OF CONTENTS

Nobody ever built a street rod completely by himself, nor did I write this book by myself. I started down the path in New Orleans over 50 years ago with two lifelong pals, Robert Rider and the late Lionel Duhon. Before and after I migrated to the West Coast in 1960, Val Pitre, Emmett Becnel, Boogie Scott, Dick Hendrix, Bob Beatty, Bruce Geisler, Terry Berzenye, John Hesford, the late Jack Garrison and a supporting cast too numerous to name kept me interested in street rodding.

I also owe a great deal to all the guys I've known—and wish I'd known—from the Southern California Timing Association, who put this game on the map in the first place. Thanks for the help.

THE COVER CAR:
BOOGIE AND JUDY SCOTT'S
BIG LEAGUE BLUE STREET ROADSTER

Charles "Boogie" Scott of Covington, Louisiana, a nationally known, NHRA-certified, drag chassis builder since the early 1960s, has also owned his share of street rods over the years. To say that his roadster is the latest and greatest is an understatement. A close inspection will soon confirm that it is not a kit car—Boogie designed, fabricated and/or modified the chassis, suspension and nearly all components!

Let's start with the rolling chassis—the side rails were built from 2 x 4 x 0.120-inch steel tubing, and the crossmembers from 1 1/2 and 2-inch square tubing. The front suspension incorporates 1952 Chevy spindles modified to accept Vega lower ball joints, top and bottom, control arms built from 1 x 0.156-inch round tubing, Aldan coil-over-shocks, JFZ Corvette rotors and single piston calipers mounted on aluminum brackets machined by Boogie.

The steering is a modified Datsun 240Z rack-and-pinion with Pinto tie-rod ends. Boogie first built the aluminum steering column, then ran the steering shaft and U-joints inside the classis tubing. The stainless steel brake lines and gas line as well as the battery cable and wiring are also run through the frame tubing!

No follower of the pack, the rearend in Boogie's roadster originally came from a 1978 Camaro, but is modified to accept Ford 28-spline axles and Ford drum brakes. The rear suspension is of the triangulated 4-link design and built from 1 x 0.156-inch round tubing with rubber-bushed rod ends and Aldan coil-overs.

When it was time for the body, Boogie chose a Speedway Motors 1927 Ford roadster fiberglass replica with a track nose. It was originally a one-piece body without opening doors or functional deck. Boogie, whose life is a "do-it-yourself" saga, drove up to Nebraska, selected the body, tied it down to his pickup and drove back home. He then proceeded to cut out the doors and deck lid, fabricate jams and install hidden hinges and electric door latches with remote openers.

Boogie hand-formed the aluminum hood, side panels, frame covers, Deuce-style dashboard, firewall, transmission tunnel, shift and hand brake consoles, rolled rear pan and windshield post and steel floor pan. He also built the hood hinges, electric hood latches, brake and gas pedals and polished stainless steel grille.

He then sprayed the car (appropriately) Big League Blue.

No, he didn't cast the engine block! It is a 4-bolt main 1994 Chevy short capped with aluminum Corvette heads and manifold and an Edelbrock 600 CFM carb. He next installed a Comp Cams roller stick and valve train, and in his spare time (no kidding) built the aluminum valve covers, air cleaner housing, oil pan, transmission pan, converter cover, radiator hoses, hose clamps, filler neck, upper and lower tanks . . . and coil and alternator brackets.

OK, Boogie didn't do it all. Engine machine work was farmed out to Don Dufour of Darr Engine/Simplex Motor Parts; the radiator was finished by Stu Henry of A-1 Radiators; the Chevy Powerglide was refurbished by Ken Perrilloux. Butch Bryant did the upholstery, Epco did the chrome plating, and Joe "Kar-2-Lo" laid on the striping. All providers are from the New Orleans/Covington metropolitan area.

The decision to build a street rod is usually the result of many stimuli—the ownership of a street rod by some admired acquaintance, street rod activity in one's community, or the casual reading of street rod periodicals. Although the interest almost always comes before the car, the neophyte builder will probably have a certain car in mind. Most of us tend to become enchanted by some idealized version of a particular make and model. It doesn't matter that the specifics change many times before the daydream becomes reality.

There was a need for an in-depth, organized overview of the major aspects of street rod building back in the mid-1980s when the first edition of this book was published. Even though millions of words on the subject had seen print since *Throttle Magazine* started the ball rolling back in 1941, most of the material was in the form of one- to four-page articles, few of which were ever collected in a single volume.

Although the contents of this book reflect my judgments and opinions about subjects most vital to the street rodder, my opinions, despite being as prejudiced as those of anyone else, are based on experience. I have been an active participant in street rodding for a number of years. During that time, I've seen many more street rods started than were ever finished. It's my goal in the revised chapters that follow to lay the groundwork that will prevent your dream from becoming a nightmare.

If you just want a good idea of what street rod building is about, this book will give you an insight as to how vintage cars are modified and reproduction cars are built from scratch. If you've already committed yourself and bought the makings of a street rod, this book will guide you along the way, and suggest what to do next.

No handbook can cover every old car or late model motor and drivetrain combination the fertile mind of the typical newcomer to street rodding can conjure up, however. What I have tried to do is to reduce many difficult choices to a reasonable—and affordable—few. What it won't do is eliminate the need to think creatively. That is the essence of this hobby.

Finally, as we go step-by-step through the potentially confusing process of merging a vintage or replica car with a garage full of late-model automotive parts and aftermarket street rod components into a safe, reliable, unique mode of transportation and personal expression, it is my fondest hope that you will enjoy yourself.

—*Frank Oddo, November 2003*

Dedicated to Lionel J. Duhon, 1934–2002.
A street rodding buddy for fifty years.

From Whence We Came

1

Muroc Dry Lake, June 15, 1941. A quartet of roadster racers gather for a "photo op" at the close of the meet. Pictured are Don Baxter, John Riley, Eldon Snapp and Randy Shinn, members of the SCTA Road Runners, a club still very much active in dry lakes and Bonneville racing.

It is widely held that motorsports began in France with the first organized race—from Paris to Rouen—in 1894. Although the interest and excitement spread quickly to the rest of the world, auto racing was largely a pursuit of the wealthy and their professional assistants. This remained the case until well after the social and economic upheaval that was World War I. It wasn't until the 1920s, a time of great expansion in the science of automotive engineering and production, that younger members of the American working class could afford a

secondhand passenger car and a few even daydreamed of glory on the racing circuit.

The history of the world may be written in the blood of wars, but the early history of hot rodding is written in the dust of dry lakes racing. The automotive manufacturing giants and much of the professional racing industry had already picked the industrialized Midwest as their home base. Southern California, however, with its unique combination of climate and geography, was destined to be the birthplace of the all-American auto

sport of modifying passenger cars for greater speed. Although it is impossible to declare which came first—street rods or hot rods—the early days of our sport were recorded.

Much of what we know comes from a handful of books. The February 1939 issue of *Popular Science* included 15 photos taken during the last 1938 dry lakes meet. *The Southern California Timing Association Racing News* was published from 1938 to 1941. And the granddaddy of the American performance magazine genre—*Throttle Magazine*—published its first issue in

1

Four-cylinder Ford engines from the mid-1920s through the 1934 production were the first mainstay of Southern California hot rodders. Even in the late 1930s—when this photo of Karl Orr in his record-setting "Modified" was taken—they were found in sprint cars, dry lakes modifieds, streamliners, and yes, street rods.

January 1941. From these sources and those wonderful early issues of *Hot Rod Magazine*, which began in January 1948 came the following historical information for your appreciation . . .

THE FATHER OF HOT RODDING

If one man can be given such an imposing title, then by all accounts it must be the revered Ed Winfield. Driven both by economic necessity—his father died when he was five—and a burning desire to learn about mechanical things, Ed started with the science of forging steel. The "Genius of Glendale" began his career in 1909 when at the age of eight years he secured employment at a local blacksmith shop.

From the smithy, he went to work for a Ford dealer. Then, in 1914 he moved to the Los Angeles facilities of the nationally prominent professional racecar and engine builder, Harry A. Miller. Ed was assigned duties in the carburetor department of the well-organized Miller complex that includ-

ed a foundry and machine shop. It was here that the fifteen-year-old lad was exposed to all forms of practical automotive engineering. By 1920, however, Ed was more or less in the speed equipment business for himself, scratch building carburetors and grinding high-lift camshafts.

In 1921, Winfield began racing his modified Ford roadster at Ascot and other California dirt tracks. No one can say with assurance that this Model T was the first street rod—Ed had been working on it since 1912—but it was most certainly the first automobile identified as such. For all practical purposes, 1920 was the beginning of hot rodding as we know it today.

Ed's racing career spanned a brief six years. Yet, during that time he built such a reputation for himself and his speed equipment, that in 1927 he hung up his driving gloves and devoted full energies to his own thriving shop and the production of high performance camshafts, carburetors and cylinder heads for Ford-based engines.

By the late Twenties, most of the Indianapolis 500 cars were running

Winfield carburetors. But, as outstanding an achievement as that was, the Winfield name is best remembered by the hot rod world for its prominence on the record-setting, cut-down Ford roadsters, which saw double-duty on the streets of Los Angeles and the dusty, dry lakes of Southern California's Mojave Desert.

THE LAKES

The first dry lake to be extensively used by Los Angeles hot rodders was commonly known as Muroc. Now, fenced off and called Edwards Air Force Base, it is home to the Space Shuttle. It lies some 100 miles north of the Los Angeles basin, just west of Highway 395. For a thousand years or more, the barren, alkali lakebed served no purpose. Although it could not support significant plant or animal life, it is often under a few inches of water during the rainy season—a dim memory of better days. Nevertheless, hot rodding—if not much else—flowered on the dry lakebed.

In the early 1920s Muroc came to life with a vengeance when some unsung performance enthusiasts realized the 22 mile long, 10 mile wide expanse was nature's gift to the straightaway racer. Not only flat and unblemished except for heat cracks, the alkali surface was hard enough on which to burn rubber, yet just slippery enough to keep an out-of-control racecar from digging in and flipping . . . most of the time. In short, it was perfect for making Land Speed Record (LSR) attempts.

In the spring of 1924, the well-known Indy 500 race driver Tommy Milton journeyed to Muroc with a 3-liter Miller powered racer, a full pit crew and timing equipment. His best

Eldon Snapp in line at a Southern California Timing Association Lakes Meet in the late 1930s. When outfitted with a modified Ford four-cylinder or flathead V-8, the 1929 Model A roadster became the prototypical hot rod. The majority of participants removed the fenders from their everyday transportation for one or two runs against the clock over a one-mile course.

speed of 151.3 mph was never recognized by the international powers—the "official" Land Speed Record of 145.89 was assigned to an Englishman, Ernest Eldridge, driving a Fiat on a public road in France on July 12, 1924.

Discouraging as that must have been, the equally famous American racer Frank Lockhart drove a supercharged 1.5-liter Miller to a speed of 164 mph on Muroc in 1927. A valiant effort, but a bit short of the official 171.02 mph record at the time. No matter, by then every young man in Southern California with a second- or third-hand car knew about Muroc. Many of them wanted to test their own machines—and driving skills—on the desert lakebed.

When the hot rods hit Muroc in the late 1920s, pandemonium broke out. With rare exception, there was no accurate timing, nor even significant organization. Often 10 or 12 roadsters would tear down the lakebed abreast. Few of the drivers knew where the "finish line" was, much less who crossed it first. Only the front-runners could see . . . the also-rans were lost in the murky cloud of alkali dust that swirled about them. Predictably, tragic results were not uncommon.

During the late 1920s and early 1930s, Muroc played host to unorganized groups of hot rodders from late spring until early fall. Even during the summer months when temperatures soared to 110 degrees, hundreds gathered to evaluate the latest modifications made to their creations.

Lakes Cars

By 1930, the Southern California hot rod/street rod, although still a very individualistic automobile, had developed enough common characteristics as to be typified. Almost without exception it was based on the Ford Model T roadster of the early 1920s.

During the heyday of the Model T—from the end of World War I until the "Crash of Twenty-Nine"—it was standard practice for adult middle-class members of the motoring public to buy a brand new car when one needed transportation. A secondhand Model T was considered too worn-out to be a good investment. Trade-ins were offered on the used car market at significant discounts—as little as $25 for one in running condition! Now, that was a small sum for wheels even in those days, and it put a driveable car into the hand of most any young man with a job.

By 1930 a fair amount of used circle track racing equipment was available. This allowed those so inclined to modify that T roadster engine with a Frontenac or Rajo overhead valve cylinder head. The Frontenac, built by Louis and Arthur Chevrolet of Indianapolis, had earned an excellent reputation which was enhanced when a Frontenac-equipped Ford racer finished fifth at the 1923 Indy 500. There were many varieties, some including single and dual overhead cams, but few hot rodders could afford even the basic overhead valve model that cost $115 new. Yet, the head appeared on several street-driven cars that ran at the lakes.

The most desired head conversions among the hot rodders were those manufactured by Joe Jagersberger of Racine, Wisconsin. The Rajo—a contraction of Racine Joe—also came in many versions. The heads that the hot rodders preferred were the valve-in-head Models B and C that were introduced in the mid-1920s. These were equipped with self-lubricating bronze-bushed rocker arms and lightweight adjustable pushrods. A new Model C head sold for $85.

The typical hot rodder's Ford Model T engine was equipped with a Winfield cam. Although there was a wide variety of carburetors available, the locally manufactured Winfield carb was also favored, along with an outside-mount magneto ignition.

The roadster body generally sat atop the frame in "high boy" fashion. As soon as finances allowed, the car was equipped with a strong Muncie gearshift transmission and a Ruckstell two-speed rear axle assembly. The latter was also a homegrown product manufactured in Berkeley, California. Worthwhile additions to the Ruckstell axle were Rocky Mountain mechanical brakes. These replaced the Ford transmission brake and operated from the T foot pedal directly to the rear wheels. It was much more reliable than the stock brake system.

The outfitting of a top-notch street T roadster turned lakes racer included

one of the popular brands of wire wheels: Buffalo, Phelps, Stewart or House. These installations were more good sense than fad—the original equipment wood-spoke wheels were likely to snap, crackle and pop during hard cornering.

ORGANIZED ROADSTER RACING ARRIVES

In the spring of 1931, a momentous event occurred—the Gilmore Oil Company Speed Trials. This was perhaps more important than the Milton and Lockhart attempts a few years earlier. It was the first sponsored, organized time trials held on Muroc. The man in charge was George Wight, the owner of the already famous Bell Auto Parts. The most significant thing about the Gilmore meet was not the 105 mph record set by Ike Trone in a Riley-equipped Model A, but the fact that sponsorship and organization brought a measure of safety and enjoyment for all.

In the months and years that followed, the hot rod sport continued to gather new adherents among the young men of Southern California. This was in spite of a generally poor public reception that was to last for many years. Neither the old folks nor the Great Depression could dampen their enthusiasm. They merely worked longer and harder for the money required to first buy a well-used Ford roadster, and then to build it into a hot rod.

WHAT IS A "HOT ROD?"

Perhaps this is a good time to define the term "hot rod." The best information available indicates that it is a contraction of "hot roadster." Hot refers to the reworking of a factory stock

engine in order to achieve an increased level of performance, or more horsepower. The flashy, well-admired roadsters were windowless open cars so popular in the 1920s and early 1930s. They were also reasonable facsimiles of racing cars when stripped of windshields, headlights, fenders and running boards—even more so when the body was "channeled" or dropped down over the frame.

At any rate, Southern Ascot Race Track, a half-mile dirt oval in Los Angeles, decided to run stock-bodied "hot roadsters" one Sunday a month beginning in May 1939. The advertising of such events used the words hot rod to distinguish the cars from professionally built true racecars. Most entries were SCTA members, although the Association disclaimed any official connection.

By the end of World War II, "hot rod" was used to describe any older car owned by a young person and modified for greater speed. It was very definitely a term of contempt.

The term "street rod" didn't come into vogue until the 1950s. In the 1930s and '40s, it was assumed that if a young Southern Californian owned a street driveable hot rod, he also raced it at the dry lakes. It wasn't until most hot rods were no longer considered weekend racecars that the street-legal driveability forced the term street rod.

Be that as it may, Muroc Dry Lake was often occupied on summer weekends in the mid-1930s by home-built cars that served as transportation during the week, and racecars on Saturday and Sunday. One's own labor was the cheapest thing around in those days. A fellow and his buddy intent on "going to the lakes" would begin by stripping down his roadster as soon as they got home from work on Friday. They would load up the trunk with hand tools, a few spare parts, a jug or two of water for drinking and cooling the engine, and a brown bag of sandwiches. They also squeezed in blankets and sleeping bags.

Sometimes, they would remove the headlights, even though they would have to drive to Muroc in darkness. When they got to the lakebed, they gathered around the various club campfires and shot the bull until sleep and dreams of astonishing speed came. At dawn, the roar of engines signaled the start of an informal meet.

In 1935, organized speed trials were given a boost when Merl Finkenbinder brought a set of electric clocks to Muroc. The rudimentary timing system was activated when a low transverse piano wire was tripped. The method worked reasonably well, but the wire was periodically broken, bringing the time trials to a halt while repairs were made.

In order to cut down on delays, the starter took a peek under each staging car to verify that all undercarriage components cleared the tripwire. While he was on his knees, the flagman often noted that some overeager racer had relied on excessive usage of bailing wire. Out of these casual examinations came the first safety inspections at the dry lakes time trials.

THE SCTA IS BORN

The summer of 1935 also brought an event that would change the random course of hot rodding forever. Although a number of men have been honored with the founding of the Southern California Timing Association (SCTA), only one was "officially" singled out by that organi-

Veda Orr's street Deuce first earned honors in 1937 with runs of 114 mph. Husband Karl Orr, already one of Southern California's top hot rod racer mechanics, was later to open one of the very first speed shops. Veda was eventually timed at more than 125 mph.

zation during its early days. The following appeared in the November 17, 1940 edition of *The SCTA Racing News:*

A Brief "Auto" Biography of Ed Adams

"Several clubs of the SCTA started when Ed Adams and some of his best friends graduated from high school. They wondered how they could keep track of each other over the years and conceived the roadster club as a solution.

The club grew to 15 members who were soon hopping up their cars. They even timed their cars and held lakes meets long before the association was formed. The roadster club was such a success that soon other clubs formed. The association was formally organized in 1938. Currently there are 28 different clubs in the Southern California Timing Association.

Ed Adams has been president since SCTA's inception. You can see him either running his Cragar Roadster through the trials or on the judges' stand taking down times."

This article clearly demonstrates that the modern world of street rodding owes a significant debt of gratitude to Ed Adams and his pals Art Tilton, Vern Hurst, Wally Parks, Jack Harvey, Eldon Snapp, et al. I must also add the various law enforcement agencies located in and around the Mojave Desert and Muroc Dry Lake. On more than one occasion, they emphasized that all dry lakes racing would be halted unless safety and organization were instituted.

A closer look at the formative years of the oldest existing hot rod organization should be of interest to you, especially if you've ever gazed green with envy at a fenderless highboy roadster or a chopped-and-channeled coupe.

The first meeting of the fledgling SCTA was held on November 9, 1937, with representatives of the Throttlers Club of Hollywood wielding the gavel. Serious hot rod racing business got under way immediately with discussions of ambulance service, club points and trophies. Over the next few months several additional meetings saw the Throttlers, Knight Riders,

★ Record Breaker

The voice of Southern California hot rodding before World War II was *Throttle Magazine*. It was a well-done periodical, covering dry lakes time trials and West Coast circle track racing. Unfortunately, it didn't survive World War II. Its last issue was published in December 1941.

Eldon Snapp and Wally Parks—who later became editor of *Hot Rod Magazine* and co-founder of the National Hot Rod Association (NHRA)—were responsible for *The SCTA Racing News*. Photographed on Sunday afternoon June 29, 1941, Wally's roadster was typical of what the pioneers of hot rodding drove.

Road Runners, Sidewinders and 90 MPH Club, Idlers, Ramblers, Gear Grinders, Derelicts and the all-black Centuries banding together into a viable association, and making preparations for the first SCTA Lakes Meet in May 1938.

That the inaugural time trials were a success goes without saying, but it was not without growing pains. At their next meeting, association members decided to further structure things. In addition to such debates over outlawing stock Ford V-8s unless they could exceed 100 mph, or whether entry fees should be raised from $1.00 to $1.50, it was decided that all coupes and sedans would be banned from SCTA events. Apparently not all hot rods were created equal. In all fairness, the ban was put in effect because closed cars were typically slower than open cars and too many such entries slowed

the progress of the meet. The coupe and sedan ban eventually gave rise to the Russetta Timing Association, which accepted closed cars, but frowned upon open cars!

STREET RODDING PROGRESSES

Hot rod racing on the dry lakes prospered in spite of bickering. Dedicated leadership and organization was the key. The early days of street rodding per se is harder to trace. It lacked organization and leadership.

The typical street rod of 1940 was a much more refined version of its 1930 counterpart. Although few powerplants were based on the Model T block any longer, four-cylinder engines still ruled. For example, of the 95 street roadsters entered in the May 19, 1940 SCTA Lakes Meet, 48 were powered by fours. Almost all of these were Model A, B, and C Fords, and 24 of them were topped with Winfield flatheads. Forty-five entries, however,

were Ford V-8 powered. The bent eight was on the verge of taking over. The remaining two roadsters were oddballs, powered by a Cadillac V-12 and V-16, respectively. They were strong runners, but the engines were too expensive to entice a significant following.

What was the mechanical description of a street rod of that era? A word-for-word item that appeared in the March 1940 issue of *The SCTA Racing News* says it succinctly:

"ATTENTION ALL
SCTA MEMBERS
Would appreciate any information concerning a stolen black '29 A Ford Roadster. License No. 5F 6318. Equipment included new B block, Motor No. DR24572. Winfield head, 6207, has been milled, twin Winfield S.R. carburetors, bowl numbers BD 5043 and BD 5045, were mounted on Alexander manifold. Also included a 281-degree Bertrand 5-bearing cam. Set of 16-inch Kelsey Hays black wheels, 700x16 U.S. Royals on front. Outside appearance as follows: Black body with no trim. Chevy headlights, two fog lights, black top, fenders and running boards, blue running lights. Anyone with information concerning this car or equipment please contact The Lancers or A. J. Lawley, 1517 S. Berendo St., Los Angeles."

We can only hope that Mr. Lawley got his car back. What about 1940 prices, you ask? The following advertisement is from the same issue . . .

"For Sale: Buick Four in '30 A, V-8 wheels, good rubber, new V-8 front axle, new 3.27 gears, Riley-ground cam, 7-to-1 compression, 1-7/8-inch

exhaust valves, new brakes, '31 steering, ran on dirt track at San Diego, 1940 license plates paid for. Cost over $300 . . . full price $75, Fred Dunn, 240 E. Chapman, Fullerton."

I don't know what kind of brakes Fred had, but a handful of the more safety conscious builders were beginning to install hydraulics. Far from common on non-factory-equipped Fords, they were considered a significant selling point.

By the way, every street roadster today has to wear a Deuce grille shell, right? Well, believe it or not, Deuce shells were so hard to find as early as April 1939 that one frustrated individual placed a 35-cent ad in the *Racing News:*

"Wanted: 1932 Ford V-8 radiator shell in fair if not good condition."

Some problems never get better, only worse. How's this for a modern day teaser? From the March 1, 1939 *Racing News:*

"For Sale: '32 V-8 touring—new cut down top, side curtains, good tires, new mains, perfect rear end, new trans . . . about $125."

Finally, for those who enjoy self-inflicted pain, the following ads from the July 1, 1939 *Racing News:*

"For Sale: '33 V-8 Roadster. '37 engine and '36 transmission. Milled heads, '38 radio, new paint and top, plenty of chrome. Motor turned 100 last races. $200.

"For Sale: '32 V-8 Roadster with battery and transmission, less engine and wheels. $60."

TIME OUT FOR WORLD WAR II

Even before the United States became actively involved in World War II, the raging European conflict had its effect on auto racing at Muroc. The eastern "shore" of the dry lake bed had, for quite some time, been set aside as the U.S. Army Bombing Range. As soon as it was apparent to the military that aerial practice was necessary, the hot rodders were told in no uncertain terms to vacate the premises.

The SCTA only scheduled four lakes meets a year and the dates were kept a secret in order to keep spectator attendance—by this time as many as 15,000—down to a manageable level. So, undaunted, the time trials were shifted from Muroc to nearby Rosamond and Harper Dry Lakes. These alternate sites were similar to Muroc, but not nearly as desirable. The worries about where to race, however, were of minor consequence after December 7, 1941.

World War II certainly left its mark on hot rodding. First, there was the general mixing of young Americans from all geographical regions. Transplanted Southern California hot rodders carried with them tales of their passion for modified Ford roadsters and coupes, and dry lakes racing. Add to that the fact that a huge number of out-of-state servicemen sailed to the Pacific Theater from the West Coast. Many of these fellows got to see at least some of the famed California hot irons first hand. And so, in the midst of a global conflict, the appeal of the hot rod was strong enough to garner devotees even though the actual pleasures were years in the future. For on December 4, 1942,

the SCTA decided to suspend all activities for the duration.

THE HOT RODS RETURN

It is reported that widespread illegal street racing started in 1945 before the Japanese signed the surrender. Recorded in the blaring headlines of every local newspaper, were the roundups of "speed-crazed hot rodders" on the streets of the semi-rural outskirts of the Los Angeles metropolitan area. Public reaction was swift and negative. A bill was introduced in the California Legislature prohibiting motorists from increasing the performance level of their cars! As far as I know, it didn't pass muster.

A meeting was held on September 7, 1945, and it was quickly decided that the Southern California Timing Association would resume dry lakes time trials as soon as practical. In addition, it was also agreed that membership would be offered to outlaw clubs if they agreed to abide by the SCTA's strict rules and regulations. Fifteen clubs with 88 active members constituted the revived Association. Wally Parks, writing in his book, *Drag Racing: Yesterday and Today,* relates the following:

"At this same meeting, in recognition of the outstanding job she had done in keeping SCTA's in-service members in contact through publication of *The SCTA Racing News,* Mrs. Veda Orr was honored with a full membership in the Association, complete with all competition privileges, since she had long before proven her capabilities in dry lakes speed trials."

Veda Orr, the First Lady of the SCTA, had indeed paid her dues. She is also the first lady of what came to be known as "street rodding." The Orrs,

7

Karl Orr opened his speed shop in the Los Angeles suburb of Culver City in 1940. "I built engines and I sold heads, manifolds, cams, carbs and ignitions. And I sold them—three or four complete sets a day!" Hot rodding was well on its way. These cars amply reflect the high quality of many pre-World War II street rods.

Veda Orr's *Hot Rod Pictorial* first saw print in the late 1940s, thanks to Floyd Clymer Publications, then "America's largest publisher of books pertaining to Automobiles, Motorcycles, Motor Racing and Americana." It is still available today in vintage auto parts stores. Veda, however, did more than just chronicle early hot rodding. She was a participant in the truest sense.

Karl and Veda, originally gained prominence among their peers in the late 1930s. Karl's story predates Veda's however. "I had what you might call a 'speed shop' back in Kingston, Missouri. That was in 1921. I was driving a 'T' with a handmade body and doing some dirt track racing at state and county fairs. Won some, and lost some. I ran a Rajo head and used the old Zenith carb, modified. We

didn't know anything about exhausts; we just ran a big old pipe. Ha, the bigger the better."

Karl's mechanical talents, as well as his driving abilities, soon brought him customers who weren't satisfied with the look-alike, run-alike Model T Ford. "The local mechanic was too busy working on tractors, and when somebody wanted something a little special, he would come to me. I would

get it for him and install it."

When Karl migrated to Los Angeles in 1923, he quickly found work in the automotive trades. Almost as quickly he found himself in the local racing milieu. It wouldn't be long before the dry lakes, with their promise of unbridled speed, beckoned him. "In 1929 I bought a '28 roadster, put on an Acme head and went to Muroc. I liked that Acme head, but it sure would knock the rods out quick. So later I got a Winfield 'Red'."

In 1935, shortly after Ed Adams and friends popularized organized roadster clubs, Karl joined the exclusive 90 MPH Club. This was an accomplishment considering its difficult membership requirement. In 1936, he married Veda and the two of them began their regular treks to Muroc, Rosamond and Harper dry lakes in search of races to run, and records to break.

And break 'em, they did. One after the other. Not just Karl, mind you, but Veda as well. Too many to list here, but in 1939, Karl pushed Veda's street-legal 1932 roadster to 121.62 mph, thereby making it the first Deuce to "officially" break 120 mph. Veda herself had driven the car to a 114.24 mph record in 1937. But it wasn't the Orr family records that were important to the hot rodders—it was the Orr family business.

SPEED SHOPS & SUCH

In the late 1930s, Karl had begun a very profitable sideline enterprise— converting gasoline carburetors over to alcohol, and rebuilding stock ignition systems into something better suited to the demands of high compression racing engines. By 1940, it was obvious that his craftsmanship was good enough to nurture a full-time business.

The Hilborn Story

More than one major automotive enterprise started on the dry lakes of Southern California. One of my favorites, however, is Stu Hilborn's Fuel Injection Engineering Company. Hilborn built his first street roadster in the late 1930s, a fenderless black 1929 Model A on Deuce rails with a 239-inch 1934 Ford V-8. In September 1941, he turned 124 mph on Muroc. In 1946, when racing returned in full bloom, he turned 139 mph on El Mirage Dry Lake.

The early records were set with an intake manifold designed by Eddie Miller, Sr. It mounted three Stromberg E single throat carbs and a dual throat Stromberg EE. Each throat of the EE carb fed one cylinder giving the effect of a five-carb fuel system. (Miller, on the right, finished in 4th place in the 1921 Indy 500.)

Never satisfied, Hilborn went on to bring his own long-held dream to fruition—the first fuel injection for a conventional internal combustion engine. To prove its merit, he simultaneously completed another project, a beautiful streamliner. In 1948, the car turned 150.50 mph at El Mirage, the first hot rod to break the 150 mph barrier.

As a result, his operation became one of the first speed shops to open its doors to the hot rodding public.

Don't misunderstand; it wasn't an auto parts store that also sold racing equipment. There were several of those already in existence. Karl's was a bona fide speed shop where high performance was its only reason for existing. Soon, business was good enough

for Veda to quit her job at MGM studios and lend her own expertise to the operation. Describing the business, Karl simply states: "I built engines and I sold heads, manifolds, cams, carbs and ignitions. And I sold them –three or four complete sets a day. I did a lot of mail order business, too."

When war came, Karl went to work at Northrop Aviation during the day

and ran the store nights and weekends. When Wally Parks and Eldon Snapp donned their uniforms, they relinquished the helm of *The SCTA Racing News* (held since 1938) to Veda. The Racing News became a one-woman newsletter, gossip column and cheering section that forever endeared her to the lakes racers.

In 1949, hot rodders and street rodders alike journeyed to the Bonneville Salt Flats to see what their racers and street rods could do on a near infinite length perfectly smooth course. Marvin Webb tried his '29 out, and turned 119.68 in D/Street Roadster Class. The plaque hanging below the license plate is from the "Hollywood Lancers," a club that eventually relocated to Anaheim.

Present day racers bring their rides to Bonneville and El Mirage aboard trailers every bit as fancy as the cars themselves. Lakes racing in August 1951 was a little less opulent. One of my personal heroes, George Bentley flat-towed his B Class roadster to El Mirage behind a 1946 Ford coupe. I proudly own the Second Place trophy George won for his 145 mph run.

THE BOOM CONTINUES

By 1946, SCTA and Russetta were back in full swing, only this time at El Mirage Dry Lake. It would be nice to report that illegal street racing had stopped, but that's just not true. Lakes meets were held with greater frequency than ever before. They often lasted all weekend and continued to draw crowds upward of 10,000. Apparently, however, that just wasn't enough.

"A guy could go street racing five nights a week if he wanted to! Hundreds of cars would show up at the Long Beach Traffic Circle. Some would head out Clark Street, others would opt for the highway near the Seal Beach ammo dump." So said Bonneville 200 MPH charter member Otto Ryssman when I interviewed him in the 1970s. There was some semblance of organization even in the midst of chaos. On Wednesday nights the street racers gathered at the Traffic Circle; other communities had their own "race nights." There was such regularity, in fact, that lunch wagons showed up for major events!

Illegal street racing was not always fun and games. Many tragic accidents occurred over the months. SCTA reacted, but threats of expulsion simply could not control the thousands of participants. Negative public opinion grew by leaps and bounds. Hot rods and hot rodders, many thought, would forever be outcasts.

ENTER *HOT ROD MAGAZINE*

If one event were singled out as the most important milestone in the history of hot rodding, my money would be on the founding of *Hot Rod Magazine*.

The foresight and courage of Robert E. Petersen and Robert R. Lindsay, co-founders of HRM, are no less astounding today than back in 1947 when Petersen and Lindsay each invested $200 in the Hot Rod Publishing Company and set up headquarters on Melrose Avenue in Los Angeles. With help from Bob Lindsay's father—a man with magazine experience—they wrote and photographed the first issue of *Hot Rod*. The initial print order was for 10,000 copies.

They had no network of distribution,

"The Lakes," just the place to take to take your girl on a warm Southern California Sunday outing in August 1951. Of course, if she thought you and she were going for a drive, and then boating, you might have had some explaining to do.

so the partners took the magazines to local racetracks and, of course, the dry lakes, and sold them like newsboys. In between sales they took photographs for the next issue.

Within two years, *Hot Rod Magazine* had secured a solid foothold on the nation's newsstands. It was well on its way to becoming the bible of the amateur speed enthusiast. Today it has an enormous circulation, and even if a smaller percentage of its pages feature pre-war roadsters and coupes, and SCTA coverage is thin, HRM will always be remembered by the faithful as the pioneer organ of their motorsport when it had a less-than-welcome name in polite circles.

LEGAL DRAG RACING IS BORN

With HRM rapidly building a nationwide readership and simultaneously preaching safe and sane hot rodding, the next development toward respectability was the use of abandoned airstrips for yet another form of speed contest—the drag race.

In 1949, the Santa Barbara Acceleration Association (SBAA) hosted a reasonably well-controlled drag race on a half-mile stretch of private road in Goleta, a small town on the Southern California coast. Three-tenths of a mile was used for the standing-start run, the remainder for shutdown. That's all that was needed. Soon, the SBAA was in the forefront

of safe hot rod racing with mandatory requirements of seat belts, fire extinguisher, crash helmet, and goggles for open cars.

The most famous drag strip that most hot rodders recall, however, is Santa Ana. More properly known as the Orange County Airport Drags and sponsored by the Orange County Racing Association, Santa Ana was for all intents and purposes the first foray into the realm of drag racing for profit. C. J. Hart, a transplanted Ohio street rodder; Frank Stillwell, a local motorcycle shop owner; and Creighton Hunter, another street rodder, dug deep into their pockets for the money to cover the expenses of one or two quarter-mile drag meets.

The inaugural event was July 2, 1950. Entrants paid $2 to run, while spectators were charged fifty cents to watch. The rest of the story is well-known. Over the following nine years, everybody who became somebody in California hot rodding had some con-

It's anybody's guess as to whether or not every roadster in line behind No. 31 in the foreground was a street rod in weekend warrior trim. Nevertheless, most of them are wearing hubcaps! The point is, a significant percentage of Southern California street roadsters (and coupes) that ran the lakes long before and for many years after WWII, did indeed do double duty.

Hubcaps not withstanding, No. 75 was a better-than-average looking racecar, so I suspect it saw a lot of street service sans the obviously temporary belly pan. Besides, dedicated racecars of this caliber often had permanent numbers rather than a quickie shoe polish ID.

tact with the Airport Drags, even if only to stand alongside the asphalt runway and watch the top shoes of the meet burn rubber. With *Hot Rod Magazine* there to promote the latest development in the quarter-century-old, dry lakes–style straightaway racing, and with the speed equipment industry eager to export its products and services beyond Southern California, the drags took off. Street rodding firmly hung on to its coattails.

ROADSTERS GET RIVALS

The street rods of 1950 weren't restricted to Ford roadsters. Gracefully designed Ford coupes and sedans had been around for nearly 20 years, now they were making a substantial dent in what had been considered the purview of the "traditional hot rod." A glance at the 1950 *Hot Rod Magazine* index identifies nine roadsters . . . yet five coupes, one pickup and one convert-

ible were also featured. That says something about expanding horizons.

There's not much doubt about the powerplant, however. It was far and away the flathead Ford V-8 backed up with either a 1939 Ford floor shift or a 1940 Ford side-shift tranny. The favorite rear end was also a 1940 unit, and even though its stock hydraulic brakes were more or less standard on the better West Coast cars, disc brakes of the Kinmont variety were featured in the May 1950 issue of HRM.

Car Shows

Another significant influence in the hot rod world was the car show. In 1948, the SCTA and Robert Petersen's Hollywood Publicity Associates joined forces to stage the first major public exhibition of hot rods and custom cars. It was a huge success from both a financial and public relations standpoint. In fact, the SCTA made

enough money to inaugurate the Bonneville National Speed Trials.

Overall changes in hot rod cosmetics were inspired by car shows. They were subtle in 1950—mild dechroming, "nosing" and "decking," but these exterior modifications marked the first time in hot rod history that something besides racing had influenced the sport's participants. That was the good news. The bad news was that the groundwork was laid for much more radical modification to pre-war Ford sheet metal. The dwindling supply of "vintage tin" was yet unnoticed.

THE HOT RODDING SPORT SPREADS EAST

By the mid-1950s, what was largely a Southern California phenomenon had grown to a full-fledged, coast-to-coast American pursuit. Hot rodding was now of age, and street rodding's reason for existence no longer depended on dry lakes or drag racing.

During those years of national growth, roadsters and coupes became hotter properties than ever. Two things limited their availability: WWII scrap metal drives and postwar jalopy racing. Scrap metal drives were in the national interest, of course, but when jalopy racing was finally recognized as predators upon the raw material of the new sport, it was almost too late. Fortunately the cars that were reasonably new at the outbreak of WWII had been babied during the lean war years. Many were still available at reasonable prices. In 1955, for instance, a 1940 Ford coupe could be purchased for about $100. And, because a recent high school graduate could easily earn $40 a week, such a purchase was well within reach.

And reach for them the young

Regardless of the GMC supercharger atop the flathead, I have to think this gentleman was a street rodder not only because of the hub-caps, but the custom Deuce shell. I don't know what he turned on El Mirage, or the next week at the Santa Ana Drags, but I'll bet nobody challenged him on the boulevard.

American male did. Sports cars, primarily Jaguars and MGs, were grudgingly appreciated—but never out loud. Their cost, however, meant inaccessibility for the great majority. But a street rod? Now that was horsepower of a different color. The 1940 Ford coupe didn't put much of a dent in the average 18-year-old's budget. In fact, there were enough bucks left over to modify the flathead . . . if one still existed under the hood.

THE FLATHEAD FADES

Just as street rodding was coming into its own, packaged horsepower in the form of stock late model overhead valve V-8s suddenly became as economical and accessible as the nearest wrecking yard. Not only that, they provided reliable horsepower. And reliability was often what separated street rods from hot rods.

Those who can remember first hand will testify that no matter how traditional a "suped" up flathead looked with its dual carbs, finned aluminum heads, acorn nut covers, and chrome-wrapped 6-volt generator, it was hard to start and harder to cool. (By the way, the spelling of "suped" is what was used in the first published accounts of dry lakes racing. It did not refer to a Campbell's product, nor the explosives used by safecrackers. It was merely shorthand for "Super," a description of a highly modified dry lakes racing class.)

On the other hand, a stock OHV Cadillac or Olds-powered street rod had 'em whipped hands down. As soon as they were painted bright red rather that the factory's dull blue or green, outfitted with finned aluminum rocker covers and a dual or triple-deuce manifold . . . man, they were accepted by even the staunchest flathead hot rodder. In the mid-1950s, traditional or nostalgia rodding was unheard of—street rodding was avant-garde in the truest sense.

That's the way street rodding progressed well into the 1960s. If put to the test, one could probably find a street rod with an OHV V-8 from every American marquee that offered one. It was a heady time of innovation, and not just in the way of powerplants. More than one stock-bodied coupe or roadster with lines considered untouchable today underwent drastic cosmetic alterations. As grotesque as many of them appear in retrospect, few voices of challenge were heard back then. Perhaps that's why sometime in the early 1960s street rodding slipped into the background in favor of plastic models, slot cars, go-karts, mini-bikes . . . and more importantly, factory muscle cars (new or used) that could be purchased on a time-payment plan.

STREET RODDING REBORN

Thankfully, the hiatus was brief. Although *Hot Rod Magazine* continued to expand its market with coverage of a wide variety of subjects including motorcycles and drag boats, another Petersen publication took stock of itself and ventured back into the street rod arena. Under the guidance of publisher Tom Medley and with the able assistance of Leroi "Tex" Smith and Bud Bryan, *Rod and Custom Magazine* almost single handedly breathed new life into the fading hobby/sport of street rodding. Consequently, the late 1960s marked the beginning of an unprecedented growth spurt that has lasted more than forty years!

The late 1960s? That was a long time ago, but not as long ago as 1920 in terms of a relatively unorganized activity. Eighty-plus years is a substantial block of time. That's why it is truly astonishing that a street rod built in the year 2004 is not significantly different from one built in 1960. Far more—and

far better—fiberglass and stamped steel reproduction bodies and frames, and commercial installation kits are now available. Yet, somehow, the basic flavor has remained. Indeed, the cars generally look the same as they did in the late 1940s. But now, more than ever, emphasis is on detail and quality construction.

One has to admit that street rodding has lost a little of its individuality, inasmuch as only small-block Chevys and Fords are serious contenders for placement under the hood, with their factory-mated automatic transmissions under the floorboards, but it has also lost its crudeness. Unless one's sole exposure to early street rodding is through contemporary car magazines, I submit that only the street rods featured in the old magazines could be considered class acts.

That is behind us now. No doubt, it's because today's street rod is rarely the sole means of transportation for its owner-builder. In the early days when one had to go to work or school in the morning, you had to keep that heap running no matter what! Today, rod builders are older and have more discretionary income to accomplish their automotive desires, and the average street rod shows it. About the only downside from where I sit is that most of them only hit the streets on the weekends.

That really doesn't count, though. The only important thing is that street rodding, after a long and often turbulent history, refuses to fade into the past.

References:

Levine, Leo. *Ford: The Dust and the Glory*. London: Collier-Macmillan Limited, 1969.

Oddo, Frank. "Karl and Veda Orr: Hot Rod Pioneers." *Street Rodder Magazine*, January 1976. pp. 34–37.

Orr, Veda. *Hot Rod Pictorial*. Los Angeles: Floyd Clymer, 1949.

Parks, Wally. *Drag Racing: Yesterday and Today*. New York: Trident Press, 1966.

Parks, Wally, and Eldon Snapp. Editors, *SCTA Racing News*, December 1938–August 1941.

Peters, Jack. Editor. *Throttle Magazine*, January–December 1941.

Post, Dan. *Model T Ford in Speed and Sport*. Arcadia, California: Dan R. Post Publications, 1956.

Unger, Henry F. "Jalopies Race on the Desert." *Popular Science*, February 1939, pp. 98–103.

VINTAGE TIN OR REPRODUCTION?

2

Choosing between vintage tin and the many excellent offerings of modern reproduction manufacture can pose something of a dilemma. The decisive factor, however, is the availability of vintage tin. Bernie Couch has owned his Deuce since the late 1940s and you couldn't pry it out of his hands with a crowbar!

VINTAGE TIN
OR REPRODUCTION?

This may be the shortest chapter in this book, but in many ways it is the most important, because it broaches the first and second of many significant decisions that await you.

Choosing the right car is no simple task. It you're the aggressive type, you may lean toward a roadster or coupe with traditional racy lines, a stark inte-

rior garnished in machined aluminum and powered by a fire breathing big-bore V-8 with polished and chromed accessories. On the other hand, you may be a more sedate street rodder with a taste for the "good life" and have visions of a moderately powered sedan, the exterior liberally coated with the finest paint money can buy, and an interior richly outfitted in leather and walnut. On the other hand, you may prefer a mix of each.

There's just no telling what any given street rod builder really wants. It doesn't matter. What matters is that he gets what he really wants.

The rod builder of fifty years ago was adamant in his desire to build a car that was first daily transportation. The fact that he frequently stepped beyond the bounds of reliability in his secondary quest for high performance didn't deter him. He was willing to tolerate a temperamental engine that was

There are still a number of worthwhile street "roddable" old cars on the market. You must be willing to pay a fair market price, however.

hard to start and overheated easily. Times have changed. Today's street rod builder is far less concerned with daily transportation. His hobby car no longer needs to have an overlay of utility to justify its existence; he wants it for its own sake. It has "functional autonomy."

It also has a mandate of perfection. In the overly glorified 1950s, perfection was rarely expected, much less achieved. Today's street rod builder, however, seriously seeks that elusive goal. He is spurred on by magazine articles that feature exquisite, professionally built, turn-key street rods with secret price tags approaching $75,000! Add to that the on-site inspection of today's better street rods at rod runs and other events, and you find the motivation for both novice and experienced builders.

What about down-to-earth street rods that are largely home-built? No question about it, they too are better than ever. Because transportation needs are lessened, builders can spend more time on planning, construction and maintenance. The result is they can have a possession worthy of pride as never before. But you'll never get there without careful planning.

That planning begins with the need to make a basic choice: build a street rod based on vintage tin—a genuine pre-1949 American production car or light truck . . . or one based on a reproduction body. Both approaches, different as they are, can be equally satisfying because both will be largely outfitted with new components and commercial kits.

At some time in the distant future, the street rod builder won't have this decision to make. The supply of rebuildable cars in even a semi-complete state will dry up. It may happen in five years, or it may take 25 years. Whatever, eventually it will happen. That's the bad news. The good news is, as the existing supply dwindles and assuming demand stays the same or even increases, newer and better reproductions will come to market. For now, however, more than enough vintage tin is still available for the serious rod builder to be faced with a choice. And yes, this is written in the year 2003!

In this book, I limit my remarks to vintage tin that has not already been

Most traditional body styles have been captured in conventional fiberglass, composite material or fresh manufacture steel. This extended cab 1930—31 Ford roadster/pickup by Brookville Roadster is a fine example of what's available today.

extensively restored, and old-timey hot rods and street rods sorely in need of refurbishing and modernizing. Reproduction cars are newly manufactured body and chassis combinations. Most of the repro bodies are fiberglass and composites, but as you know, metal reproduction bodies are now a reality.

Body Style

The first consideration in the vintage tin vs. reproduction controversy is that of body style. Those who seek the traditional street rod—fenderless Ford 1927–34 roadsters—have to accept the fact that these cars were never produced in significant numbers. Although genuine Ford roadster, phaeton and convertible bodies appear from time to time in the marketplace, the asking prices are quite steep for the better ones, and ridiculous for poorer specimens. An original steel 1927–41 Ford open car body that is in only mediocre condition will sport a price tag at least that of a quality fiberglass body ready for paint.

It is well known that coupes and sedans from the late 1930s through the late 1940s are far more available than open cars. Yet, because of their complexity of construction, reproduction coupes and sedan are more expensive than reproduction roadsters!

The final consideration is the cost of quality metal repair. Unless the buyer-builder is a body and fender professional, restoration expenditures must be added to the purchase price of the car. The reality of the situation is that most of the available vintage tin has been picked over for the last 50 years.

If your cap is set for a vehicle that's not available as a reproduction, then book passage to the next major swap meet.

For the most part, the cream of the crop is long gone. What is left today is often what was rejected yesterday. Consequently, considerable metalwork is required to bring the body up to par, and guess what, the rehabilitation of coupes and sedans is usually more extensive and expensive simply because they are larger and have more "working parts!"

The Bottom Line

At one time, reproduction bodies were so crude they wouldn't accept original windshield posts, door hinges, trunk handles and the like without major reworking. Today, not only will reproduction bodies readily mate with original or quality reproduction components, many are offered with the needed operational hardware already installed.

Therefore, when price and availability are considered, it's fair to say that the quality-built fiberglass, composite or steel reproduction body is superior to almost all moderately priced "as is" vintage tin currently available. Shortcomings exist only in the mind of the restoration enthusiast for whom genuineness and originality are uppermost, and whose mind is closed on the subject.

Others, certainly more pragmatic, are less adamant in their demand for originality. They consider the big picture—a street rod is a significantly modified, custom-built vehicle that has been designed to suit their tastes and personalities. Period. For them, the difference between vintage tin and fiberglass is murky. Their ultimate choice must be between an affordable vintage car that is immediately available and a reproduction assemblage that can be ordered at leisure. Otherwise, they will never advance beyond the daydreaming stage.

3

FINDING AND EVALUATING VINTAGE TIN

Prewar Fords are still available. These coupes can certainly be brought back although the "basket case" is rough, and parts are missing. Reproduction catalogs offer a vast array of sheet metal components for many "real steel" models. Nevertheless, study the catalogs carefully before you tender an offer on a rebuildable body. You always want some idea of what you will have to spend after you purchase it. As you have no doubt already found out, there are no inexpensive popular models of old Ford roadsters and convertibles, and coupes aren't that far beyond. By the way, those with legitimate titles command a premium.

Let's now examine the pros and cons of choosing vintage tin as the basis for your street rod. The first major hurdle is simply finding an old car or pickup, but simply finding any old-timer won't do. Chances are, you want a specific make and model that's in satisfactory condition and offered at a realistic price.

SOURCES FOR FINDING VINTAGE TIN

Locating one, as relatively easy as that may be in a street rod–rich area such as Southern California, can be very difficult in other parts of the country, but vintage tin is out there. Even today, more than 80 years after the beginning of hot rodding, old cars still abound. Although they're not there

just for the asking, if you don't ask, you don't get! So, start looking.

Fellow Rodders

The best starting place is with your friends and acquaintances . . . and their friends and acquaintances. Although it helps, they don't have to be street rodders. It's surprising just how many folks know the whereabouts of old cars.

18

Magazine ads are something else. Many cars offered in the automotive monthlies seem to excite great enthusiasm in the hearts of their owners. Prices and descriptions often boggle the reader's mind. True street rod material appears, but as often as not, it seems as if the vehicles advertised were bought new and stored in hermetically sealed garages the following day for the sole purpose of being offered at grandiose prices sixty or seventy years hence. At least the ads read that way to me.

Rod Runs

Cars that are offered for sale at rod runs, car shows and similar events are usually already built. Their sale will finance the next car (or house) the owner wants to build, and normally won't be of more than passing interest to those intending to build their own. Completed cars offered for sale, be it on the street or in magazines dedicated to buyers and sellers, are all too often covered with more than a little "fairy dust." Buyer beware.

Swap Meets

One of the most enjoyable ways of searching for basic street rod material is window-shopping at auto swap meets, car shows and race events. Automotive swap meets are still not a nationwide occurrence, but they become more widespread every year. They are sometimes held in conjunction with major rod runs and car clubs and local street rod associations sometimes sponsor them. Whichever, they are always fun to attend, whether you go as a buyer, seller or just a spectator.

Big swap meets such as those at Hershey, Reno and the LA Roadster Show invariably draw high-dollar

Fast disappearing, but still a good resource for roddable vintage tin is the tucked-away vehicle that a long-time owner always meant to restore for himself . . . but just never got around to it. Rural areas are rife with old pickups that offer the makings of a great rod. Best of all, the early pickup is usually the most economically priced, and an ideal "starter" rod for a younger fellow with a family. Often, there is no other way for a less affluent first-time rod builder to get into the game. Caution: Don't reveal your plans when shopping. Some would-be restorers will flat-out refuse to sell if they think you're a "dirty-neck hot rodder."

Although "old" might be a 1986 automobile to most people, after a bit of education, they quickly get a handle on what you want and are just as quick to advise you of what they know. Everybody loves a treasure hunt.

Some years ago, a friend of mine was downright shocked to learn that his secretary's husband had a 1939 Ford coupe stored in their garage. Her husband acquired it more than a decade before with the intention of transforming it into a street rod. Unfortunately, he never got around to it. A chat with him that night led to a tentative agreement. The coupe and sundry pieces were towed away the next Saturday morning after three hours of garage clean-up and the transfer from his pocket to theirs of two crisp one hundred dollar bills!

Print Advertising

The easiest hunting, of course, is a diligent perusal of newspaper advertisements and ads in periodicals that offer special interest cars for sale. Some metro newspapers have Antiques, Classics and Racecars sections in the classifieds that virtually "let your fingers do the walking." After a phone call to verify or investigate the specifics, you may be on your way.

Most sellers advertise cars beginning in the Sunday edition. Usually, that edition is on the stands by Saturday afternoon. So, buy the paper as early as you can. You could be the owner of some fine vintage tin 16 hours before the not-so-slick buyer crawls out of bed, gets the paper, then discovers that his "find" is already gone.

On the other hand, extremely popular open cars such as this 1940 Ford convertible will invariably bring the highest dollar no matter what condition they are in. It didn't matter to this happy purchaser. He wanted a '40 ragtop, and he found it. Believe or not, this picture was taken just a few years ago. The car had been sitting in the seller's Orange County, California, backyard untouched since the early 1960s!

street rods from miles around. Nevertheless, there are usually an equal number of half-finished rods, stockers, clunkers and other more reasonably priced beginner cars on the auction block. The upside of such events is that there are competitive and realistic prices. Some cars, however, are there to be shown rather than sold. That accounts for the occasional stratospheric price tag.

The beauty of the show-and-sell aspect of automotive events is efficiency. Many potential buildables are on display in one place. Even if you don't find a car that interests you, you can make comparisons. In addition, cars you see will spark new ideas for future street rod material shopping. Moreover, as you begin to develop comparative-shopping experience, you'll learn one very important thing: It pays to be choosey. Resist paying more than you can honestly afford.

More important, only buy what you want! If you really want a 1936 coupe, please don't buy a 1935 coupe because it is "close" to what you have your heart set on. The next piece of advice is more difficult to follow . . . Don't panic with joy and buy the first or second car that looks as if it may satisfy your needs. Often, another potential candidate may be exactly what you want. The tricky part is this: You may not live long enough to find the perfect car! This is where one's own measure of good judgment comes into play.

Your Own Backyard

A far less efficient method, but one that has paid dividends for many a rod builder, is to keep an eye open when driving around in the normal course of your day. Be ever on the alert for that semi-abandoned old car sitting in a backyard, stuffed away in the dark corner of an open garage, stored—and

forgotten—behind a fence in an industrial area, or planted in a rural area. Sometimes what you find will be an abandoned street rod project, or one with progress delayed long enough to pass for abandonment. Who knows, you may be able to talk the owner into selling. Experienced rod builders develop selective perceptibility—an uncanny ability to spot an old car camouflaged in the brush. In short, develop the habit of keeping an eye open for vintage tin when you're on the road.

Wanted: Old Car or Pickup

If, by some cruel twist of fate you can't find the car of your dreams, there's one last desperate thing you can do: advertise. Don't enter into this lightly however, for there's danger in placing such an ad. You will be vulnerable to the price gouger. He knows you're anxious because you went to the extreme of advertising, so he figures you must be willing to spend a bundle on the car you want. Right? This is okay if money is no object. However, nobody wants to be "had."

When you finally find what you think may be that "just right" car, you must be able to separate the wheat from the chaff, that is, accurately appraise the condition of the offered car. Then, if it meets the standards you've set, you must deal effectively with the seller.

Essentially, the era of the unmodified stocker with an asking price of less than several thousand dollars is gone. It became outdated in the early 1970s when high inflation took the country by storm. Sure, occasionally some lucky rod builder stumbles across that legendary low-buck gennie a soldier off to the wars stored away in an Arizona garage soon after Pearl

Don't sweat the engine and transmission, no matter what the current owner says. Simply plan on completely rebuilding what's there (if you like it) or installing a brand new power package.

Integral firewalls are far more important to overall body strength than many early rod builders realized . . . until it was too late! A body with a near perfect firewall is a rare find. This one is fairly solid although those gaping holes above the stock battery location are a bit hard to figure out. Beyond that, junk batteries seep acid and a good inner fender panel is worth its weight in gold. Fatigue cracks, which are common, are relatively easy to repair

Rust begins and accumulates in the most unexpected places. Chances are no one would have thought to look for it in the roof if telltale scaling wasn't surrounding the windshield.

Harbor. However, if you hold out for such a find, plan to spend most of your days watching other street rodders drive by!

In reality, good-quality vintage tin only changes hands after the owner receives a princely sum. Moreover, like it or not, prices for complete pre-1949 Fords are only going up in the future. Fortunately, a reasonably com-

plete car in good condition will invariably be the most economical car to build in the end. It's no secret that original parts are very costly. In addition, one of the biggest expenses facing the street rodder is the cost of basic metal work. As a result, money saved up front by buying a solid, complete car can be spent on other costly items such as paint and upholstery.

Unfortunately, not every would-be street-rod builder starts with a stash of discretionary money. Most find it easier to work on the fender-a-month plan than to accumulate the necessary funds before beginning the build. They anticipate, justifiably, that their finances will allow them to acquire parts and services on a piece-meal basis over time.

Additionally, if he put his time and talent into a street rod that's in the mainstream of popularity, he can re-pocket a greater percentage of his original outlay than most hobby-type projects. (Try selling an unfinished boat!) So much for broad economic considerations, let's get on with shopping for the best vintage tin your money can buy.

ARE STREET RODS AN INVESTMENT?

One of my pet peeves is the misuse of the term "investment." An investment is defined as "property acquired for future income." In short, it is expected to reap you a monetary profit. On the other hand, street rod building is a hobby, profitable only in terms of pleasure. So, spend your money thoughtfully and prudently, but not with the thought that you're making a blue chip investment. If the latter is of more interest to you, the average bookstore abounds with books on investing.

How about those fellows who buy and sell half-finished street rods and boast of profits? I am skeptical of their accounting procedures. I doubt if they've tallied every nickel they've sunk in the car, or kept records of the hours spent acquiring the needed parts and assembling their most recent "gold mine."

There's no denying that there are a few street rod entrepreneurs who have the finances, experience and shrewdness to buy street rods at bargain prices and quickly turn them over, earning a substantial profit with little or no additional work. They are good businessmen, and more power to them. This is not to say that even the average builder, who wisely purchases an old car, cannot recoup most or all of his cash outlay if he's forced into a premature sale. The simple fact is old cars have a quasi-antique status. As a result, they usually appreciate.

This interior is about as pristine as one finds in a veteran street rod neglected for a long time. Nevertheless, it's a good idea to pull up old carpeting or floor mats. It wouldn't hurt to yank the seat cushion out as well. Another potential interior problem is the insides of the doors . . . they are usually rusted. Repairs are difficult and expensive. Missing door and window hardware can be a headache, as well.

BASKET CASES

When looking at possibles, keep in mind one factor. All of the cars are old. Many parts will be worn, ruined or missing. For the majority of novice street rodders about to tackle their first car, a vintage basket case, which is a disassembled car accompanied by boxes of miscellaneous parts, is most likely what fits their budget. The enthusiastic expectation that they will acquire the missing pieces often encourages them to close the deal on an incomplete package.

Although buying a basket case is often a good way to go, it has its prob-

lems. I can't be there with you as you nose through the boxes that you hope hold the makings of a street rod, so this chapter spells out some of the harsh realities my friends and I have learned over the past 50 years.

Earlier, I spoke of cars in the mainstream of popularity. This is important because popular cars are not only the easiest to sell; more parts—original and reproduction—are available for those that have a long reign of popularity. For example, although Chevrolet consistently outsold Ford during the '30s and '40s, ask any Chevy fan how easy it is to find fenders and grilles, much less interior trim.

Another interesting point about Fords: Although 1937 was a very good year for Ford with 1,037,476 passenger cars and light trucks built, and 1940 was a mediocre year with only 638,109 units, it's much easier to find parts for a '40 Ford than a '37! This is due in part to the fact 1940 models were newer at the advent of World War II, which brought domestic auto production to a halt for almost four years. Cars were garaged or babied through the war years to keep them alive. Consequently, 1939–41 cars were in better shape after the war. More importantly, their styling has been favored by street rodders for a long, long time.

I'm not alone in my opinion that cars favored by the early hot rodders—Ford roadsters and coupes of the classic years—were the ones saved from World War II scrap drives. After all, who would have risked being called unpatriotic for the sake of a Ford sedan or a non-Ford of any description?

The point is, as you stand there in some cold, dark garage in Boise, don't deceive yourself into thinking that finding the missing parts you mentally list will be easy. Don't assume that any parts are insignificant. More than one street rod project has died during the initial building stages because too many parts were unobtainable. Completeness is the cardinal rule when shopping for street rod material! What isn't there when you pack those boxes and trailer that purchase home is going to have to be found and paid for later on. Those later purchases—total cost unknown—can add dramatically to project expense and completion time.

BE PREPARED

When searching for rebuildable tin, there are some items you should have on hand. Start with a high-powered flashlight. You'll need one when you're in a dark garage and down on your knees peering at the underside of a floorboard! With this in mind, conduct your inspection trips during the day just in case you'll be able to roll the car out into the sunlight. A far more realistic appraisal can be made then.

Another handy-dandy thing to have is a pocketknife. You'll need it to discreetly poke into oxidation bubbles. There's no other way to evaluate the extent of under-paint rust. Additionally, a small toolbox with the standard assortment of wrenches and screwdrivers will come in handy.

Finally, carry along a shop coat, creeper, a small 1-ton bottle jack and jackstand. Don't buy a 60-year-old car without inspecting the underside. It's "buyer beware" all the way.

WHAT AWAITS THE SEARCHER

There are two kinds of old cars you'll be inspecting: those that have been

A few extra parts is always a plus, but that not withstanding, the inside of the trunk is often a good predictor of overall body condition. Inspecting is easy, just be sure to remove those wooden panels over the tool storage area. They're rain catchers, and 'tis a very rare old-timer without some problems under them.

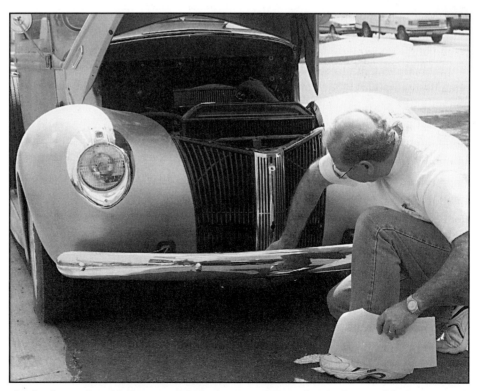

A wise buyer does his homework before money changes hands. Some critical parts such as reproduction grilles are readily available for some models, but not all of 'em! Research the model you are interested in before the purchase is finalized.

23

Oh, those pesky rain channels. Enough moisture will have accumulated in most any old car or truck to present a problem. They are one of the most difficult of all areas to repair when they are rusted through.

modified significantly and those that haven't. Of the two groups, the latter is certainly the more rare, particularly with open cars, coupes and pickup trucks. The pendulum can swing either way when it comes to sedans.

The Unmodified Car

Let's take a closer look at the rare example—an old car that somehow reached and stayed in retirement without major surgery. Begin your inspection of what's behind the FOR SALE sign by listing the missing bolt-ons.

The ideal car will include original fenders, hood, grille, doors, deck, bumpers, mounting brackets, bumper guards, running boards, door and deck handles, exterior chrome or stainless trim and interior trim. Otherwise, you may never get your project completed because half of the needed items were missing. If you're not sure what parts are supposed to be there, do your research before you go hunting. There

are too many possibilities for me to provide a parts list for every model that could conceivably be turned into a street rod. However, use the list at the end of this chapter as a guide, then make your own to ensure that you get the needed parts. Do your homework, and then take a close look. The condition of a part isn't necessarily as important as its presence. For example, the door of a late 1930s car may include dozens of impossible-to-find items from a window crank and door latch to special screws.

THE WHOLE ENCHILADA

Again, completeness is the primary concern! Yet, completeness is the simplest aspect of a vehicle evaluation. What you see is what you get. If you know what parts should be included with the car, walk around it with your list in hand and take notes. If there are boxes of parts, go through them and make an inventory. Check the list

against an antique auto parts catalog to determine the cost of replacing any missing items.

After you've satisfied yourself on the completeness of your find, the difficult part begins: evaluating the condition of what's there and "guesstimating" the cost of any farmed-out repairs.

Fenders

Start with the fenders. If they are bolted to the body, look for rust-outs at the lower corners, points of attachment, and in and around headlight and taillight buckets. Check the inner panels carefully for signs of metal fatigue.

Exterior Body Panels

Next, check the exterior body. There are three major areas of concern: drip moldings, lower front and rear quarter panels, and rear deck panel. The first, and usually the most difficult to deal with are the roof drip moldings. These metal stampings are spliced between the roof and side-panel seams, and are extremely difficult to repair.

Other critical body areas are the lower front and rear quarter panels. Inasmuch as they are in close proximity to the wheels, they are exposed to road contamination such as salt and water. Through the years, the channels inside the body immediately behind the quarter panels accumulate considerable moisture and, as a result, eventually rust away. Carefully inspect these prime areas with your pocketknife. Although replacement body panels are available, you want to know as much as possible about the extent of the needed bodywork before you make the purchase, not after the car has been stripped and sent to the metal smith.

Another major problem area is the

As pointed out earlier, the evaluation of the engine, transmission and radiator is not particularly important—unless you plan to drive the vehicle for awhile before getting started on the project. Even then, condition is only critical if you plan to keep and rebuild them. Otherwise, these items will only become "excess inventory" in your home shop. The No. 1 consideration is what was done to the firewall and chassis to install them!

Be careful sitting behind the steering wheel. There is often a mystical feeling that sometimes clouds your judgment. Even the experienced rod builder is whisked away on a magic carpet of fantasy.

rear deck panel. Here, moisture accumulates down in the inner panel where it does its dirty work. As Neil Young said, "rust never sleeps."

Many times the seller will have liberally coated the body with gray primer. This is usually not done deceitfully, but in a misguided attempt to protect the metal. As discussed later, inexpensive primers are not sealers. Consequently, moisture penetrates through to the metal. Not only that, primer makes it difficult to visually judge the waviness of a panel.

Check the remainder of the body exterior by hand. You don't need the sophisticated touch of the experienced auto body man to detect ripples, waves and other expensive-to-repair flaws. Even the more subtle ones are relatively easy to detect by slowly running your hands over the sheet metal—if it feels as lumpy as a corncob, it will take many hours of hammer work, filling and block sanding to get a smooth, ripple-free surface worthy of paint. Adjust your offer to buy accordingly.

LIFT THE HOOD

After you are satisfied with the exterior, look under the hood. Unless you're considering hopping up the original powerplant—which may be the case with a flathead—chances are you won't care about the engine or its remains. It's a waste of time to check out a powertrain that isn't exactly what you want. In fact, you're better off if there's no engine at all. It will be easier to inspect the overall condition of the engine compartment. Check the condition of the firewall, inner fender panels and hood latching hardware.

SIT INSIDE

Next, slide behind the steering

Door hinge areas are another place to check. They are banged about quite a bit through the years, and are sometimes crudely repaired. Look with a critical eye, remembering that every repair will increase total cost.

wheel. If you wondered why I didn't suggest you do this first, it's because there is a magic spell that descends upon a budding rod builder when he takes hold of the wheel. It's too easy to lose touch with reality. All of a sudden, you're no longer sitting on disintegrating upholstery that's been home to a tribe of spiders for ten years, or peering through a dirty and cracked windshield. You're in the car of your dreams.

Even the experienced street rodder can be whisked away on a magic carpet of fantasy when he's behind the wheel. Dented sheet metal straightens out, faded paint suddenly gains depth, and a pitted hood ornament with flaking chrome gleams. Don't fall for it. Instead, you need the sobering effect of the exterior evaluation before you place yourself directly in the path of temptation.

Interior Evaluation

Begin interior evaluation by pulling up the remnants of the floor mats.

Scrutinize the sheet metal that lies hidden beneath. Even in the driest climate, you'll find far more rust than you expected. But is it all the way through?

The most common floorboard rusting occurs from the scuff plate inward for about 10 inches. If it's only surface

scale, chances are you won't have a major repair job. You may even be able to do all of the restoration yourself. To be sure, poke around with your knife.

It is unrealistic to expect a floorboard with no rust, but you have to quantify what's there. Of course, the bigger the hole, the more expensive the repair. Moreover, although excellent floorboard repair panels are available, installation is a major repair job. Look for two things: insurmountable difficulties and bargaining points. You certainly shouldn't buy a turkey, nor spend one dime unnecessarily.

Take a close inventory of the cockpit. Again, forget the condition of the upholstery. If the original seats are still there, are they rebuildable? Replacing them with late-model bucket seats is a possibility, but often at the sacrifice of proportionality. The original seat in a coupe or sedan seems to be the only one that "looks right."

Inspect the dash. This has always

Nothing beats the human hand for detecting surface irregularities. When surveying a potential purchase, take notes. Later when you are mulling it over at home, you'll be better able to weigh factors that will help you make the right decision.

As indicated a number of times, purchasing any old car or truck requires a strong emphasis on completeness. Although there is an ample supply of reproduction parts for early Fords, availability of parts for any other make is not, and probably never will be as extensive. On the other hand, even Ford enthusiasts should not be complacent . . . just try to find a decent stock rear fender for a 1940 pickup!

wheel openings. When street rodders adopted wide aluminum wheels and rear tires, they suddenly found that the combination wouldn't fit under the rear fenders. Sooo, out came the tin snips! Often, the results were sadly amateurish. Therefore, if you elect to retain those stock fenders, you're going to have to restore them.

Another common sheet metal headache is an equally crude attempt to heal rusted drip moldings. This was typically done by slicing off the molding and leading in the seams. Another popular sheet-metal modification during the '50s and '60s was to blank-out the side windows and enlarge the smallish rear window of a pre-war coupe. If you don't like such modifications, you may later find out you've bought a ticket to some expensive bodywork.

been a favorite area of modification. The worst situation would be the complete removal of the original and substitution of, say, a 1950 Olds dash. (I actually saw this swap in a 1940 Ford pickup. Yuk!) Forget the gauges, you should have something to work with depending upon what you plan for the dashboard. The more interior hardware present, the better off you are. Although many reproduction items such as door handles and window cranks are available, many parts such as window moldings are still swap-meet items . . . and expensive.

Plan to replace the window glass. Chances are the original glass is foxed—turned brown—and is useful only as patterns for the glazier to cut new glass.

SIDESTEP SHOT RODS

In all of the foregoing, I described an

original car, not a hot rodded more-or-less stocker, foxtails and Sears seat covers not withstanding. However, no matter how old a car is or the weather conditions it was subjected to while abandoned, the most serious problems found are usually those that resulted from crude modifications, not neglect. Barring the car that is a total rust-out, the hot rodder of old has all too often left a bitter legacy. He may have saved that roadster body from the scrap-metal drive, but he did it on his own terms. That can mean anything from welding the doors shut to cutting out the floorpan in order to channel the body.

Problem Areas

After a careful inspection of the exterior sheet metal, let's look at a few problems typically found in hot rodded cars. One in particular is the rear-

Modifications and Mayhem

When looking over an old street rod, first lift the hood. Inspect the inner fender panels, firewall and chassis. If the original transmission is still in place, it's a sure sign the engine swap was done a long time ago. One of the most common and frustrating sights encountered in an engine compartment is the gapping hole a former engine-swapper left in his eagerness to provide clearance for a big late-model engine and automatic transmission. The latter is typically the reason why parts of the floorboards and chassis look like they swallowed a hand grenade!

As often as not, excess quantities of metal were removed from the lower part of the firewall and midsection of the chassis. After the damage was done, the holes were crudely patched to keep engine fumes from engulfing

Nothing takes a beating like an old truck's cargo bed. True, the makings of a complete reproduction bed is as close as your telephone, but you may find that an entire repro bed will cost you half as much as the purchase price of the whole truck!

driver and passenger. Anything can be repaired. Nevertheless, you must ask yourself, "At what cost?"

Firewall Modification—Firewall modifications can be a real tragedy. For example, I've never understood the 1950s craze to stuff the battery into the firewall instead of the trunk. As a result, many firewalls were butchered. Today, most rod builders agree that such modification should not be done. The restoration of such a critical panel will drive up the cost of a project. By the way, "critical" is just the right word for many old car firewalls because they originally served as a structural component. Careless metal snipping may have created problems you can-

not see, such as increased metal fatigue in the entire cowl area.

Clutch-and-Pedal Assembly—The thought of butchered firewalls calls to mind a modification of similar consequences: the poorly mounted and unsupported post-1948 hanging clutch-and-brake pedal assembly. If such an installation was performed on a car you are considering, don't think that merely removing it and patching up the holes will correct the problem. It is more than just a question of cosmetics. You may also find stress cracks radiating 6–12 inches from where the cylinders bolted, and along the firewall to the body seams.

In general, the cost of repairing a

firewall is directly proportional to the amount of metal previously removed, but don't be overly concerned with small holes an eighth to a half-inch in diameter. Through the years, former owners may have mounted all sorts of things to the firewall. The repair is tedious, but not expensive. You'll be able to repair most of these even if you're not particularly skilled in metal finishing.

Clear away the cobwebs along both inner fender panels and note what you see and feel. This is a prime area for metal fatigue, but simple welding is often the only fix required. Not so simple to repair are bulges a previous owner might have beat into the panel to provide generator clearance. Firewall-to-distributor clearance was another favorite modification for old-time hot rodders to practice their black art of ball peen hammer metalwork.

POWER CORRUPTS

There's no telling what engine or transmission combination you'll find in an old hot rod. Popular cars, particularly early Ford coupes and roadsters, have been powered by every V-8 to come out of Detroit. If it looked as if it made horsepower, the adventuresome would somehow figure a way to shoehorn it in the engine bay.

Problem Engines

Problem engines, however, have traditionally been the early Oldsmobile, the big Chrysler Hemi and the entire Ford OHV V-8 line from the 1954 Y-block to date. Installation of any of these has all too often been an open invitation to a cut-and-hack party. The least you can expect is modification to the lower firewall and fender panels, particularly if the previous builder installed headers.

Never buy an old car or truck without a thorough inspection of the chassis and general underside. The number of potential problems is extensive. They may not deter your purchase, but you should know about their existence. Often you just have to get down and dirty and slide under. Watch out for spiders!

If the former street rod appears to have been the victim of an unhealthy engine swap, take a peek at the firewall and floorboards from the cockpit side. This is particularly necessary if the engine is still in place, thus restricting your vision from the engine compartment side. You should know now what was done to get the engine installed, and what you must undo when it's removed.

Don't be alarmed simply because the frame was altered. What's important is the quality and quantity of workmanship. Check to see if the X-member or any major part of the chassis has been weakened. Were big chunks crudely burned away or were neat incisions made? Were any strengthening brackets or fishplates welded in that might have prevented stress cracks in hidden areas? Is there a lack of such precautions that would make you stop and wonder? Can the previous modifica-

tions be reached for easy repair? Not everybody plans on replacing the frame or even pulling a heavy sedan body off the original chassis for major repairs.

Sometimes you can't see well enough to tell if a chassis was butchered. However, because the original automatic transmission often was installed with an OHV engine, you can imagine what it took to stuff a fat '53 Olds Hydro or '66 Chrysler Torqueflite into a slim prewar frame. There is a brighter side, though. Perhaps the workmanship is good, and better yet, the transmission swapped may be close to what you've planned on installing.

ROLL UNDERNEATH

If all looks like a "go" so far, it's time to look at the underside. First, jack up the car and support it firmly on jack stands. Never get under a car that's

supported by only a jack. The consequences can be fatal. Be sure the car is firmly supported by gently rocking it. Now, armed with your knife and flashlight, get on the creeper and roll underneath.

Carefully inspect the lower rear deck panel and slowly work your way toward the firewall. Caked-on grease and road tar are usually positive signs. Oil-based deposits protect the metal frame and floor pan. A dry chassis, on the other hand, won't have this protection. It may be badly rusted. Light surface rust is nothing to panic over, but do some discreet scraping here and there. Look for weak spots or actual rust-throughs in the frame and floor pan. Check in corners and pockets, particularly under the trunk. Rain and moisture accumulate inside the trunk, and those back-end tool compartments in prewar cars frequently rust through to the underside.

Also, check for collision damage while underneath. 'Tis a rare 60-year-old car that hasn't been rear-ended at least once. To get the inside story, check the rear of the frame and the underside of the lower rear deck panel for signs of repair. Collision damage isn't the only problem; the quality of repair work done way back when is equally important. Actually, if the car was damaged and repaired from the period of its manufacture until about 1955, chances are the repair work was done with some semblance of care. Normal standards of workmanship were higher in the days before the quickie insurance company–oriented collision shop. In the 1960s, the quality of non-custom body and fender repair fell off dramatically.

If you find repaired damage, look for plastic filler seeping through ice-pick

29

holes, metal wrinkles that were not hammered out—just puttied over— and twisted frame horns that snitch on crude and ineffective attempts to pull them straight.

Not only do some rod builders want to retain the original chassis, they may also want the original front suspension, particularly devotees of 1932–48 Fords. If you're among this group, carefully inspect the radius rods, spring perches, axle and spindles. If the radius rods were split, was a decent job done? Or, were the rods heated, bent and twisted out to hook up to big plates welded to the sides of the frame rails? If so, this could mean expensive repairs, or a search for costly replacement parts. In effect, the car would not be complete.

As you continue your inspection, I hope you find at least as many good points as bad ones. Rust is to be expected in any old car, but the ravages of a thoughtless 1950s-era builder who believed old Fords would be around forever is sometimes heartbreaking.

You'll usually find that parts of the frame were removed to provide clearance for dual exhausts. It was as if muffler shops of the day couldn't bend tubing to go around anything. Instead, they cut the offending frame member

away. Most minor alterations won't affect frame strength, although structural integrity is what you must always keep in mind. Nevertheless, crude or excessive cutting can spoil the looks of a chassis, and ours is a hobby that places great emphasis on the appearance of otherwise mundane mechanical components.

I haven't said much about the rear axle assembly. Whereas front suspensions were often only partially modified with a dropped axle or tubular shocks, even the most casual hot rod enthusiast quickly learned that the original rearend wouldn't take much power. Inspect any welded-on brackets on the rear axle housing from a design and an execution standpoint. How are the springs and shock absorbers mounted? Are the brackets for traction bars crudely welded to the frame? Yes, it's true. It seems like everything was welded on years ago. Nothing was merely bolted to the frame.

FILLING IN THE BLANKS

Up to this point, emphasis is placed on the condition of what's there, and what it will cost to repair it, be it a basketcase or a running car. However, as I've said all along, that is the easy part.

It's much more difficult to determine what isn't there and what it will cost in time and money to replace the missing components.

If you plan to build a Ford-based street rod, the reproduction parts industry will be a lifesaver. In addition, the situation is getting slightly better for Chevy-based street rods. Not so for everybody else. If you have your heart set on an uncommon street rod, more power to you, but make sure the car has all of its original body and trim components.

Finally, although I've emphasized buying as complete a car as possible— in keeping with the long-term trend of maintaining exterior originality—I haven't spent much time discussing mechanical aspects. The assumption is that you are planning on incorporating modern engineering and reliability into the powertrain, suspension and steering. After all, that's what street rodding is all about. Therefore, you may be better off purchasing a complete body and frame with little or no running gear. In that case, you are paying for what you will use, not for the privilege of hauling away the seller's junk.

VINTAGE TIN CHECKLIST

Parts to look for and inspect when evaluating the complete condition of an old car.

FRAME: Complete, no significant damage? Yes ___ No ___
Front Horns: Modified? Removed ___ Damaged ___
Front Crossmember: Modified? Removed ___ Damaged ___
Center Member: Modified? Removed ___ Damaged ___
Rear Crossmember: Modified? Removed ___ Damaged ___
Rear Horns: Modified? Removed ___ Damaged ___
Matching Title Papers: Yes ___ No ___

BODY: Complete, no significant damage? Yes ___ No ___
Roof Drip Moldings: Good ___ Rusted ___
Quarter Panels: Good ___ Rusted ___
Deck Panel: Good ___ Rusted ___
Firewall: Complete, no significant damage: Yes ___ No ___
Floorboards: Good ___ Rusted ___
Body trim: Complete, no significant damage? Yes ___ No ___

FRONT FENDERS: Complete, no significant damage? Yes ___ No ___
Front Fender Inner Panels: Good ___ Rusted ___
Headlight Assemblies: Complete, no significant damage? Yes ___ No ___
Headlight Rims: Good ___ Rusted ___
Headlight Buckets: Complete, no significant damage? Yes ___ No ___

FRONT BUMPER: Complete, no significant damage? Yes ___ No ___
Front Bumper Brackets: Complete, no significant damage? Yes ___ No ___
Front Bumper Guards: Complete, no significant damage? Yes ___ No ___

GRILLE: Complete, no significant damage? Yes ___ No ___
Grille Guard: Complete, no significant damage? Yes ___ No ___
Grille Guard Stiffeners: Complete, no significant damage? Yes ___ No ___

HOOD: Complete, no significant damage? Yes ___ No ___
Hood-Spring Assemblies: Complete, no significant damage? Yes ___ No ___
Exterior Hood Trim: Complete, no significant damage Yes ___ No ___
Interior Hood Hardware: Complete, no significant damage? Yes ___ No ___

COWL VENT: Complete, no significant damage? Yes ___ No ___
WINDSHIELD-WIPER: Complete, no significant damage? Yes ___ No ___

DOORS: Complete, no significant damage? Yes ___ No ___
Exterior Trim: Complete, no significant damage? Yes ___ No ___
Inside Door Hardware: Complete, no significant damage? Yes ___ No ___
Window Frames: Complete, no significant damage? Yes ___ No ___
Interior Trim: Complete, no significant damage? Yes ___ No ___

RUNNING BOARDS: Recoverable, no significant damage?   Yes ___ No ___

DECK LID: Complete, no significant damage?   Yes ___ No ___
Deck Lid Trim: Complete, no significant damage?   Yes ___ No ___
Deck Lid Spring: Complete, no significant damage?   Yes ___ No ___

REAR FENDERS: Complete, no significant damage?   Yes ___ No ___
Taillight Assemblies: Complete, no significant damage?   Yes ___ No ___
Taillight Lens: Complete, no significant damage?   Yes ___ No ___
Taillight Buckets: Complete, no significant damage?   Yes ___ No ___

REAR BUMPER: Complete, no significant damage?   Yes ___ No ___
Rear Bumper Brackets: Complete, no significant damage?   Yes ___ No ___
Rear Bumper Guards: Complete, no significant damage?   Yes ___ No ___

GAS TANK: Complete, no significant damage?   Yes ___ No ___
DASHBOARD: Complete, no significant damage?   Yes ___ No ___
STEERING COLUMN: Complete, no significant damage?   Yes ___ No ___
PEDAL ASSEMBLY: Complete, no significant damage?   Yes ___ No ___
SEATS: Complete, no significant damage?   Yes ___ No ___
WINDSHIELD FRAME: Complete, no significant damage?   Yes ___ No ___
WINDOW FRAMES: Complete, no significant damage?   Yes ___ No ___

REPRODUCTION BODIES

4

Henry certainly never envisioned the reproduction of his beloved Model A in fiberglass. I'm sure, however, that he would have appreciated the endurance of his legacy no matter what the medium.

FIBERGLASS BODIES

Although Ford experimented with soybean plastics for automotive use as early as 1939, plastic resins reinforced with spun-glass fibers weren't seriously explored until World War II ended. In 1946, several small boat manufacturers began experimenting with synthetic plastic hulls. The word "Fiberglas," a registered trademark of the Owens-Corning Fiberglas Corporation, was coined to describe that company's products for the marine indus-

try. As with many words, however, it has entered the lexicon with a slight variation in spelling to generically identify a medium made from plastic resins and a woven glass-fiber cloth.

It isn't too surprising, then, that the first complete plastic-bodied car was designed and built by the Glaspar Boat Company for a U.S. Army major in 1951. It was premiered at a Los Angeles auto show where it captured the attention of Detroit's professionals, amateur sports car builders, racers . . .

and hot rodders.

Original prewar roadsters were reasonably available in 1951 and more coupes were still driven by middle-aged folks than by street rodders when the Korean Conflict broke out. Therefore, although interested, the boys in T-shirts and blue jeans didn't look into the fabulous potential offered by fiberglass back then. There wasn't much incentive to do so.

Custom sports car body-builders did, though. The first was the Devin

Company of E1 Monte, California. Coachcraft, Kellison Engineering, La Dawri, Track Craft, Victress and other West Coast manufacturers soon followed.

By the early 1960s, street rodders were acutely aware that the demand for original roadster bodies had greatly exceed the supply. Few however, were in a position to do anything about it . . . with the exception of the late Tex Collins. Tex had founded a company to make reproduction stagecoach bodies for the western movie and television industry. An offshoot of that company was Cal-Automotive, and Tex began manufacturing and marketing a reproduction 1929 Ford roadster body.

Admittedly, many early fiberglass creations were of dubious quality. In fact, some were quite flimsy. I recall not wanting to spend a single day in one, much less all my street rodding tomorrows. Thankfully, few of those old repros are still around—and offered for sale. If you are considering buying a fiberglass car, be sure to determine its age!

Modern fiberglass is an excellent material for a reproduction street rod body in many ways. It affords high resilience, reasonable strength, corrosion resistance and light weight. Current reproductions faithfully replicate the early roadsters, coupes and sedans. Moreover, although prices naturally reflect high quality, they are within the reach of serious enthusiasts. Best of all, the nonprofessional finds it easy to work with fiberglass.

Basic Fiberglass
Construction Technique

Although approaches vary slightly from manufacturer to manufacturer, most commercial fiberglass street rod

bodies begin the same way. The builder pulls a mold off an original steel body. Before this is done, however, the steel body must be prepared so it has a flawless surface. As the male mold, any existing flaws will be transferred directly to the female mold. Because the female mold must be made in sections, molding clay is used to make dams for parting lines. A heavy coat of automobile body wax is then applied and polished to a hard film. After the waxing, a special parting agent is sprayed on. The female mold is then built up from the male. This is done by applying several coats of pure resin containing a high percentage of catalyst to make it cure quickly.

After the last coat of hot resin cures, the mold-builder applies a half-ounce surfacing mat saturated with a slow-curing resin. Mat is used because it's easier to sand should any imperfections have to be removed from the finished mold. A layer of 3-ounce mat and one of 10-ounce cloth usually follows.

When the body is completely encased in fiberglass, a braced framework is built around the mold to hold each section in its correct relative positions. This is because the assembly will be jostled about constantly during this process. In addition, there must be no hint of sag in the female mold when it's lifted from the body.

Imperfections on the inside surface of the female mold must be filled with a mixture of resin and glass fibers, and then sanded smooth. With the completion of the female mold, the manufacturer can start building reproduction bodies.

Basic body-building materials are the same as those used for constructing molds—a combination of spun glass

and synthetic resin. The glass is available to the manufacturer in several forms: mats, cloths and continuous strands. The mat is a fabric made from either chopped or continuous strands of fiberglass bound by resinous adhesives. It varies in weight from a feathery 3/4 ounce to a hefty 10 ounces per square foot. The cloth is woven from continuous strands of fiberglass available in 6- to 12-ounce weights. Those at the lighter end of the scale—6- and 7-ounce cloths—are most commonly used. A very heavy fabric known as woven roving is used to ensure high structural strength.

Regardless of form, fiberglass only serves as reinforcement, hence the term fiberglass-reinforced plastic (FRP). The other half of the equation is the plastic or synthetic resin bonding agent. The most common resins are polyesters, although occasionally epoxy is used where extra strength is needed or when the fiberglass is to be bonded to steel.

Building the Conventional
Fiberglass Reproduction Body

To manufacture a typical street rod body, the inside of the female mold is first sprayed with a gel coat. It contains a waxy substance that facilitates the eventual removal of the body shell after it hardens. Following the gel coat lamination, lay-up begins—the building up of the layers of fiberglass that form the body.

Body strength depends on the amount of fiberglass reinforcement used. Relative amounts of resin and fiberglass can be varied to meet whatever the manufacturer specifies. Quality is not simply a question of quantity though; the arrangement of the fiberglass fibers is just as important. If all the fibers were laid parallel to each other, there would be great longitudinal strength, but little lateral strength. If, however, the fibers are laid at right angles to each other, overall strength is doubled. Strength is further enhanced when the fibers are arranged randomly. Often, the combined strength of bi-directional and randomly arranged fiberglass is preferred for building a street rod body.

Because major manufacturers of reproduction street rod bodies work with the same raw materials and basic techniques, it's easy to assume that there are no significant differences between their products. Advertising claims aside, that's not entirely true. Sophisticated techniques, once prohibitive for low-volume manufacturing, have come to the fore. The structural integrity and durability that exists today would withstand even the most bone-rattling chase in a mid-1960s "hoss opera."

Hand lamination is the oldest and most laborious method of manufacturing fiberglass panels. Varying layers of mat and cloth are used to build the body up from the gel coat. Resin is applied with a paintbrush. This combination of mat and cloth forms easily into the corners and curves of the mold. Mat, which is used first, imparts substance and thickness depending upon how much resin is brushed on. The bi-directional woven pattern of the cloth, which is applied after the mat, gives even strength to the panel.

Methyl ethyl ketone peroxide (MEK) is used as a catalyst to accelerate the hardening of the resin. It induces heat and, as such, must be very carefully and sparingly stirred into the resin at an average rate of 20cc per gallon at room temperature. The

American Streetrod & Performance chose the Chevrolet 1934 Coupe, Cabriolet and Phaeton to interest buyers of non-Ford building material. The Cabriolet body is available with stock-width doors on a 107-inch wheelbase frame or with doors that have been "stretched" 4 inches for easier entry and exit.

manufacturer must constantly monitor shop temperature and adjust the amount of MEK accordingly. Normally, it takes about 30 minutes for the catalyst to harden the resin. During this time, the laminator must work rapidly to eliminate air pockets and gently squeeze out excess resin. Hand-laminated bodies consisting of up to 65-percent fiberglass have traditionally been considered the strongest available in terms of the fiberglass-to-resin ratio.

One quality-enhancing technique is a vacuum or pressure bag in the mold that squeezes out excess resin and entrapped air. This provides uniform shell thickness and improves the smoothness of the paint surface much like high-production matched molds. Another, and perhaps more significant improvement, is the addition of reinforcement materials to back up the fiberglass mat and cloth.

Some manufacturers use steel-tube "birdcages" within the fiberglass shell. Others insert oak between layers of fiberglass, some use an acoustical

foam sandwich in the floorboards, and still others use strips of previously cured fiberglass. In fact, fiberglass construction alone is not strong enough for a street rod body. The technology has vastly improved over the years, though, and it is obvious that new and better means of structural reinforcement will be developed in the future.

MANUFACTURERS OF FIBERGLASS BODIES

American Streetrod & Performance
7323 NE Gilsan Street
Portland, Oregon 97213
(503) 255-1607; Fax: (503) 255-1659
Website: www.americanstrod.com

The Blue Oval Boys may be hesitant in admitting it, but there is another early car marquee out there with a very significant following. In the Chevrolet line, the 1934 Coupe, Cabriolet and Phaeton seem to be the most popular. No wonder, then, that ASP chose these three full-fendered honeys to excite

Older hot rodders will always remember the early Willys coupes that all but dominated the quarter mile in the 1960s. Not only were they fast, they looked like they could be driven on the street. This Antique & Collectible Autos 1940–41 Willys coupe could just be the car that turns an ex-drag racer into a street rodder.

Brinkley Manufacturing's Zipper Roadster is based on the traditional 1932 street rod, yet it's doors are a discreet 10-inches longer and it sits atop a 106-inch wheelbase frame specifically designed for the car. Add the optional hardtop, and voila! you have a sleek coupe for those rain-threatened wintry days!

Antique & Collectible Autos
35 Dole Street
Buffalo, NY 14210
(716) 825-3990, Fax (716) 823-0048

The typical street rodder's "knee jerk" answer to the question of which car epitomizes the genre will be the 1932 Ford roadster. It is equally true that A & C Autos is quick to point out their fiberglass laminate Deuce with its reinforcement of heavy woven roving is one of the most durable bodies in the industry. All high-stress areas of the body are reinforced with roving, and the doorframes and dash are supported with hardwood and plywood inner structure for solid stability. A & C likes to cover the bases, however, and the 1934–35 Chevy coupe in their stable attracts far more than a passing glance when a jaded rodder ambles by. That's not all, folks. Street rodders with a drag racing memory going back to the 1960s will forever have a warm spot in their hearts for the prewar Willys coupes that all but dominated the quarter mile in those days. The A & C Autos sleek 1940–41 Willys coupe just might be the car that turns an ex-drag race fan into a practicing street rodder. A & C Autos have more than 20 years experience in the conventional fiberglass industry including Kevlar carbon fiber applications.

Brinkley Manufacturing
P.O. Box 2337
Oregon City, Oregon 97045
(503) 632-1932
www.brinkleymfg.com

The Zipper Roadster, while based on the traditional 1932 street rod, has several distinctive styling features that set it apart from its completely stock-appearing brethren. One is its curved

interested buyers. During manufacture, the company laminates heavy core mat into several layers of fiberglass on large panel areas such the top, floors, doors, deck lid and quarter panels to assure strength and prevent flexing. All bodies are reinforced with a steel cage structure, and the floor is further underlaid with a 1-inch square steel tubing structure. The Cabriolet body is available with stock width doors on a 107-inch wheelbase frame or with doors that have been "stretched" 4 inches for easier entry and exit. This modification lengthens the wheelbase, and the body is therefore fitted to the longer (112-inch) Phaeton chassis.

Bill Keifer's famous Fad T California Custom Roadster kit is a sure way to go from the garage to the boulevard in record time. All you have to do is assemble the package and install the drivetrain of your choice!

frameless windshield and the "no-cowl" hood and side panels. The body is actually 2 inches longer than a stocker with 10-inch wider doors, but it sits atop a 106-inch wheelbase frame (which is specifically designed for the car). The result is impressive, but discreet. Not quite so discreet is the Stretched Deuce Roadster. This one is tweaked a full 6 inches longer than stock, and is fitted to a 112-inch wheelbase chassis. Adding further to creature comfort is the fact that the doors open to a 90-degree angle for effortless entry and exit. All hinges and latches are factory-installed and inspected. Brinkley also offers steel reinforced 1932 "Vikki" Phaetons, 1933 Roadsters and 1933 "Vikki" Phaetons with a full complement of fenders and hard tops.

California Custom Roadsters
15094 Sierra Bonita
Chino, California 91710
(909) 393-4005
Fax (909) 393-4228

CCR, known for many years as the place to go for plans and patterns for the ever-popular "Fad T," offers everything else to move from the ground up—fiberglass bodies, perfect-fit frames, and the proper steering and suspension. All you have to do is assemble the Fadster as per detailed instructions and add the drivetrain of your choice! Of course, they also build complete, turnkey cars in their shop.

Coach & Chassis Works, Inc.
1445-A Babcock Blvd.
Pittsburgh, Pennsylvania 15209
(412) 821-1900, Fax (412) 821-5099

In numbers, fans of mid-1930s Dodge and Plymouth passenger cars and light trucks may be smaller than other street rod practitioners. No big deal, what they lack numerically, they make up for in enthusiasm. Moreover, equally enthusiastic are the folks at Coach & Chassis Works. Armed with statistics and specifications, they want to bring Plymouth and Dodge street rodders up to speed with regard to the objects of their affection. Such knowledge is not trivia, either. It is important to a fellow turning a dream into a highway bound reality. The 1933 Dodge

Series DP, in production from November 23, 1932 to April 1933, had a 111 1/2-inch wheelbase. Those made after April 1933 had a 115-inch wheelbase. The extra length was reflected in the front sheet metal design. The 1933 Plymouth PC series production ran from April 14, 1933 to December 5, 1933. The 107-inch wheelbase was dropped early in the year and replaced with the PCXX 108-inch wheelbase. Only 43,403 cars rolled off the line. The PD 112-inch wheelbase used a modified 1933 Dodge model DP 111 1/2-inch wheelbase chassis. Front fenders and hood panels were juggled to construct a new car without designing a new body! Well, Coach & Chassis Works wants their potential reproduction body customers to know they have all these bases covered. They offer fiberglass 1934 Plymouth and Dodge Coupe and Convertible bodies with a filled roof and cowl vent, a recessed fire wall, a smooth floor with steel tubing laminated into it. (The body is bolted to the chassis through this sub-frame.) All body reinforcing steel is welded into a unit using approximately 80 feet of 1 x 1-inch, and 1 x 2-inch steel tubing in the body and sub-frame.

The so-called "Glamour Era" 1933–35 Dodge trucks were produced in substantial numbers, about 191,000 units. (Just try to find a rebuildable one today!) These "Commercials" rode on a chassis originally designed for a passenger car. If this is the honey you've been looking for, Coach & Chassis Works offers a reproduction 1933–35 Dodge Pickup with a filled roof and cowl vent, recessed firewall, and smooth floor. Construction is identical to the coupes and convertibles.

Finally, although the early Plymouth

Deuce Customs of Australia distributes their products in the US of A through Geoff Mitford-Taylor (GMT) of Huntington Beach, California. This 1934 roadster is just one of their extensive 1928–36 Ford reproductions.

The J. B. Donaldson Company, with over 30 years experience in fiberglass manufacturing, offers handcrafted, oven-cured 1935–36 fiberglass bodies fitted with a steel inner framework. Coming or going, Donaldson's reproduction 1936 Ford roadster (of which only a few thousand originals were built) combines the essence of an "old ragtop" with all the mechanical improvements of a modern street rod.

and Dodges may be the C&CW flagship models, their showroom also highlights a 1932 Ford 3-Window Coupe!

Deuce Customs of Australia/GMT
17782A Metzler Lane
Huntington Beach, CA 92647
(714) 842-2824

Not to be undone by his American mates, Geoff Mitford-Taylor of GMT, a New Zealand native, but well-known in Southern California street rod cir-

cles for his sheet metal artistry, is also the US distributor for the fiberglass reproduction bodies manufactured by Deuce Customs of Australia. At the time of this writing, the team offers a dozen or so Ford-styled reproductions to the rod builder: One each from the 1928, 1932, 1934, and 1936 Roadster lineup; a 1932 Tudor and Sedan Delivery; the ever popular 1932 3- and 5-window coupes; a phantom 1932 "Tudor Phaeton," and a 1933–34 Tudor and Sedan Delivery. Now, a trip

to Australia to look over their wares would be a great vacation, but if all your spare cash is going into your rod project, get in touch with Geoff at his Beach City hangout.

J. B. Donaldson Co.
2533 West Cypress Street
Phoenix, Arizona 85009
(602) 278-4505; Fax (602) 278-1112
Website: www.jbdonaldsonco.com

The mid-1930s were good years for Ford, and over two million 1935–36 models were sold. Even so, not enough Roadsters and 3-Window Coupes are left to satisfy today's street rod builder. Thankfully, the J. B. Donaldson Company, with over 30-years experience in fiberglass manufacturing, has the wherewithal to satisfy those with the itch. Their 1935–36 fiberglass bodies and parts are handcrafted and fitted with a steel inner framework. Then they are oven-cured to prevent blistering, warping, and something not often mentioned—fiberglass odor.

Downs Manufacturing
715 North Main Street
Lawton, Michigan 49065
(616) 624-4081, Fax (616) 624-6359
www.downsmfg.com

Jim Downs founded this street rod body company some twenty years ago, and as they enter their third decade, they have increased their manufacturing facility from 3000 to 28,000 square feet. From this complex comes a product line of over forty different body styles plus custom designs! That's a bunch, guys! All of Downs Cabriolets, Coupes, Roadsters, Phaetons, Sedans, Victorias, Convertibles and Pickups are hand-laminated, and fitted over a steel sub-structure. All are

Few 'glass body manufacturers can claim 25 years or more in the business. The team running the Gibbon Company can, however. Kyle Bond, son of the founder, uses all that experience to offer a variety of body styles, but this 5-Window coupe is one of his favorite ways to promote the company's products.

equipped with D.O.T. approved bear claw safety latches.

Gibbon Fiberglass Reproductions
132 Industrial Way
Darlington, South Carolina 29532
(843) 395-6200; Fax (843) 395-1953
Website:
www.gibbonfiberglass.com

Sharing the limelight with a handful of other 'glass body manufacturers who can claim 25 years or better in the reproduction business, is the team running the Gibbon Company. Dwight Bond started the ball rolling back in 1971, and his son Kyle took over the presidency a few years ago. Continuity of management is always a plus. A big plus, too is the variety of body styles offered. For starters, there's the 1928–29 Roadster, the 1928–29 Roadster Pickup, the 1930–31 Tudor/Phaeton, and the 1930–31 Closed Cab Pickup. Jumping into the V-8 years, there's the 1932 Roadster, 3-window Coupe, 5-window coupe, Cabriolet, Tudor Sedan, Sedan Delivery, Roadster Pickup, Cabriolet Pickup, 4-Door Phaeton; the unique channeled 1933 Viper Roadster Coupe and Tudor, the 1933–34 Roadster,

Tudor Sedan, 3-window coupe, Roadster Pickup, 4-Door Phaeton, 1937 Club Cabriolet, Rumble Seat Cabriolet, and last but not least, the 1939 Convertible.

Lone Star Classics, Inc.
580 Aviator Drive
Fort Worth, Texas 76179
(877) 572-2277 Fax (817) 439-5722
Website: www.streetrodcountry.com

This Texas based company has been in the kit car business for ten years, and for most of that time, they were primarily known for classy Cobras and the "Route 66" Corvette. Now, the LS32, a traditional looking High Boy Deuce roadster just might become their new flagship. The body is constructed of Triax® weave and Coremat® reinforced fiberglass, supported with a full steel substructure, and finished in sandable gel coat. In fact, the LS32 was recently voted one of the best new kits by Petersen Publishing. The company offers full kit cars, complete but unassembled cars (as opposed to a kit), and options such as fenders and running boards. Lone Star is very proud of their ability to provide a budget-minded rod builder with the opportunity to buy a part at a time, or a complete car. The LS32 is designed to be installed on a dedicated street rod reproduction chassis manufactured by Cornhusker Rod & Custom.

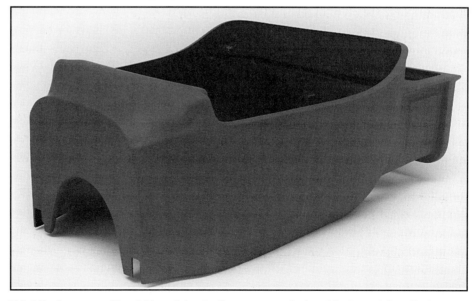

Total Performance Street T roadster bodies are manufactured in two styles. Both come complete with floor, firewall, custom dash and hidden doors, and are fully reinforced with 1-inch square tubing. They are specifically designed to fit the Total Performance Pro Street chassis.

Wescott's Auto Restyling is justifiably proud of its 1939 Ford convertible coupe. Although a little difficult to appreciate in the jam-packed shop, the classic lines of this sought-after body style, and the work it takes to make a relatively complex project function as it should, is readily apparent. Wescott was one of the first reproduction body manufacturers to use steel internal support structures to reinforce critical stress areas.

Total Performance
400 South Orchard Street
Wallingford, CT 06492
1-203-265-7107
Website: www.tbuckets.com

Mickey Lauria's Total Performance has been in the T-Bucket Biz in a big way since 1971. The company offers frames, bodies, driveline components, accessories, and on and on. In fact, their hefty catalog ($7) reads like a wishbook for nearly everything spelled s-t-r-e-e-t r-o-d!

Rat's Glass
844 Collie Cove Ct.
Friendsville, Tennessee 37737
(865) 995-9126; Fax (865) 995-9126
ratsglass@aol.com;
Website: www.ratsglassbodies.com

Rodders in the Tennessee area are accustomed to seeing a big red GMC Hotshot pulling a big red step-down trailer into events all through the Mississippi Valley. Well, it isn't Santa, it's a local 'glass body builder known as "Rat." I won't even try to guess how

he came by this moniker, but I personally think "Rad" is more appropriate for his Speedstar line of radically redesigned coupes and roadsters based on early Ford styling. Rat's oak and steel reinforced offerings are available with swept back '34ish grilles, track noses and all sorts of neat optional features such as lift-off tops, chopped tops and the like. As this is written, word is that there will soon be an equally radical Vickie available.

Wescott's Auto Restyling
19701 S. E. Highway 212
Boring ,Oregon 97009

The middle and last name alone should give you some clue as to the tenure and background of Dee Wescott. He started a body shop way back in 1954 and quickly became the place to go in the Pacific Northwest for quality "Restyling" as the art of reconfiguring automotive sheet metal was known in those days. A number of first-rate "customs" rolled from his shop into the pages of car mags.

Moreover, he rolled up a reputation second to none. His initial journey into the world of fiberglass began with contemporary Corvette repair, but the lure of mail order with its national marketing opportunities quickly led him to introduce 'glass reproductions of early Ford fenders. For street rodders and restorers, the discouraging, never-ending search for already rare original replacements was reduced for all but the die-hard purist. The more practical types, unwilling to spend years on wild-goose chases, were now able to bring completed projects from the garage to the boulevard.

Wescott's entry into the building of a full-on reproduction body rapidly advanced from his first offering in 1969—a 1931 Model A coupe replica with doors that opened and closed properly, to a '31 roadster in 1971. Ultimately a Deuce roadster made its debut in 1975. The rest is "histoire," as they say, and today Wescott's Auto Restyling catalog features a stable that includes the 1926 Roadster, 1928–29, 1930–31 Roadsters and Phaetons, 1928–29, 1930–31 Roadster Pickups, the 1931 coupe and the 1939 and 1940 convertibles! Lord only knows what else is on the drawing board.

Wescott's is more than just a prolific styling leader, however. They were one of the first to use steel internal support structures patterned after the Corvette to reinforce critical stress areas. These structures are bonded to the one-piece body shell. A shell, by the way, that was laminated in a steel-reinforced, square and level mold.

BUYING A USED 'GLASS BODY

Fiberglass street rods with twenty years of service are at every swap meet with a "For Sale" sign taped to the windshield. On the other hand, they may be offered in a terse, 10-word advertisement in the Sunday classifieds. If you encounter either, you owe it to yourself to investigate; the car may well be a super deal. But then again . . .

To determine if that 'glass rod looking for a home has a hand-laminated body, look for an unupholstered panel, usually found inside the trunk. Check the inside surface. You should detect a coarse, cloth-like texture. The backside of a body built years ago by the spray lamination method is typically smooth, but shows random 'glass fibers. This once popular method—done with a "chopper gun"—was faster and less expensive compared to hand lamination. A multi-strand fiberglass rope was fed into a special spray gun. The rope was shredded—or chopped—into short strands, mixed with catalyzed resin and sprayed into the gel-coated mold. The coat had to be applied evenly or the body would have weak areas.

Even when you know which body-construction method was used, you still only have half of the story. The skill and craftsmanship of the street rodder who later reinforced it and fitted it to the chassis is often the difference between something that's worth buying and something that's best forgotten.

The exterior of the body, and the fit and function of the doors and deck lid can reveal a lot about these fellows and just how conscientious they were. For example, can you see or feel any major surface imperfections? Is there any evidence of cracking? Are the finish coats of paint as smooth as a baby's backside—as they should be—or can you see or feel ripples and waves? An

upholstered fiberglass body is difficult to fully evaluate, but not impossible. For example, run your hand over the body to check for surface imperfections. Be super critical when evaluating door and deck-lid fit and operation.

One problem often encountered with old, poorly unreinforced fiberglass bodies is warpage. It takes about a month for fresh fiberglass to completely harden. During this period, precautions must be taken to prevent the body from sagging or twisting and taking a set, both when it was manufactured, and later during the time lapse when the buyer received it and when he and his buddies fitted it to the chassis. If this mating wasn't prompt enough, the body could have assumed a shape that simply wasn't compatible with either the chassis or other components. There is also the ever-present possibility of shrinkage, which can range from one percent to as much as six percent, depending on the quality of the resins used.

All fresh fiberglass bodies should be fitted and secured to the chassis as soon as possible to prevent warpage and minimize shrinkage. If this wasn't done on the rod you're looking over, it may be an insurmountable task to right the wrongs. For this reason, avoid buying a previously owned fiberglass body, even one of modern manufacture, that's been sitting unsupported by either a chassis or major bracing for any but a very short length of time. Fiberglass bodies are one-off items with unique fitting problems, as you'll discover when you install one on your unique chassis.

Since the beginning of fiberglass street rod bodies, manufacturers have come and gone. Today, those who cater to the street rodder have solidi-

fied their position in the market by turning out high-quality parts. The fiberglass-replica bodies and components listed are suitable for street rod purposes. Prices vary depending on the sophistication of manufacture and options chosen. All manufacturers provide catalogs or brochures that answer typical questions asked by prospective customers. Many have websites and email addresses where specific questions relating to their products are answered. All are quality products on which you can base your project, but keep in mind that by their very nature, fiberglass reproduction bodies will still need some degree of fine-tuning before they are ready for paint. Just how much fitting and extra reinforcement will be required varies not only from manufacturer to manufacturer, but from body to body.

REPRODUCTION BODIES MADE OF COMPOSITE MATERIALS

"Composites" entered the manufacturing world in a big way during the 1970s. The use of carbon fibers arranged at various angles to enhance rigidity and resistance to fatigue under stress has made even more gains since then. In fact, they have become the replacement material for a significant number of items formerly made of steel, aluminum and fiberglass.

It wasn't until the late 1990s, however, that composite reproduction street rod bodies began to appear, and for the same reason composites gained so much attention in industry at large—lightweight and strength. Consequently, more and more repro roadsters are beginning to show up at major rod events. Construction-wise, composite bodies have no gel coat. As

41

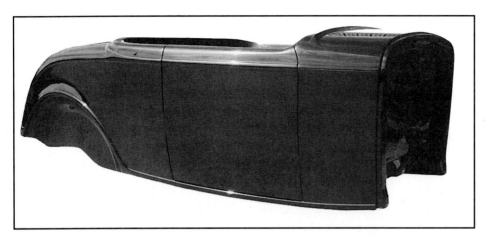

Harwood's forte is the traditional 1932 Ford roadster. The body is hand-laminated and reinforced with porcelain ceramics and honeycomb composites.

a result, there is only a one-percent air void beneath the surface thereby reducing heat buildup (and subsequent distortion) to a minimum. Because the process avoids the expansion and contraction found in fiberglass—a downside that sometimes leads to surface "spider" cracks requiring repair—its staunch advocates go so far as to claim it is the most durable of manufacturing materials for an automobile body. Only the future will tell, but this much is for sure . . . composite materials already have more than just a toehold in the repro rod body market.

MANUFACTURERS OF COMPOSITE BODIES

American Street Rod Designs
324 Home Avenue
Maryville, Tennessee 37801
(865) 982-3091; Fax (865) 983-4418
www.americanstreetrod.com

If you've ever slid behind the wheel of a stock Model A or its big brother the 1932 Ford, and you even have the beginning of "middle-aged spread," well, you know why tilt steering wheels were invented! I suppose folks were smaller and thinner in Depression Era days. Nevertheless,

you don't have to be a "fat cat" to appreciate the smooth cowl, hand-laid composite body manufactured by ASRD. The cockpit and doors on their Deuce roadster body have been lengthened a discreet two inches for extra ease upon ingress or egress. Deciding there is a market for innovations such as that doesn't come from by guess or by golly, it comes from experience in the world of real street rodding. In addition, the folks at American can point to a solid twenty-one years of hand-crafted fiberglass experience. If further proof is needed, the company's all hand laid composite 1932 3-window coupe body should suffice. It comes with the traditional 2.5-inch top chop, a smooth dash fitted and installed, power windows (with glass!) installed, and a several other features, both standard and optional.

Cutting Edge Composites
P.O. Box 45, Building 45
Albany, Prince Edward Island
Canada, C0B 1A0
1-800-204-33343

Cutting Edge started out as a manufacturer of housings for high-tech Magnetic Resonance Imaging (MRI) machines used in the medical commu-

nity. How they got to aftermarket reproduction bodies for the street rod community is anyone's guess! Nevertheless, they have come up with several new construction methods that have intrigued street rodders looking for something different. The composite process Cutting Edge uses was originally developed for the US Navy, and it is more properly called "resin infusion molding." In this process, dry fiberglass mat is placed in an open mold that has been waxed and sprayed with gel coat. CE utilizes "quadraxial weaving" which lays out the individual fibers of a given part in four directions, and "needle-punched layouts" in which the component is needle-punched with glass fibers in three directions with the individual strands placed a quarter-inch apart across the entire surface. The mold is then sealed in a plastic bladder to which are attached resin feed and return lines and a number of flexible lines leading to a powerful vacuum pump. The resin is vacuum drawn into the mold, and throughout the fiberglass, at the rate of three gallons per minute. In three quarters of an hour, the resin begins to gel, and the "transfusion" is halted. The body cures in the closed mold. According to company officials, the net result is greater rigidity and incredible resistance to fatigue under stress, with up to 30,000 pounds per square inch compressive strength at a quarter-inch thickness. Reproduction bodies made thusly can withstand considerable loads without noticeable fatigue.

Cutting Edge offers no less than 17 different bodies based on the styling of the 1932, 1934, 1935 and 1936 Ford models including stock and chopped Coupes, Sedans and Vickies, in addition to the ever popular stock-looking 1932 roadster.

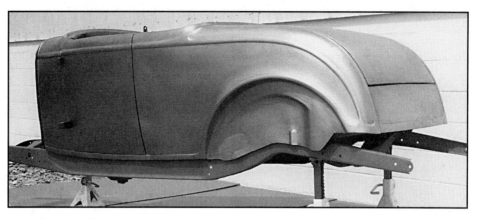
Brookville's All-Steel ™ Deuce Ford roadster bodies are fabricated from heavy gauge steel just like the originals.

Harwood Street Rods
13240 Hwy 110 S
Tyler, Texas 75707
(903) 561-6338

Gary Harwood traces his fiberglass and composite manufacturing pedigree back some 27 years. In the quarter century since he entered the high performance and street rod industry, his products have continually undergone improvements in both technology and quality, no small factor in his receiving the Composites Fabricators Association ACE Award for Excel-lence a few years ago. Harwood's forte is the traditional favorite in the 1932 Ford genre—the beloved roadster, with his Deuce 3-Window Coupe and Tudor Sedan/Sedan Delivery not far behind. Harwood Street Rods' hand-laminated bodies are reinforced with porcelain ceramics and honeycomb composites, and are dimensionally accurate for a glove-like fit on a factory-fresh reproduction chassis, or a dimensionally stock 1932 chassis in excellent condition. Nevertheless, several street rod features amply assist the novice owner-builder along the way. One is the fact that the compound double channel firewall is recessed to provide adequate clearance for all popular engine installations, and the Harwood-designed steel steering column support is laminated to the inside of the firewall.

Superior Glass Works
31816 Ona Way
Molalla, Oregon 97038
Mailing Address: P.O. Box 1140
Mulino, Oregon 97042
(503) 829-9634; Fax (503) 829-6634
www.superiorglassworks.com

Superior is a company eager to cap-ture both ends of the street rod/hot rod spectrum with a line of street and drag race bodies. Street versions include the "Trac-T Roadster," styled after the '27s that were so popular in the late 1940s and early 1950s on Southern California dirt ovals, a 1932 "Smooth Victoria" and 1932 3-window coupe, both offered in stock height or with a 2-inch chop. Then there is their 1933 "Hi-Tec Low-Boy Roadster." Other interesting products include a 1933 Willys Sedan Delivery, a 1937–38 Chevrolet Sedan Delivery, 1937–38 Chevrolet Cabriolet, and guess what, a reproduction of the ever popular 1936 Mullins Trailer! All built of fiberglass/composite with steel reinforcement. Several models come with hidden hinged doors; all have hinged deck lids and hood assemblies. Package deal chassis are also available. Their race versions include a 1934 Chevrolet Roadster (fiberglass or carbon fiber), a neat looking 1933 Willys Coupe, a 1933 Willys Sedan Delivery, a 1940 Willys Coupe and a 1937 Chevrolet Coupe.

ALL NEW METAL STREET ROD BODIES

Finally, we have now come full swing in the world of street rod body manufacturing. From the original domestic automobile industry came the originals, and not even a foresighted icon such as Henry Ford could have envisioned just how enduring would be this upstart offshoot of America's infatuation with the Model T and the V-8, even though he lived to witness the birth of *Hot Rod Magazine*. If he had, he may have punched out another couple thousand 1932 roadster bodies for a later sale.

Since he didn't, a few modern entrepreneurs put their capital on the line and jumped headlong into the street rod market with steel reproduction bodies and panels. Once a fledgling sub-industry, several manufacturers are in full swing. The manufacturing process itself holds no mysteries, however. In truth, it is quite similar to the manufacture of Henry's production in the 1930s without the advantage of a full-bore assembly line!

METAL BODY MANUFACTURERS

Brookville Roadster, Inc.
718 Albert Road
Brookville, Ohio 45309
(937) 833-4605
www.brookvilleroadster.com

Family owned and operated, BRI has been an industry leader in

I first saw HR&H's "Dearborn Deuce" down at Terry Berzenye's Specialized Street & Performance facilities in Huntington Beach, California. Crowded as his shop may be with myriad street rod works in progress, I couldn't have been more impressed with the genre's unique steel reproduction of the enormously popular 1932 Ford 3-window coupe.

1928–32 Ford steel reproduction bodies for more than ten years. All BRI bodies are made of the same gauge steel as the original Fords, and all panels are interchangeable with original panels. The completed bodies are hand assembled in their 52,000 square foot facility. Brookville has a marketing approach that is difficult to counter— "avoid the hassles of reconditioning a body that's been rusting for years and is full of body filler!" Their Model A offerings include a 1928–29 and a 1930–31 Roadster in the "Hi-Boy" styling. As an added feature, they offer a frame designed to handle a late model drivetrain. Not satisfied with only an A-bone selection, they next unveiled an All-Steel™ 1932 Ford Roadster body. Again, these handsome reproductions are made from heavy gauge steel just like the originals.

The company also manufactures critical sheet metal components such as a recessed firewall that enables a builder to easily install an oversized engine in his 1928–31 Model A. The heavy gauge stamped-steel firewall is engineered for proper fit and function.

BRI also offers stock Model A firewalls.

Stepping to the rear of the ever-popular Model A Pickup, BRI builds exact reproductions of original beds, and a number of different options including a special version that is 8 1/2 inches shorter than an original bed. Other options include stainless steel bed strips, a tailgate with or without the Ford script, and your choice of an assembled or unassembled unit. Bed components are manufactured with such detail that they will interchange with originals.

Want a comfortable breath of fresh air? Look into BRI's "ultimate 1930–31 Roadster pickup with the extended cab." The back of the All-Steel ™ cab is extended to provide more interior room along with a stretched body look. The front of the bed is shortened to match the cab, and uses stock running boards, aprons, and fenders.

What's that you say, you don't need a completely new car? Well, few components in 70-year-old street rod bodies take a daily beating worse than the

doors. BRI's reproduction 1928–31 roadster doors are made of heavy duty steel, and look, feel, and fit exactly like originals with all correct bracing inside and out.

Hot Rods & Horsepower, LLC
11 Business Park Drive
Branford, CT 06405
203.481.1932
www:hotrodsandhorsepower.com

Introduced in the summer of '02, the "Dearborn Deuce" as HR&H calls the first steel 1932 Ford 3-window replica, is an amazing sight to behold. Suffice it to say it was designed, engineered and built with state-of-the-art technology. It features a chopped top, filled cowl, recessed firewall, flat floor pan with a trans tunnel and clearance for a 9-inch Ford back axle. Hidden hinges for the doors and deck lid add a touch of custom styling. There's much more, however. Optional fenders of course, plus a 1-inch dropped grille shell, and a smooth 3-piece hood with louvered side panels. There is also a compatible, fully boxed 109-inch wheelbase frame with a notched front and "C-ed" rear.

Real Steel, Inc.
4440 S. E. 174th Avenue
Portland, Oregon 97236-1384
(503) 665-2222, Fax (503) 665-2225
www.realsteel.com

Five years ago, this division of Steve Frisbee's Auto Restorations was but a twinkle in the owner's eye. Steve built his reputation as a restorer of concourse-quality antiques and classics. Today one could say it is a classic example of the "tail wagging the dog." He owns the dies, which are kept in Detroit, and he phones in his manufacturing orders for the raw stampings.

Real Steel's 1933–34 roadster body fits the stock or reproduction frame, and is designed to receive the small- or big-block engine of your choice

They're shipped to Portland, where his 17-man crew does the trimming and other necessary finishing to turn them into parts that can be pulled "off the shelf." For the customer who wants a "turn key car," painting, upholstery, etc., is done in-house . . . unless the customer wants to finish the project in his own garage. Real Steel's 1933–34 roadster body package features a smooth floor, a custom firewall for small- and big-block engines, and fits the stock or an identical aftermarket frame.

AND THEN THERE ARE THE CARS THAT COME IN KIT FORM

In the 1920s, an automotive enthusiast with a few loose dollars in his overalls could order all the components he needed to build a speedster. He found advertisements in adventure magazines telling him he could convert a Ford Model T frame and engine into an early version of today's street rod. Using goodies from Ed Winfield and compatriots, lo and behold, he could build a road job that would run almost as well as a real racecar. It could easily whip the daylights out of his neighbor's stocker . . . and scare the devil out of the whole darn town.

The earliest of the modern kit cars is the Fad T Bucket serendipitously popularized by real-life street rodder Norm Grabowski in the famous *Life* magazine photo taken at a Southern California drive-in and later by the character Kookie in the late 1950s TV series "77 Sunset Strip."

The beauty of kit cars is two-fold: you can save time by making one major purchase; and most of the tough fabricating and welding work is already done. As a bonus, a kit car can be purchased at what amounts to a discounted price!

Today, most kit cars come with high-quality bodies, be it fiberglass, composite materials or steel. Examples of cars in kit form include not only the 1923 Fad T, but 1927, 1929, 1932 and 1933–34 Ford Roadsters, and early Chevrolet Roadsters. It is a good bet that more models will be added to the list as demand increases.

5 The Workshop, Tools & Equipment

Kevin Goitia's spacious home workshop is an admirable example of comfort and convenience with room for a driver and a builder. Well-lit and easily maintained, it is more than a place of toil, it is a sanctuary. That rollaway chock full of hand tools goes right to where the work is, saving numerous steps and much time. (One never really appreciates wheels until you have to move something that doesn't have 'em!)

FIRST, A PLACE TO WORK

There is no option: you must have a place to work to build a street rod. This means converting all or part of your garage, or renting storage and work space somewhere else. The latter has its advantages, particularly if the rental is in an industrial area. Noise is usually not the problem it can be in a residential area. Of all the difficulties I've encountered in my years of street rod building, complaints about noise have been the most vexatious!

Rented work areas aren't trouble free, however. They have their problems, too. First is cost. Every dollar handed over to a landlord is one less for the car. Second, there's a tendency to rebel against paying for the necessary modifications and maintenance of a cold, dark industrial building because you don't own it. This, of course, is the age-old dilemma of renters everywhere. However, more important than economic considerations, no matter how convenient the away-from-home shop may seem at first, convenience is sometimes an illusion.

It takes time to drive to and from the

46

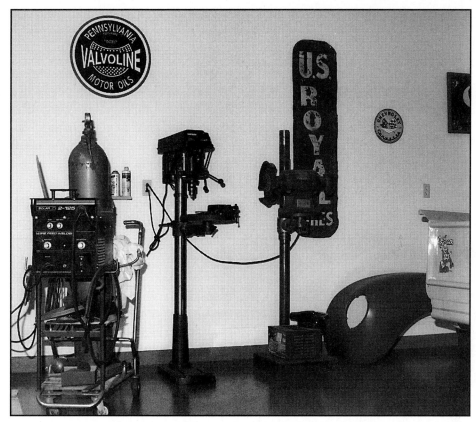

Stationery equipment such as a drill press should be allotted ample elbow room. The space isn't wasted however; that's where you temporarily store a mobile welding outfit when the drill press isn't in service.

Almost every rod builder is going to face welding tasks. Because of the obvious fire hazard, and potential eye damage for unexpected and unwary "spectators," extra care must be taken. Plan the shop to accommodate the work. That is, you need to be able to provide at least five feet clearance all around you, and you must be able to erect a temporary curtain or shield to prevent visual flash burns.

shop. Tasks that could be done in 20 minutes on impulse suddenly aren't worth leaving the dinner table for and don't get done. Delays like that can drag out construction time, causing frustration. Also, no matter what you haul to the shop, you'll always leave something home. Murphy's Law applies. Either you lock up, go back, and retrieve it, or you do without until tomorrow.

For these reasons and more, I heartily recommend the home workshop over all others unless you are totally without usable space. No matter how quickly that rod can be built, or how little or how much work is farmed out, you'll spend a great deal of time in that shop. In fact, that part of the house known as the garage, carport or basement is where you'll dedicate yourself

to completing your self-appointed task—building your street rod.

A good workshop is essential to a home-owning street rodder even if you are only minimally involved in the upkeep of your house or family car. In light of the high cost of professional work, you must be prepared to deal with a multitude of maintenance problems—both major and minor—that naturally occur over time. In the case of a street rodder, however, the shop is not considered a place of labor. It is, in fact, a refuge that usually becomes a source of pleasure, sometimes a secondary hobby.

There is, of course, only one ideal place to put your street rod workshop: smack dab in the center of an air-conditioned and heated 1000-square foot building with hot and cold running

water, a shower, fridge and a microwave oven. The less fortunate of us, however, can make do with a bit less.

You probably have access to at least a single-car garage, maybe a two-car garage. (If you are an apartment dweller or similarly "marooned," you must be creative—very creative!) Let's take a look at a variety of possible locations from the ridiculous to the sublime. Chances are you will fall somewhere in the middle.

Street rods have been built under a carport with tools and parts kept in a waterproofed 6 x 10-foot storage shed in temperate zones such as the rain-soaked Southeast and the sun-baked Southwest. Such facilities are hardly ideal, but as long as there's a concrete slab available for easy mobility, a long enough extension cord

Storage shelves and cabinets, and of course lots of workbench top, are critical not only for work itself, but for organization. Countless minutes, adding up to valuable hours can be saved when there is a designated place for everything . . . and everything is returned to its designated place!

and enthusiasm to carry the project through, it can be done.

A ground level basement with an auto entry may be dark and dingy, hot in the summer, cold in the winter, and home to a host of creepy, crawly things year round, but it's a step up. The work area should have a minimum 8-foot ceiling with pipes and electrical wiring running between the joists and not below. Anything less will detract from a comfortable work area.

If flooding is a threat, make sure interior walls are insulated and grades around the house slope away from the exterior walls. Also, make sure the gutters and downspouts are in good condition. If there's any question at all about drainage, install a runoff channel around the footing of exposed walls. You don't want to be flooded out.

A fiberglass-insulated false ceiling can be built to mask wiring, ductwork and plumbing. It'll also improve lighting. Roll fiberglass insulation between the uprights can be used to minimize the effects of adverse weather—hot, cold or wet—and soften that late-night noise that accompanies a street rod project.

Building a street rod in a narrow single-car garage is significantly more convenient than either, and many successful street rod projects have come from such humble surroundings. Not all are exactly the same width and length, but 10 x 20 feet is about average. The typical pre-WWII American passenger car, on the other hand, is about 6 feet wide and 18 feet end to end, so not much room is left for workbench, tools, and major ready-to-install components such as the engine

and transmission. The rule of thumb is that car storage—even temporary—requires enough space so that one of its doors can be fully opened, with a minimum of 18 inches to spare. The rest of the space is yours to fill with workbench, tool chest, shelves, small parts cabinets and, yes, even a tiny fridge and microwave oven without eliminating the hot-water heater, washing machine and clothes dryer.

The secret to accomplishing this end, of course, is to reduce the bulk of the car by removing the hood, bumpers, fenders, running boards and the like for as long as possible. Also, keep the car mobile as long as possible so it can be rolled back and forth or outside while workbench tasks are performed. Organization and compactness of your facilities is the key to a work-friendly home shop.

The next step up the ladder of desirability is the two-car garage. Such is more or less standard on houses constructed since the 1960s. It typically started as an empty shell measuring 20 by 22 feet, more or less. Illumination was nothing more than a single 100-watt bulb hung in the center of the exposed-beam "ceiling." Nonetheless, well-organized remodeling can transform such a shell into an ideal workshop for your street rod project.

Maybe you're one of the lucky ones whose house has a three-car garage. Such an abundance of elbow room is almost an embarrassment of riches, but is a true delight to behold. The problem with a big home workshop is avoiding the temptation to fill it with two or even three unfinished street rod projects! Don't laugh. I've seen it happen.

For many, the ideal automotive workshop is an existing structure that's completely detached from the house. Quite often, unused outbuildings and, yes, barns can be turned into facilities second to none with regard to space and convenience. One of the most usable backyard street rod workshops I've ever been in is a remodeled stable!

Finally, there's the custom-designed-and-built home workshop. I've visited one or two such awesome quarters. Imagine an area spreading over 1200 square feet and equipped almost as well as a professional shop. Obviously, such lavish facilities are left to those who can afford them. We'll set our sights on more realistic facilities with no less utility.

Likewise, I shall not deal with the potential of club or cooperative shops because they simply don't work out in the long run. Bitter feelings are the usual outcome, even though the best street rodding is built around the buddy system. Street rod workshops, like the kitchen, are best commanded by one captain.

PLANNING THE SHOP

Regardless of the location and size of your shop, it should be well planned, with an efficient and logical organization of storage, tools and work area. A hobby auto shop, just as its professional counterpart, should have the car at the center of the work area and tools organized in common clusters wherever practical. This is generally called the U-shaped plan.

The primary considerations in the placement of major power tools such as the drill press, electric welder and, to some extent, the air compressor, are power supply, clearance and frequency of use. Some electrical tools work best in a corner, some along the wall, and some need clearance on all sides.

Another major consideration in planning the placement of tools is the predictable order of their use. Metal fabrication, for instance, proceeds from storage of materials, to cutting, to assembly and to finishing. Fabrication tools, then, should be placed in this order.

Placement of the workbench(es) and tool chest, even if the latter is on a rolling cabinet, is of major importance. I've found that a workbench—no matter how short or narrow—on each side of the car is almost indispensable. The best place for the tool chest is directly in front of the car. Engine work eventually becomes the most frequent task and the hand tools are always within easy reach.

Sketch It

It's always best to work out things on paper. Moving heavy equipment on paper is much easier than actually doing it. Your sketch doesn't have to be fancy, only to scale, usually 1/4-inch to the foot. Remember to sketch in items that will go on the walls and hang from the rafters.

First, draw out the exact floor plan. Include locations of windows, doors, electrical outlets and permanent non-shop equipment such as water heater, washbasin, washing machine and clothes dryer.

Next, make an inventory of the tools and equipment you now own and those pieces of equipment you expect to add during the time it takes to build the car. Make 1/4-scale cardboard cutouts of each. Space them out on the floor plan, keeping in mind the existing electrical outlets and clearance requirements.

When you have all the major items positioned, determine where you'll put

additional electric power, special lighting, and a telephone. Pay particular attention to items that may require the services of a professional tradesman. For sure, have a qualified electrician install the 220-volt service and any complicated overhead wiring. Moreover, if you didn't know, the telephone company likes to run their own lines.

While planning, keep in mind that the typical workshop grows through the years and you will have to accommodate new tools and even changing interests. In other words, plan for expansion and stay as flexible as possible.

Power

Chances are that when you first walk through your shop-to-be, you'll notice that it is sadly deficient in terms of electric power and illumination. More often than not, any changes will be an improvement. It may be that minor additional wiring will make the shop usable. On the other hand, few older basements or garages are equipped with 220-volt service. Such service is needed for an arc welder and air compressor.

Older garages usually have two-prong ungrounded outlets, and often even single-service outlets. You don't have to be an electrician to replace the ungrounded outlets with three-prong duplex outlets. Simply shut off the power to the box and replace the old outlets. Run a wire from the grounding terminals of the new outlets to any metal pipe or conduit that leads to the real ground (dirt).

It's possible that your basement or garage has multiple 110-volt circuits, but don't bet on it. A well-equipped workshop should have at least three 110-volt circuits and one 220-volt circuit just for the shop. A washing machine, electric clothes drier or water heater in the shop area should have its own power source, independent from that for shop equipment. Lighting and power circuits should also be independent. Nothing is more distracting than lights that dim when the air compressor kicks in, or worse, go out and leave you in the dark.

The circuit is the power line that runs from the circuit-breaker or fuse box to the outlets. Each 110-volt circuit to the workshop—including those for the lights—should be able to handle at least 20 amps. A single 40-amp circuit is barely adequate if several power tools are ganged into it. If more than one tool is in operation at once, the circuit may be overloaded. Likewise, a 220-volt air compressor and small arc welder should be serviced with an internal double-trip 40-amp circuit. There's no excuse for a "blown fuse" in a first-class workshop.

Your local building codes may allow you to do your own wiring provided you have a permit and have the job inspected afterwards. Building materials stores usually have several different "Home Wiring Made Easy" books in their electrical section. Otherwise, have it done by a professional contractor.

Regardless of how many outlets you may have on your walls, you'll still be short one or two in some unanticipated corner. Heavy-duty extension cords are okay, but extension outlets, either commercial offerings or homemade, are more versatile. Making your own is easy because all the materials are available at your building materials store. All you need is the cord, a 4 x 4-inch metal box and cover, and a pair of duplex receptacles. Once finished, plug the extension into a wall outlet, and then take your power to where it's needed.

Lighting

For some reason, the home-building industry saves pennies when installing lights in a new garage or basement. Even houses built today with price tags well into six figures will have one naked 100-watt bulb in a cheap ceramic fixture in the center of the garage or on the wall above the laundry area. Such lighting doesn't fill the minimum requirements of a workshop. You'll need all the illumination you can squeeze under the roof. Not only that, lighting is surprisingly cheap. That 100-watt bulb the generous contractor left you draws 1-amp; a fluorescent tube will give you two to four times the light with the same current draw!

The cost of lighting, however, should not be a consideration. You should have ample illumination in your shop for safety. If you can't clearly see what you're doing, you'll be the proverbial "accident waiting to happen." There are more than enough opportunities to skin knuckles, bang elbows and thump your head while building your street rod. Good lighting is also a necessity for improved work efficiency. Errors are easy enough to make without inviting the gremlins to take liberties.

How much light should you have? A good rule of thumb is two 4-foot, 40-watt fluorescent tubes for every 100 square feet of floor space with supplementary incandescent lighting at power tools such as a drill press or band saw. Fluorescent lighting, which produces soft shadows, is good for general overhead lighting. On the other hand, incandescent bulbs are best for pinpoint or spot lighting on power tools. Additionally, you should have several clamp-on reflector lamps and drop lights for under car and tight areas that nothing else will illuminate.

Can you get your shop too bright? Not really. If the fluorescent fixtures (with reflectors) are evenly spaced and the walls and ceiling are flat white, there's little chance of glare. In fact, glare is not a consideration unless one part of the shop is more than three times as brightly illuminated as another.

The Walls

Depending on where you live, your shop will have uninsulated, cement block walls or frame walls with 2 x 4-inch studs ribbing light-absorbing black-felt lining. Neither is desirable. Masonry walls are porous and should be treated to seal out damp and cold. Not only that, heat will radiate from your body to the walls, even if it's not cold outside.

Plug any holes or cracks in masonry walls and coat their interior surfaces with powder-type block filler and sealer. Follow this by installing 2 x 2-inch studs, placing them vertically on 16-inch centers on the interior walls. Most building-materials stores carry a special adhesive that works better than fasteners for securing the studs to the walls.

Even shops in the mildest climates will benefit from insulated walls. Exposed studding is easily insulated with either 3-inch thick roll or batt fiberglass matting. You can usually wedge it in between the studs and it will stay there. If the fiberglass doesn't have a vapor barrier, first install 2-mil polyethylene sheeting to prevent moisture from penetrating.

If insulation from dampness is particularly critical as it is in the Pacific Northwest or Deep South, you may have to go to the added expense of mineral wool insulation blankets. Your city or county building department can give you advice in such cases.

After you've wired your shop and insulated its walls, finish it off with paneling. There is a variety of inexpensive 4 x 8-foot panels suitable for the workshop. Choice depends largely on your bank account and tastes, but there are construction considerations.

Half-inch thick gypsum wallboard backed with foil eliminates the need for the additional polyethylene vapor barrier. It also provides rigidity and additional soundproofing. Some wallboard is also vinyl covered, making it washable—a real plus for a workshop.

Shop-grade plywood, 1/4 or 3/8-inch thick, provides excellent rigidity and is a fine sound-deadening material. Its surface, however, is usually knot-filled, rough and not attractive.

Another low-cost paneling is pegboard, a perforated hardboard. It is most popular with those who like to hang their tools on the walls. Of the several grades of pegboard, only the more expensive are rigid enough to resist warping and withstand ordinary use.

Every building materials store has economy 1/8-inch thick fiberboard panels with at least a dozen different printed patterns. Quality varies from low to decent. Sometimes just finding enough warp-free panels for a project can be a problem.

Somewhat higher in price are 1/4-inch hardboard panels with vinyl or plastic coatings. One of my favorites is an off-white plastic-coated panel designed for lavatory usage. They are durable, and can be cleaned with sol-

Several coats of easily maintained high quality concrete paint on your shop floor is the best approach for this active area.

vents or soap and water. Admittedly, they have an antiseptic look, but the high degree of reflectivity for improved lighting puts them near the top of my list. The hospital atmosphere is easily subdued with posters and pictures.

If you want the ultimate in class, and are willing to pay the extra bucks, there are the better plywoods with a veneer of real furniture wood. There's no doubt that the most beautiful shops are outfitted this way.

Whether you choose wallboard or paneling, installation is simple. Lighter weight paneling can be attached to the studs or furring strips with adhesive, eliminating the need for nails. If you use nails, special painted ones are available.

Install the first panels in a corner of the shop. Be aware that the corners of a garage or basement usually are not finished with the greatest of care, and are frequently out-of-plumb. To get a satisfactory fit, and to allow for electrical outlets and other projections,

hold the panel in position and carefully measure and mark trim points.

Extra framing around water, gas or electric meters may be required. Straight-line cuts and holes are easily made with a power saw and sabre saw, but be sure to use the recommended blades to avoid ripping the panel up. Panels, usually installed vertically, should be secured on all four edges with their intersecting edges beveled slightly for a neat fit. If you install pegboard panels, use fiber washers to space them out a quarter-inch from the studs to make room for the tool hooks.

The Ceiling

Unlike most other hobby workshops, those for working on a car require considerable room overhead for such tasks as pulling engines. In addition, if your workshop has living quarters above it, you should soundproof the ceiling. If headroom is sparse, you can fasten 1 x 2-inch furring strips to the joists and install 1/2-inch-thick acoustical ceiling tiles.

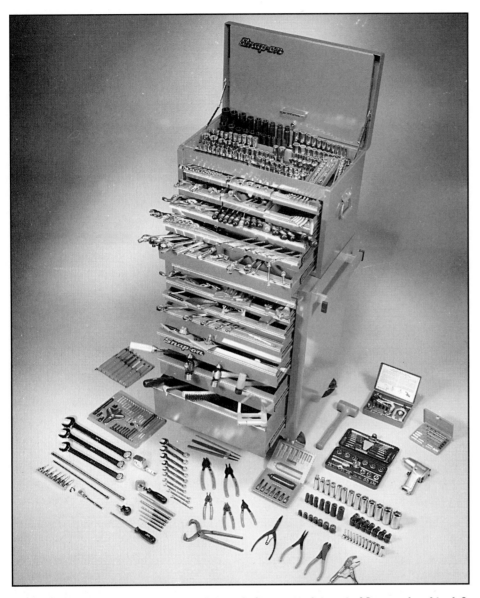

Breathes there a rod builder who hasn't lusted after a complete set of Snap-on hand tools? I think not. Although I wouldn't exactly call this assembly basic, after studying its contents carefully, there aren't many items that won't be useful over the years. After all, a rod builder eventually becomes a rod maintainer. The economic reality is that a substantial amount of money can be saved by a one-time full set purchase.

information on how to deal with specific problems.

The Floor

I suppose that you, like most street rodders, have worked in the dirt on some street rod task. So, I needn't tell you it ain't no fun! A smooth, crack-free concrete floor is the only way to go. Your creeper and floorjack will then roll freely without dropping a wheel in a crevice and coming to an instant halt. And, although a floor is strictly utilitarian, it doesn't have to be ugly . . . at least not any more than necessary.

Some guys go to the trouble of tiling their shop floor. It is handsome in the beginning, but after inspecting the battle scars of many years of labor in my shop, I suspect that you could spend an awful lot of time maintaining a tiled floor. Stay with concrete with several coats of high quality concrete paint.

Concrete must be thoroughly cleaned before painting, so review the manufacturer's directions. In general, trisodium phosphate is recommended, but "muriatic" acid—the old-fashioned name for hydrochloric acid—may be required to properly prepare an old, extra-grimy surface. However, be aware of the dangers of using muriatic acid. Always wear rubber gloves and substantial eye and face protection. Prevent splatter on yourself at all costs, and the surrounding walls as much as possible. With regard to paint application, a big roller on a long handle is easiest on the back and knees.

The street rod workshop offers a secondary challenge that should be met with a degree of enthusiasm. How far you go depends only on how elaborate you want your surroundings. Now, let's look at what it should contain in

These tiles come in various sizes and shapes, and can be installed with a special stapler you can rent at the building materials store.

Even where overhead sound-deadening is not critical, a ceiling or a false ceiling is worthwhile for reflecting light. Inexpensive lightweight panels can be nailed to the joists and painted flat white.

A more creative approach may be necessary if access is required for overhead storage, plumbing pipes or heating ducts. In such a case, you can install a well-supported length of 3/16-inch wall (2 7/8-inch O.D.) steel tubing (not pipe) for engine removal, then build a suspended ceiling below it. Again, building materials suppliers offer a wide variety of fiberglass and plastic ceiling panels, installation hardware and, best of all, practical the way of tools and equipment.

TOOLS AND EQUIPMENT

Once your workshop is ready to go, you must stock it with the tools and equipment needed to do the work. However, just as you don't need 1000 square feet of workspace, you don't need a full complement of professional tools and equipment. Many special tools and expensive pieces of seldom-used equipment can be rented or borrowed. Nevertheless, you should have your own set of high-quality hand tools and basic power tools.

Hand Tools In General

It's been said that Henry Ford built his tools by hand before he built his first car. Whether this is true or not, it certainly illustrates that you can't build a car without basic tools. As to what constitutes the basic set of tools, there is no agreement. It depends on the work to be done.

There are hand tools of every description. You can easily spend $5000 without duplicating any. So, before you decide which tools to get, ask yourself the following questions about each:

• Should I get the expensive or cheap version?

• How often will I use the tool?

• Is it cheaper to rent, or will an outright purchase cost less in the long run?

• Should I buy each tool individually or should I get the complete set?

These are tough questions. To help with making a decision, here is my response to each:

Cheap vs. Expensive—To say that these are relative terms is true, but that's a cop-out, so let's get one thing out of the way first. Starting with the low end of the scale, those bins of low-

priced imported items that are found in most auto parts and hardware stores contain junk. I don't use that word loosely, either. Since I bought a pack of drill bits from one of those "junk bins" way back in the early '60s—only to have the first one I used bend—I've refused to even accord them the title "tools." I just call 'em junk. If it doesn't have MADE IN THE USA on it, the tool doesn't go in my tool chest.

Most American hand tools are of good quality, but there is often a substantial cost differential between Brand A and Brand B. If you look closely, you can see why some sockets have thicker walls than others do, excluding those specially designed and labeled THIN WALL for particularly tight places. Some screwdrivers have stouter shanks and tougher handles. Some ratchets boast better fit and finish. In short, quality shows if you look.

Your street rodding project doesn't end on its maiden voyage—you must maintain that creation of yours. Therefore, think long-term and buy first-class tools! You will use each tool from a basic set of ratchets and sockets, screwdrivers, wrenches and pliers a thousand times in five years. The only question that remains is this: what does the basic tool set include?

This is tricky, and you may not have the answer even when you find yourself renting something for the second or third time. Nevertheless, you must "guesstimate" when multiplied rental fees will equal the purchase price—and act before then. Also, keep in mind that when you purchase a tool, it's yours. Then, again, you shouldn't spend money on an expensive tool you'll only use once or twice in 10 years.

Individual vs. Set Purchase—

WRENCHES

They come in a wide variety of configurations: Open End, Box-End, Combination, 6-point, 12-point, angled heads, offset heads, "S" shaped, and half moon. Start with standard flat wrenches in the following sizes, and add to your collection as needed. (All measurements in inches).

1/4, 5/16, 3/8, 7/16, 1/2,
9/16, 5/8, 11/16, 3/4,
13/16, 7/8, 15/16,
1, 1 1/8, 1 1/4

Adjustable: Standard Thin Jaw
4, 6, 12

Tubing Wrenches
3/8–7/16
1/2–9/16

Beware of the urge to become a "tool collector." Otherwise, you may not have enough money left to finish your street rod on schedule. Carefully evaluate each item in a set of tools with regard to frequency of use and unit price. For example, a super set of sockets will often contain several items with limited use. Simply add up the unit prices of the pieces you know you'll use time and again. Compare that against the price of the complete set. If the price of the full set is close to the sum of the important pieces, and you get the odd-ball pieces for little or nothing, the full set is a good buy. Otherwise, buy only what you need, and when you need it.

Wrenches

Most rodders agree that you must have a set of wrenches ranging from 1/4 to 1 1/4-inches in 1/16-inch incre-

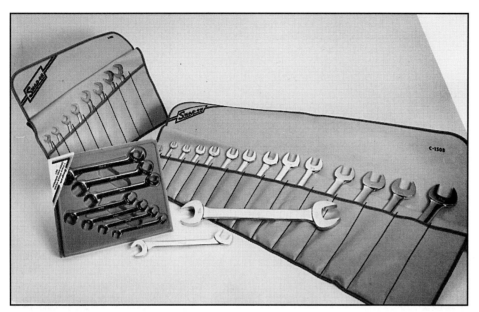

Wrenches are about as basic a hand tool as one can find, however, a wide variety, in both working size and configuration exists. The "open end" is for fast work in tight areas.

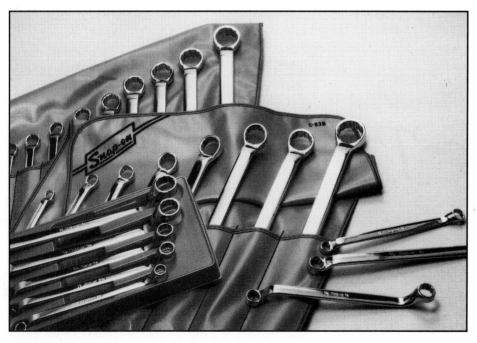

On the other hand (no pun intended), "box" wrenches are designed to put the finishing touches on the job. That is, one is best advised to always use a box end for final tightening when a specific torque spec is not required. Even an inexperienced builder quickly learns just how tight, "tight" should be. Nevertheless, along the learning curve there will be fewer "rounded" nuts and bolts and skinned knuckles when a box end is used.

ments. However, don't take the miserly approach when building your street rod if you want it to be any fun. Therefore, rather than see how few tools you can get by with, list what a well-rounded collection should include using the photos and tables as reference.

A complete set of open-end, box-end

and combination wrenches is about as basic as you can get. Even if you never acquired a ratchet and socket set, you could handle about every nut-and-bolt assembly and maintenance task to be found on your car. The handle length of each wrench increases relative to the nominal opening size to allow more leverage (torque) on the larger nut or bolt.

Open End—The open-end design is for relatively fast work. Their heads are typically angled at 15, 30 or 60 degrees to the handle to improve access and clearance. Most manufacturers offer a variety of styles with straight and curved, short and long handles, in various head thicknesses. The greater the variety you acquire, the greater the range of applications with which you can deal.

Box End—A box-end wrench cannot be used with the speed of an open-end, but for given sizes it can be used to apply more torque. This is because a box-end wrench exerts a force on all six corners of a standard hex head rather than two.

There are two basic box-end wrench designs. The six-point box allows for a new bite every 60 degrees; the 12-point needs half the rotation, or 30 degrees for a new bite. Twelve-point box-end wrenches are useful in confined areas where wrench rotation is half of the six-point. However, a six-point box wrench is best for applying greater torque because the bearing area of the wrench flat is greater, reducing the chance of rounding off the corners of the hex. Box-end wrench heads are angled 15 or 30 degrees to the handle to allow for maximum grip and knuckle clearance. Handle shapes and lengths are various.

Real versatility, however, is obtained with combination-end wrenches.

RATCHET & SOCKET SETS
1/4-inch Drive:
Ratchets:
Standard Handle (4–5-inches long). Long Handle (6–7 inches). Long Handle, Flex Head. 18-inch Speeder Handle. 3-, 6-, 14-inch Extension Bars

Six-Point Sockets:
Standard and Deep 1/8, 5/32, 3/16, 7/32, 1/4, 9/32, 5/16, 11/32, 3/8, 7/16, 1/2, 9/16 inches

Universal Joint 3/8-inch Drive:
Ratchet:
Standard Handle (7 to 8 inches long). Long Handle (10 to 11 inches long). Long Handle, Flex-Head. 15-inch Speed Handle. 3-, 6-, 12-inch Extension Bars

Six- and 12-Point Sockets,
Standard and Deep: 3/8, 7/16, 1/2, 9/16, 5/8, 11/16, 3/4, 13/16, 7/8-inches
12-Point Flexible Sockets, Standard Length: 7/16, 1/2, 9/16, 5/8-inches

1/2-inch Drive
Ratchet: Standard Handle (10 inches long)
Speed Handle (20 inches long)
Breaker Bar (18 inches long)
Sockets: 6-Point:
Standard and Deep: 5/8, 11/16, 3/4, 7/8, 13/16, 15/16, 1, 1 1/8, 1 1/4-inches

The 3/8-inch and 1/2-inch drive ratchets and a full range of sockets is nearly indispensable for fast, efficient work. Start with them, and add the 1/4-inch drive when the need arrives. You'll never be able to anticipate all of the sockets you'll eventually want, so expect to purchase an odd one now and then.

These feature a variety of offset and/or angled box-end heads on one end and open-end heads on the other. An experienced tool twister can use a combination wrench very effectively by quickly running the nut down with the open end, then applying final tightening with the box-end.

Ratchets and Sockets
Professional mechanics and street rodders can thank the Snap-on Tools Corporation for their 1920 invention that revolutionized the knuckle-busting trade. Socket wrenches and their many accessories are indispensable for a wide range of fastener removal and installation jobs.

Ratchet Drives—There are three ratchet drives you should have in your tool chest: 1/4, 3/8 and 1/2 inch. These dimensions measure the square projection from the ratchet or breaker-bar handle and, of course, match the square holes in the sockets. Ratchets are available in a variety of handle lengths from extra-short stubbies to real "pry bars," 1- or 2-feet long that allow maximum leverage. There are ratchets with flex-heads, bent handles, flat handles and plastic handles, but the one with the plain old standard handle is what you'll reach for most often. The standard 1/4-inch drive ratchet is about 4 1/2 inches long; the average 3/8-inch drive is typically 7 1/2 inches long, and the average 1/2-inch drive is about 10 1/2 inches long.

Note: A good rule of thumb to use when using your socket set is this: bolt-shank diameter determines drive size. The bigger the bolt, the bigger the drive and vice-versa. For instance, avoid tightening a bolt with a 1/4-inch shank with a 3/8-inch drive ratchet, or a bolt with a 3/8-inch shank with a 1/2-inch drive. Assuming you apply the same force as you would with the proper ratchet, using one that's too large will over-torque and strip the bolt. Also, using a ratchet that's too small will break its internal mechanism if you apply the force necessary to tighten the bolt correctly!

Sockets—At the "business end" of

SCREWDRIVERS

Standard

(Measurements in inches.)

1/8 x 2, 1/8 x 4, 1/4 x 1 1/2, 1/4 x 4, 1/4 x 6, 1/4 x 8, 1/4 x 12, 3/16 x 4, 3/16 x 9, 5/16 x 1 3/4, 5/16 x 6, 3/8 x 12.

Phillips

(Measurements in inches.)

0 x 2 1/2, 1 x 3, 2 x 1 1/2, 2 x 4, 2 x 8, 3 x 6, 4 x 8.

PLIERS

Interlocking Pliers: 6 and 12 inches with plastic grips and jaw heads set at 45 degrees provide easier access to obstructed areas.

Combination Jaw Slip-joint Pliers: 6-inches with plastic grips.

High Leverage Diagonal Cutting Pliers, Needle-Nose Pliers: 6-inches straight and bent nose, with plastic grips.

Vise-Grip® pliers: 7 and 10 inches.

Tempting as it may be sometimes, please don't use pliers on nuts and bolts. There are literally hundreds of tasks for which they are the "right tool," so a good variety pays off.

the ratchet is the socket. As your street rod building skills develop, and you take on new and different sub-projects, you'll continue to find new and useful sockets that are best suited for doing uncommon jobs.

There are four basic sockets in 6- and 12-point configurations, just as with box-end wrenches. The standard-length socket is two to three times the nominal size; deep sockets are three to five times the nominal size. These, combined with the three basic drives, nominal sizes and configuration varieties, provide many sockets from

which you can choose! The best way to deal with the overwhelming variety of sockets is to study the tool catalogs, and if a special job does come up, purchase the special socket.

Screwdrivers

Street rods are not built with nuts and bolts alone. There are always screws with different heads with which you must contend. As such, a good complement of screwdrivers is necessary.

The most important thing to remember when using a screwdriver is that slot or "X" in the screw head is a definite length, width and depth. Therefore, you shouldn't grab just any old screwdriver just as you wouldn't grab any wrench for installing or removing a nut or bolt. Using the wrong screwdriver could damage it or the screw head.

The screwdriver blade should use the entire available screw head surface. Examine closely the shape of the standard slotted screwdriver. Note that the tip of the blade has nearly parallel

sides. Hollow-ground screwdrivers have parallel surfaces. Whatever the tip type, it should wedge snugly into the slot.

Most, but not all screwdrivers carry identifying marks. Unfortunately, there isn't a standard identification system or a ready reference for ordinary slotted screws. Sears Craftsman slotted screwdrivers are cataloged by slot dimension and blade length such as 3/8 x 12 inches. Only the slot size appears on the handle. Snap-on, conversely, stamps a code on the handle which is useless for quick identification unless you look it up and memorize or chart it on the wall near your tool box. Otherwise, the guy under the car is left with the trying experience of shouting big, little or medium to his partner who's handing him the tools. Ultimately, he must develop an eye for screw-slot sizes so that at a glance he'll be able to choose the screwdriver that will give a snug fit. Fit, by the way, is particularly critical on old, rusted screws, the likes of which are found on old, rusted cars.

The situation is better with regard to Phillips and Pozi-Drive screws. Once you learn what a No. 0, 1, 2, 3, and 4 Phillips or Pozi-Drive looks like, you can ask for a specific screwdriver.

Pliers

The choices can be overwhelming when it comes to pliers. There are at least 35 different styles from which to choose! Those listed should be adequate to get the job done. Caution: Pliers are near the top of the list in terms of readily available low-cost imports. As with other hand tools, use top-notch American-made brands. Among other problems, the two halves of imported cheapos have an annoying way of slipping past the detents and pinching fingers!

Electric Power Tools

I'm sure I don't have to sing the praises of electric power tools. I can't imagine that anyone would trade his electric drill for a brace and bit, or a bench grinder for a rough-cut hand file. Or even a power hacksaw for a hand hacksaw (for those with a fat pocketbook). Nevertheless, for those of us on a limited budget, some power tools are far more necessary than other power tools.

At the top of the list are power drills. You'll need two: one with a 3/8-inch max chuck and one with a 1/2-inch max chuck. A heavy-duty Black and Decker, Craftsman and Skil—to name some top-notch brands—will last a street rodder many years. Economy power drills, even those with good brand names, usually won't live through the construction of one street rod.

The same is true of grinders, both hand-held and bench-mounted. The

ELECTRIC POWER TOOLS & EQUIPMENT

Electric Drills: Heavy-duty, high-torque 3/8- and 1/2-inch drill motors with reversible switches for backing out bits.

Drill Bits: Minimum 1/16 to 1 1/2-inches in 1/16-inch increments. New high-tech nitride-coated titanium bits are expensive, but outlast ordinary bits seven-fold.

Drill Press: Free-standing or bench-top model with minimum 1/2-HP motor and four speeds. Drill press vise a must.

Utility Lights: Cord-reel droplight that mounts to the ceiling or wall with minimum 25-foot long cord.

Bench Grinder: Heavy-duty model with at least 1/2-HP motor that will accept 6 X 3/4-inch wheel. Variety of aluminum oxide and wire-brush wheels.

Arc Welder: Minimum required is 225 amps, A-C unit, allowing you to weld 1/16- to 1/4-inch thick steel. Welder should include cables and electrode holder. Protect yourself from intense heat and light. Economical facemasks included in most starter outfits are not adequate, so replace with one of higher quality. Heavy-duty gloves are also required; leather apron is highly desirable.

Portable Electric Disc Sander/Grinder: Low-cost, light-duty models are tempting, but they don't last. Get a heavy-duty, 1-HP sander/grinder that will take a 7-inch disc. Also, get a variety of discs.

Bench grinders come in several sizes, but avoid the light-duty models. A grinder in the one third to half horsepower range is adequate, unless you anticipate more need than just rod building. In that case, you may want to consider the larger industrial grade types.

heavy-duty models will withstand considerable use; inexpensive ones won't. If you buy the best, chances are you'll never have to buy another one.

Pneumatic Power Tools

Soon after you start your project, you'll find that there aren't enough minutes in each of those precious weekend hours, even with ratchets or speed handles. Eventually, you'll conclude that you're not only working too slow, you're working yourself too hard.

Professional mechanics solve both problems by using quality pneumatic

The air ratchet is likely to become one of your favorite tools once you grow accustomed to it. Just be sure to always use a hardened (black) socket. Chromed sockets, particularly the thin wall variety, will crack.

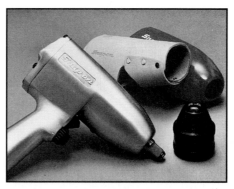

No home shop should be without a 3/8-inch drive "butterfly" impact wrench. The pistol type is mighty handy as well.

tools. 'Tis a rare shop indeed where the most prominent noise isn't the staccato breep, breep of the impact wrench or air ratchet.

Most street rodders are aware of the time-saving feature of pneumatic tools. Few, however, know that with minimum care, air tools are amazingly durable, outlasting their electric-powered counterparts four to one. Moreover, they are economical!

To design a pneumatic-tool system for your workshop, you are best advised to first determine the needs at the working end of the air hose. Start with the types and demands of the air tools, and then buy an air compressor that will supply the needed volume.

Determine what is needed in the way of tools now . . . and in the predictable future. A pneumatic system is a permanent, long-term fixture in the shop and, although most of the components are not expensive—as power tools go—the cost is far from insignificant.

The Air Compressor—This is the most expensive item in a pneumatic system. It's also the most difficult to choose. Compressors on wheels are best for the home shop even though they will probably remain in the same corner forever. Dust, dirt, debris and

even rolling sockets will eventually hide behind them. They come in a variety of models, and common ratings are 1/3, 1/2, 3/4, 1, 1 1/2, 2, 3, 4 and 5 horsepower.

Usually, the lower-rated compressors are powered by a 110/120-volt electric motor. A 220/240-volt motor or gasoline engine usually powers bigger compressors. Then there's the compressor itself. These have single- or twin-cylinders. Compressors with two cylinders normally require a minimum of one horsepower for efficient operation.

Horsepower notwithstanding, the most important compressor specification is its volume—standard cubic feet per minute (scfm) at a given pressure—pounds per square inch (psi). Typical portable units are delivery rated at oddball figures such as 1.7, 2.7, 3.2, 3.4, 6.4, 7.3, 7.8 or 9.3 scfm. About the next biggest non-stationary compressor is rated at 15.3 scfm. Pressure ratings run from 40 to 175 psi.

Naturally, more power is needed to deliver high volume and pressure, but as pressure demands increase, volume delivery drops. Therefore, many units have dual ratings, such as 7.8 scfm at

40 psi and 6.3 scfm at 90 psi.

Another major consideration is the air storage tank. Like most tanks, air compressor tanks are rated in gallons. The 7 1/2-gallon compressors that are frequently on sale are too small for the automotive workshop. A 12-gallon compressor is better, but 20–30 gallons is best. In other words, when you are considering air supply, the more the better.

A 1 1/2-horsepower compressor delivering at least 7 scfm should be the minimum for your workshop. These units usually require a single-circuit 220-volt line. Thanks to the big merchandising chains, compressors in this range are readily available and reasonably priced.

Air-system horsepower, as with street rod horsepower, costs money. That's why you should anticipate your current and future needs before you make a purchase. To do that well, means you should understand the volume and pressure demands of the pneumatic tools you are planning to purchase.

Pneumatic Hand Tools

Probably the first air devices that come to mind are air ratchets and impact wrenches. Many are often sold as a package deal with popular air compressors. Working with these tools is a real pleasure and, if you buy "industrial grade" models, they should last a long time in your workshop.

Maintenance of most air tools is very simple. All that's usually required is a few drops of special oil in the gullet each time the tool is used, and a moisture-free air supply. If these considerations are met, your air tools will last years. If not, the best tool will rust internally.

It may not have the glitz of some of the other tools in the home workshop, but a hefty vise securely mounted on a substantial workbench is almost as useful as a visiting buddy when you need a helping hand. If space (or money) is tight, a bench-mounted drill press is a viable substitute for the significantly larger (and more expensive) stand-alone unit. It can also be stowed away when not needed.

Most auto shop air tools require 8 scfm or less. Only very large ones such as a 1-inch drive air wrench or heavy-duty sander/grinder require a substantial air supply, of 12–20 scfm. Of those, only the sander/grinder will be useful in your shop. However, with a 20-scfm demand—requiring a 5-horsepower compressor—it's impractical for most home workshops. An electric sander/grinder is more versatile even though it is heavy.

Any tool in the 7–8 scfm range will have no air supply problem. In fact, most useful tools use 4 scfm or less. That means a 1 1/2- to 2-horse compressor is easily capable of performing most street rod building chores.

Overextending air tools usually doesn't cause them any damage. Once the tool reaches its capacity, it just blows air past a built-in safety valve. The exception to the rule is the air ratchet. If overextended, it's possible to strip the internal gears. Follow the rule of thumb I gave with regard to hand-ratchet size versus bolt size when using a pneumatic ratchet.

Note that the maximum working demand of an air tool is not necessarily a constant demand. Many tools have built-in regulators to reduce the air supply (power) for light-duty jobs. Also, most air-tool manufacturers offer add-on inline regulators for tools not originally equipped with regulators.

One thing I have to tell you, though—continued use of air tools is addictive. Once you become accustomed to them, you'll never want to pick up a hand tool again. About the only drawback I can think of is that the outside world could care less about your speed and efficiency. The breep of the air ratchet, particularly late at night, tends to generate neighborhood hostility!

THE WORKBENCH

It's been said that the workbench is the most indispensable item in a workshop. Although I can't go quite that far, I believe that you should invest in a substantial workbench immediately after you purchase the basic hand and power tools.

There are many types of true workbenches. You can either build a workbench or purchase one. A bench can be built out of a solid, heavy-duty wooden door, or you can convert an old wooden or metal office desk. Plans for workbenches abound in craft and do-it-yourself woodworking magazines. Sears, Home Depot, et al and tool supply houses are ready resources for light- to medium-duty workbench kits that come unassembled.

The best deals, however, are often used industrial workbenches. Good leads to these can be found in the newspaper classifieds under Tools and Machinery. For example, I bought my favorite bench for a very reasonable price from the surplus yard of a large Southern California aircraft manufacturer. Wise buying is easy, too. It's hard to go wrong on a used workbench. Look 'em over and rock 'em a bit to judge their steadiness. If one isn't to your liking, move on to the next one.

Workbench heights range from 30 to 34 inches and widths from 24 to 30 inches. Lengths are equally as variable. Available space often dictates width and length maximums, but the height should be determined by what physically suits you. The working surface should be at your hip joint so you can work comfortably without bending over.

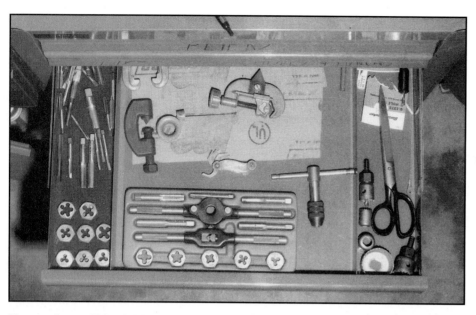

Your car is, or will be, held together with threaded fasteners—hundreds of them! Although old or damaged nuts and bolts should be discarded in general, you're still going to need to tap chassis holes, build brackets, or chase the threads on some irreplaceable component, etc. In short, you need a complete set of taps and dies, including several "pipe" sizes.

Don't forget a thread gauge. In no time at all, you'll be able to glance at a fastener and recognize the thread count, but it never hurts to verify. The old rule always applies—measure twice, cut once.

HAMMERS

Ball-Peen: 8 and 16 oz., Brass Tip: 16 oz. and 8 oz.

PUNCHES & CHISELS

Flat Chisels: 5/16, 7/16, 1/2.
Center Punches: 5, 6, 7.
Pin Punches: Point sizes 1/8, 3/16, 1/4

If possible, position the workbench lengthwise in the shop with a minimum of 18 inches clearance at each end. If you have gobs of room, move the bench away from the wall, so you'll have access to it from all sides. Once in place, avoid using your bench as storage place for tools. No matter how large its working surface, keep permanent space-stealing equipment off. Some industrial arts references caution you to not permanently attach a vise or grinder to a general-purpose bench. Regardless, I have broken both rules. The impact is lessened, though, because I have two benches. You may find that space in your shop is so limited that you must use your best judgment and compromise the ideal.

The bench should be level in all directions, so level that a marble placed in the center of the work surface won't roll off. There should be ample electrical and compressed air outlets within reach. The bench top or working surface should be of either tough end-grain wood or one of the many available durable synthetic industrial materials. A sheet metal surface is OK. Just make sure you place a rubber mat on top if you repair any electrical appliances on the bench.

Lighting over the bench is important. It should have at least a four-foot fluorescent light overhead plus one or two incandescent lights nearby that can be clamped on for close work. Finally, because a bench occupies considerable floor space, use the dead space above and below it for storage. Just leave enough foot and head room for comfortable working.

MISCELLANEOUS TOOLS:

There are many more tools that would be nice to own, but start with those previously listed. As you progress through your project, you'll quickly discover which additional tools are worth having even though they may not be basic or necessary in the strictest sense.

• Ratchet-Head Torque Wrench, 30–200 ft-lb.
• Tap & Die Set: 1/4 to 5/8-inch UNC and UNF threads..
• Hacksaw: Heavy-duty 12-inch model with front-end grip and blade tensioner. Maintain a good supply of high quality blades in all major varieties.
• Taper-Bit Screw Extractor Set: Should contain at least 1/8, 9/64, 7/32 and 5/16 inch sizes.
• Brake-Adjusting Tools: Check tool catalogs for items designed for specific brakes.

A low-cost tool that is valuable time and time again in street rod building is the magnetic angle finder.

• Bolt-on Type Axle Shaft Puller: Required to break loose Ford and GM axle shafts.
• Scrapers: Tool chest should contain several scrapers and putty knives with 1-, 2- and 3-inch blades.
• Electrician's Wire-Stripping and Crimping Tool.
• Extra Deep C-Clamp: At last four each of 6-inch capacity.
• Crankshaft-Damper Puller.
• Measuring Tools: 35-blade combination master feeler-gauge set in standard sizes with extra brass blades for electronic ignitions; 25-foot measuring tape.
• Files: High-grade alloy steel; minimum set should include 6- and 12-inch round files, bastard cut; 6-, 8-, 10- and 12-inch mill files, bastard cut; 6- and 10-inch triangular files, bastard cut; 6-, 10- and 12-inch half-round, bastard cut. File handles must be installed on every file.
• Tube Cutting and Double Flaring Tools: Set should include tubing cutter

If you plan on doing any engine work, you must have a half-inch drive torque wrench. Its value in general street rod maintenance is debatable although alloy wheels should be torqued down.

and small bender.

...AND EVERYTHING ELSE YOU'RE GOING TO NEED Eventually!

• Tool Storage Units: Tool chests and roller cabinets should be of high quality and as large as possible. (They can never be too large, only your workshop can be too small.)
• Hydraulic Floor Jack: High-quality US-made, minimum 2-ton capacity and 24-inch lift; steel wheels with ball bearings; rear swivel casters; and removable handle.
• Hydraulic Axle Jack (Bottle Jack): High-quality US-made, minimum 1-ton lift capacity and 4- to 5-inch lift.
• Jack Stands: Minimum of four heavy-

duty stands with tripod base; 2-ton minimum load capacity; ratchet type preferred.
• Creeper: Washable finish, ball-bearing casters; built-in tool tray and large diameter caster wheels.
• Steel Chain Hoist: Minimum 2000-lb. capacity.
• Safety Equipment: Clear polycarbonate face shield; goggles with polycarbonate lens.
• Heavy-duty dry chemical fire extinguisher suitable for Class A, B, and C fires.
• Bench Vise: Heavy-duty model, 4- to 5-inch-wide jaws that open at least 6 inches with a swivel base that rotates approximately 160 degrees.
• Parts Washer: Small, inexpensive portable parts-washing bins are available in many auto supply stores. Use with nonflammable solvent.
• Standard Oxyacetylene Gas-Welding Outfit: Basic gas-welding set should include torch, cutting attachment, regulators, hoses, strikers, goggles, tip cleaners, a variety of welding and cutting tips. Two-stage regulators are preferable over single-stage type. They deliver constant gas flow to torch within a wide range of cylinder pressures without the necessity of making constant adjustments to compensate for dropping cylinder pressures. However, if your budget is limited, single-stage regulators will work.

6

TEARING DOWN VINTAGE TIN

It's very tempting to blow everything apart as soon as you get your newly purchased vintage tin home or to your off-site workshop. It's not always the most prudent thing to do, however.

OK, you took the plunge. You bought an old car and now you are ready to turn it into a street rod. There it sits, more-or-less in the middle of the driveway. What do you do now?

Start by removing all the debris from the car. Vacuum out those cobwebs, dirt and critters that thought they found a permanent home. This is where a shop-type vacuum cleaner comes in handy. Then give your old car the bath of its life. After all, it hasn't had one in years. Scrub it well. While it's drying, inspect it closely. I hope you won't be disappointed by what you purchased after your inspection. It does happen, though. That's why rescission clauses are put in contracts. None here, though. What you see is yours.

Consider how far you will go with your project. Are you going to completely rebuild the car, or will you settle for an engine and transmission swap? If you take the easy way out and do a light restoration job, remember that simple projects have a way of growing. I always advise beginners of Oddo's Rule of Three: No matter how long you think it will take—multiply it by three. Unfortunately, the same holds true for car building expenses.

As you progress, you'll find that one thing invariably leads to another. That is, if you install a highly modified engine and heavy-duty transmission, you must install an equally healthy rear axle assembly. Or, if you change the steering gear, you will have to modify the steering linkage and steering column. Moreover, if you install power disc brakes on the front, you should install better brakes at the rear. That's the way the story goes whenever you set out to build or modify anything. It's called the snowball effect. Like a snowball rolling downhill, a street rod project tends to grow as it "rolls" along.

Nevertheless, you're committed, so set your ratchet to OFF and begin the disassembly.

THE TEARDOWN

Dismembering an old car seems simple enough. You just take it apart, clean and repair all the pieces, then screw 'em back together after the engine and driveline swap modifications are completed. It's almost that simple, but unless you are well organized, you'll lose half the small parts. Also, unless you have a "perfect" memory, you'll forget how and where some of them go back together. There are other pitfalls as well. Rendering a car immobile is one; insufficient storage and workspace is another.

Parts Storage

Often it is best to keep the basic body and frame intact down to and including a working front and rear suspension. Many tasks are best completed with a mobile and semi-intact shell.

After you've organized your immediate work area, set up long- and short-term storage areas. If your long-term storage is under the fabled shade tree, you'll need to cover everything with heavy-duty plastic sheets. If you bought a complete car, you will have loose fenders, bumpers and the like to store. They must be stored in a secure, dry area.

If you have the room, install sturdy shelving for storing smaller parts. Good used heavy-duty shelving is often available at second-hand industrial equipment dealers. Most any size or height will do—they are adjustable. Avoid the flimsy, light-gauge shelving sold at discount hardware and building supply stores.

Take Notes

Get yourself a large bound notebook. Collect a number of coffee cans and boxes (lots of small ones are better than a few big ones). Get several packages of heavyweight, clear plastic interlocking sandwich bags and a fistful of shipping tags and adhesive labels. Many bolts and nuts on your old car are for unique applications and should be identified accordingly. Although you may intend to replace them, some items may not be available new, used or reproduction, so try to remove and store each as if it's the only one in existence. Count on it. If you get careless and lose or ruin any part, it will be irreplaceable!

Take It Easy!

When turning an old car into a street rod it is best not to immediately disassemble everything. The gung-ho approach where the builder rips the body off the chassis in the first week is fine, but only if you already know exactly what you're going to do and how to do it. If you're not sure which engine and transmission you're going to install, keep the basic body and frame intact with a working front and rear suspension. This not only retains mobility, but also will later allow you to mock up tentative engine and powertrain swaps.

Disassemble Thoughtfully

Once you've centered your car in the work area, begin disassembly by removing the bumpers, bumper guards and brackets as a single unit. Keep these and other major subassemblies in one piece for as long as possible. Even bumpers, as simple and uncomplicated as they may seem at first, can be confusing when all the nuts, bolts and brackets are dumped loose in a box. Replace all bracket-to-body attaching nuts and bolts in the bracket ends and finger-tighten.

Whip out that handy digital camera and take photos of anything you're likely to forget six months or more from now. Take as many notes as you think necessary. Again, don't trust to memory. Sketch or trace bumper brackets. Many are similar in appearance, but are specifically designed for left or right, front or rear, or deluxe or standard models. Put loose nuts or bolts in a tough plastic bag and tag the bag.

Lightly wire-brush rusted areas, then spray them with Cosmoline Corrosion Preventative. (This is one handy product, well worth searching out. It is made by the Aervoe-Pacific Co. of Gardnerville, Nevada, and is found in better auto parts stores. It provides an excellent corrosion protection by leaving a non-sticky, transparent, amber film that protects parts in prolonged storage, inside or outside. It is easily removed with any petroleum-based solvent.)

A second-best approach is to paint them with cheap "rattle-can" enamel. Don't worry about the color and don't

If your long-term storage is under the fabled shade tree, you'll need to cover everything with heavy-duty plastic sheets. If you bought a complete car, you will have loose fenders, bumpers and the like to store. They must be stored in a secure, dry area. Avoid the temptation to just put them in your backyard even if it does make a great area for a kid to explore.

use primer. Too many rodders think ordinary primer is a protective coating. Not so! On the other hand, cheap enamel is an excellent surface sealer although it's not as easily removed as Cosmoline when necessary.

Next, remove the hood, all four fenders and running boards. Clean and store the chrome or stainless steel trim items. Keep the hood-latch assembly and headlight buckets intact. Outdoor storage is OK for major sheet-metal parts, but before you put them outside, hose off whatever was missed when you washed the car, and then allow everything to dry. Again, wire brush and spray-paint bare metal with Cosmoline or enamel. If the fenders or hood were primered, but not painted, lightly sand the primer before enameling.

With that done, drain and remove the fuel tank. The tank may have to be shifted to one side and twisted slightly before it drops out. As soon as you fig-

ure out the combination, write it down in your notebook. The more notes you make now, the fewer mistakes you'll make when the car goes back together. Drain any gasoline from the tank, and then blow out the remaining vapor. A gas tank that's been drained, but not purged of gasoline vapor is the most dangerous. Use compressed air for this. Afterwards, seal the outlets with duct tape, not masking tape.

Next, remove the seats and floor mats or carpets. Again, return all nuts and bolts to their holes or bag and tag them. Obviously, you don't store seats or any upholstery outside. Keep the seats out of the weather and dry at all costs. If you're out of indoor storage, borrow an unused garage corner from a friend, relative or neighbor. And even though they're stored indoors, cover them. Old shower curtains work well for this.

ENGINE & TRANSMISSION REMOVAL

After you've completed the preliminary body disassembly, and cleaned and stored all bits and pieces, turn your attention to the engine and transmission. Access to them will be easier now that the surrounding sheet metal has been removed.

Remove the battery and drain the fluids from the radiator, engine and transmission. Then disconnect all hoses, lines, wiring and linkages. You can now remove the radiator, engine and transmission. Store the radiator in a safe place even though you don't plan on reusing it. I'll get back to it when we discuss the cooling system.

Sometimes a rod builder has acquired a car with a good late-model engine that he plans to reuse. Storing it involves more than throwing a piece of plastic over it to keep off dust. Moisture will enter through open valves, rusting valve seats and cylinder walls. The gasoline in the carburetor bowl will evaporate, leaving behind a thick varnish-like residue.

If you expect the engine to immediately start after sitting idle for the duration of your project, then treat it like the expensive piece of equipment it is. Start by draining the oil and removing the filter. ("Old" oil, with its accumulation of acids, will attack the bearing and bearing journal surfaces it was supposed to protect.)

Refill the crankcase with fresh detergent oil and a polymer additive such as STP. (The lubricant must cling to the rings). Install a new filter. Now, run the engine long enough to circulate the clean oil throughout. Then drain the coolant while the engine is still warm.

Remove the carburetor and drain every drop of fuel. Liberally squirt

Most removable body parts can be protected and stored easily, but be careful if you opt to keep the original fuel tank. It must be completely opened to the atmosphere and all resident vapors blown out before sealing and stashed away.

Sometimes the car comes with a perfectly good engine that the builder plans to reuse as is. Storing it involves more than throwing a piece of plastic over it to keep off dust. Moisture can enter rusting valve seats and cylinder walls. Media blasting is an easy and economical may to clean it up. Then it can be painted, and sealed indefinitely in plastic pallet wrap. Wrap is sold in rolls at better hardware stores. Media blasting is described in detail in the chapter on body restoration.

When it comes time to remove a "flexy flyer" like a floorless, previously channeled roadster body, or an integrally weak 1939–41 pickup cab, a dimensionally accurate framework should be built to keep warping or further fracturing to a minimum. If you don't think you can do the job properly, bring the undisturbed chassis and body assembly to a competent body shop. Believe me, this is cheap insurance, and will save time and money down the road.

light machine oil or gun oil in the passages and pour some in the bowls. Finally, seal the carburetor in two plastic bags and store it.

Next, remove the distributor, water pump, fuel pump, spark plugs, intake and exhaust manifolds, and core plugs, commonly known as freeze-out plugs. Spin the crank a number of times and force compressed air through each water-jacket opening in the block and heads, and intake and exhaust ports. This will ensure the water jackets are as empty and dry as possible. (Don't forget your safety glasses.)

Rotate the crank some more and, while doing so, squirt oil into the intake and exhaust ports. This will rustproof the valve seats and faces. After this, pour fresh oil into each cylinder to get a good coating on the walls and piston rings. It isn't necessary to remove the valve lifters, but pour oil over them.

After this profuse oiling, spray a liberal dose of demoisturizer, or water-dispersant oil, such as DOM, CRC or WD-40, into the ports and cylinders.

Immediately replace the spark plugs and tape up the lifter valley, intake and exhaust ports. Duct tape, commonly called racer's tape, works best for this. This will keep out dirt and moisture, and seal the demoisturizer in the engine. Finally, loosen the rocker arms enough to close all the valves. This seals each cylinder and minimizes valve-spring load.

Disconnect the battery, drain the oil from the engine and manual transmission (fluid, if it's an automatic) and remove the engine and transmission as a unit. Once out, separate the transmission and engine. Set the engine on a dolly or mount it on an engine stand. Bolt on the rocker covers (if it's not a flathead) and intake manifold.

Put it in a clean, airy spot, and wrap it well with plastic sheets or heavy-duty trash bags. Unless you are going to rebuild the transmission, wrap it up as well. You can forget about the engine and transmission for now, knowing they'll be in good condition come reinstallation time.

What if your engine isn't worth sav-

ing? Maybe you'll have to pay someone to haul it away! However, if you're going to rebuild the engine or transmission that came with the car—or one you've acquired along the way— you should still protect it from rust and corrosion. This is best done by leaving the engine or transmission assembled. The grime and crud will do a fair job of inhibiting rust. Further protect it by draining the fluids and drying it out. Then seal the engine or transmission in plastic sheets or bags.

BACK TO THE CAR

After all of the foregoing is squared away, buy or design and build a stout tow bar if you don't already have one. You'll need this for towing your car to various shops before it can move under its own power. Even if you have access to a car trailer, it's often easier to flat tow.

The first place to tow your prize is to a steam cleaner. Find one that shows more than a passing interest in doing a careful and thorough job. Tell 'em a little about your project and how important it is to you. Practice this verbal routine now. Many rod builders have learned the hard way that too many steam cleaners, sandblasters, metal smiths, painters, and repair shops don't care enough to do more than an average job. If it's top-quality work you want, let your enthusiasm rub off on them!

When you get your car back home, carefully look it over. If you made the right purchase, you won't be disappointed or disenchanted with what you see with her "makeup" off.

THE STREET ROD CHASSIS

The street rod chassis must bridge the gap between decades old body styling and a modern drivetrain with a bit of nostalgia thrown in for good measure.

ORIGINAL FRAMES

The modern street rod chassis is a true hybrid. It must function as a precise platform for an original body . . . and it must be significantly modified in order to handle a modern V-8 and the accompanying drivetrain. Also, if an independent front or rear suspension is anticipated, the frame must be reconfigured to accommodate mounting of either. In short, the frame is the essence of street rodding—the bridge between the old and the new.

In the early days of street rodding, builders recognized that the straight and narrow open-channel Ford Model T or A frame was hopelessly inadequate for even the moderate horsepower developed by hot four bangers and lukewarm flathead V-8s. They were quick to note that the curvaceous 1932 frame with its K-member was a major departure from the simple rails and 90-degree crossmembers that preceded it. Alert backyard builders were equally quick to acquire a Deuce

frame for their Model A roadster. It didn't hurt matters that it was a beauty in and of itself.

Early rod builders realized that their frame must handle the increased loads and stresses of their new hot engine. They did their best by using the most modern hardware available. You must do no less. You owe it to yourself and your passengers to put the safest, most reliable frame possible under that vintage body, original or reproduction.

If you have, or will elect to use a

reproduction street rod frame, there's no need to learn how to inspect, repair or modify an original chassis. If you detect a hint of encouragement in my words, you're right. I've done a major chassis rebuild in the past, and believe me, saving up the bucks for a repro frame is easier than slaving over a twisted, rusted piece of iron that has outlived its usefulness! You know what you have, so you are the judge. Nevertheless, before you can make an objective decision as to what constitutes a safe and reliable frame, you should know your options.

Although I won't encourage a novice to build a frame from scratch, every street rod builder should be aware of two design factors. The so-called X-braced frames of the mid-1930s were a belated recognition of basic structural engineering, that is, triangulation is the key to rigidity. Triangulated frame members provide much more torsional rigidity than rectangular members.

The second point of major significance is that an open-channel frame must have a very large cross section to provide even mediocre rigidity. Boxing a channel section, which is closing in the open side of the channel with a steel plate of equal thickness, increases the strength of the member significantly.

A frame and body are separate structures that must be free to move relative to each other, although slightly. Consequently, a body should be mounted on a frame over soft rubber pads to isolate it from as much vibration as practical. Furthermore, although engine and suspension attachments must be strong, they too should be mounted to the frame with rubber or urethane bushings. They should never be mounted directly to

the frame.

Many street rods are now built with fiberglass bodies. Consequently, a super-strong frame is required. Why? Unlike steel bodies, even fiberglass bodies with steel reinforcement add little or nothing to the overall integrity of the vehicle. If you doubt this, ask a roadster owner whose car doors pop open every time he crosses the railroad tracks, or the poor soul who has to replace cracked windshields with regularity. So, forget an open-channel frame if you're going to use a 'glass body.

If you purchased vintage tin, decide whether or not the original frame is repairable. If it is, clean it up, locate the predictable problems, get replacement parts and practice repair techniques. If the frame isn't repairable, or if you've concluded that the repro frame is best for you, you can choose from among the list of manufacturers and their wares.

If you're dealing with the remnants of an original frame, it is a good bet you would live to regret a rebuild. Bail out sooner, rather than later. The longer you stew over the dilemma, the more costly—in both time and money—your unusable frame will become. I don't want to sound too gloomy, though. Not all original frames are refugees from the scrap heap, just a lot of them.

The Very Early Ford Frame

Let's face it, all Ford Model T frames still in existence and unattached to an original Model T are junk. Do anything you want with the one you have . . . except put it under your street rod. A variety of replacement frames is available. Few are true reproductions for reasons stated

above. Most are fabricated from a combination of rectangular and round tubing. A few duplicate the original specifications, but many have kicked-up rears, making them suitable for a variety of modern rear suspensions. So, if you are building a Model T-based street rod, think 100 percent reproduction.

I also recommend doing the same if your car will be Model A based. The stock Model A frame is a little better than the T, but it is still a ladder-type design with two straight open channel side rails approximately 100 inches long. Three cross members—front, center and rear—are riveted to the side members with each corner reinforced by gusset plates or brackets. Front and rear crossmembers serve as spring mounts. Separate body-support brackets are riveted to the side rails.

Model A frames were built from 5/32-inch thick pressed steel. Thanks to rust, you may find yours to be a tad thinner. Even if not rusted, an original Model A frame is so old and inadequate for handling the loads imposed by a modern engine, the amount of work required to bring one up to par justifies going to a repro frame in nearly every case.

Nevertheless, you may be one of those rod builders who have a cherry Model A frame and is willing to put the extra hours into it, particularly if you're planning to build a channeled roadster rather than a High Boy. And, since massaging this sinfully simplistic frame design into a suitable street rod structure is a time-honored pursuit, you should know about two of the more important construction options—"kicking the rear" and boxing the rails.

Kicking the Rear—Of course, common sense dictates that nothing will be gained by jumping headlong into a major frame modification before you know what front and rear suspension you will use. You should also know what you want the car to look like. "Kicking" or "Z-ing" the frame up in the rear allows the body of the car to be dropped as low as practical and still retain the rear transverse leaf spring.

In this operation, the frame is cut just forward of the rear axle. A new section of channel is spliced into each side rail. This is done so the rear quarter of the frame, inclusive of the rear crossmember, is repositioned 5 to 8 inches higher than the forward three quarters. Although this severely reduces trunk volume, it provides ample transverse spring clearance over the rear end.

*Boxing the Rails—a*s mentioned earlier, greatly increases frame strength. It all but eliminates sagging and twisting of the side rails. A cardboard pattern of the frame area to be boxed is transferred to 1/8-inch thick sheet stock. A few street rod component manufacturers still catalog precut boxing plates that need only minor trimming before they are welded in place. Inasmuch as most of this work (if not all of it) requires the skills of a competent welder to insure strength and avoid warpage, the novice is again well advised to consider a reproduction frame.

The Deuce Frame

The 1932 Ford frame is a tough one to deal with. For almost as many years as the hobby is old, it has been the favorite means of support, not only for the classic Deuce body shell, but fenderless Model A roadsters and coupes as well. When it was still a teenager, the stock frame was adequate for

hopped up flatheads. However, by the time it had reached its "majority" and early OHV-engine swaps were applying higher loads to its handsome rails, metallurgical deficiencies began to show up.

There was another problem as well. The original K-type crossmember couldn't handle the longer and larger automatic transmissions. As a result, out came the hacksaws and torches—another practice that's about as old as hot rodding. Many frames were butchered to make room for the massive automatics. Once clearance for the transmission was achieved, the K-member was too flexible and unstable. Lengths of angle iron were often welded to it in an attempt to restore stiffness.

Nevertheless, the 1932 frame was a big jump forward from the Model A, even if it still had no rearward support. Although this latter problem was solved the next model year, no frame has ever supplanted the Deuce for sheer grace and beauty in the misty eyes of the tradition-bound street rodder.

The value some street rodders still place on an original frame is unrealistic, however. It isn't a rare work of art. It's just an assembly of mass-produced stamped-steel rails and crossmembers that have now been faithfully reproduced. The desirability of an "original" should not be confused with that of an original body. An original 1932 Ford steel body in most any condition will justify the economic cost of its restoration. It is a rare work of art.

Still, the frame is an important piece of working hardware that shouldn't be clouded with sentimentality. An original '32 Ford frame that isn't in use should be sold to a restorer who will unleash no more than a 65-horsepower flathead within its confines.

The 1933–36 Ford Frame

What I said about the '32 Ford frame also applies to 1933–36 frames. When the 1933 model was introduced, the frame was a significant improvement over what had gone before—it was the first Ford issue with a true X-member. Although it hasn't nearly the charisma of original Deuce rails, there are still those who take great pride in pointing to a clean factory-built frame. If it's near perfect, I'll go along with the program. If not, you will be ahead in terms of time, effort and money if you save up for even a bare-bones reproduction.

The 1937–48 Ford Frame

Here I do an about-face. Ford frames from the 1937–1948 era were well designed and built. Aside from those that have rusted away or have been butchered—and many have—a 1937–48 Ford frame is easily repaired at a moderate cost by a skilled welder. There are, however, some original frames along the automotive swap meet trail that may be better than the one that came with your car. An empty frame at a swap meet is well worth looking over.

Prices for average-condition 1937 to 1940 frames are often higher than those for 1941–48 frames. However, a choice frame will bring a pretty penny due to the demand for these very popular models. (And no longer are there any unpopular early Ford cars!) Postwar models—1946 through 1948—are usually the least expensive, and they are the least likely to have been butchered.

Other Frames

Admittedly, I've left out non-Ford frames. After all, over a thousand dif-

69

To determine if a frame is square, measure it diagonally from factory bolt hole to bolt hole, and side to side. If both measurements are within 1/16-inch, the frame is square. If not, the frame should be straightened professionally. Furthermore, if the jackstands are square and level, there should be no gaps between stands and frame.

ferent marques have been on the scene in the U.S. alone since the 1890s. Then there are several old foreign roadsters or coupes that have been converted into street rods. The variety is near endless. Nevertheless, when it comes to the specifics of converting this or that to a street rod, it is simply not practical to go beyond the traditional Ford choices. Although there are a few reproductions, the non-Ford rod builder often must settle for the following generalities of clean-up, inspection and repair.

Removing the Body

Whatever original frame you start with, clean it thoroughly. To do this,

you must first remove the body and running gear. That means further disassembly and, unless you have or build a body dolly, immobility of the body proper. A body dolly is nothing more than a small frame with wheels on which you set the body so it can be rolled around.

Caution: Remember what I said about frameless roadsters and convertibles? Well, if you have a woodie, removing the body from the frame can result in disaster. Most old woodie bodies are very weak, and when unsupported, the wood can break and deform the metal structure. Therefore, great care must be taken to provide adequate support for the body prior to any disas-

sembly beyond removing the fenders and doors. Some builders, in fact, don't risk removing the body. Instead, they restore and modify the frame with the body left in place. A tall order, indeed. To say nothing of the risk of fire.

A body dolly is worthwhile regardless of how small or light the body is. After all, if you remove it from the frame, you must wrestle with all that sheet metal one way or another. However, if you followed my earlier advice, you've already removed and stored the hood, doors, seats, deck lid, fenders, running boards, gas tank, engine and transmission. The body is much lighter with these components removed.

Build Your Own Dolly—A crude but effective body dolly for a roadster or similar lightweight can be made from 2 x 4s. If your car is heavier, such as a four-door sedan, better use some well-seasoned 4 x 4s. Measure the length of the body from the firewall to the rear deck panel, and the width at its base. Build a slightly longer and slightly narrower rectangular frame using long carriage bolts for fasteners. Put flat washers under the nuts. Bolt a quality caster of adequate capacity on each corner and you're in business. It'll take a few hours and a little money to do it right, but you'll never regret having the dolly once it's done.

Now the tough work begins. Find all of the body-attaching bolts and remove them. Don't be surprised if a few are reluctant. Chances are the body bolts have been rusted in place for as many years as the car is old. To help with loosening them, squirt penetrating oil on each and let it soak for several minutes. When you think you've removed them all, try lifting each corner of the body an inch or two.

Don't strain too hard, though. It's likely that you overlooked one or two bolts, cables or other things that pass through the body and frame. Find the problem and correct it.

Once the body is free, you should be able to lift each corner. When you're satisfied it is ready to come off, put some soft drinks in the frige and call at least three friends. Ask 'em if they'd like to come over and "hoist" a few. You needn't tell them that the "few" is a few hundred pounds.

When all are in place and ready, gently pick up the body, carefully step over the frame rails and carefully lower it onto the wheel-blocked dolly. Padding and contour-cut 2x4s placed under the midsection and other unsupported locations will help prevent sagging and stressing. The idea is to help the body, particularly if it is an open model, retain its shape and still be mobile. Roll the body out to the farthest corner of the shop. Next remove all suspension components, brake lines and the many bits and pieces of hardware attached here and there. You can now take a good look at the frame.

Frame Inspection

Chances are you won't be terribly impressed. Maybe just depressed once you see how much damage occurred to your frame over the years. If it looks hopeless now, now is the time to decide whether to order a repro frame, or enlist the services of a professional welder. If you're not quite sure if you want to embark upon its restoration yourself, it's at least time to clean it up for a more careful inspection.

There are several ways you can go about it, but first put the frame on four jackstands and closely inspect it from one end to the other for tell-tale signs

Significant straightening and miscellaneous repairs to an original chassis are best done by a shop equipped with a frame table because heat can induce unpredictable warpage.

of collision damage. Check for cracks, splits and other irregularities. Get a couple of "rattle cans" of gray primer and shoot all the bad spots you see. Mark tears and questionable areas with chalk or grease pencil arrows. Photograph and make notes in your car diary of anything you must remember. Look closely between and behind double-wall sections. Once you've checked the topside, flip the frame over and repeat the process.

You won't be able to detect every flaw at this stage, but certainly the major ones. Once they're identified and listed in your diary, you can contemplate them at your leisure. All of this thoughtfulness, of course, is merely a systematic way of determining what must be done to restore your frame to its factory-fresh state. Repair must take place before any modifications are made to fit the engine and

mount the new front and rear suspensions.

Stripping the Frame—Don't take the frame down to bare metal until you're ready to start work on it. Otherwise, the surface will rust and you'll have more work to do. Even though you can rent portable sandblasting equipment, or purchase a small handheld blaster, I don't recommend you try to sandblast something as large and bulky as a chassis at home. (A small handheld blaster is great for small parts, however.) When you're ready to begin the cleanup in earnest, farm the job out to a commercial company. Depending on availability in your area, talk to a conventional sandblasting company, or one that uses powdered walnut shell media, mild acid stripping or the Redi-Strip® franchised electrolytic derusting process. Media blasting and the two chemical

Sometimes modern upgrades such as an independent front end are planned for an older street rod that is only undergoing partial restoration. Unless you know the rod's road history intimately, a professional frame analysis is worth the additional cost. It makes no sense to weld a new crossmember into a tweaked chassis!

stripping processes are such boons with regard to cleaning precious sheet metal, that I've devoted a substantial part of another chapter to their processes. You may as well get familiar with them now.

Whether the frame is sandblasted or chemically stripped, it is ripe for immediate re-rusting shortly after the process. To protect it, get what you need before you take it to the rust-removal "palace." A product used at body shops—PCL Pro-Etch (PN 195A) and the necessary catalyst Part B (PN 195-B)—works very well. A quart of each will be plenty.

Immediately after rust removal, spray the entire frame. A substantial coating is good for six months as long as you keep it garaged. Before you preserve the frame, though, once again inspect it closely. Pay particular atten-

tion to obvious stress areas where high-load components such as the steering, suspension, engine and transmission mount. Metal fatigue is caused by dynamic forces pulling, bending, twisting and compressing the frame over time.

Check closely around the rivets. Cracks frequently begin just under rivet heads and radiate outward. After you've found the cracks, don't lose track of them. Make a few annotated sketches in your trusty notebook and after you have given the frame its temporary preservative job, mark them with a daub of red paint.

With the exception of a few tiny cracks under rivet heads and similar high-stress points, finding many of the predictable problems in an old frame won't require the deductive abilities of a Sherlock Holmes. Big ragged holes

testify as to their exact location. Nevertheless, sometimes a frame can be in bad shape literally. Sometimes? Make that many times! Damage is not always obvious, either. Often, a frame is twisted only a quarter inch or so out of alignment. That is plenty even if you can hardly see it.

If yours doesn't quite "look right" and you suspect that it is indeed out of shape, don't panic. Just start looking for a good body-and-frame man. You need a skilled craftsman who sincerely appreciates old automobiles and who is ready and willing to work on one. These fellows are around, and usually their reputations are well-known within the street rod community.

As you might imagine, early street rods are particularly vulnerable to frame damage even from a relatively minor collision. If the effectiveness of the original X-member has been lessened by crude modifications, even a moderate blow can upset the side-to-side alignment of the frame . . . and everything attached to it.

The reason you need more than a casual tradesman to do a frame alignment is that he must have a thorough mastery of modern sophisticated frame equipment. The basic instrument for many years, however, has been the precision frame gauge—a unit composed of two cross bars moving in opposite directions through a center assembly. The gauge has a sighting pin in the exact center of the assembly, and when three or more are hung from a frame, the operator can read the degree and direction of misalignment.

Diamond Check—The first thing the technician will do to a suspect frame is run a diamond check. A diamond-shaped frame—one that is out of square—is not always easy to see. The center section must be true so the remainder can be compared with it. So, he checks for a diamond condition by setting up his special gauges, one just behind the front crossmember, and one just before the rear crossmember.

With a square frame, the center pins in the sighting bar of one gauge will align with the pins in the other gauge. If the frame is not square, the line of sight will be at an angle to the frame centerline, and the center pins in the other gauge will be to one side of the line of sight.

The diamond check is particularly useful for early Ford frames if the car was ever struck broadside or on a front or rear corner. As I said, improper modifications to the crossmember makes things worse, but even normal, trouble-free driving for 60 plus years is likely to distort the frame. Builders of 1946–48 Ford-based street rods have less of a problem. These heavy X-membered cars are much less prone to the condition.

Other checks the frame specialist should make include one for twist of the central section, one to ascertain that the full length of the frame conforms to the original center, and level-flatness of the overall frame.

Datum Line—Another critical test of frame trueness is the datum line. Here the height of each frame rail is measured by sighting across the topside of the gauge cross bars and reading against a vertical scale. Finally, measurements are taken to ensure that the front and rear suspension radius rods or lower control arms are correctly positioned and that any suspension crossmembers are of the correct width. Problems here can create prob-lems with front or rear wheel alignment later.

A precision frame gauge, however, only tells the frame man what's wrong and how much. The machine that corrects frame-alignment problems is the frame aligner. It's a large machine that steadies one frame rail while it exerts a force on the opposite rail. Every good body shop has one.

Frame Repair

Ordinarily a frame can be pulled (straightened) cold, but occasionally heat must be applied. Unfortunately, once a riveted frame has been damaged, it cannot be fully restored without welding. The rivet holes are stretched at the time of impact. Consequently, one way to keep a once-damaged frame in proper realignment is to heat and hammer down the loosened rivets and then weld the crossmembers to the frame rails while the frame is supported by the frame-alignment machine.

Frame alignment isn't just for the wreck-damaged street rod. It is also good for a frame that will receive substantial repair or modification. I'll discuss that later. For now, let's look at—and start working on—some of the "shot" rodder–caused frame damage you may encounter.

The first step is to place the frame securely on four jackstands, each adjusted to the same height. You'll also need six large C-clamps and several hefty Vise-Grip® locking pliers. Four 6-foot lengths of heavy-wall 1 x 3-inch rectangular tubing will also come in handy.

The next thing to do is find a smooth, level area on your workshop floor. This part of rod building is literally from the ground up, so you must have a level surface on which to place the jackstands. In short, don't build in

a new problem by welding your frame on a floor that's uneven due to low spots or settling cracks. Make sure the jackstands are positioned in the same places across from one another and that the frame remains level.

With help from a friend, measure diagonally from both front and rear corners of the frame. The diagonal measurements will be equal if the frame is perfectly square. When measuring, it's very important to measure from the same reference points on both side rails. The best points are factory boltholes or rivets because the rails were stamped originally, and those are the only holes you can depend on being in exactly the same location on both sides.

Both diagonal measurements should be within 1/16-inch. If not, you already have a diamond problem and, depending upon its magnitude, you may have to seek the services of that professional frame-alignment tech before you go further.

With the frame sitting on four leveled jackstands, you shouldn't be able to slide a sheet of typing paper between it and any of the jackstands. If you can, or worse, if you can see daylight between any of the two, the frame is "tweaked," or twisted. The amount of twist will determine the effort required to reduce it. A minor gap—and that is defined as up to an eighth inch—can be corrected at home when you're welding in new crossmembers.

If the gap is really bad, you may be better off getting it pulled back into alignment before you do any welding. Welding alone will make things worse. Adding stiffness to a tweaked frame with such procedures as boxing, Z-ing or replacing crossmembers, makes

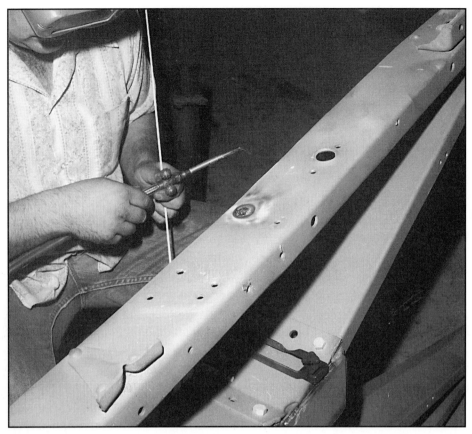

Minor repair work doesn't always require the professional touch, however. Unnecessary holes smaller than a half inch can be repaired with special brazing rod that melts at about 800 degrees.

realignment much more difficult.

Once you've determined your frame is square enough to proceed, you can begin the welding repairs. Frame material is too thick for gas welding, so electric welding is required. (Wire feed or heli-arc is preferred.) If your frame is in average condition, there are a number of operations you should undertake. Because such operations vary with regard to the danger of introducing misalignment, start with the simplest—hole filling.

Normally, filling holes won't tweak the frame, and it will afford you safe passage as you unravel the metallurgical mysteries of your particular frame. For example, forty different steel alloys were used in the manufacture of the Model A! There's no telling what might be lurking in the crystalline

innards of the frame you have!

Installation of a reproduction front or rear crossmember or a replacement X-member, is trickier than filling holes, but still relatively easy on frame alignment—if you follow the up-coming advice. The same goes for tubular engine mounts and rear-suspension coil-over shock mounts.

Probably the most critical operation—in terms of potential frame warpage—is welding in boxing plates. Nevertheless, to be on the safe side, you should ensure against warp-age every time you apply high heat to the frame.

The best way to repair or modify a frame is with an accurate frame fixture . . . period! Unfortunately, you probably don't have access to one. Moreover, you can't run to the frame-

alignment shop every other day. Therefore, you'll have to use a little ingenuity. To help prevent warpage, position something heavy on the front and rear of the frame before you do any welding. If heavy enough, this will keep the frame from lifting off the jackstands or shifting around when you are welding, pounding or grinding on it. Although crude looking, a rear axle assembly or old engine block chained to the frame on each end will work fine.

Replacing a stock front or rear crossmember with a new reproduction or one designed for an independent suspension is a common street rod practice. However, removing the old crossmember is time-consuming. In addition, the longer you work on it at one sitting, the more apt you are to apply excessive heat or force. So, before you remove any major frame component, trim two pieces of rectangular tubing slightly longer than the frame width and clamp them on the top and bottom of the rails. Next, cut out a section from the center of the old crossmember. With the load lessened on the side rails, burn or grind off the rivet heads and drill them out. You should now be able to remove the remainder of the crossmember with relative ease. During this operation, make sure the side rails are held firmly in place.

With the frame rails clamped and "loaded" make the necessary measurements and trim the replacement member to size and shape. By the way, a certain amount of gentleness is necessary when a new frame section is being fitted.

I am not going to try to teach you how to weld or work metal. I really don't have to, there are a number of good, how-to welding books available.

Tungsten Inert Gas (TIG) is best when installing boxing plates with minimal distortion. Conventional home-based welding is possible if you proceed slowly and deliberately. As with so many frame repair decisions, the builder must weigh his level of skill against the cost of professional work.

However, I should mention the fact that the amateur frame builder's most common mistake is trying to use a welding rod that's too big. The consensus is that 1/8-inch rod is just about right. It is approximately the same diameter and thickness of the frame material to be welded. Moreover, if you are not sure about the correct welding heat range, don't experiment on a good part of your frame. Practice welding on an old crossmember or other metal scrap cut from the frame. By the way, after you've finished welding, don't remove the clamps before the welds have cooled enough to touch.

Boxing

Boxing an old frame is one of the biggest headaches with regard to maintaining frame alignment. Keeping the front and rear of the frame loaded will lengthen the time required to complete the job, but will minimize frame warpage. As mentioned earlier, boxing plates can be cut from steel sheet stock

or, precut plates can be purchased from one of the street rod components companies. Before you start welding in the boxing plates, hand fit them in the channels to make sure the frame flanges are flat and there are no apparent interference problems. Gentle heating and some hammer work may be in order.

Once you're satisfied with their fit, determine if there are any places on the inside frame rail where you will bolt brackets or components. If so, weld in nuts or small sections of 1/4-inch plate. Later, you can drill and tap the plate with the desired thread. If, however, you elect to weld in pre-threaded fasteners, remember that heat distorts the threads. This means that the threads must be chased before you can run a bolt through. Consider also that it's easier to fill in unwanted holes before you begin the boxing process.

Typically, a frame is boxed between the front crossmember and the start of the X-member, and in the area of new crossmembers. Boxing the full length

of older rails is not normally done for street rod applications. The danger of distorting the rails is too great. Fully boxed is a common term, but it usually refers to boxing that begins just behind the front crossmember, goes to the firewall area, around the center crossmember, and around the rear crossmember. The plates should be fitted part way into the opening of the framerail C-section. Push the plate in with about half of the top and bottom edges exposed. This will allow you to lay in a substantial fillet weld along the edges of both pieces of material.

When everything looks right, start welding from the center of the plate, skipping back and forth toward the ends. Lay eight-inch beads at a time— no longer—changing from side to side of the frame. This will balance out any warpage.

Depending on your skill as a welder, you may be able to do the whole job without turning over the frame, but that's needlessly cutting corners. When somebody looks at the finished job, chances are he will look at the bottom side edge. So, for maximum neatness and ease of welding, flip the frame over to do the bottom. This means repositioning the ballast, but it will be worth it.

Make sure the welds are cool before you unload or move the frame. If you take your time, you should be able to do all the foregoing work without warping the frame significantly. Nevertheless, when all major frame modifications have been completed, check frame alignment.

The cost of straightening a badly damaged frame, even one as simple as the typical early Ford, can cost several hundred dollars. A frame that is found to have a minor tweak or one that has

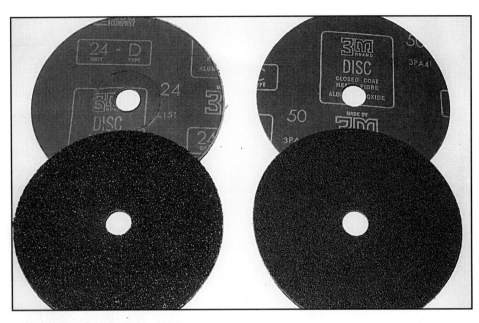

Abrasive discs are used for cleanup, scale or rust removal, smoothing out ragged torch cuts and rounding off sharp corners.

been warped by careless welding can be made right for less. Even so, it's worth it to take precautions to ensure that what you do is done right. The key here, as everywhere else in the construction of a street rod, is patience.

REPRODUCTION FRAMES

Much, it not all, of the previous advice can be skipped if you elect to use a reproduction frame. The reproduction frame industry, which followed closely on the heels of the reproduction body industry, is a blessing to the street rodder. Whether the average fellow realizes it or not, repro body and frame manufacturers—most of 'em street rodders themselves—breathed life back into a near stagnant hobby. Desirable vintage tin, except for half-ton pickups, was no longer in the affordable range. Not only that, the hope of finding a good chassis at an affordable price (plus the cost of repair and modification) was also demanding more time than ever. In the early 1970s, unless the average working guy

already owned a decent car, it was becoming more likely that he would not be able to enter the street rodder ranks. The reproduction body, chassis and replacement parts industry put an end to the fears of a dismal future.

The chassis end of the repro street rod business began with basic rectangular tube frames built for "Fad T" roadsters back in the late 1950s. They were not reproduction frames in the true sense of the word, but they were up to the task of safely supporting the lightweight fiberglass body, a mild V-8 engine with the bare necessity driveline and suspension components.

A great many early Fad T rectangular tube frames simply were not designed for the hairy supercharged V-8s stuffed into them. Fortunately, most of the Fad T drivers didn't dare let it all hang out. The powerful engines were there mostly for looks. Today's street rod builder is just as interested in looks, but he is a far more practical fellow. He keeps his engine mild, and most of the time, he can judge what's excessive horsepower

for a given frame. If there's any question, he knows the repro chassis manufacturer will make recommendations.

Reasonable facsimiles of original frames began auspiciously about 30 years ago when the pioneers of today's street rod industry began manufacturing the parts necessary to restore butchered originals.

The first repro frame parts were for the Ford Model A and 1932. As mentioned earlier, the 1932 K-member took the brunt of punishment handed out by unknowledgeable hot rodders of an earlier day. One of the first replacement components to hit the scene was Dick Hendrix's "Chassis in a Box"—a bolt-in X-member for the Deuce. The kit was designed so the rod builder could bolt its eighth-inch mild-steel channel sections into the frame following removal of what was left of the original center section. (It was also neatly packaged and easily shipped in a box, hence the name.) Although the "forelegs" of the X-member were longer than their stock counterparts, they fit in the position of the original K-member. The transmission saddle, however, was moved rearward and the rear legs, which had no counterparts in the original frame, bolted to the side rails through existing holes. The net result was a great amalgamation of the good looks of the stock 1932 chassis, but with the desirable engineering of the later X-member frames.

Along about the same time, Jerry Kugel of Kugel's Komponents started marketing precision-formed reproduction front framerail sections. Jerry's replacement rails were designed to accept the Jaguar independent front suspension. With or without the special crossmember and fancy cat's paws, they were near-exact duplicates of the Deuce front "horns" that took such a beating during the early years of hot rodding.

Front horns weren't the only mangled members of the stock 1932 Ford frame. As popular as it is today, the High Boy Deuce sitting tall and mighty atop a full-length frame wasn't always the street rodder's favorite. If the truth were known, the channeled roadster—cut down as low as it could go—was what early street rodders considered the "in thing." If that seems strange, just recall the ride height of everything else in the 1930s.

Channeling, of course, is an extensive operation. It entails cutting out the floor pan, dropping the body over the frame and moving the body hangers up. The floor pan is then rewelded back in. The driver and his passengers, in effect, sit right on top of the frame. Unfortunately, the channeling of a 1932 Ford was not done without "bobbing" the back end of the frame—the last 18–20 inches were unceremoniously chopped off.

All that changed in the early 1970s, when the High Boy look caught fire on the West Coast. More than one oldtimey "channel job" underwent an uplifting retrofit.

Two men are primarily responsible for the big jump forward in reproduction frames. They are Ed Moss of Total Cost Involved Engineering and Roy Fjastad of the Deuce Factory.

By the time the former circle-track racecar builder Ed Moss brought his Model A frame to market, there were enough patch pieces and crossmembers available to completely refurbish either Model frame. Using the pieces, many a rod builder spent hours welding on a sad frame in an effort to bring

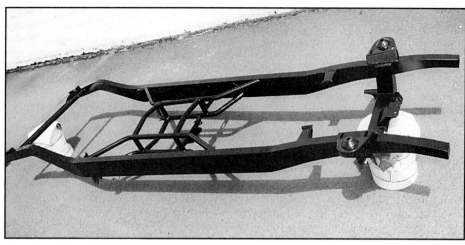
American Streetrod & Performance.

it back to life. Ed changed all of that in one fell swoop. His labor of love was a dimensionally exact duplicate of Henry's 1928–31 frame, but fabricated from 2 x 4-inch mild steel rectangular tubing. It was now fully boxed "from the factory." The reproduction deviated from the original in other ways as well, particularly since it incorporated a redesigned K-member that stretched out in the direction of the rear crossmember. It was, and is, a product for the street rod market. Model A builders loved it from the start.

It wasn't long after the Total Cost frame was publicized that another former racecar builder surprised the street rod fraternity. Roy Fjastad jumped in feet first with perfect replicas of the 1932 right and left frame rails, precision die-stamped on a 1000-ton press. This was expensive mass production just like the big boys do it, hence the company name, "Deuce Factory."

What must have seemed like real gambles to Ed and Roy ultimately proved to be wise business moves. They and their colleagues have given the street rod hobby the kind of future it never would have had otherwise.

MANUFACTURERS INDEX
American Streetrod & Performance
7323 NE Gilsan Street
Portland, Oregon 97213
(503) 255-1607; Fax: (503) 255-1659
Web Site: www.americanstrod.com

This company has the early Chevrolet passenger car line well covered. Their 1934 and 1937–39 frames come in two versions, one with a 107-inch wheelbase, another lengthened to 112 inches to fit their extended Cabriolet and Phaeton bodies. Features include boxed steel rails with rear spreader bar, tubular center section and Mustang II front crossmember welded in place.

The 1932 Ford chassis from ASP features die stamped, one piece, cold-roll formed steel frame rails with stock side reveals. The rails are boxed full length and include a welded-in tubular center section. The round tube rear crossmember is fitted with upper coil-over shock mounts. A stamped steel front crossmember is installed. Frames are assembled and welded in a holding fixture and include welded-in nut plates for body mounting. Also catalogued are frames for 1933–40 Ford

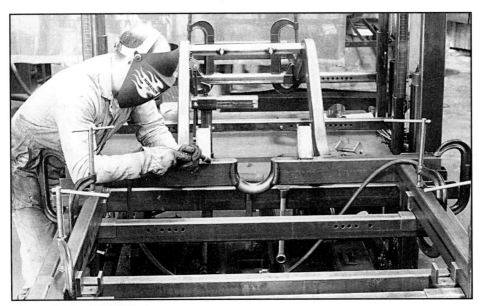
Art Morrison Enterprises.

passenger cars and pickup models with boxed steel frame rails, rear spreader bar, tubular center section and Mustang II front crossmembers.

Antique & Collectible Autos
35 Dole Street
Buffalo, NY 14210
(716) 825-3990, Fax (716) 823-0048

A & C Autos manufacture their own frames for their reproduction bodies. Builders of other car brands nevertheless may want to contact the company for specific chassis information. A & C Autos' rails are fabricated from 10-gauge cold-finished mild steel. They are reproduced from original designs, plasma cut to eliminate warpage and assure uniformity, and MIG and TIG welded for strength. Holes in the rails are precisely located and predrilled. Blind holes have nuts welded in place for ease of assembly.

Access holes are cut in crossmembers for ease of routing exhaust, brake lines and fuel lines. Their lineup includes the following:
1934–35 Chevy 3-Window Coupe (107-inch wheel base)

1932 Ford Roadster (106-inch wheel base)
1934 Ford 3-Window Coupe. (112-inch wheelbase)
1940–41 Willy Coupe (102-inch wheel base)
1941 Willys Pickup (102-inch wheel base)

Art Morrison Enterprises, Inc.
5301 8th Street East
Fife, Washington 98424
(800) 929-7188, (253) 922-8847
Fax: (253) 922-8847
www.artmorrison.com

Morrison has a sophisticated, high-tech approach to reproduction chassis manufacture. Their specialized equipment replicates OEM contours and eliminates the need for special body-mounting outriggers. Their "bumper-to-bumper" perimeter-style PROfile 2 x 4-inch rectangular (.120-inch wall) frame rails are precision-formed in-house using proprietary multi-axis mandrel-bending equipment. Being able to bend tubing in both horizontal ("hard") and vertical ("easy") planes allows them to config-

ure the components to conform to the original shape. The components are then fixture-assembled and welded.

Morrison's comprehensive database includes specifications for over 100 car and light truck makes and models, with more being added all the time. The following lists the most popular street rodding choices:

Buick: 1940–41 Special/Roadmaster.

Chevrolet: 1934–36 Coupe, Sedan; 1937–39 Coupe, Sedan; 1937 Sedan Delivery; 1940 Coupe, Sedan; 1941–48 Coupe, Sedan.

Chrysler/Dodge: 1935–38 Coupe, Sedan; 1939–42 Coupe, Sedan; 1946–48 Coupe, Sedan.

Ford: 1933–34 Coupe, Sedan, Cabriolet; 1935–36 Coupe, Sedan, Roadster; 1937–40 Coupe, Sedan, Convertible; 1941–48 Coupe, Sedan; 1935–41 Pickup.

Oldsmobile: 1937–38 Coupe, Sedan; 1939–40 Coupe, Sedan; 1941–47 Coupe, Sedan.

Plymouth: 1934–38 Coupe, Sedan; 1939–42 Coupe, Sedan; 1946–48 Coupe/Sedan.

Pontiac: 1939–41 Coupe, Sedan; Willys 1933 Coupe; 1936–37 Coupe; 1939 2D Sedan.

Whew! And that's not the best part. Should your particular vehicle not be listed, Morrison will send you a form to fill out that includes all necessary dimensions.

California Custom Roadsters.

Coach & Chassis Works, Inc.

California Custom Roadsters
15094 Sierra Bonita
Chino, CA 91710
(909) 393-4005, Fax (909) 393-4228

The staying power of the "Fad T" is nothing short of incredible. Having first seen the light of day in the late 1950s, it's still going strong! Bill Keifer's version of the T-bucket chassis may not have been the first offered via mail order, but it sure ranks amongst 'em! Alone among its compadres, CCR sells complete plans for building the frame, mounting the steering, motor, and either a conventional rearend or a Jag IRS

Coach & Chassis Works, Inc.
1445-A Babcock Blvd.
Pittsburgh, PA 15209
(412) 821-1900, Fax (412) 821-5099

This fiberglass body manufacturer builds frames for their own Plymouth and Dodge coupes, convertibles, and pickups. A builder of an original car in need of a new chassis would do well to discuss their problem with Coach & Chassis Works, Inc. They offer basic "Perimeter Frames" for the models indicated below. Each comes with a center K-member, stock front and rear crossmembers or an optional IFS and IRS crossmembers.

1933 Plymouth and Dodge, 112-inch wheelbase

1934 Plymouth, 108-inch wheelbase
1934 Plymouth, 114-inch wheelbase
1933–35 Dodge Pickup 112-inch wheelbase

Cornhusker Rod & Custom, Inc.
RR 1, Box 47
Alexandria, NE 68303
(402) 749-1932, Fax (402) 749-1933
www.cornhuskerrodandcustom.net

These guys, noted for their Ford flathead endeavors, custom build 1928–40 frames with tubular X-members and a variety of component options.

GMT
1824 Metzger Lane
Huntington Beach, CA 92637
(714) 842-2824
www.gmtmetal.com

Geoff Mitford-Taylor, the man behind GMT, builds a 1932 frame, but not just any ol' frame. His patented design features recessed channels with removable panels that shroud wiring, fuel and brake line. The corners are welded in, and function as virtual boxing plates.

Harwood Street Rods
13240 Hwy 110 South
Tyler, TX 75707
(903) 561-6338

Harwood manufacturers their own chassis for original 1932 Ford cars. The significantly redesigned tubular 10-point K-member fits stock bodies and all flat floor aftermarket bodies.

Heinzman Street Rods
1305 North "C" Road
Phillips, NE 68864
(402) 886-2275, Fax (402) 886-2998

John Heinzman has been in the rod building biz for over thirty years and

Cornhusker Rod & Custom, noted for their Ford flathead endeavors, build 1928-40 frames with a variety of component options. Pictured is the traditional 1932 High Boy with the conventional 9-inch rear.

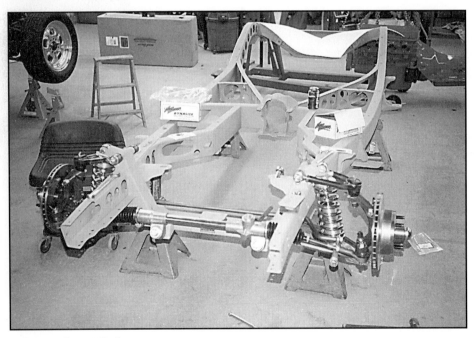

Heinzman Street Rods.

manufactures several different early Ford frames in a precision holding fixture. He starts with Deuce Factory 1932 frame rails and adds a die-formed front member, 1 1/4-inch and 1 1/2-inch tubing center crossmembers and braces, a rear crossmember set up for Eliminator coil-over shocks, and front and rear spreader bars. The frame is finished off with 3/16-inch boxing plates. His 1933–34 chassis is built in a similar manner with 10 gauge frame rails. The company will also rework the customer's original frame, assuming of course, that it is in good condition.

This one accepts the "flat-fendered" 1941–48 Ford and Merc body. These larger cars are becoming quite popular with the easy living set that appreciates creature comforts in a street rod.

**The Rod Factory
3131 N. 31st Avenue
Phoenix, AZ 85017
(602) 269-0031**

The Rod Factory manufactures complete frames for Model T roadsters and 1928 through 1940 passenger cars, plus a full line of chassis components for the 1936 through 1940 Chevrolet.

The 1928–31 chassis is equipped with a dropped axle front crossmember, and an optional 2-inch raised and narrowed rear crossmember for a lower stance. The 1932 Ford frames are cut from 11-gauge cold-rolled steel using CO_2 laser technology. They are built in a precision holding fixture, heli arc and MIG welded to original dimensions, and boxed full length. Frames can be ordered set up for Aldan rear coil-over shocks, or the Corvette or Jag IRS.

The center crossmember in the 1932 and 1933–34 chassis allows adequate transmission clearance, and the front crossmember for dropped axles has a 6-degree pitch to help insure correct alignment. The 1935–40 chassis has an optional Mustang II IFS with parallel leaf spring rear with coil-overs.

**SAC Hot Rod Products
633 W. Katella St.
Orange, CA 92867-4627
(714) 997-3433, Fax (714) 997-3693
www.sachotrod.com**

Now headed by Roy Davenport, SAC has been engaged in the manufacture of street rod components for over a quarter century. Their 1934–40 Ford frames have earned an enviable reputation, and are used by many premier rod building companies.

Total Cost Involved, Inc.
1416 West Brooks St.
Ontario, CA 91762
(909) 984-1773, (909) 391-1526
www.totalcostinvolved.com

Ed Moss originally built his company around the reproduction 1928–31 Model A chassis. It retains the dimensions and profile, but its contoured 2 x 4-inch, 0.125-inch wall, rectangular tubing construction provides a stronger base that the original. The stock front crossmember is standard, and body and hood latch brackets are included.

An IFS crossmember is optional. A choice of four rear crossmembers includes stock, coil-overs, Corvette and Jaguar.

The company's 1932 frame features full-length boxed reproduction rails with rectangular K- and X-members for strength and rigidity. The 1-inch lower Model A type front crossmember is standard and the IFS crossmember is optional. There are four optional rear crossmembers—stock, coil-over, Cor-vette and Jag. A special contoured rail that follows the 1928–29 Model A

body line in the cowl area is offered for those who wish to build one of the most traditional of all street roadsters.

Total Cost's 1933–34, 1935–40 Ford passenger car and 1935–1941 pickup frames also feature full length boxed rails with rectangular tubing X-members for strength and rigidity. The stock-type front and rear crossmembers are standard on all models. An IFS front crossmember and rear crossmembers for coil-over, Corvette or Jag suspensions are optional.

8

STREET ROD ENGINES

There's simply no disputing the fact that the Chevrolet small-block V-8, in any one of many factory displacements, has graced the hold of more street rods than all other engines combined since 1955 . . . if not since 1925!

If there's one thing that can be credited for bringing street rodding into existence, it was the demand for more power! In the early days of hot rodding, speed was the only thing that mattered. Of the countless worn-out four-cylinder powered Model T and A roadsters that fell into the hands of young men with mechanical talents, almost all of them received some kind of high performance modification ranging from the installation of a bigger carburetor all the way to dual overhead cam conversions.

Then, in the decade following the appearance of Henry's 1932 Ford flathead V-8, nearly all vestiges of the original T, A, B and C four-bangers were gradually eliminated in favor of the bent eight. When that was accomplished, the focus of hot rodding was on the flathead V-8 going from 21- to 24-studs and the addition of rudimentary, but effective, commercial speed equipment. Along the way, engine swapping became—and has remained—a significant concern.

As Henry's engineering staff improved the flathead, and displacement grew from 221 cubic inches in 1932 to 255 cubic inches for the 1953 Mercury, engine swapping was relatively simple. The only difficulty involved the popular late 1920s Model T and 1928–31 Model A chassis. The original four-cylinder cars used completely different engine and transmission mounts . . . and the art of engine swapping was advanced.

Early swappers still had it relatively easy, however. They only had to fabricate new front engine supports and attach them to the frame rails. Since it wasn't practical to use the Model T or A transmission with the flathead (the bolt patterns are different), the equally improved transmission was installed along with the engine. Of course, that meant that a rear mount had to be fabricated. In addition, new clutch linkage was required, a throttle linkage devised, and on and on . . . Finally, when a legal exhaust system was deemed necessary, street rodding proper had arrived.

It wasn't until the early 1950s that engine variety began to spice up the lives of street rodders. Oldsmobile, Cadillac and even Studebaker V-8s suddenly looked interesting. Within a few years, the mighty Hemi had made its debut. By the middle of the decade, the small-block Chevy had entered center stage. Today, a few of the old favorites are still very much with us, but the rules of the game have changed. Brute horsepower is, in most

From any angle, the Chevy comfortably fits in wherever an original flathead V-8 formerly resided. Best of all, it doesn't require an open account at the local speed shop to get it moving. A mild cam and a basic 4-barrel carb make it a strong performer on any boulevard.

cases, not as important as it once was.

"Driveability" is on the rod builder's mind more than it ever was in the "hot cam" 1950s. Even so, there is no shortage of healthy engines from which to choose. Big-city wrecking yards are full of powerful modern engines although the most modern American and foreign engines are laden with "electronic engine management" paraphernalia with which even mechanically astute hobbyists can't come to terms. We'll have more to say about this later.

A WORD ABOUT "STOCK" PERFORMANCE

Prior to 1971, an engine's SAE net horsepower and torque was still determined on the manufacturer's dyno under ideal conditions with no power-robbing accessories such as an alternator, power steering pump or air pump attached. Consequently, the resulting figures were not representative of normal operating conditions. In short,

engine-output figures were inflated. Nevertheless, that was what was used in advertising copy.

In 1971, the California legislature started a "Truth in Advertising" campaign that put severe limitations on the horsepower and torque claims that could be made. Eventually, the only horsepower ratings quoted nationwide were those obtained with all accessories connected and with the automatic spark advance in operation. By 1974, the published ratings were decreased even more because by then the manufacturers had to indicate how much power was available at the driving wheels.

This is not to say that the true horsepower and torque developed by engines built from the mid-1970s to the early 1990s did not actually drop. Hardly. Emissions controls, low compression, and retarded ignition timing all but destroyed the concept of high performance except in advertising copy. The point is, if you're considering one of these de-tuned V-8s; don't be misled by published horsepower and torque figures. If you want to get the most out of an engine, you will have to consider installing an aftermarket cam, ignition and induction, and as always, a good exhaust system inclusive of headers.

With that said, let's get on with the search for a powerplant. The best resources for used, but rebuildable engines are your friends and acquaintances, swap meets and, of course, wrecking yards. The latter is the most efficient.

Most metropolitan automotive dismantlers specialize. For instance, some wrecking yards feature only GM products, others FoMoCo or Mopar. Still others deal exclusively in imported cars and parts. Not only that, because their primary customers are commercial repair shops, and shops are mostly concerned with relatively late-model cars, many wrecking yards inventory vehicles no more than ten-years old. What this means is a bit more resourcefulness may be necessary if you're interested in a good, rebuildable engine (and transmission) more than ten years old. Nevertheless, start your search in big-city wrecking yards, and then move out to non-specialty wrecking yards in rural or semi-rural areas. Usually two or three will be within a reasonable distance from your home.

There are two reasons these are good places to start: First, a few telephone calls can be used to find suitable candidates, or indicate the scarcity thereof. You'll also get an idea of the going rate for your desired engine. Prices quoted should not be considered a baseline, however, but rather a top-dollar figure. The true baseline is free

or next to nothing! Yes, there are freebie engines out there. I've even had them delivered to my shop!

The second reason is that when found, the engine will very likely be complete—often with the transmission attached. Best of all, it may still be in the donor car. The value of completeness should be apparent. However, the desirability of finding an engine still in the car may not be apparent.

An engine in the hold will probably be protected from the elements, especially if the car has its hood in place and the air cleaner is atop the carb. In addition, you'll be able to check the mileage on the odometer, stick a finger in the exhaust pipe, and look for damage suffered in a front-end collision. In short, you can better evaluate the history and condition of an engine that has not yet been removed.

It doesn't even matter whether the yard pulls the engine for you or permits you to do the dirty work. Either you save time and effort, or you get to pocket—with their permission—those little bits and pieces of hardware that could save you bucks and time later on down the road.

SWAP-MEET MILLS

The next step up the ladder of cost-conscious engine shopping is the swap meet. At big swap meets, you'll find a good selection of popular engines: dozens of Chevy small-blocks, several small-block Fords, and a smattering of most everything else.

The main advantage of touring swap meet aisles includes lower prices, occasional home delivery of your purchase, and the availability of engine accessories at little or no extra cost. The most significant disadvantage is

you'll seldom get return privileges, something that many wrecking yards toss into a package deal. Still, the ability to haggle over prices from the driver's seat—and that's exactly your position as a buyer at the swap meet—is a significant factor. You can bet the seller doesn't relish toting that quarter-ton plus piece of cast iron back home.

Finally, street rodding is not a hermit's hobby. Very few practitioners go it alone. Every rod enthusiast has like-minded friends; so look to them when you begin your search for an engine. Let's face it: by their very nature, street rodders are hoarders of what the ill-informed often call junk. You've probably heard it at one time or another from your spouse: "When are you going to get rid of these junk cars, junk parts and junk engines!" It is true, though, if you've been into street rodding for long, you'll have accumulated what I call surplus inventory. Fortunately, most of us can usually be persuaded to part with some of it when the greenbacks are flashed.

The advantage of buying from a friend or acquaintance is a fair, often well-below market price. Most rodders will not knowingly sell a friend an engine that's not rebuildable. This is not to say you shouldn't exercise prudence; it's just that if you can't trust your friends, you'd better move to another neighborhood.

The major pitfall of buying an engine from an acquaintance is that it may not be complete. Familiarize yourself with what goes with the engine you plan to install.

Always assume that you must completely rebuild whatever used mill you purchase.

Regardless of how good it looks on the outside, completely disassemble,

There're two things that most street rodders desire, sometimes secretly—a combination of performance and dazzle. Performance you can get from a supercharged engine, and a polished blower adds the dazzle. If you really want to knock 'em out, throw in a polished stainless steel firewall! A word of caution relative to the 351 cid Ford Cleveland engine, so impressively showcased in this Deuce coupe. The 351C engine series performs best on the street when stock heads designed for a single 4-venturi carb are swapped out for those designed for 2-venturi carbs. If you want the glitz of dual 4-venturi induction, rework the carbs to get the total cubic feet per minute (CFM) fuel delivery as low as possible.

inspect and rebuild it. Otherwise, you'll end up pulling it out so you can do what you should've done in the first place. Besides, even the most mild-mannered street rodder wants to make some modifications to his powerplant.

PRUDENT ENGINE MODIFICATIONS

Although the quest for speed was the original motivation of street rodding when the hobby was young, modifications made for the sake of speed alone are now relatively insignificant. Nevertheless, a modified powerplant is simply the heart and soul of any street rod, regardless of whether you are taking the traditional path or are dreaming about a rod with engineering

as modern as tomorrow. Questions to address in this respect concern the type and degree of modifications you may want.

First, last and always, the cardinal rule for a street rod engine is reliability. The overly zealous pursuit of high performance will lessen reliability proportionally. Guard against temptation as you peruse speed equipment catalogs. No matter how powerful or handsome, an unreliable engine doesn't belong in a street rod.

The other side of the coin is driveability—that comfort zone for you and your passengers when you are just cruising. It includes a minimum of engine commotion, exhaust noise, road vibration, transmission jerkiness,

or excessive fuel usage. Trust me—the attempt to maximize horsepower has lessened the driveability of more street rods than anything else has.

A middle-weight street rod (2500–3200 pounds) rarely benefits from more horsepower than the typical bone-stock 300–350 cubic inch V-8 can produce in pre-smog-control guise. Valve timing is roughly comparable to what was stock in 1965, only now it's called RV or mileage timing, which is in the neighborhood of 240° duration and 0.425-in. lift. Mild? You bet. Not only that, a 600-cfm four-barrel carburetor has two primary and two secondary venturis that can be adjusted both to the lean or rich side to compensate for altitude changes—and 550 to 600 cfm is all the carburetion that's needed for a 300 to 350 cubic inch engine. An ignition system capable of operating at 6500 engine rpm will top off the engine requirements.

The engine specifications in the above paragraph describe the engines I've run in my 2900-pound street coupe over the past 30 years. (Not the ones I ran 40 years ago!) Today I use a hydraulic cam whether I'm running an automatic transmission or a manual four-speed. Anti-pump hydraulic lifters work for me. Even when I run three carbs with progressive linkage they are pinched down to about 600 cfm total delivery.

Is my engine down on power? No! I love high performance as much as the next guy does. In fact, you'll find my racecar and me at Bonneville every August and on El Mirage Dry Lake for most SCTA dry lakes meets. However, I depend on my street coupe for routine transportation, usually racking up 1000–1500 miles a month. That means I need a smooth, tractable and, above

The bottom line for the novice street rodder on a budget remains a mild small-block with emphasis on cosmetics and visual appeal.

If more suds are required, there's always the step up—a big-block Chevy . . . with a blower . . . and nitrous! And still it fits. Of course, this '40's hood had to be opened up, but most other modifications were very discretely accomplished.

With that said, let's go right to the undisputed engine favorites in the practical street rod world: the Chevy and Ford small-block V-8s, and, to a lesser extent, a few big-block models, plus the engine that refuses to die, the Ford flathead V-8.

THE CHEVROLET LINE

Old-time street rodders read from the Book of Tradition and worship at the shrine of the Ford flathead, and Ford small-block street rodders are equally proud of their Henry heritage. They have a strong desire to keep it all in the family. Nevertheless, the small-block Chevy V-8 is the favorite of most, bar none! It is installed in more street rods than all other makes and models combined. So, let's start with it.

The small-block Chevy was introduced in 1955 as a 265 cubic inch, 90-degree, overhead-valve V-8. It had a 3.75-inch bore and 3.00-inch stroke. The two-barrel-carb version developed 162 horsepower at 4400 rpm and 257 foot-pounds of torque at 2200 rpm; the four-barrel version developed 180 horsepower at 4600 rpm and 260 foot-pounds of torque at 2800 rpm. From the beginning, it was apparent that the little V-8 was a high winder rather than a stump puller. Moreover, because more drag races have been won with rpm than brute torque, it suited the hot rodders of the day just fine.

Two years after its debut, the Chevy was boosted to 283 cubic inches, then to 327 in 1962, 350 in 1967, and 400 cubic inches in 1970. In 1967 a short-lived 302-cubic inch version was slipped in and a 307-cubic inch version was introduced in 1968. All models were well received, with the exception of the 400-cubic inch engine. It

all, reliable engine.

Of course, when the demand for fire-up-and-keep-going reliability is decreased to once or twice a week, there's a lot of time in between for maintenance. One can tolerate an engine on the edge of immoderation.

Therefore, if your car will see limited service, you have a bit more leeway when it comes to engine modifications. Nevertheless, if you want to spend more time on the road than in the garage, keep modifications to a minimum.

Never discount the entrenched popularity of late 1950s street rod styling. Call it nostalgia if you like, but this multi-carbed Chevy small-block in a roadster is a "poster boy" for the classic look. No easy-to-install V-8 delivers more useable street performance.

Still, brute big-block power with air conditioning comfort appeals to a significant number of street rodders. That's the beauty of this hobby, there's room for everybody who is willing to work at achieving his goal.

an outstanding performer, this performance is contained in a package that is almost the same size and shape and weight as the Ford flathead V-8—the engine it replaced in 90 percent of all street rods built before 1955. Where it differs, the nod is in favor of the small-block Chevy!

Big Blocks

Although not used in the numbers of those just described, there is one Chevy V-8 that street rodders wanting strong performance have long been partial to—the big-block. At last count, it found a home in about 5 percent of the street rods currently on the road. This engine is for those who like their horsepower with hair on the chest. Introduced in 1965 and available in its early years in both 396- and 427-cubic inch versions, the big-block Chevy has never failed to satisfy the ego of any rodder who could afford to regularly replace rear tires.

Contributing in large part to the big-block's awesome power is its cylinder-head design: canted valves and efficient intake and exhaust ports. The valves are tilted away from each other, a design that minimizes bends in the ports, thus increasing intake and exhaust- port flow.

Dimensionally, the adaptability of the big block is surprisingly good; it's only one inch wider and a half inch longer than the flathead! It is, of course, heavier than the flathead, weighing in at about 685 pounds compared to the late flathead's 569 pounds. One hundred pounds is a downside, of course, but it can be accommodated if the front suspension is upgraded with heavier springs.

never gained much of a following among enthusiasts because of the subtle but significant performance reductions required by the expansion of the block to a displacement never envisioned by the original designers.

Today, the 350 reigns supreme due to its superb performance potential, but

complete engines of every displacement are readily available, and the tremendous supply of aftermarket equipment of every description, both new and used, promises to keep the small-block Chevy in the vast majority of street rods for many years to come.

Not only is the small-block Chevy

It wouldn't be cricket to lead you to believe the Chevy V-8 is the only Bowtie worth considering. In fact, the Chevrolet six cylinder was Ford flathead's truly fierce contemporary competitor in postwar Dry Lakes racing. I have it on good authority (the late California Bill Fisher) that the Stovebolt, when massaged by knowledgeable hands, truly gave the V-8s a run for their money. (Photos courtesy Patrick's Antique Cars & Trucks)

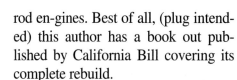

The quintessential street rod engine is the Ford flathead V-8. It was the indisputable powerplant of choice from the mid-1930s to the mid-1950s. Its popularity stalled with advent of the overhead valve engine, but it has refused to pass quietly into the pages of hot rod history. This very modern version of a 1949–53 8BA sports early style (59AB) Edelbrock heads plus an electronic ignition and alternator. Photo courtesy Motor City Flathead.

THE FORD LINE

First the Flathead

In the 1980s, and to everyone's amazement, it was realized that the Ford flathead V-8 had simply refused to die. It is in fact, still used by about ten percent of current street rod builders! That's a substantial number. Building a modern flathead, however, is fraught with danger.

Before you purchase either a 1946–48 59AB or 1949–53 8BA Ford or Mercury flathead, demand a money-back guarantee based on having the block thoroughly de-rusted and completely Magnafluxed by a competent automotive machine shop. All internal parts and speed equipment you may want are currently available for the venerable gran'daddy of street

rod en-gines. Best of all, (plug intended) this author has a book out published by California Bill covering its complete rebuild.

The Modern Ford Favorite

Not all street rodders pour gleefully over well-worn early *Hot Rod Magazines* and get misty eyed, or grab the Chevy V-8 and run. A significant percentage chooses to install the more awkward 302/351W small-block Ford V-8. They maintain that Henry's products form the backbone of street rodding, and as such, they should be outfitted with power by Ford, albeit a significantly more up-to-date Ford. Who can argue with them? Certainly not I.

Windsors

The FoMoCo Windsor small-block series came in 221, 260, 289, 302, 351-cubic inch displacements. It is technically described by the company as being the skirtless, thin-wall, 90-degree "V" family. This design is compact and lightweight, features it shares with its crosstown rival. Like most overhead-valve V-8s of the last 50+ years, the small-block Ford block is over-square—the bore is greater than the stroke.

Ford was the first company to develop precision thin-wall casting techniques to control warpage and bore misalignment, and they made the most of it in their early advertising copy. When the high-performance 289 was

On the other side of the popularity aisle sits the blue oval boys. Nothing but a Ford engine in a Ford car for them. The 260/289/302 cid mills in the thin-wall castings series really got them serious back in the 1960s and they haven't quit yet.

introduced, it was rated at 271 horsepower. The fact that it weighed only 480 pounds was shrewdly pointed out.

Although a variety of displacements in the stock block is still available in wrecking yards, the Windsor 302 and 351 are the most popular. (The Windsor 351 substantially differs from its cousin the 351 cubic inch Cleveland. Their city designations grew out of the foundry locations.) The Windsor engine is more compact, and even though it weighs closer to 500 pounds, it is still lighter than the 580-pound small-block Chevy.

The standard 302 is more plentiful than the 351W and, when mildly modified, is certainly adequate for the average street rod. The major reason it falls behind in popularity relatively to the small-block Chevy is not its performance potential. The problem is the small-block Ford's front-mounted oil pump and appropriately configured oil

pan. This makes it far more difficult to install in the 1932–48 Ford than the rear pump/rear sump small-block Chevy.

Most small-block Ford engine-to-early Ford chassis installations require the slightly more shallow dual oil sump pan first used in Bronco and Econo Van models. With this setup, the oil-pump pickup is moved rearward, just behind the center of the engine. Installations in the Model A and 1932 Ford are not quite as diffi-cult as in later model Fords with a stock chassis, however. At one time, the firewall had to be modified, but with the advent of redesigned aftermarket water pumps and the near commonplace independent front suspensions, more Ford-based street rods have modern Dearborn power than ever before. In addition, the small-block Ford has a front-mounted distributor that makes for easier servicing.

CRATE ENGINES

Up to now, we've been talking about buying a used engine with the intention of hauling it down to the local automotive machine shop for reconditioning. Whether the machine shop re-assembles it or returns a box full of parts to the rodder for home assembly depends on the skill of the street rodder. The last fifteen years, however, has seen Detroit capitalize on an old idea—the so-called "crate engine."

For years, production engine rebuilding shops have maintained a ready-to-go stock of popular models in their inventory. All a fellow with a dead player had to do was drain the oil, remove the carburetor and other accessories, and yank it out of his car with the assistance of a buddy and a handy rental yard cherry picker. After the long-block was eased down upon a sandwich of cardboard in the back of a pickup, they drove over to the shop. A couple of hours later they were bolting a replacement back in the car.

Today's rod builder has it even easier. There's no searching for a rebuildable engine to pluck from a wrecking yard and haul to a machine shop. A core or a trade-in isn't needed. He can pick the engine of his choice from a catalog or the Internet, order all the high-performance components he desires installed professionally, and consummate the deal over the phone with nothing more than a credit card. The engine will be delivered to his garage door in a few weeks.

Detroit and aftermarket high-performance component manufacturers are competing for the street rodder's favor with an exciting line of crate engines all the way from bare bones short blocks to package deals that are fully accessorized and ready-to-go.

Computer controlled engines made their debut in the mid-1980s and quickly advanced to fuel injection and throttle bodies that made amateur mechanics accustomed to plain ol' carburetors scratch their heads. Even Detroit had problems in the beginning, but the engineers soon sorted them. The average street rodder must do his homework to make them perform reliably.

Chevy Crate Engines

GM Performance Parts offers several complete engines as well as a wide array of accessories. Prices and choices change with the years, but for the beginning street rodder who has enough challenges with which to deal, yet knows he wants to run a Chevy, I recommend the small-block 350 HO Deluxe. This is a long block, with 9.1:1 compression ratio cylinder heads. The intake manifold, carb, distributor, water pump, torsional damper, and automatic transmission flexplate can be added at the time of installation. These are newly manufactured engines, mind you, not rebuilds. This particular model reliably delivers 350 horsepower and 380 foot-pounds of torque when you stretch it out.

Edelbrock—One of the most venerable names in hot rodding is Edelbrock, and their line of Performer Crate engines is available in three horsepower versions: 310, 320, and 410. Edelbrock starts with an all-new Chevrolet 4-bolt main, Goodwrench 350 cid short block. Then they work their magic by adding your choice of cam, cylinder heads, intake manifold, and carburetor. Rest assured, however, all of the components are designed to be compatible and reliable. Again, with the novice street rodder in mind, I suggest a review of intake manifolds, carburetors, and ignition components in the Performer line, and the aluminum Performer heads with 70 cc, 8.5:1 compression ratio combustion chambers. These are designed for low- and mid-range power, the neighborhood in which the cruising street rodder lives.

Ford's most interesting crate engine is a 302 cid with a hydraulic roller cam. It is a new long-block assembly which means you will have to provide the timing cover, water pump, damper, oil pan and pick-up. No problem, though. Street rod installation requires a mix and match of these parts anyway.

Ford Crate Engines

If Chevrolet is on the crate engine bandwagon, you can be certain that Ford is also in there pitching with an array no less imposing. If you want to let your imagination run rampant, get the latest Motorsports catalog and salivate over the variety offered. (I did.) If, however, you are a novice street rodder, and all you want to do is take that old car for a ride with fresh FoMoCo power, carefully review the 5.0l/302 GT-40-320 HP Performance long-block engine assembly. This, too, is a brand new engine with streetable 9:1 compression ratio aluminum heads, and a compatible high performance hydraulic roller cam and matching roller lifters. It is a long block, however, which means that you get to choose the intake manifold and ignition. As with most Ford engines, it comes with a front sump oil pan and pickup although it is equipped with the Explorer "short style" timing cover and water pump. As is explained in a later chapter, small-block Ford engines do present a few, but surmountable street rod installation problems.

AND THEN THERE ARE THE TRULY MODERN ENGINES

We've all seen the TV ads with computer-rendered graphics showing pistons pumping up and down in step with scads of valves dancing to the tune, "electronically managed." No carbs or distributors are to be found. Everything is computer-controlled.

Rodders with late model "grocery getters" have been known to go out to the garage, pull the hood, and just stare at the modern wonders the Ford and General Motors Engineering Departments came up with a few years before the turn of the century.

When they are watching, spouses have also been known to say in no uncertain terms, "Don't get any ideas!" Maybe yes, maybe no. Nevertheless, as one of the above, I have taken a tape measure to the 32-valver in my wife's car . . . and done a little daydreaming. There's no harm in daydreaming is there?

Some rodders, however, are not satisfied with daydreaming. They want the very latest powerplant under the hood of that old car on their side of the family garage. Most (I hope) understand that the installation of an electronically managed engine is likely beyond their level of amateur automotive mechanic skills. Not that it should deter them. They simply have to be willing to swallow a little do-it-yourself pride and be willing to pay for the expertise they don't possess. The installation of a computer-controlled engine is not the place to "learn by doing."

If that's the direction in which you want to go, here is a taste of what is currently out there. You'll have to wait for the introduction of the "Fall Models" on TV to know what's coming next season.

Ford Modern Engines

The 1991 Single Overhead Cammer—FoMoCo called their modular 16-valve engine SOHC "Sophisticated power: The most advanced engine in its class" when it made its debut in the 1991 Ford Crown Victoria and

The Nineties saw an abundance of fuel-injected, high-tech engines hidden beneath a maze of wire, sensors and plumbing in stockers, but street rodders were impressed with their performance. The Chevrolet line again topped the popularity poll even though a reliable installation required more professional expertise than ever before.

Mercury Grand Marquis. No doubt it was, after four decades of American production car engines with only overhead valves. This breed of "deep-skirt block design" cast iron and aluminum engines displaces a mere 4.6 liters (280 CID) with its bore and stroke of 90.2 mm x 90 mm. The SOHC short-block features four-bolt mains, a forged crankshaft and forged, sintered (powdered) metal connecting rods. Innovations to be sure in an upscale grocery-getter, but the engine's overhead cam design, one that allows the spark plug to be located near the center of the combustion chamber for more efficient burning, is what brings back memories of Ford's 1960s Racing Program. Roller "finger followers" put the intake and exhaust valves in contact with the camshaft lobe. Performance-wise, the reduced valve train friction and weight provides a substantial increase in power and efficiency.

By 1991, of course, Ford's "sequen-tial electronic fuel injection" (an injector for each cylinder) was old hat, but the "distributorless ignition" wasn't. The conventional distributor was gone, and in its place was a separate coil for every two spark plugs.

Cutting edge it was, but it was just the beginning.

The 1993 Dual Overhead Cammer—Ford introduced a 32-valve DOHC in the 1993 Lincoln Mark VIII. It was the first DOHC, 4-valves per cylinder, engine and the first all-aluminum V-8 engine Ford had ever built for the general motoring public.

The 4.6 DOHC engine shares some design features with the SOHC engine, the bore and stroke is the same, but the gravity-cast aluminum block with pressed in, cast iron cylinder liners is a few pounds lighter. With 280 horsepower at 5500 rpm and 285 foot-pounds of torque at 4500 rpm, it develops more power out of the same displacement. The deep-skirt block has extra metal in the bottom end for

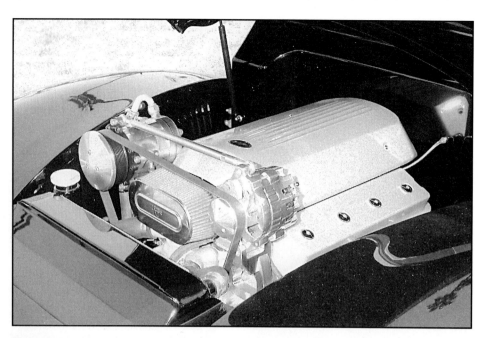

Even street rodders accustomed to seeing a high-rise induction system atop the Chevrolet small block have to admit there is nothing more pleasing than an ultra clean installation.

increased structural integrity, and six bolts are used on each of its five main bearing caps—four vertical, and two horizontal. Again, the crank and connecting rods are forged, but the latter are made of sintered metal.

Because it is a DOHC, two intake and two exhaust valves service each cylinder. There is a primary intake valve, and a secondary intake valve, but the exhaust valves open and close at the same time. An aluminum front cover seals off the cam drive chain. Finally, a re-engineered fuel injection delivers the juice.

If the above is not enough "latent content" to foster aqueous nocturnal dreams, Ford introduced an even higher performance 4.6-liter DOHC engine for the Mustang Cobra in 1996. This one delivers 305 horsepower with the addition of "high port" aluminum heads and longer duration cam timing.

GM Modern Engines

The Chevy LT1—The LT1 first saw the light of day in the 1992 Corvette.

Its 346 cid displacement typically delivers about 300 horsepower and 330 foot pounds of torque. The aluminum cylinder heads have redesigned ports and combustion chambers.

The water pump is gear-driven off the cam and directs coolant to the heads first, where it can efficiently eliminate hot spots in the combustion chambers. The Opti-Spark System "distributor" is mounted below the water pump behind the harmonic balancer. It is controlled by an optical sensor for ultra accurate timing through the entire rpm range by means of an Engine Control Module (ECM) and sensors strategically placed on the engine. Spark timing is adjusted instantly to avoid detonation. The LT1 engine uses a multi-port fuel injection that is lower and more efficient than earlier inductions.

The Chevy LS1—The production LS1 5.7 L (346 cubic inch) aluminum block engine debuted in the 1997 Corvette. It too is slightly smaller than

the veteran 350 CID block with 3.90-inch cylinder bores, but a longer 3.62-inch stroke. Obviously, it is no slouch as it is rated at 345 horsepower. It can also be found in the 1998 Z28 and Pontiac Firebird.

With its clothes off, it admittedly is a little disconcerting in that the distributorless ignition system uses eight individual coils mounted above the rocker covers. Fortunately, fancy sheet metal masks the ignition wiring and coils.

The LS1 has a programmable flash memory that controls spark timing and fuel delivery via input from sensors. It does not use a replaceable chip, but the memory can be modified at a Chevy service center. If you come by yours by way of a wrecking yard, be sure to get all of the wiring harness and connectors, and the Powertrain Control Module (PCM). GM Performance Parts does offer an LS1 engine installation kit, however.

The rest of the engine's technical data is just as impressive. The 6-bolt main block is fitted with flat-top lightweight pistons, sintered metal rods, a nodular iron crank, a 0.500-inch lift/200–203-degree duration hydraulic roller cam, a single bore throttle body atop a composite intake manifold with tuned runners, a cast aluminum oil pan and tubular long-style exhaust manifolds.

By the way, there is another feature that you should know about. Although it uses a conventional cooling routing (as opposed to LT1's "reverse flow") the coolant inlets and outlets are so low, an air-bleed system must be used to eliminate any air bubbles that may become trapped in the cylinder heads.

As I said, the current crop of American V-8s are the stuff of which dreams are made. I, too, as a "motor-

The most modern American V-8s are the stuff of fantasy for many street rodders. Discussions with professional mechanics engaged in high-tech engine swaps with sophisticated shop equipment to help them along have convinced me that the novice builder working at home, and determined to do as much as he can on his own is best advised to pass on these engines in favor of the older and more basic powerplant for which his high school auto shop course prepared him. To encourage readers who are relatively new to this game to try their hand at such a complex engine swap at home would be a disservice. If you could study this installation at the point in time that I did, I think you might agree!

head," have had my share of fantasy. However, after discussions with mechanics who are engaged in high tech engine swaps, I've concluded that although computerized induction and ignition have proven their worth in a stock production car, it simply takes an experienced professional with sophisticated shop equipment to persuade a hybrid to function as it should. Leave some computer wire dangling and the engine may run so poorly you'll have sleepless nights. Worse, the engine may not start!

In my considered opinion, the novice rod builder determined to do as much as he can in his home garage without professional assistance is best advised to pass on the latest trick FoMoCo or GM engine (and transmission) in favor of the older and more basic powerplant for which his high school auto shop course prepared him. To encourage readers who are relatively new to this game to try their hand at such a complex engine swap at home would be a disservice.

9

THE AUTOMATIC TRANSMISSION

The automatic transmission has been with us since before World War II, but few street rod builders seriously considered its use until the 1960s. In fact, the Hydra-Matics, Powerglides and Ford-O-Matics of the 1950s were more often the butt of a bad pun: "Slip 'n' slide with Powerglide, Hydra-Mush and Ford-O-Slush!" The custom-car buff, however, always on the lookout for something a little different, found the early automatics worth the time and effort, particularly in low, channeled jobs. Clutch operation can be a bear when you're almost sitting on the floorboards.

By the late 1960s, even street rodders took another look. It wasn't that automatics had improved all that much. It was the gradual change in street rod driving habits—fewer and fewer cars were built with the intention of drag racing. Street rods were becoming a legitimate form of family recreation. As such, they were often driven by the distaff side of the family who favored the convenience of the automatic. Today, the vast majority of street rods powered by a V-8 are backed up with an automatic transmission. Inasmuch as automatic transmissions are now far better than ever, it's safe to assume that the percentage will hold.

INSIDE THE AUTOMATIC

The full performance and fuel economy potential of the automatic trans-

Terry Berzenye puts the finishing touches on The FoMoCo C-4 I've run off and on in my coupe for many years. The C-4 is a decidedly "old fashioned" tranny, but it continues to serve me faithfully.

mission has largely been reached today. Indeed, some passenger car and light truck manufacturers provide a heavy-duty towing warranty only with automatic transmissions. If you choose an automatic, it will be the most complex single component in your street rod. Therefore, you must have a basic understanding of its operation even though you may never have

94

the desire to repair or modify it yourself. With that in mind, let's take a quick look at the anatomy of the generic automatic transmission and its major components.

The Torque Converter

The transmission—automatic or manual—multiplies engine torque and delivers it to the differential via the driveshaft. The workings of a manual transmission and clutch are relatively easy to understand. The automatic, although it performs the same function, isn't so easy. It does its work through fluid pumped under pressure, and then delivers its output to the remainder of the drivetrain.

The torque converter, that fat, round reservoir of dark red liquid that installs between the engine and transmission, is a sophisticated fluid coupling, a device consisting of two rotating members. Essentially, it transmits the power developed by the engine through fluid to the valves, clutches, bands and gear sets of the transmission proper. The fluid coupling is sometimes called a fluid drive, but we'll just call it the converter from here on out.

The converter contains within it the pump or driving member. When rotated, its vanes develop fluid pressure and flow. This fluid pressure and flow causes another component within the coupling—a driven member called the turbine, to rotate. The stator, a freewheeling fluid "propeller," redirects fluid flow in the direction of rotation at low engine rpm as it leaves the turbine, thus assisting the rotation of the impeller and multiplying torque approximately 2:1.

Although there is no direct mechanical connection in the converter, it is to the remainder of the automatic trans-

mission what the pressure plate and friction disc are to the manual transmission. The torque converter, however, is attached to the engine crankshaft through a flexible driving plate. The flexplate, as it is often called, is not a flywheel. Engines equipped with automatic transmissions do not have true flywheels.

Conventional torque converters have varying rates of slippage. Efficiency is determined by the amount of slippage, 85 to 90 percent being acceptable for many years. Looking for something better, manufacturers developed "lock-up" torque converters. There is a clutch and damper assembly in modern lock-up converters, and when acted upon by fluid pressure, a 1:1 ratio between the engine and transmission is developed, thereby lowering engine rpm. The result is better performance and fuel economy.

Stall Speed—"Stall speed" refers to the rpm at which the torque converter transfers the power from the engine to the transmission. Drag racers using an automatic transmission want a torque converter that most closely matches the peak torque rpm of their engine. It puts more power to the ground more quickly. Experienced street rodders, however, know that driveability is better achieved with a lower stall speed. As we have seen in the chapter on engines, the practical street rodder should choose his "speed equipment" wisely. In this case, discuss stall speed minimum and maximums with the camshaft provider.

The Hydraulic System

The lifeblood of an automatic transmission is the 15–20 quarts of low-viscosity, dark red hydraulic fluid pumped throughout its die-cast veins

and arteries. The heart of the system is the fluid pump, usually located just behind the converter. When the engine is running, it turns at crankshaft speed.

The pump supplies the torque converter with pressurized fluid. It also routes fluid through the transmission cooler, which is normally in the engine radiator in a stock car. Heat is transferred from the fluid to the engine coolant. Accessory fluid-to-air coolers are sometimes used to supplement or replace the radiator cooler.

The pump also supplies pressurized fluid to the valve body, the brain of the transmission. The valve body contains most of the various transmission control valves and a multitude of check balls and other bits and pieces. The job of the valve body is to shift the transmission automatically or manually by operating the clutches and/or bands.

The Gear System

The muscles of the automatic transmission are the various planetary gear sets and hydraulically applied multiple-disc clutches, clutch pistons, servo pistons and brake bands. The planetary gear train in the automobile has been with us since the days of the Ford Model T transmission. Basically, it consists of an internal ring gear and a central, or sun gear mounted on a shaft with three or more planetary pinions encircling it and meshed at all times with it and the ring gear. Most conventional automatic transmissions are based on a patent filed by Howard Simpson in 1955. The Simpson three-speed automatic transmission features a compound planetary gear set (one for second gear, one for reverse) and shares a common sun gear. Multiple-disc clutches, sprags and roller clutches drive the various members of the planetary gear set, while bands hold the members. The particular arrangement of the clutches and bands determines the gear ratios. Ford's C-4 and C-6; Chrysler's 904 and 727, and GM's TH 200, 350, and 400 all utilize Simpson's design.

Power Flow

When running, the engine spins the torque converter and turns the input shaft. The input shaft of the typical automatic is splined to the forward-clutch cylinder, which engages the forward ring gear. This, in turn, rotates the forward planetary pinions on their shafts. In low gear, torque is transmitted from the planetary pinions to the sun gear.

In second, however, the sun gear is locked to the transmission case by an intermediate band. Force applied by the ring gear causes the planetary pinions to encircle the stationary sun gear. The sun gear rotates the planetary pinion carrier that is splined to the output shaft and thereby transmits torque to the differential.

In high gear, the forward-clutch cylinder is engaged, and the input shaft drives it, causing the forward ring gear to transmit torque to the forward planetary pinions. Because the reverse-high clutch is also engaged, the pinions cannot rotate and torque is transmitted directly—a 1:1 ratio—to the output shaft and on to the differential.

In reverse gear, the forward clutch is released, the reverse-high clutch is engaged, and the rear ring gear rotates in a counterclockwise direction. When in reverse, gear reduction is approximately 2:1.

WHICH TRANSMISSION?

This, obviously, is the most critical question. If you've chosen a popular V-8, you'll have a number of different transmissions that will fit the back of the block. Most of them would be good choices for a street rod except for their size and weight. In addition, some are more expensive than others are, with no appreciable increase in usefulness to the non-racing street rodder.

The best street rod automatic is always the one that is most mechanically compatible with the particular engine chosen, and in general, that is the one the factory installed with the engine. Everything fits with perfection, and there is no need to modify the bellhousing, grind the starter base or rework the flex-plate. Best of all, it is equal to the task of withstanding stock engine torque, even when the stocker is mildly massaged.

In recent years, however, rodders have installed more modern transmissions behind older performance engines. The previous expectation that it should simply be light and generally fit the car without major alterations to the chassis was sometimes too limited. Several of the newer transmissions are well worth the extra cost and the relatively minor modifications required for street rod installation.

Nonetheless, I would be amiss if I left out at least a discussion of a few time-honored automatic transmissions that are still selected by experienced rodders. Aside from that, Chevrolet Powerglides and Ford C-4s may exist in running street rods recently purchased from previous owners. Current owners may wish to retain the existing transmission in keeping with the philosophy that one doesn't fix what ain't broke.

On the other hand, it is neither practical nor purposeful to cover every possible transmission just as it is not practical or purposeful to cover every possible engine an avant-garde street rodder may wish to consider. The transmissions discussed are what most of today's street rodders are using.

Finally, as with all street rod automatic transmission installations, an external transmission cooler and a transmission temperature gauge is a hedge against overheating. Transmission temperatures that exceed 220-degrees doom the gearbox to failure. Most rodders are fanatics about changing engine oil. Be the same with the transmission, and when you drain the old hydraulic fluid, take a good look at it. If it is dark brown and doesn't smell right, have the trans checked immediately.

CONVENTIONAL GM AUTOMATIC TRANSMISSIONS
The Powerglide

GM has produced dozens of passenger-car transmissions since the introduction of the small-block Chevy V-8 in 1955. Although that number can be reduced to a manageable few for the modern street rod builder, the aluminum case Powerglide that came with the 1962 327 cid small-block is still very much with us. It weighs a mere 150 pounds. The light-duty version of the Powerglide is built around a two-speed compound planetary set with a first-gear ratio of 1.82:1. The heavy-duty version has a first-gear ratio of 1.76:1. High gear in both is 1:1. The 1962–64 versions have a shorter tail shaft than the later V-8 versions.

The Turbo Hydra-Matic 350 & 350C

The TH-350 has been an extremely popular transmission among street rodders for decades. They can be found in a great many 1969–86 GM automobiles as the factory installed them when light- and medium-duty service was anticipated. It came in two case styles beyond the common Chevrolet bolt pattern—a dual Chevy/Olds-Buick-Cadillac-Pontiac pattern and an Olds-Buick-Pontiac pattern. The TH 350 is a fully automatic three-speed with a compound planetary gear set, four multi-disc clutches, two roller clutches and a band to provide the required friction elements to control the planetary gear set. The 1983 series TH 350C has a four-element hydraulic torque converter and a planetary gear set. The designation "C" indicates the inclusion of a converter clutch, which provides mechanical lockup under cruise conditions for improved fuel economy. Dry weight is approximately 125 pounds.

The friction elements couple the engine to the planetary gears through fluid pressure providing three forward speeds and reverse. The three-element torque converter is of welded construction and consists of a driving member, a turbine and a stator assembly. When required, the torque converter supplements the gear assemblies by multiplying engine torque.

The converter-clutch assembly consists of a conventional three-element torque converter with a converter clutch. The converter clutch is splined to the turbine assembly and, when operated, applies against the converter cover to provide a direct coupling of the engine to the planetary gears. When the converter clutch is released, the assembly operates as a conventional torque converter.

The later model TH 350s have been

The popular 1969–86 TH-350 is a fully automatic three-speed. The 1983 series (TH 350C) has a converter clutch, which provides a mechanical lockup under cruise conditions.

used behind most GM V-8s in street rods for a number of years now, and there doesn't appear to be a significant lessening of its popularity even with the advent of its overdrive competition. About the only fault one might find in the TH 350 and in most automatics, is that they use fluid accumulators to delay and soften shifts. Whenever high performance is desired, rodders install a shift-programming kit so shifts will be more positive. The Trans-Go "Tow and Go" is quite popular in that the shift is firm, but still comfortable.

The Turbo Hydra-Matic 400

Hydra-Matic transmissions were the first domestic automatics, premiering way back in 1939. The earliest, and all the subsequent Hydra-Matics, had four forward speeds until a three-speed version was available on several 1961 Pontiac models. The more modern three-speed Turbo Hydra-Matic 400 was used in heavy-duty applica-

tions into early 1980s GM products. It is a fully-automatic unit consisting of a three-element torque converter and a compound planetary gear set. Three multiple-disc clutches, two one-way clutches and two bands provide the friction elements required to operate the planetary gears. One of the major differences setting the TH 400 apart from most other transmissions is the sprag clutch, a one-way clutch that takes the place of additional bands. It rotates freely in one direction and locks up in the other. The torque converter, multiple-disc clutch and one-way clutches couple the engine to the planetary gears through fluid pressure in specific combinations to provide three forward speeds and reverse.

External-control connections to the transmission include a manual linkage to select the desired operating range, engine vacuum to operate the vacuum modulator, and an electrical signal to operate an electric-detent solenoid. The vacuum modulator is used to sense

The Turbo 400 has long been a favorite behind street rods with big-block Chevy power. It is a more than a little long-in-the-tooth, but parts are readily available and its popularity shows no sign of waning. Models from mid-1960s Buicks, Cadillacs and Oldsmobiles use a variable-pitch stator in the torque converter for better cruising and acceleration.

CONVENTIONAL FORD AUTOMATIC TRANSMISSIONS

The C-4 Dual Range

The C-4 Select Shift Cruise-O-Matic automatic was first used in 1965 in medium- and light-duty applications beginning with the 289 cid small-block and eventually the 302, 351W and 351C. It has not been manufactured for many years, and there are better choices. However, it is still a viable choice for the budget-minded rod builder not wanting to pay the price for the latest AOD to install behind an older, carbureted 302 or 351W engine.

It has a conventional torque converter, compound conventional torque converter, a compound planetary gear set, two multiple-disc clutches, a one-way clutch and a hydraulic control system. When in Drive, the transmission will upshift automatically to intermediate and then to high as the throttle is depressed from the idle position. Conversely, the transmission will downshift automatically as vehicle speed drops to 10 mph. The driver can also force a downshift from high to intermediate at speeds below 65 mph by applying full throttle.

The C-4 has been offered on all Ford passenger cars with the aforementioned powerplants through the mid-1980s. With its aluminum case, the dry weight is a miserly 110 pounds.

The C-6 Dual Range

The Ford C-6 was originally used in medium- and heavy-duty passenger cars and pickup trucks with 351C-4V, 351M, 400, 427, 428 and 429 cubic inch engines. For a while, it was also used with the 302. The latter is diffi-

engine torque to the transmis-sion automatically. The vacuum modulator transmits this signal to the pressure regulator, which controls line pressure so that torque requirements of the transmission are met and correct shift spacing is obtained at all throttle openings. The detent solenoid is activated by an electric switch at the carburetor.

When the throttle is opened sufficiently to close this switch, the solenoid in the transmission is activated, causing a downshift at speeds below

70 mph. At lower speeds, downshifts can occur at lesser throttle openings without the use of the electric switch.

In the Chevy version of the TH 400, forward gear ratios are 2.48:1 in first, 1.48:1 in second and 1:1 in third. Some transmissions, however, have a low gear of 2.97:1 and a second gear of 1.56:1. This transmission is bulkier than the TH 350. Nonetheless, it is still frequently used with big-block Chevys and many high-performance small-blocks.

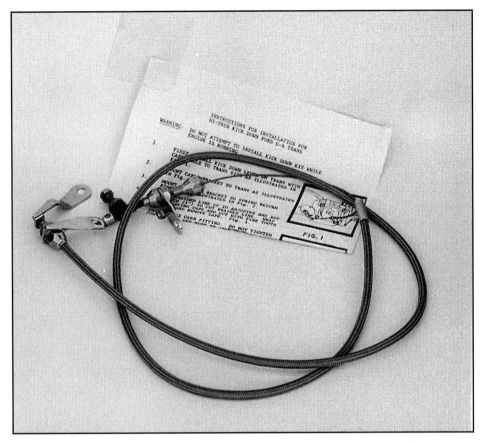

All conventional transmissions use a "kick down" cable connected to the throttle controls to determine shift points. Pictured is Lokar Performance Products' offering.

cult to find, however. As there are rodders who want Chevy big-block megapower, there are rodders who want Ford big-block power, particularly those building the larger 1946–48 models.

All dual-range Ford automatic transmissions are designed for both automatic and manual shifting. The C-6 is no different. It has a conventional torque converter, compound planetary-gear set controlled by one band, three disc clutches and a one-way clutch.

Forward speed gear ratios are the same as the C-4 except for reverse, which is 2.18:1. The C-6 also uses a low-and-reverse plate clutch instead of the low-and-reverse band used in the

C-4. Valves in the hydraulic control system are also similar to the C-4, but in no other way should the C-6 be equated with its smaller brother.

The typical prewar street rod simply doesn't demand a powerhouse engine or transmission, but the additional bulk and weight can be easily tolerated in the immediate postwar Ford passenger cars and pickups. For those, the 429/C6 is a tough combination to beat.

SHIFT-PROGRAMMING THE CONVENTIONAL STOCK TRANSMISSION

The conventional automatic transmission was originally designed to cater to the luxury desires of the mass market. As such, it shifts gears without

any fanfare, smoothly and softly. This is great if you're not a performance buff and don't miss the minor concussions of a four-speed manual gearbox. Nonetheless, if the shifts seem too mushy, the cure lies in the valve body, that part of the transmission that determines the shift points and the hydraulic pressure triggering them.

Gradual shifts are not the only irritant either. There is the questionable stock design parameter called gear overlap. This is where one gear is engaged slightly before the previous gear is fully released. The intentional state of being in two gears at the same time makes for a smoother shift, but it generates a lot of unwanted heat. The older Ford and GM transmissions all exhibit this condition to one degree or another. The solution is the transmission shift-programming kit. There are several types manufactured, and they all offer about the same performance.

A shift-programming kit minimizes overlap by speeding the release of the previous gear and hastening the application of the next one. There is no hesitation or delay in either upshifts or downshifts. Typically, the shifts are firm, but not unpleasant.

Most of the kits contain modified separator plates, spool valves and pressure-regulating springs. They can usually be installed without even removing the transmission from the car. Generally, if you can change the transmission filter and fluid in your car, you can install a shift-programming kit in-car. All kits come with complete, understandable instructions. Just be advised that you shouldn't use a competition shift-programming kit on the street. Shifting will be too harsh. Only install a kit designed for high-performance street use.

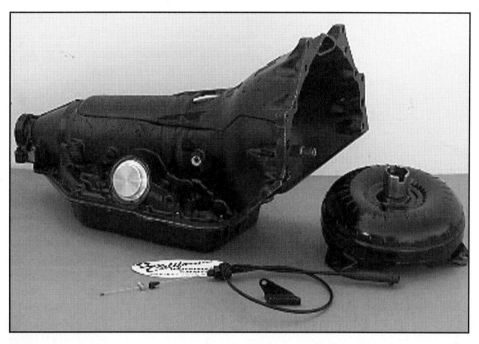

Art Carr changed the name of his company to California Performance Transmission, but he hasn't changed the name of his game. Known best for his modification of the 700-R4, he has turned his attention to what he calls the "Ultimate 4-Speed Automatic." It is, of course, the 200-4R, a tranny long overlooked for street rod usage. After Art's skillful massage, the 200-4R can handle up to 800 horsepower and shift into overdrive at full throttle! Although that may not be what the average street rodder is looking for, it certainly belies a common belief that the 200-4R is a wimp. The transmission has a multiple bolt pattern that not only fits Chevrolet transmissions, it will also mate to several models of Buick, Cadillac and Pontiac. The 9-inch HD Mega Torque Converter (PN 19930) is balanced to 2 grams. The California Performance package (PN 12251) includes extra clutches with high-performance friction material, a 16-pack third gear and a 6-pack fourth gear clutch.

GM AUTOMATIC TRANSMISSIONS WITH OVERDRIVE

The Turbo Hydra-Matic 200-4R

In the late 1970s, General Motors began development of a line of versatile transmissions with low first gears for around the town, plus an auxiliary overdrive for highway-bound fuel economy. The 200-4R was their first automatic overdrive, appearing in 1981 behind a number of V-8 engines. It did not enjoy a particularly good reputation in the early years, but that is not the case today. Many well-respected transmission specialists such as Art Carr have overcome any shortcomings with aftermarket improvements.

Today, the 200-4R can easily handle 350 normally aspirated cubic inches.

The 200-4R is a fully automatic unit consisting primarily of a three-element hydraulic converter with a converter clutch, a compound planetary gear set and an overdrive unit. Five multiple-disc clutches and a band provide the friction elements required for the compound planetary gear set and overdrive. The hydraulic system is pressurized by a variable capacity vane type pump to deliver the working pressure required for the friction elements and automatic controls. Fully automatic changing of gear ratios is determined by vehicle speed and engine torque. A throttle valve cable controls line pressure and gear shifts. A vacuum modulator is not used, so proper cable adjustment is critical. (More about this later.)

The beauty of the 200 R4 is its compactness and lightweight. As such, it is a natural in rods based on Model T and A dimensions where such mundane problems as exhaust placement are common. As with all automatic transmissions, the rule of thumb is to look for the latest model. The 200-4R is no exception.

The Turbo Hydra-Matic 700-R4

The 700-R4 debuted in the 1982 Corvette and was later installed in the 1983–84 Camaro and Firebird lines. Since the Chevy V-8 is the street rodder's first choice, the attached transmission often finds a home under a vintage hood. Beyond that, virtually any power package emanating from a Corvette is considered "highest performance," so the 700-R4 is well worth considering.

The 700-R4 is a fully automatic transmission consisting of a 3-element hydraulic torque converter with the addition of a torque converter clutch. The pressure plate is operated by hydraulic pressure created by the fluid in the rotating converter. The friction pad binds under this pressure to a surface on the converter cover, thereby coupling engine power to the gear sets and providing additional torque multiplication when required. A variable capacity vane-type pump provides the operating pressure required for the operation of friction elements and automatic controls. The converter drive and driven members operate as one unit when applied.

Two planetary gear sets, five multiple-disc clutches, two roller or one-way clutches and a band are used to provide the friction elements needed to produce four forward speeds, the

The 700-R4 automatic transmission contains a 3-element hydraulic torque converter with the addition of a torque converter clutch. The converter drive and driven members operate as one unit when applied. The gear ratio changes are fully automatic in relation to the vehicle speed and engine torque and provide the proper gear ratio for maximum efficiency and performance at all throttle openings. Look for one manufactured after 1987.

last of which is the overdrive. The gear ratio changes are fully automatic in relation to the vehicle speed and engine torque and provide the proper gear ratio for maximum efficiency and performance at all throttle openings.

Earlier 700-R4s had teething problems. The factory, however, made sufficient changes through the years to render the 700-R4 capable of handling all street performance needs. Look for one manufactured after 1987. Nevertheless, the TH 700-R4 functions best when subjected to a few, but significant aftermarket modifications such as those pioneered by the Southern California-based high performance transmission specialist, Art Carr.

FORD AUTOMATIC TRANSMISSIONS WITH OVERDRIVE

The AOD

The Ford automatic overdrive introduced in the mid-1980s is the transmission of choice for a street rod equipped with a 302 or a 351W engine of that era, if for no other reason than it was factory-installed behind them. The four-speed unit incorporates an integral overdrive. The transmission will start and remain in low gear when selected manually. In the "3" position, it upshifts automatically through the entire three forward speeds. In the "D" position, it automatically selects the appropriate time to shift into overdrive.

In the 1:1 ratio third gear, 40% percent of the engine torque is transmitted

hydraulically through the torque converter and sixty percent is transmitted mechanically. This split-torque gear train reduces the hydraulic losses associated with the torque converter. When the transmission is in overdrive or fourth gear (0.67:1 ratio), all torque is transmitted through the direct-drive input shaft. This full mechanical lock-up completely bypasses the torque converter and eliminates the usual torque-converter slippage. The most significant advantage of the automatic-overdrive transmission is that it allows lower engine speeds for greater fuel economy.

As can be expected, some modification to AOD is a good idea when high performance is demanded. Several aftermarket trans specialists replace the stock third-gear clutch drum and five-clutch assembly with a larger six-pack drum. Furthermore, the stock piston has two seals. A piston with four seals is installed when a firm two-three shift is desired. The stock diameter 3/16-inch AOD pump stator-support lube hole is also enlarged to 1/4-inch to increase hydraulic fluid flow to the planetary gear set.

THROTTLE VALVE CONTROL CABLES

An automatic transmission with a built-in overdrive is obviously desirable, but there is one significant drawback—a poorly adjusted throttle valve (T.V.) cable sometimes called the "kick down" cable. All conventional (non-electronic) transmissions use some type of linkage connected to the throttle controls to determine shift points. With conventional transmissions, however, maladjustment merely results in improper shifting. Not so with the automatic overdrive.

The four–speed Ford automatic overdrive incorporates an integral overdrive (0.67:1 ratio). All torque is transmitted through the direct-drive input shaft. This full mechanical lockup completely bypasses the torque converter and eliminates the usual torque-converter slippage.

The automatic overdrive transmission is extremely sensitive. The geometric relationship between the throttle and the throttle valve plunger is critical. Improper throttle valve cable adjustment not only leads to altered transmission function, it can cause the transmission to fail completely. In the stock setup, the T.V. cable snaps into a bracket at the rear of the carburetor. Few street rodders, of course, are satisfied with the stock setup, and even fewer have access to factory manuals.

Fortunately, the aftermarket street rod industry has come to the rescue. There are several brands of throttle valve tuning kits for the TH 200-4R and 700-R4, but the one we had a close-up look at is the "T.V. Made EZ" kit made by Bow Tie Overdrives of Hesperia, California. A separate kit is designed for the Edelbrock Performer, Holley and Demon carburetors. Each includes a carburetor mounting plate, an adjustable T.V. cable, three plates that correctly position the cable end to the linkage, a special drill bit and the necessary fasteners. Detailed installation instructions are included. The company also recommends (and

offers) an inexpensive transmission pressure gauge. With the appropriate kit, the street rodder can accurately position the cable at home before his new rod hits the asphalt. Just remember, it is critical to complete the basic cable installation before the car is driven. It can be fine-tuned afterwards to obtain the desired shift firmness.

FULLY ELECTRONIC OVERDRIVE TRANSMISSIONS
The GM 4L60E

Time and automotive technology marches on, and since the early 1990s domestic auto manufacturers have directed their automatic transmission engineering progress largely to gear boxes that are connected to the engine and fuel induction by a computer rather than by mechanical means. In the GM line, the fully electronic are the 4L60E and the 4L80E, but the latter has received the most attention from street rodders.

The 4L80E uses two electric shift solenoids to control transmission upshifts and downshifts. A Torque Converter Clutch/Pulse Width Modulated (TCC/PWM) solenoid

controls fluid acting on the converter clutch valves. These solenoids are turned on and off by a Vehicle Control Module (VCM) which receives signals from various transmission sensors including engine speed and throttle position, transmission speed, hydraulic pressure and transmission fluid temperature. The VCM has onboard diagnostics to identify parts and circuits, which may need further testing. Of course, a dedicated laptop computer is needed to access the onboard computer.

The Ford E4OD

In the large Ford-design electronic transmission, input signals from sensors are sent to the Powertrain Control Module (PCM). The PCM can determine when the time and conditions are right for a shift or converter clutch application. The PCM can also determine how much line pressure is needed to optimize shift feel.

The PCM controls transmission operation through five electronic solenoids consisting of four On/Off solenoids for shifting and torque converter clutch control, and one variable-force solenoid for line pressure control. All components are part of the transmission solenoid body. The PCM has built-in self-diagnostic capability, with fail-safe code and warning code displays for the main input sensors and solenoid valves. Again, a dedicated laptop computer is needed to complete the diagnosis.

Should You Go Electronic?

Computerized transmissions are complex, but not delicate gearboxes that can handle all the power the modern breed of efficient engines can put out. For those interested in even more

GM's 4L60E is essentially the same as the 700-R4, inclusive of gear ratios, but it is electronically controlled. GM Performance Parts offers installation kits for 700-R4 trannies. www.spoperformanceparts.com

power, several aftermarket companies offer complete, modified transmission packages. Computer chips are available to make them shift any way you'd like. Are they the be-all, end-all for the street rodder, then?

Opinion is somewhat split. I talked with one professional street rod builder who makes no bones saying he doesn't recommend them for street rods unless the builder is well-versed in electronics, and is willing to pay the price for an aftermarket reprogrammed computer module. Another shop owner, who specializes in their installations smiled, and said the home builder had better purchase "the steering column and dashboard in addition to the engine and transmission package." Therein lies the biggest problem. The engine and transmission is just that, a package. There is no simple mix and match combinations as in the far less complex "good old days" of street

rodding. In fact, the latter resource person showed me three attempts at street rod installations by three shops in which something had gone awry, and the jobs had to be outsourced to him. It is true that any competent diagnostic shop or new car dealer can dial into the stock system and determine a given problem, but only in stock applications for which there are detailed factory manuals.

In time, of course, new and better aftermarket adaptations will be available, but for now, the rod builder (novice or moderately experienced) on a limited budget, is best advised to stay with engine and transmission installations with a proven record of reliability in a street rod. Farming out complex work to a specialty shop can get expensive in a hurry.

10

THE MANUAL TRANSMISSION

There will always be a significant minority of street rodders who seriously consider a manually shifted transmission. Pat Massey of Anaheim Gear is the primary resource in Southern California for up-to-date information on today's practical options for the street rodder.

There was a time in street rodding when no self-respecting driver would be caught with anything but a manual transmission. The most commonly used transmission in Ford-based rods was either the 1939 box with a floor-shifter or the 1940–48 box with a steering column mounted shifter. Preference in performance circles went to the '39 and the "Kustom Krowd" favored the space-saving column mount. In fact, the term "stick shift" at that time (1946–60) was reserved for the far more positive 1939

setup.

Soon after the introduction (and subsequent popularity) of the powerful overhead valve V-8s, the inherent weakness of the Ford transmission quickly became apparent. Weekend racers turned to tough, early Cadillac-LaSalle and Packard manual transmissions, but most street rodders used "adaptor plates" and grudgingly accepted the periodic failure of the relatively weak 1939–48 Ford gear set. Today, nobody but flathead traditionalists would even consider a 1939–48

transmission. The fact remains, however, some rod builders seriously consider a manually shifted transmission.

Although the decision as to which engine is favored comes quickly and easily, the same rodders are not at all sure which slam-shifter will best meet their needs. Beyond that, the mere fact that components can be bolted together doesn't ensure that they will work together. More than one builder has experienced grief with a mismatched flywheel, clutch assembly, and starter. The apparent simplicity of the back of an engine block and front of the transmission bellhousing can be deceiving. As always, I'll try to whittle the choices down to a manageable few.

Unlike the automatic transmission, the dynamics of the flywheel, clutch and manual transmission are fundamentally familiar to most rodders. The amateur rod builder, however, is still uncertain about many details, to say nothing of problems that may not have occurred to him. Before you seek any in-depth answers, you must re-acquaint yourself with those critical components collectively called the drivetrain that begin at the back of the engine and end at the rear wheels.

THE TRANSFER OF POWER

Some type of drivetrain was recognized as a necessity early in the development of the horseless carriage. After a few feeble attempts to connect the engine directly to the drive wheels, automobile designers realized that the internal-combustion engine needed torque multiplication to accelerate from a dead stop, and up steep grades. At low rpm there wasn't enough power to put a car in motion, much less launch it with the authority even a 19th century stage driver expected. Then there was that other problem—the need to disengage the engine from the drive wheels when the vehicle was at rest or the driver was changing gears.

That two-fold task—harnessing the engine's power and propelling the car—is exactly what the drivetrain does. It is accomplished by first temporarily releasing the engine from its grip so the latter can efficiently develop its power. Then it allows that power to gradually and controllably flow to the driving wheels.

The simplest means of doing this is

A high-quality, 30 to 40 pound, low-carbon, hot-rolled, steel-billet flywheel is best for street rods weighing 2000 pounds or more. The type clutch pictured is the Ford Long style with nine coil springs, a hexagonal-shaped cover and drop forged release levers with a centrifugal force weight at the outer end of each lever. Pressure plate load from the weights increases with engine rpm. Although shifting at high rpm becomes increasingly difficult, the Long style has gained favor because of its superior air circulation and ability to dissipate heat.

the conventional manual transmission drivetrain. Four major components are incorporated: a clutch system, a gearbox with manually selected ratios, a drive shaft, and a differential/rear-axle assembly. The following paragraphs describe the basics of each.

The Flywheel

The purpose of the flywheel is simply to keep the crank turning at a constant speed while the engine is between power strokes. Consider a single-cylinder four-stroke (cycle) engine. Power is produced only 25 percent of the time—during the power stroke. Therefore, 75 percent of the

time our single-cylinder engine expels exhaust gases, draws in a fresh air/fuel mixture, and compresses the charge. During these strokes, and laboring under frictional and inertia losses, the crank slows, but suddenly another power stroke comes along and accelerates the crank back to speed.

This uneven flow of power can be smoothed by adding mass to the crankshaft to increase rotating inertia. Inertia resists any change in speed or direction of travel. Consequently, the heavier the flywheel, the more resistant it is to changing speed.

Recalling the writings of Newton, which you no doubt diligently pored over in high school, a motionless object wants to remain at rest, but once it is set in motion, it resists attempts to speed it up . . . or slow it down . . . or change its direction. The flywheel, therefore, acting under the principle of inertia, resists the engine's tendency to speed up during the power stroke. It also resists slowing down during the exhaust, intake and com-pression strokes. In effect, the flywheel minimizes the effect of power impulses by absorbing some of the energy during the power stroke and releasing it during the remainder of the operating cycle.

This is exaggerated in a single-cylinder engine, but although the power impulses in a multi-cylinder engine overlap and produce a smoother power flow, additional leveling off is desirable, still making a flywheel necessary. The flywheel performs other functions, as you'll soon read about. Before I broach that subject, however, let's look at the minimums for a street rod flywheel.

Stock cast-iron flywheels, by and large, are just fine for Uncle Mert, but you should not use one unless it's of the nodular cast-iron variety. Many are on Detroit muscle cars.

To determine what a flywheel is made of, hang it by a rope or wire and tap it lightly with a hammer. If it rings like a bell, it's nodular cast iron or steel. However, if it's more like a thud, the flywheel is made of gray cast iron. Don't use it. Even ordinarily conservative street rodders have been known to over-rev mildly modified engines, and more than one cast-iron flywheel has been known to come apart with the fury of a hand grenade!

In general, a high-quality, 30–40-pound, low-carbon, hot-rolled, steel-billet flywheel is best for street rods weighing 2000 pounds or more. Aftermarket flywheels manufactured from stress-relieved low-carbon steel reduce the possibility of concentrated carbon deposits, which, through usage, can become harder than steel and ultimately prevent uniform sur-face wear. Uneven wear, of course, leads to poor disc life and erratic performance. Low-carbon steel also minimizes the danger of carbon embrittlement.

For street applications where a high degree of stored flywheel energy isn't necessary, specifically in rods weighing less than 2000 pounds, a high-quality aluminum flywheel may be just the ticket. Most Grade A aluminum flywheels are machined from forged 6061 aluminum alloy—T6 or better—with a heat shield, or high-friction bronze insert.

OK, inertia, and a convenient place for the starter ring gear aside, the flywheel also serves as a mounting and friction surface for the clutch assembly. The pressure plate provides one friction surface, the flywheel the other.

The Clutch Assembly

The primary purpose of the clutch assembly is to couple and uncouple the engine to and from the drivetrain. However, it is designed to slip a little during engagement. Positive engagement at any engine speed above a slow idle and zero vehicle speed would result in a possibly harmful impact to the drivetrain components. Once coupling is achieved, the clutch must quickly stop slipping and maintain sufficient friction against the flywheel and pressure plate friction surfaces to transfer full power to the transmission input shaft and on to the driving wheels.

One of the two major clutch assembly components is the friction disc. Most original equipment and high-performance street discs are of the unbacked facing type with cushioning. The friction material is riveted to a wavy thin steel disc called a marcel. Sandwiched thusly between the two pieces of friction lining, the marcel provides a degree of compressibility to smooth out clutch engagement.

Another means of softening the shock of power transfer is a hub with coil springs positioned concentrically around it. These allow slight torsional movement between the center of the disc, the hub and the lining.

The second major clutch assembly component is the pressure plate, a relatively complex unit manufactured in several different designs. In general, the pressure plate consists of a ductile steel or cast-iron face plate or pressure ring, a set of springs and a set of release levers or a one-piece slotted-steel stamping called a diaphragm, and a stamped steel cover.

There are three basic pressure plate designs. The type used in Ford cars for many years is known as the Long style. This pressure plate typically has nine coil springs. It is easily recognized by its hexagonal-shaped cover and the way its drop forged release levers extend toward the center. There's a centrifugal force (CF) weight at the outer end of each lever.

Unlike static plate load supplied by the springs, pressure plate load from the CF weights increases with engine rpm. Although shifting at high rpm becomes increasingly difficult, the Long style pressure plate has gained favor because of its superior air circulation and ability to dissipate heat.

Borg-and-Beck—The Borg-and-

The Borg-and-Beck style pressure is a full-circle design, with stamped-steel release levers, and twelve coil springs. Centrifugal-assist rollers between the cover and pressure ring are used. (They do not have weights on the release levers.) The only drawback of this design is cover distortion during release at high rpm.

The diaphragm pressure plate has a one-piece, slotted, dish-shaped spring. The spring incorporates the release levers. The diaphragm pressure plate has low pedal resistance, and performance models have no problems with high rpm shifting.

Beck style pressure plate is recognized by its full-circle design, stamped-steel release levers, and twelve coil springs. They do not have CF weights on the release levers. Instead, centrifugal-assist rollers between the cover and pressure ring are used. The biggest drawback of this design is cover distortion during release at very high rpm.

The diaphragm type of pressure plate does not use coil springs, but rather incorporates a one-piece, slotted, dish-shaped (Belleville) spring. This spring also incorporates the release levers. A diaphragm pressure plate is easily recognized by the many tab-like release fingers. It has low pedal resistance, but in stock form, has problems with high rpm shifting. Street performance diaphragm pressure plates don't share this problem.

In the operation of a clutch—the mechanical coupling and uncoupling of the engine from the drivetrain—the throwout (release) bearing becomes part of the clutch assembly even though it's part of the clutch linkage.

One of the primary considerations in an engine swap that includes a manual transmission is clutch pedal travel and effort and the linkage needed to operate the throwout bearing.

When the clutch pedal is depressed, a pivoting lever, or fork, moves the throwout bearing forward. As the bearing moves, it operates the release levers, which moves the pressure ring away from the disc. Once unloaded, the disc moves back slightly from the flywheel on the splined transmission input shaft and disengages from the engine.

Releasing the clutch pedal moves the throwout bearing away from the pressure plate to force the clutch disc against the flywheel. The clutch assembly and flywheel can once again revolve as a single unit, transmitting torque through the transmission and on to the rear wheels.

If you are planning on a high performance engine, use a top-quality SEMA-approved high performance street flywheel and clutch. Even occasionally winding out the engine in low gear can push a stock flywheel and clutch assembly to its limit—possibly beyond.

SELECTING A MANUAL TRANSMISSION

Most transmissions in the low priced passenger car of the immediate post-WWII era were of the selective type with combination sliding gear and constant-mesh features. "Selective" refers to the ability of the driver to choose (select) a gear without progressing through intermediate gears. This type of transmission has shift rails and levers that can be moved through a gate from one rail to another in an H-pattern. The driver can select any one of the gear positions from a central (neutral) position.

The term sliding gear refers to gears that move fore and aft on internal splines. When the driver moves the gear selector, the splined gear is pushed along a shaft until its teeth mesh with the teeth of another gear.

If you are old enough to have learned to drive in a car with an early three-speed gearbox, you may recall that you had to come to a complete stop before you could downshift into first gear. That's because first gear was the sliding type. If you tried to cheat and force the transmission into first before you were completely stopped, you were rewarded with a grinding gear clash . . . and an unhappy stare from your dad.

Constant mesh refers to gears that are constantly in mesh, remaining in a more-or-less fixed position. Engagement is accomplished by means of sliding sleeves (sliders) and synchronizing devices that match gear speeds before engagement occurs, thus preventing clash. Second and third gears in the old three-speeds used constant-mesh gears. Providing the synchronizing devices were in good condition, you could shift gears without worrying about raising the hackles on dad's neck.

Now, let's look at how major transmission components work together. The splined transmission shaft that pilots in the back of the crankshaft and slips into the clutch hub is called the main drive gear or input shaft. It is in constant mesh with the countershaft gear, commonly called the cluster gear because it has a number of gears clustered together in a solid assembly. The main drive gear and cluster gear rotate as soon as the clutch is engaged to a running engine whether or not the transmission is in neutral.

When the clutch is disengaged, the driver selects first one, then another forward speed in a modern transmission. He is not actually moving the gears—they are in constant mesh—he is moving sliders that are fitted with

Flathead enthusiasts, have wisely abandoned the traditional 1939–48 transmission in favor of something a lot more reliable such as this Ford muscle car Top Loader 4-speed. The icing on the cake is the Jeep CJ topside shifter. It is the most positive gear selector I have ever used.

brass friction devices (synchronizers) that match the speed of the two gears so they can be engaged. Torque can then be transferred smoothly through the main shaft and to the output shaft, then on to the differential and driving wheels.

How Many Forward Speeds Are Needed?

Does the typical street rod with an average of 300–350 cubic inches of engine displacement need a mega-forward speed manual transmission? Of course not. When I was young and foolish back in the mid-1950s, I drove my 365 cid Cadillac powered 1940 Ford coupe all over town for a year using only second and high! That big displacement (by contemporary standards) Caddy put out a bundle of

torque. I was running a common wide ratio 1939 Ford transmission and a super-low 4.44:1 rear gear with 28-inch tires. It wasn't a bad performer on the local drag strip with slicks and was somewhat comfortable—again, by contemporary standards—on city streets. Nevertheless, it was far from being an efficient drivetrain by modern street rod standards. (I eventually stowed that 4.44:1 rear under the house, using it only for drag racing. A 3.78 became my street rear.)

Most experienced street rodders are aware of the fact that even a big displacement engine that develops a lot of torque is a better performer with a "close-ratio" four-speed than a three-speed. Close-ratio, of course, is the key, as any bread truck driver with a "granny-geared" four-speed will tell you.

One of the class acts in transmissions is the Doug Nash Engineering five-speed. The street version of this racing transmission is housed in an aluminum case with optional extension housings and input shafts available for Ford and GM applications. Even more exotic manual transmissions with six forward speeds are on the market.

				SUPER T-10 RATIOS
1st	**2nd**	**3rd**	**4th**	**Description**
2.43	1.61	1.23	1.00	First design special close ratio (T-10)
2.64	1.75	1.23	1.00	Special competition (T-10x)
2.64	1.75	1.33	1.00	Special competition wide ratio (T-10W)
2.88	1.75	1.33	1.00	Second design, extra-low ratio (T-10Y)
3.44	2.28	1.46	1.00	Second design, ultra-low ratio (T-10U)

Close-ratio gears are those that have less of a ratio spread from one forward speed to another. For instance, the 1965–73 Ford top loader four-speed was originally available in both a close- and wide-ratio version. The gear ratios in the close-ratio box are:

First: 2.32:1
Second: 1.69:1
Third: 29:1
Fourth: 1.00:1

The ratio spread between First and Second is 0.63; the spread between Second and Third is 0.40 and the spread between Third and Fourth is 0.29.

On the other hand, the wide-ratio version is, respectively, 2.78:1, 1.93:1, 1.36:1 and 1.00:1, with spreads of 0.85, 0.57, and 0.36.

In terms of performance differentials, there is less of a spread in engine rpm from First to Second to Third to Fourth. And, because the whole idea of engine performance is to keep engine rpm up, there's less rpm drop or loss when a close-ratio box is delivering the horsepower goods. In other words, with the close-ratio four-speed, your engine will operate within a narrower rpm range when accelerating up through the gears.

If Four is Good, Why Not Five?— Good question! And indeed, as we've seen with the current crop of modern five-speed or four-speed with overdrive-transmissions, Detroit is certainly giving the street rodder options. Theoretically, a five-speed is much better choice over the four-speed in the same sense that the four-speed is a better choice over the old fashioned three-speed. And so it goes with the number of forward speeds increasing up to road racing standards. The price tag on the newest mega-speed transmissions, of course, is high and is likely to remain so.

Unfortunately, many of the modern aluminum-encased high-tech multi-speed transmissions cannot withstand the punishment delivered by an older model, large displacement, high torque engine. The old standby Muscle Car four-speeds built from the mid 1960s through the late 1970s are often a good choice for the rod builder with an appetite for performance. They are rugged and, although many are well worn, most rebuild parts are available.

Multi-speed transmissions are fully synchronized, constant-mesh transmissions, and any deeper delving into the innards of the generic manual transmission is of little value to street rodders. You've probably chosen your engine by this time; so let's take a look at what goes best with it.

Practical Classic Street Rod Transmissions

*The Super T-10—*The first Super T-10 transmission came out in the mid-1960s, and a "heavy-duty" version came out in 1972. Improvements, and as you can see from the chart, a variety of ratios have been added to the line through the years. The 1966 and later GM Super T-10 has 32 splines. Nevertheless, the only real reason to install one today is if you already own it.

*The Muncie—*One of the best General Motors four-speed transmissions for street rod use is still the venerable aluminum-cased Muncie produced from 1963 through 1974. This transmission was the first performance manual four-speed from the BigThree. It is easily recognized by its seven-bolt side cover. There are three major versions: a heavy-duty close-ratio series, a high-performance close-ratio series, and a standard wide-ratio series.

Muncie four-speed transmissions manufactured from 1963 to 1965 are known as the M20 and have a 7/8-inch diameter countershaft seated in 80 needle bearings.

The Super Muncie, or rock crusher—so called because of its noisy, but strong gear set, or tooth angle—was introduced in 1965 as an option with the 396 big-block. It has a one-inch countershaft. This transmission is more properly known as the M22.

In 1966, the factory increased the close-ratio high-performance and wide-ratio standard transmission countershaft diameter to 1 inch and increased the number of needle bearings to 112. Close-ratio boxes of this period are coded M21; wide-ratio transmissions retain the M20 designation.

Responding to the need for greater torque input, GM increased spline count on the main drive gear from 10 to 26 in the 1971 models of the high-performance close-ratio and standard wide-ratio Muncie. The original 27-spline output shaft was also replaced with a 32-spline output shaft.

One of the problems with an old Muncie, however, is the press fit of the counter shaft through the case. It wears out over time. Either the case can be repaired or a new one ordered. I should also mention that there is an aftermarket Muncie close ratio rebuild pack that upgrades any older Muncie M20 or M21 to an M22. It is also available in a wide ratio with the coarse-cut gears, so you get the strength of the M22, and what some rodders feel is better drivability.

The Ford "Top Loader"—In 1964, Ford introduced their fully-synchronized, constant-mesh, four-speed passenger car transmission. The new model was so well accepted that less than a year later the company began phasing out the Borg-Warner T-10. Both close- and wide-ratio gearing was available.

MUNCIE TRANSMISSION RATIOS

1st	2nd	3rd	4th	Description
2.20	1.64	1.27	1.00	Early close ratio (1963–65)
2.56	1.91	1.49	1.00	Early wide ratio (1963–65)
2.64	1.75	1.33	1.00	Super Muncie (1965–74)
2.52	1.62	1.24	1.00	Close ratio (1966–74)
2.52	1.88	1.46	1.00	Wide ratio (1966–74)

An aftermarket Muncie close ratio rebuild pack is available to upgrade any older Muncie M20 or M21 to an M22. It is available in both close and wide ratios.

FORD T&C TOP LOADER TRANSMISSION RATIOS

1st	2nd	3rd	4th	Description
2.78	1.93	1.36	1.00	Wide ratio (1964–73)
2.32	1.69	1.29	1.00	Close ratio (1964–73)
3.29	1.84	1.00	.81	Overdrive (1977–78)
3.07	1.72	1.00	.70	Aluminum case overdrive (1979–86)

The Ford transmission is different from other modern passenger car four-speeds in that it is serviced through a removable sheet metal cover in the top of the case. The shifting forks are mounted in bosses cast into the side of the case, one feature that makes this transmission stronger than those with removable side plates do. This design feature is also responsible for the nickname "top loader," which it has been known by since its introduction.

BORG-WARNER T-5 RATIOS (Ford Application)					
1st	2nd	3rd	4th	5th	Description
3.35	1.93	1.29	1.00	0.68	1983–85 5-liter V-8
2.95	1.94	1.34	1.00	0.80	1985 Motorsport

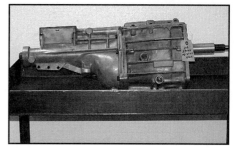

The Borg Warner T-5 five-speed transmission originally came in 1980—85 Ford Mustang/Mercury Capri Sports Coupes and 1983–85 Thunderbird/Merc Cougar V-8 powered Intermediate passenger cars. It is the modern choice for Ford power street rods but an aftermarket bellhousing is needed to mate the gearbox to older Ford engines. According to Pat Massey, in order to get the clutch to work properly in an earlier vehicle you have to use an aftermarket bellhousing such as McLeod. "Several versions are available with hydraulic or mechanical clutch linkage. They've got them set up for the exact depth of the input shaft that bolts to the front of the B-W case." The pilot bearing and clutch splines are the same as the earlier Ford trans (.667 and 1 1/16-inch). The diameter of bearing retainer is standard Ford.

The nice thing about the T-5 is that it has been used in so many different vehicles, a savvy shop like Anaheim Gear can mix and match different parts to make it comfortable in an early car or pickup. For instance, the shift selector in the stock Ford passenger car trans would come out under the bench seat of most full height early cars. According to Pat, "The best way we've found to resolve that is to use the interchangeable Chevy S-10 tail housing, output shaft and speedometer gear. In effect, the trans is Ford from the main case forward, but the back end is Chevy S-10." This hybrid moves the shifter galley about 6 inches closer to the gearbox where it is easily reached. Naturally, the drive shaft will have to be modified to accommodate the Chevy output shaft and the Ford rearend pinion flange.

As with the Super T-10, if you already have one, it is certainly worth rebuilding. Seeking one out is another story. Restorers of Ford muscle cars have driven the price up.

Practical Modern Transmissions

The Borg-Warner T-5 Five Speed— Call it modern merchandising if you wish, or some other catchy phrase such as "outsourcing," it doesn't matter. There is a decided move on the part of many manufacturers to buy services and components from outside venders for their brand name products. Detroit is no different. Since the mid-1980s, one major transmission manufacturer—Borg-Warner—has been supplying essentially the same gearbox to both Chevrolet and Ford. It is simply called the "T-5." Unlike many handsome aluminum-cased transmissions hanging on the back end of four cylinder and V-6 engines, both domestic and foreign, it has the ability to withstand the torque output of a healthy V-8. I knew that, but I wasn't fully aware of its chameleon-like attributes until I visited Pat Massey at Anaheim Gear, a family-owned and operated business specializing in standard transmissions, and best of all, willing to work with street rodders.

The centerpiece of the T-5 five speed is the gear case. With the exception of a few minor ratio differences in the forward speeds, the same gear case is used in many Ford and Chevrolet passenger car and light truck models. The primary differences lie in the input and output shafts, tail housings and speedometer hookups. Naturally, the bellhousings are designed to fit each company's engine block.

If you do not already own one of the classic transmissions, Pat's advice is to strongly consider the T-5. It is "fresh,"

BORG-WARNER T-5 RATIOS (GM Application)					
1st	2nd	3rd	4th	5th	Description
2.95	1.94	1.34	1.00	0.73	Various V-8 models
2.95	1.94	1.34	1.00	0.63	Various V-8 models

The T-5s factory-installed in V-8 powered Chevrolets have the standard Chevy bolt pattern which mates to any Chevy bellhousing. The pilot shaft has 26 splines like the Super T-10 or later model Muncies. The pilot bearing and retainer is the same for all Chevy/GM applications from 1955 up. This later model Chevy has a Ford style tail housing.

Beyond an easy match-up to the engine you're installing, the only reason to pick one T-5 transmission over another is slightly different ratios among applications. (See corresponding charts.) By the way, there are several optional factory handles. Some are screw-on; some are bolt-on, depending on the tail housing. Hurst also makes a short throw shifter with a raised pivot point. Beyond that, one could modify an older, taller, Hurst shift handle to work in most cases.

and parts are readily available. The advantages that accrue to street rodders with their never-ending desire to shuffle the deck when upgrading an old car or pickup should be obvious. Take a look at the photos and you'll see what I mean.

When street rods doubled as weekend drag cars, cast iron and cast aluminum bellhousings were banned at the race track. That was well and good, and in fact, don't even think about going to the Antique drags today without a SEMA-approved steel "scatter shield." However, is it necessary on a boulevard cruiser that will never see a "Christmas Tree?" No. If you are planning to run a high quality aftermarket flywheel and a McLeod street performance clutch assembly as I do in my coupe, the stock bellhousing is fine.

SUSPENSION AND HANDLING CONSIDERATIONS

11

Want a quick, but safe test of your street rod's suspension and handling? Drive over a railroad track at 30 mph.

Shortly after you've found and purchased a suitable body and frame, you must come to terms with planning and designing the rest of the car. Moreover, nowhere will your ingenuity, inventiveness and building skills be put to a more demanding test than when dealing with suspension and steering systems and the resultant handling.

Technically, an automobile's suspension is comprised of the springs, shock absorbers and locating linkages that connect the front wheels and rear axle assembly to the frame. An examination of what the factory installed under pre-1949 Fords—by far the most popular street rod building material—is a good place to start.

THE EARLY FORD FRONT SUSPENSION

In the more primitive, non-independent front suspensions, particularly those under early Fords, there's a full-width axle—typically a curved I-beam. Kingpins are used at each end of the axle to mount and pivot the spindles for steering. The kingpin leans inward at the top and outward at the bottom. This angle reduces steering-wheel kickback and increases straight ahead stability. It also causes the body and frame to rise slightly as the wheels are turned in either direction, with a detectable increase in steering effort.

The spindle assembly is a combination steering knuckle and stub axle-spindle. It accepts and supports the wheel hub and bearings, and has an

113

The engineering of the early Ford suspension is outdated, but most owners of fenderless street rods on the road and under construction refuse to give it up.

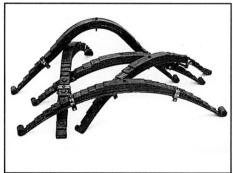

The most common spring in general use has long been the leaf-spring bundle—a combination of two or more leaves. Leaf springs come in a variety of shapes. The traditional transverse (buggy) style used in early Ford suspensions is but one.

arm to which the tie rod is connected. The function of the tie rod is to transfer steering motion from one steering arm to the opposite one. In the oldest Ford tradition, a drag link runs from the Pitman arm on the steering gear shaft to one spindle. Ford passenger cars (and many light trucks) used the worm-and-roller Gemmer design through the 1948 models. Ford also used lever-action Houdaille shocks long past their prime. The Ford Motor Company simply never veered from the solid front axle during Henry's lifetime. True, it is inexpensive and durable, but regardless of springing or damping, it was and is still a relatively poor design with a major shortcoming: When one wheel is deflected by road irregularities, the opposite wheel is affected; not as much as the first wheel, but enough to cause a perceptible difference in handling. Worse, if steering components are worn, severe front-wheel wobble can result. So severe, in fact, that sometimes the car must be brought to a complete halt to stop the wobble.

With the above in mind, the only reason for using an I-beam front axle in a modern street rod is simply tradition. No excuses need be made, nor is

Boogie Scott, a professional dragster chassis builder, designed and built his own IFS.

The petite Corvair steering box is a long-time favorite in lightweight roadsters.

an elaborate justification for running an archaic front suspension necessary. The I-beam axle looks "right" under a fenderless street rod. To many street rodders, the engineering deficiencies are not important.

THE INDEPENDENT FRONT SUSPENSION

If, however, you were to look under the front sheet metal of most non-Ford passenger cars starting in the late-1930s, you would find something quite different from the beam axle and leaf spring—an independent front suspension (IFS) with either coil or parallel leaf springs. An independent front suspension allows each wheel to move up and down . . . well . . . independently. Gone are the solid I-beam axles and kingpins. In their place is a variety of linkages and ball joints.

Independent front suspensions were originally designed with a pair of suspension locating links in the shape of the letter "A" for each of the front wheels. The bottom A-arm was longer than the upper A-arm and the two were

non-parallel. The legs of the A-arms were attached to the frame, and rubber bushed; the wheel spindles were attached to the points of the A-arm with pins and bushings, and were able to move up and down freely.

Significant design variations appeared regularly through the early years of the development of the independent front suspension. First, the legs of the A-arms were spread farther apart for improved load distribution and durability. In later designs, a straight control arm combined with a compression or tension strut was used instead of a bottom A-arm. This strut, which is attached to the control arm near the spindle, runs forward or rearward to a mounting bracket. Variations on this latter design are used in many American passenger car front suspensions.

There are other types of independent front suspensions, of course. You've heard of the MacPherson strut. After all, it is the most popular front suspension in the world. It may well be on your very own "grocery getter," particularly if it has front-wheel drive. If so,

you may have considered it for a street rod project. The sliding strut/coil spring/shock absorber unit to which the wheel and brake assembly is connected will work in theory on a lightweight street rod. Practicality is another story because of the high mounting position of the strut. To my knowledge, no one has ever made a serious attempt to mate one to an early car. It's just as well.

The same holds true for Ford's Twin I-beam light truck front suspension. It actually consists of two straight axles, each pivoted at the opposite side of the chassis from the wheel it supports. It is as massive as the MacPherson strut is delicate. Nevertheless, it, too, fails to find a home under the early chassis. As a matter of curiosity, Terry Berzenye of Specialized Street and Performance and I took some preliminary measurements of the down-sized Twin I-beam IFS used under the front of a 1985 Ford Ranger. Forget it. The basic passenger car stamped-steel control arms with their coil springs nestled between the upper and lower arms, or the more sophisticated street rod industry's redesigns with coil-over-shock units are best for street rod use.

STEERING SYSTEMS

With this overview fresh in your mind, let's look at steering. Making the front wheels turn left and right is not a matter of major consequence as long as the car utilizes the traditional rigid - beam axle, a steering arm attached to each spindle, a tie rod with adjustable, flexible ends to connect them, and some kind of triangulated linkage connecting one wheel to a steering mechanism.

In its most basic form, the steering is nothing more than a system of reduction gears between the steering wheel

115

With rack-and-pinion steering, turning motion is transmitted through a shaft to a pinion gear. The pinion is meshed with a straight gear—the rack. Rotation of the pinion is converted into lateral sliding motion by the rack. The rack is located between the front wheels, and short tie rods attached to each end and transmit steering wheel movement.

and the steered wheels. Reduction gears, by the way, are needed to give the driver enough mechanical advantage (leverage) to generate the force necessary to steer the car.

You may wonder if gears of any kind were in that rusted pre-WWII hulk you muscled into your garage. Back in the 1920s and '30s when straight-axled, buggy-sprung Fords were less than 3000 pounds, the tires were tall and skinny. Their plain-Jane manual steering, crude as it may appear today, was adequate.

Design-wise, things took a turn for the worse when independent front suspensions were introduced. The conventional tie rod simply couldn't handle the job when each front wheel went its own way. Early attempts to coordinate two independently sprung wheels and a single steering box resulted in a morass of bearings, ball joints, long arms, short arms, idlers and dampers, all moving in arcs that would baffle a geometry professor.

In time, of course, a host of engineers worked the bugs out of the independent

front suspension. Improved bushings were developed and low-friction bearing materials, such as nylon were introduced. Steering gear boxes also made great strides. Today's heavier cars, regardless of their origin, will either have recirculating ball-and nut or rack-and-pinion steering gears. They all come with power assist, as well.

The recirculating ball-and-nut design came from General Motors' Saginaw Steering Gear Division. Although it was conceived for the 1940 Cadillac, it hasn't changed much since. Internally, a long worm gear positioned at the end of the steering shaft is fitted with a large, coarse-threaded nut. The grooves in the worm and inside the nut are machined to accept a number of loose ball bearings that perform the function of conventional threads, but with much less friction and a better ability to absorb steering gear loads. As the car is steered to the right or left, the ball bearings circulate around the worm, changing direction when the steering wheel changes direction.

In modern light- to middleweight, rear wheel drive cars, however, the recirculating ball-and-nut steering gear has all but disappeared. The steering gear of choice is now the rack-and-pinion. It is simple in construction and it takes up very little room.

With the rack-and-pinion, turning motion at the steering wheel is transmitted through a steering shaft to a pinion gear. The pinion is meshed with a straight gear—the rack. Rotation of the pinion is converted into lateral sliding motion by the rack. The rack is positioned laterally between the front wheels, and short tie rods attach each end of the rack to a wheel, transmitting right and left steering movement.

The ratio between steering wheel turns and the full left to right sweep of the front wheels is low, resulting in quick steering action. Furthermore, the driver gets a better "feel" of the road than he would with a conventional steering gear.

Rack-and-pinion steering does have its drawbacks, however. For one, more effort is required to steer at slow speeds and when parking. The driver also gets more feedback—harshness or kickback—through the steering wheel because of lower friction in this type of steering gear. Power assist, of course, negates this.

Wheel Alignment

To get on down the road without ruining the tires requires a practical application of geometry to the art of front-wheel alignment. The front wheels on a car may look as if they are sitting at 90 degrees to the ground but they aren't. They are leaning either inward (negative camber) or outward a slight bit (positive camber). If the wheels are sitting straight up, camber

Wheel alignment is more than simply insuring directional stability; it also relieves the driver of the need to make continuous steering corrections. Although only light pressure on the steering wheel should be enough to keep the vehicle headed on a straight course, a slight resistance is needed to give the driver something to turn against, thus reducing the tendency to over-control. On the other hand, a certain amount of counterforce is also needed to help return the wheels to the straight-ahead position when coming out of a turn. There's one more vital concern—friction between the tire and the road. In short, wheel alignment plus steering geometry (the operating angles of the suspension system) provide directional stability, easy steering, and normal tire life expectancy.

is zero, or 90 degrees to the ground. Although slight, most passenger car front suspensions have some positive camber specified.

The wheels, however, do have a fair amount of toe-in. The front of the tires are closer together than the rear. Initial toe-in is intended to compensate for the toe-out caused by slight deflections in the steering linkage created by drag on the tires as the car moves down the road. Don't confuse this toe with toe-out during turning—Ackerman steer—gained with steering linkage geometry. This is done to turn the inside wheel more because it turns around a "shorter" radius that the outside wheel. Toe-out increases and the turning radius tightens, or gets smaller.

Then there is caster, the angle of the

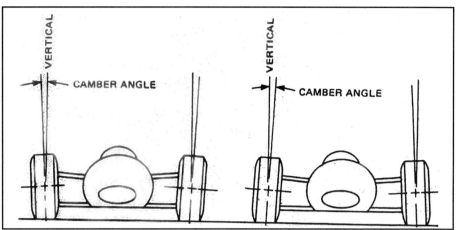

Caster, camber and toe-in are the three basic suspension settings. Camber is zero when the tire sits perfectly square to the road surface, positive when it leans out at the top, and negative when it leans in.

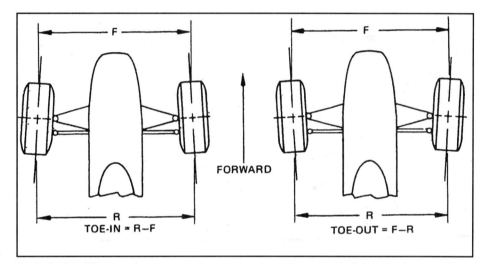

Toe-in is the difference between measurements from the centers of tire treads at the front and at the rear. If the front measurement is less than the rear, the tires are toed in, vice versa, if the front measurement is greater.

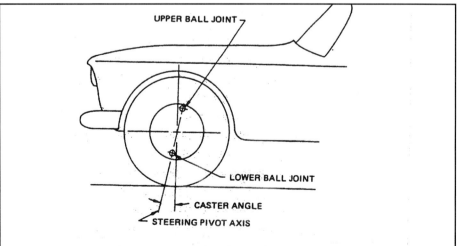

Caster angle is determined by the steering pivot axis (the line drawn through the kingpin or upper and lower ball joints). As viewed from the side, if the axis leans back at the top from vertical, caster is positive, negative if vice versa.

117

kingpin as viewed from the side. It is negative when it leans toward the front of the car at the top, positive when leaning to the rear. Positive caster forces the front tires to point straight ahead as the car travels down the road with little effort on the part of the driver.

THE REAR SUSPENSION

Although there's a 99-percent probability of finding an independent suspension under the front of any post-1949 American passenger car, there's less of a chance of finding an independent rear suspension although the numbers are increasing gradually.

Hotchkiss Type

The rearend under all American cars with rear wheel drive from 1949 until recently has been some version of the Hotchkiss type, and often suspended with parallel semi-elliptical leaf springs. Loosely speaking, these springs take the shape of half of an ellipse. This suspension on a conventional, strong, one-piece axle housing and a gear carrier is a workhorse and still a great combination for a rodder on a budget.

Although the Hotchkiss rearend was popular with cost-conscious manufacturers, it has shortcomings in performance applications. It is bulky and heavy, and consequently has a high unsprung weight—the weight on the road side of the springs and shocks. In addition, the springs "wrap up" under hard acceleration and braking loads. As drag racers learned a long time ago, wheel hop is a problem that must be controlled by some type of traction-assisting device.

Coil Spring

There are several versions of rear

The most popular street rod friendly rearend is the Ford 9-inch Hotchkiss type, and it has been suspended in a variety of ways.

Starting in the late 1950s, the 9-incher was suspended by means of the original transverse spring. Old-fashioned, you say. Well, let me be honest with you, the one I ran for more than 15 years rode quite well. Nevertheless, street rodding is as much of a game of chance as anything else is.

suspensions that incorporate coil springs instead of leaf springs. Coil spring rear suspensions use control arms and/or some type of linkage to locate the rear axle. Linkages used include the Panhard rod, sometimes called a track bar. It is a long, transversely mounted link that goes between the frame and axle to control lateral axle movement. Watts linkage, similar in function to the Panhard rod, is a more complicated, straight-line

mechanism. The Panhard rod describes an arc when it goes up and down. The Watts link has an idler at the axle with two links, one going to each side of the frame or body. Conventional coil springs have lost out to coil-over-shock suspension units, however. They are easier to install and are better looking.

Independent Rear Suspension

Just as with an independent front

In the mid-1960s parallel semi-elliptical leaf springs caught the fancy of rodders. Ordinarily, semi-elliptical springs are multi-leaf, but one modern street rod components manufacturer (James J. Durant) offers a friction-free single leaf semi-elliptical.

The coil-overs, Jaguar independent rear suspension, and locating linkages are all illustrated in this shot of a well-detailed T-bucket chassis.

Coil-over-shock suspension units are about as clean as they come, even though they require lateral locating linkage. No problem though, full kits are available from most vendors in the street rod market.

suspension, the wheels of an independent rear suspension move independently. In rear-wheel drive cars with this type of suspension, the differential cage is mounted to the chassis—to reduce unsprung weight—and the wheels are driven by shafts pivoted at the differential carrier.

There aren't many varieties of American or foreign manufacture independent rear suspensions that are practical for street rod applications. If

you've been eyeballing some old sports cars in the local boneyard, you probably noticed their independent rear ends. Chances are they are the swing-axle type. Used under early VWs, Corvairs and Sprites, the assembly consists of a pair of axles in housings with the wheel and brake assemblies fixed at the outboard ends. The axles are free to pivot up and down at the inboard end, or at the third-member housing. Each half axle is as long

as practical in order to minimize camber change, which can be extreme at times. This can cause rapid tire wear.

Worse, swing axle rear suspensions have a high roll center, the point about which the wheels swing. This creates a tendency of the car to "jack up" while cornering, causing severe oversteer—and sending the back end sliding out of control. Swing axles are outdated and not in use any longer, but they are relatively inexpensive and therefore might be appealing if money is tight. If you have been thinking about adapting one into a rod with a narrow chassis such as a T-bucket or Model A, forget it.

If you assumed that the most popular sports cars on the American road in the last forty years—Corvettes and Jaguars—would have the finest independent rear suspensions, you'd be right. They and a few other not-so-exotic imports use a version of the double A-arm rear suspension.

The pivot axis for each wheel is near 90 degrees to the car's centerline. In this layout, the roll center is low and camber change is much less severe than the swing axle. Most use coil

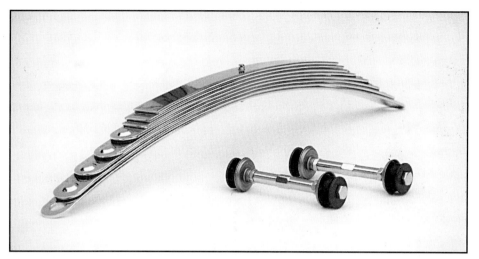

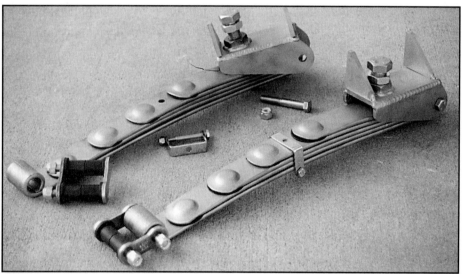

Pictured is Posies' multi-leaf Corvette spring and adjustable hangers for street rod use. Below it is Posies' "Elippta Slide" adjustable quarter elliptic kit. (Quarter elliptics first came to prominence on track roadsters.) Photos courtesy Posies.

components industry to come up with new versions. More about that later, suffice it to say if you want the best rear suspension under your rod, your desires will be well rewarded if you choose an IRS.

AIR SUSPENSION

Another system has intrigued street rodders in recent years—air suspension with automatic leveling. Domestically, these first appeared in high-end production cars in the late 1980s. Typically, street rod installations consist of an air compressor, a compressor relay, an air dryer, an exhaust solenoid, a control module, a height sensor, adjustable shock absorbers and the air lines and fittings connecting the compressor to the shocks. A lot of hardware to be sure, but the aftermarket street rod industry, as they always do, has cleaned most of it up, and made the parts prettier. Complete air suspension packages are available in kit form as well as an option on rolling chassis built by some rod shops.

I'll discuss the more practical of the above systems at length in later chapters, but for now, let's define some of the suspension system's critical components.

A CLOSER LOOK AT THE BASIC HARDWARE
Springs

As mundane as they may appear, the springs are those significant, elastic components that flex under load, but return to their original configuration when the load is removed. They allow the vehicle to travel more comfortably by allowing the wheels to comply with the irregularities in the road. Sometimes the springs also provide full or partial wheel location.

spring/shock combinations, or as in the case of some Corvettes, a single transverse leaf spring. Control rods and lateral linkages tie the wheel assemblies to the chassis.

These systems are costly to manufacture, but they are the best handling rear suspensions so far devised. The double A-arm rear suspension is also one of the best looking. You know this if you've ever looked under the rear of a street rod with a Jag IRS. That's not the only reason the Jag unit was one of the very first street rod IRS adaptations, however.

It and the Corvette are the two most frequently adapted production car independent rear suspensions because their design configurations and dimensions are just about perfectly matched to the early Ford's frame. Matched, that is, after a few modifications and one of the street rod installation kits.

The supply of early Jag units has dwindled over the years, and rodders have tired of waiting for Corvettes to appear in the wrecking yards. The demand for a good-looking, reliable IRS hasn't abated, however. In fact, the demand has driven the street rod

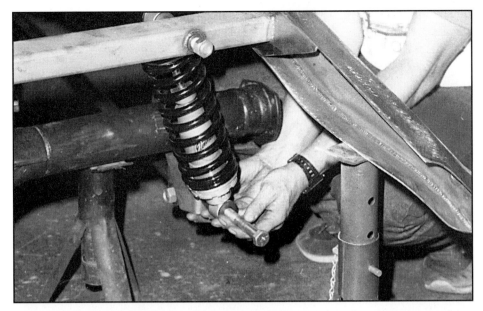

Coil springs and coil-over-shock suspension units both provide basic suspension services, but the coil-over additionally provides shock absorption. Its relatively small size, attractiveness and the ease with which it accommodates rear as well as front end needs has made it a street rodding favorite even though installation requires lateral locating struts.

Functionally, the torsion bar is a long straight unwound coil spring. Yet, it is the most efficient spring used in suspension systems. Spring action is accomplished by a twisting of the bar. Pictured is a Harry Nicks chassis.

Regardless, there are three basic types: leaves, coils and torsion bars.

Leaf Springs—The most common spring in general use has long been the leaf-spring bundle—a combination of two or more leaves. Leaf springs come in a variety of shapes: the traditional transverse (buggy) style, semi-ellipti-cal, quarter-elliptical, and cantilever. There is also the GM-resurrected fiberglass-reinforced mono-leaf spring used under some Corvette models. Barring such high-tech approaches, however, the steel leaf spring remains the manufacturer's delight—it is cheap to produce and works reasonably well.

Not great, mind you, but reasonably well.

The reason for this so-so rating is that automotive springs are technically judged and compared in terms of energy stored per unit of weight. The typical steel leaf spring only stores 300 inch-pounds of energy per pound. This measure is one of efficiency and not to be confused with spring rate—or load per unit deflection.

Spring rate refers to the force in pounds required to compress a spring one inch. A spring with a 200-pound per inch (lb/in.) rate requires 200 pounds to compress it one inch, 400 pounds to compress it two inches, and so forth. Furthermore, spring rate should be relative to the weight of the car; the lighter the car, the lower the rate and vice versa. It is wheel deflection—how much the wheel travels from full rebound to normal ride height—that is important. It governs ride quality.

Coil Springs—Conventional coil springs are more efficient than leaf springs. They store approximately 700 inch-pounds of energy per pound of spring weight. Therefore, a friction-free coil spring weighing less than half that of a multi-leaf spring will do the same amount of suspension work. Ten to twelve feet of wire is used to wind the typical automotive coil spring. When the coil is compressed, the wire twists. This is how the energy generated by the movement of the suspension is stored. That's the good news. The bad news is that some of the weight advantage is lost when you consider that leaf springs do double duty. The conventional coil spring does not locate the rear-axle assembly, a leaf spring does.

That disadvantage disappears when

Ford cars were equipped with lever-action Houdaille shocks well into the 1940s. As awkward looking as they are, they do indeed work when they are in tip-top condition. Although street rodders haven't used them in years, vintage auto parts stores still carry parts and rebuild kits for restorers. Street rodders, of course, have long preferred what used to be called the "aircraft" type.

the coil is reduced in size and wrapped around a shock absorber. The double-duty capability of a coil-over-shock absorber suspension unit coupled with its relatively small size and the ease with which it accommodates both an independent suspension and a convention rear axle assembly has made it a street rodder favorite. Of course, its attractiveness is no small plus. A conventional rearend with coil-over-shock suspension units still requires some type of lateral locating struts.

Torsion Bars—The most efficient type of conventional springing used in suspension systems is the torsion bar. Careful quality control and the finest spring steels must be used in their manufacture, factors that drive up production costs. Functionally, they can be thought of as nothing more than an unwound coil spring. The long straight bar is fastened to the frame at one end and to a suspension component at the other. Spring action is accomplished by twisting of the bar. Few suspension systems offer the elegance of those that utilize torsion bars. As such, they are close to ideal for use in a street rod.

Torsion bars can store 1000 inch-pounds of energy, more than three times that of the leaf spring. They are not without drawbacks, however. Carefully engineered space allocation is necessary, as is the avoidance of nicks or surface scratches. Surface irregularities create stress risers that will lead to cracks and eventual failure.

Unlike most other types of suspensions, torsion bar suspensions usually have built-in methods for adjusting ride height without altering spring rate. Subtleties such as this make a torsion bar suspension the advanced rod builder's first choice when the design of the car permits it, and the cost is not prohibitive.

Shock Absorbers

Moving right along in our discussion of suspension system components, we come to the shock absorbers. As critical as springs are, adequate ride cannot be achieved with them alone. At rest, the weight of the car compresses the spring a given amount. This is called static deflection. As the car moves over road irregularities, the springs compress. Once past a bump, the springs try to extend from their compressed position. In doing this, they go past their original position and thrust the chassis upward. Without shock absorbers, a vicious oscillation would be set in motion. If this oscillation becomes too severe, the wheel may leave the road surface or the frame may drop . . . or both. Even if he has the saddle stamina of Teddy Roosevelt, the driver will soon grow weary. Worse, he may lose control of his car. The solution is the shock absorber, that component in the suspension system that restricts and damps suspension movement. Although some operate on friction or compressed gas, the simple telescoping hydraulic shock is what most rodders use.

Standard direct-action, double-tube shocks are velocity-sensitive damping mechanisms containing hydraulic fluid that is forced through a multi-stage system of restricting valves and orifices during suspension movement. The inside tube is considered the working tube because the shock piston moves in it. Surrounding this tube is an outer tube that contains fluid in reserve, thus the name "reserve chamber." The resistance to fluid movement is what retards spring (suspension) motion and oscillation. The heat energy generated is dissipated into the shock body, the fluid in the reserve chamber, then out to the surrounding air.

Gas Shocks—The high-pressure gas shock, one incorporating a pressurized gas chamber that acts against the fluid to resist foaming is movement sensitive—it begins damping the instant the suspension moves. It also runs cooler because the working component is exposed to the air. Therefore, it's ahead

The Monroe Load-Leveler combines a heavy duty shock with an auxiliary coil spring for additional stiffness. If you find your suspension is too soft, you can beef it up with Load-Levelers. They are not the same as coil-over-shock suspension units, however, and are not intended to stand alone.

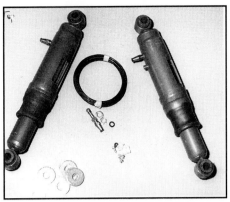

Air shocks similarly add stiffness to the suspension by means of pressurized air in an internal bladder.

Anti-roll bars resist body roll by transferring the load from an inside wheel to the outside during turning. As factory issue, they've been on the front end of rod-popular cars since the 1940 Ford with its stock Houdaille shock absorbers premiered. Too much anti-roll bar can cause steering problems, however. Properly designed commercial kits such as Chassis Engineering's anti-roll bar for street rods with the Lincoln Versailles rear take this into account.

of the game and superior to the conventional double-tube shock described above.

Work Cycle—The work cycle of a shock—single or double tube—is divided into two phases: compression, where the piston is thrust down in the cylinder displacing fluid through the valves into the opposite chamber; and extension, where the piston is pulled up, forcing the fluid back into the original chamber. Changes in pressure and fluid movement are controlled by piston movement, the displacement of the piston rod, the area of the valves, and the amount of restriction to fluid movement through the valve or orifice system.

DeCarbon Shocks—A somewhat different shock absorber was invented by one Dr. DeCarbon. It has a single tube in which the piston moves; there's no reserve chamber. A floating piston in the tube is backed up on the side opposite the working fluid by gas under high pressure. Consequently, there's no need for the conventional reserve chamber to compensate for displaced fluid during shock-piston movement.

Anti-Roll Bars

Frequently used on both front and rear suspensions, anti-roll bars resist roll by transferring load from an inside wheel to the outside during turning maneuvers. The anti-roll bar is confusing, not because of what it does, but for what hot rodders have called it through the years: sway bars, anti-sway bars, roll bars, stabilizer bars and who knows what else. Well, the most accurate term is anti-roll bar.

In resisting body roll and resulting weight transfer, the anti-roll bar makes the outside wheel work harder, thus decreasing its cornering ability. There is a caveat, however. "Too much" anti-roll bar on the rear suspension can cause oversteer, a tendency of the vehicle to spin while turning. On the front, too much anti-roll bar creates understeer, or push. This is the tendency of the vehicle to go straight ahead while turning.

VEHICLE DYNAMICS AND HANDLING

That's what the engineers call it, and it's a neat sounding phrase. It refers to the science of what makes a car handle. However, what does that mean to

you? Well, the old hot rod action movies of the 1950s portrayed inadequate vehicle dynamics dramatically—a pair of fenderless roadsters winding through the rugged Southern California mountains at high speed. Burning rubber on the straights and fishtailing in the curves, until finally one driver miscalculates, loses control of his car and goes sailing over the cliff to his death.

Old movies often incorporated a gloomy object lesson. In *Hot Rods to Hell* and others of its kind, the message seemed to be that hot rodders were brainless adolescents who drove flashy little cars that were unsafe in the final analysis. The fruits of their labors were bitter, indeed. Yet, as campy as many of the old movies were, they weren't too far off base when they dealt with the handling characteristics of more than a few early street rods. Unfortunately, some modern street rods are still being built as if they will only be driven in a straight line.

If the job is to be done well, you

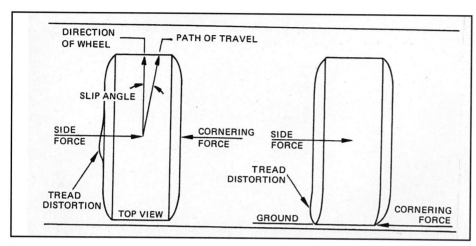

This drawing from HPBooks' *How to Make Your Car Handle* illustrates what happens "when the rubber meets the road." The tire distorts during cornering and must be turned more sharply than the path it travels. The difference between the turning angle and the tire path is the slip angle.

must be acquainted with the basic concepts of vehicle dynamics and the kind of hardware you plan to put between yourself and the highway. I certainly don't recommend racing on public roads, but you must work toward achieving the best road handling possible for a modified sixty-five-year-old car. You may not end up being able to compete with a Porsche on its stomping grounds, but you can build a street rod that will corner almost as well as it will accelerate!

As soon as you start doing your research, however, you'll be immersed in concepts and terminology that are both scientific and mystifying. Vehicle dynamics, for example, is the science of what makes a car handle. Handle? Yes, that's a difficult concept to define. Some say it's simply when your car does what you want it to do. At any rate, you know when you have it . . . and you know when you don't. Inasmuch as it is commonly accepted that in a two-wheel-drive vehicle, rear-wheel drive handles best, the street rodder is halfway there because that's the way street rods are built.

Weight Distribution

Another commonly accepted axiom of automotive design is that any car with rear-wheel drive will handle best with a rearward weight-bias. Racecar builders and some sports car manufacturers have achieved this fundamental advantage by placing the engine and drivetrain behind the driver or passenger compartment. It is a simple matter to obtain the rear weight-bias thusly if it fits within other design requirements. It's not that easy when you're out to build a typical street rod. Weight distribution counts, however, not necessarily the location of the hardware.

With this in mind, it behooves you to keep the front end of your car as light as practical, and to shift whatever you can to or toward the rear. Although not many American cars have been built this way, several models of the Corvette and some station wagons have nearly as much weight on the rear axle as on the front. This was done on the Corvette through engine and passenger-compartment location. On wagons, it was accomplished with additional weight in glass, sheet metal and structure over the rear wheels. The

street rodder's problem is that aside from the battery, there aren't many heavy components that can be shifted toward the rear. This problem is greatly accentuated in a lightweight roadster. Therefore, it is not outlandish to at least consider a hundred (yes, a hundred) pounds of securely mounted lead ballast in the trunk. It won't take up as much space as you might think and beyond that, you will increase ride comfort as well, because you will be changing the "sprung to unsprung" weight ratio.

Dynamics

If you will recall your high school physics, Isaac Newton declared that any mass—such as an automobile—once in motion, must be acted upon by some external force in order to change direction or velocity. That is, for every action there must be an equal and opposite reaction.

With regard to cars, the forces of reaction are applied primarily by the ground and, to a lesser extent, the atmosphere. Furthermore, the ground forces are generated through and limited by the friction of the tires. In fact, although inertia forces—acceleration, deceleration and centrifugal—act on the mass of the car, and are spread out according to the distribution of the car's weight, a significant percentage of vehicle dynamics is in some way or another related to the tires.

Picture in your mind our *Hot Rods to Hell* roadster going around a curve. Centrifugal force is applied at the car's center of gravity, but the roadster's tires are providing a reactive force by virtue of their friction with the road. As long as these two forces are equal, the roadster will maintain its equilibrium. Ah, but should centrifugal force

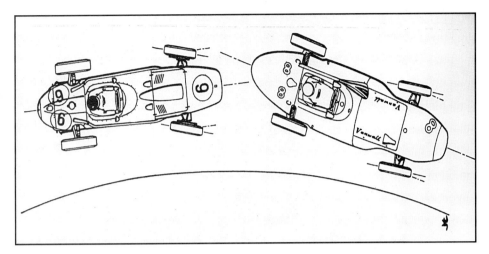

Both racers are following the same line, but the leader is oversteering. The follower, however, is understeering. Slight understeer is generally best for street use. Courtesy *Road & Track Magazine.*

get the upper hand, that is, should it overcome the force of the tires, it's a quick trip off the road.

As important as the equality of the sum of the forces is to our understanding of handling, that isn't all of it. The sum of the moments—forces applied at a distance—must also be equal. If those turning moments are not equal, the roadster will spin out—either around its center of gravity, or either axle. However, don't trouble yourself about these sophistications. There are simpler things to concern you.

Tires

Although automotive dynamics are primarily based on the above considerations, there is that crucial variable—the aforementioned tires. To further your understanding of an automobile in motion, let's look at the characteristics of tires.

First, let's assume that frictional forces are the same in all directions. If two or more external forces are acting on a body, the net or equivalent single force cannot be greater than the limit of friction—fancy wording to explain why a sliding tire is incapable of steering a car. In short, the tire must be

rolling, not sliding in order to maintain directional stability.

While rolling, tires must provide driving or tractive forces, cornering or sideways forces and braking forces. Together or separately, they cannot be greater than the tire's limit of friction. This limit of friction, sometimes called the coefficient of friction, is defined as the sliding force applied to a vehicle, divided by the vehicle's weight. More accurately, this is called "grip" when applied to tires. Now, although friction is never zero when two surfaces are in contact, it is common practice to simplify problems in mechanics by assuming it to be zero. Likewise, for tires on any ordinary paved surface, grip is about 1.0, a number that is close enough to be held true.

Therefore, a wheel and tire that is capable of supporting 1000 pounds will develop a side force of 1000 pounds before it slides. What all this means is that from the standpoint of friction, weight distribution alone has no effect upon the balance of a car while cornering. So, the next time a buddy tells you that the heavy end of a car will break loose first, tell him that's a common misconception.

Slip Angle

From there, we come to one of the least understood factors influencing handling, the all-important slip angle. Slip angle is the difference, measured in degrees, between the direction the wheel is traveling, and the direction in which the wheel is aimed. If the slip angle is greatest at the front, the car understeers. If it's greatest at the rear, it oversteers.

Understand that slip angle is not created by the tire's sliding or slipping—the tires are changing shape. An inflated tire is an elastic body, and when it is subjected to a strong side force, it deflects. If it is rolling and cornering on a flat road surface while it is in its deflected or out-of-shape condition, it will diverge from the path that it would have otherwise taken, the path that the driver steered into. In other words, the roadster pilot of the old hot rod movies cranked the wheels to the right, but the rod understeered and sailed over the cliff!

Don't draw too many conclusions. If the rear tires experienced excessive slip angle from excessive deflection, the car would've gone backward over the cliff. The result would've been the same. If the tires deflected the same—neutral steer—the roadster would have negotiated the corner, assuming all four tires maintained traction. In other words, slip angles, centrifugal forces and the intended path are all interrelated and form the basis for vehicle dynamics.

Although centrifugal forces and the angle of the steered wheels are major causes of slip angles, they are not the only causes. Wind gusts can easily affect slip angles, as can irregularities in the road surface. In addition, there

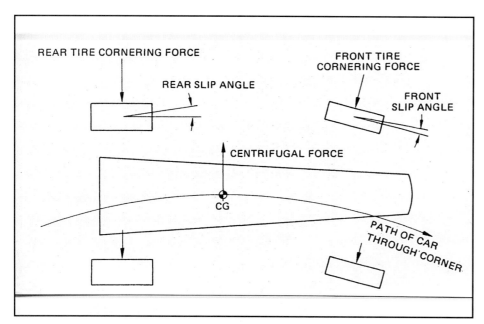

The sketch shows a car rounding a right-hand curve at speed. The slip angle of the rear tires is greater than the fronts, an oversteer condition. Only the outside slip angles are shown because the outside tires do the majority of cornering work.

are the changes in the attitude of the tires to the road surface because of suspension deflection and geometry, particularly camber. Then there are changes in vertical force or pitch—the fore and aft rocking motion which alternately compresses the front springs while extending the rear springs, all of which are caused by acceleration, deceleration and resulting weight transfer.

Rearward weight bias is accepted almost without question. If the rules allow, racing cars are rear-engine, rear drive with about 64 percent or more of their weight on the rear wheels. Should you then build your car in the conventional manner, then determine the total weight, front axle weight and rear axle weight at the local truck scales, to calculate how much lead ballast should be added in the rear to make it handle? Although this is exactly what my racing partners and I did a few years ago with our Bonneville Salt Flats blown gas roadster, the street sit-

uation is not the same. We were after traction, not cornering ability. Although it was just a straight-line runner, under full boost, that extra 900 pounds of lead in the rear helped it handle pretty well at over 200 mph!

Beware however: Too much weight can hurt handling on the street.

Although weight distribution by itself is immaterial with regard to good or bad handling, if a tire is made to work harder, its slip angle increases. The same occurs by adding weight-induced load to a tire rather than doing it "artificially" with an anti-roll bar. Excess weight, just as too much bar at the rear, will cause oversteer. The same holds true at the front when understeer is created. This is a good news/bad news situation, but a couple hundred pounds in a street rodded early pickup (notorious for poor handling) is worth considering.

You can compensate for weight-induced steer at either end of a vehicle by adding or increasing anti-roll-bar

size at the opposite end of the vehicle. Or, you can increase tire size at the end that has excess slip angle. For the basic street roadster or coupe, however, rearward weight bias usually improves handling simply because of the extreme forward weight bias.

Acceleration and Deceleration

Let's look at some other advantages of rearward weight bias—acceleration, for instance. It is true that the rear tires are given an extra "bite" in a rearward weight-biased car. Look what the move to rear-engine dragsters did for their times. In the same vein, traction is further enhanced by the weight transfer from front to rear.

What about braking or sudden deceleration? Well, there's certainly an advantage here. Any vehicle, particularly a street rod with an equal or even a slight forward weight bias, must do most of its braking at the front. Very little braking is done by the rear wheels. The front brakes quickly heat up while the rears remain cool, but almost useless. The situation improves with a rear weight-biased car. Weight transfer is somewhat offset and braking is more equally distributed to both the front and rear wheels.

What about those annoying slip angles we discussed earlier? If you're building your street rod from scratch, you can begin to compensate for the differences that occur between front and rear slip angles in three ways—tire design, suspension design and vehicle proportions.

Tire Selection

Of these, tire design and selection is paramount. Although I already mentioned tire size, a tire's basic structure—radial, bias ply, tread configuration and "rubber" compound—can also be used to balance front-to-rear slip angles. Just installing tires with slightly better cornering characteristics, coupled with higher pressures and wider rims at the heavy end of the car, can significantly improve handling. Unfortunately, if you put bigger tires on the front rather than on the rear, the drive-in crowd will look at you as if you were crazy. It's just one more reason for figuring out how to get a rearward weight bias.

Roll-Couple Distribution

As mentioned above, one way of balancing slip-angle differences between front and rear wheels is to deal directly with the distribution of lateral dynamic forces. These occur in cornering as the vertical forces from the inside wheels transfer to the outside wheels. The vehicle "rolls" on its suspension due to lateral (centrifugal) forces. The rate of force transfer at the front or rear is expressed as a percent-

age of the total. This is called roll-couple distribution.

Just as anti-roll bars can be used to tailor roll-couple distribution, spring rates can also be used. This includes using stiffer springs at the front of a rearward weight-biased car or a stiffer bar at the front. The latter is preferable. The anti-roll bar twists in roll, but does not twist when both wheels hit a bump at the same time. "Better" tires at the rear can also help in reducing oversteer.

CONCLUSION

Although I've only touched briefly on vehicle dynamics, I hope you've gotten more from the discussion than merely confusion. It's a deep and difficult subject. However, I've pointed out a few of the more important points and I hope I've left you with a little practical knowledge. This knowledge will prove helpful when you begin to wade through the suspension kit catalogs and the maze of components that make up a street rod suspension system.

12

THE EARLY FORD FRONT SUSPENSION

The early Ford suspension was outdated when street rodding began in the late 1920s, but its classic good looks keep new builders returning to it year after year.

The traditional front suspension used by the Ford Motor Company from the Model T through the 1948 passenger car line consists of a one-piece triangulated radius rod commonly called the wishbone, a solid axle, and a transverse leaf spring. The gently curved axle is nothing more than a forged steel I-beam incorporating steering knuckles with yokes—called

spindles—fitted at the ends. The wheel and brake assemblies are mounted with bearings on the spindles and supported at the axle boss with kingpins.

The transverse spring is securely U-bolted to the frame's front crossmember. Shackles link the ends of the spring to perches at the axle. The spring shackle studs were of the rubber type through 1932; later models used

an improved lubricant-impregnated fabric. The entire assembly pivots in a single ball joint at the midpoint of the chassis.

The spring is mounted above the axle on pre-1935 models and ahead of it on subsequent models. A reduced spring rate for a smoother ride was achieved by lengthening the spring when it was moved ahead of the axle.

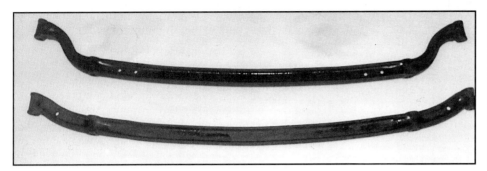

It isn't difficult to spot a dropped original axle. The "S" curves at the axle boss are noticeably narrowed. This is a natural occurrence in the process of maintaining the original width.

Other minor design changes were made through the years, one of which was the slight widening of the spring base—the mounting points at the axle—in 1940. An anti-roll bar was also added to control side-sway.

Nevertheless, as faithfully as this arrangement has served countless thousands of motorists, and subsequently street rodders, for nearly eight decades, it has a major fault shared by all solid axle suspensions—gyroscopic procession. When one wheel hits a bump, its angular deflection is transmitted through the axle to the other wheel. A spinning wheel reacts like a gyroscope. If it is tilted, it tries to resist the tilting force, hence causing the shimmy with which every traditional street rod pilot is all too aware.

This gyroscopic action causes the axle to dance like a teeter-totter. When one wheel bounces, it causes the opposite wheel to bounce. This sets up a self-generating back-and-forth motion that can only be stopped by stabbing the brakes or slowing the vehicle, sometimes bringing it to a complete halt if the conditions are severe.

Other faults commonly attributed to this suspension include the erratic movement of the axle assembly from braking and cornering forces. These movements usually come from excessive wear and/or inappropriate modifi-

cations to the radius rods. In short, the pre-1949 Ford passenger car front suspension is outdated, inefficient, and to those accustomed to the soft ride of the modern automobile, harsh.

Street rod builders have access to far more modern front suspensions, yet a substantial number will stay with the I-beam axle and transverse spring suspension on the front end. Why is that? Well, it is traditional, and as such, it just looks right on street rods, particularly fenderless roadsters.

TRADITIONAL MODIFICATIONS
The Dropped Axle

Beauty is in the eyes of the beholder, and for a very long time street rodders have seen greater beauty in a car that's lower in the front than one sitting on an even keel. In less complicated days when few rodders considered anything other than a Ford-based front suspension, the choice was between a stock axle and one with a greater-than-stock arch. The dropped axle was designed to lower the front ride height of the car two to three inches. Smaller tires accounted for another inch or so. The lowered front end is still very much with us, and so is the demand for dropped axles.

You may have the problem of not knowing exactly what to look for as

FORD MOTOR COMPANY AXLES, 1928–1948

1928–31: A relatively straight axle with only a 2.75 inch arch; 51.875 inches long with radius rod centers 36.250 inches apart. Radius rod bosses are 2.250 inches thick.

1932: A prominently curved design with 4.50 inch arch; 51.750 inches long with radius rod centers 36.562 inches apart. Radius rod bosses are 2 inches thick.

1933–36: Slightly thinner I-beam than 1932 axle, but dimensionally the same.

1937 Tubular: Lightweight tubular axle used only in the 1937 Model Fords powered by 60 horsepower, 136 cid V-8. It has a 4.50 inch arch and is 50 inches long with radius rod centers 38.50 inches apart. Radius rod bosses are 2.50 inches thick. (Only passenger car axle produced by Ford during the transverse spring era that wasn't an I-beam.)

1937–41: Standard I-beam axle with a 4.375 inch arch; 49 inches long with radius rod centers 38.50 inches apart. Radius rod bosses are 2.250 inches thick.

1942–47: The most prominently curved of the Ford I-beams with a 5.375 inch arch; 52 inches long with radius rod centers 40.750 inches apart. Radius rod bosses are 2.250 inches thick.

1948: Dimensionally the same as 1942–47 models, but with an extra hole in the I-beam web between the kingpin boss and radius boss to accommodate mounting of tubular shock absorbers.

you wander up and down swap-meet aisles in search of a used dropped axle. This is understandable because there can be more than one name for the same product, or worse, more than one product with the same name. As a result, many an unwary buyer has purchased an axle that did not quite fit as planned.

It's no wonder. There were five major varieties of Ford passenger car beam axles manufactured in Dearborn between 1928 and 1948. In addition, a number of aftermarket axles were reworked during the early commercial years of hot rodding. Add to this the several different axles being scratch-built today, and it is easy to see why there's so much confusion.

One thing for sure: We know that the original concept of a dropped axle—ends that have been reshaped to raise the spindles and thereby lower the car—is the brainchild of Abe Kobeck in San Diego back in the late 1930s. The dropped axle gained its fame, however, through the aggressive mar-

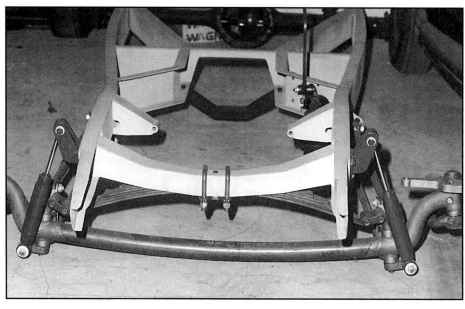

There's so much confusion about the original "Bell" axle and modern reproductions, that it serves no useful purpose to try to distinguish between the two. Suffice it to say that this is what they look like, and that a brand new one purchased from a reputable dealer is your most prudent move.

keting efforts of Ed "Axle" Stewart, also of San Diego, beginning in the 1940s. The so-called "Dago axle"—evolving from Diego—became so popular that virtually all early Ford-based street rods were built with them until the Mustang independent front suspension gained a following in the

mid-1970s.

For many years, dropped axles were actually modified stockers. The first of these were the stretched jobs, which can be identified by the slight narrowing in the middle of the S-curve, the short section between each wishbone boss and kingpin boss. Next came the forged, dropped axle, where the S-curve is a constant width. Some axles were "filled," that is, the open sections at the ends of the I-beam flanges were boxed, creating a rectangular cross section. They were at the height of street rod fashion during much of the 1950s. Whether or not the axle was filled, it was at least polished and chromed, with the hollow of the I-beam between the wishbone bosses neatly painted red.

Before the end of that decade, though, the "Bell" axle had made its name. It wasn't a dropped stock axle, though. It was a fresh, new axle manufactured by an auto parts company headquartered in Bell, California. The original Bell axle is not seen as often as reworked stockers because it was a

Dropped and "filled" axles, in which the open sections at the ends of the I-beam were boxed, were all the rage during the early 1950s. The axle was then polished and chromed, and the hollow in the center painted red.

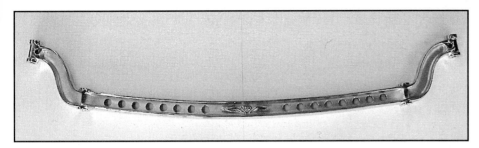

This Super Bell reproduction dropped axle has been "drilled" by SAC, a custom touch that recalls the early days of drag racing with its emphasis on weight reduction.

relatively expensive item back then.

Today, several different types of dropped axles are manufactured from scratch, and a company that started reshaping original axles in the '50s—MorDrop—is still going strong.

How Low Should You Go?

The purchase of a dropped axle for a street rod front suspension requires some forethought. A front-end drop of 2 to 4 inches is the most desirable, but some brave souls have gone as low as 6 inches. However, if you plan to do a lot of driving on less than glass-smooth roads, it's best to err on the side of moderation. There are other considerations as well.

When a front end is lowered, the entire frame and body is tilted (raked) forward. Naturally, any suspension components secured to the frame will also be angled forward. For example, front wheel caster angle will be decreased and headlight beams shortened. Fuel level in the carburetor- float bowl will also be affected, and the gas gauge reading may be upset.

Moderate changes won't cause major problems, but if compensating changes aren't made, too much rake well affect driveability and tire wear. Putting it mildly, properly changing the rake of that old Ford the right way will take a lot of work.

In stock form, early Fords tend to

oversteer—rear tire slip angle is greater than the front when cornering. This condition is worsened when the front end is lowered. The best solution for a traditional beam axle is a front anti-roll bar based on the 1940 design. Smaller front tires also help. You can also run lower pressures in the front tires and higher pressures in the rears. The bottom line is that when it comes to driving a modified car, it behooves you to know its particular characteristics and drive accordingly. Pay close attention to "seat-of-the-pants" cues that tell you when you are on the edge.

Camber is not significantly changed with a dropped front end, but caster and toe-in are. So, no matter how slight the rake, have the front end realigned. Re-aim the headlights, too. The change in carb angle shouldn't be a problem, but you'll have to familiarize yourself with changes in gas gauge readings.

Disassembly

Installing a dropped front axle in a stock Ford radius rod assembly is difficult. Original matings aren't easily changed. In fact, few components of an old car are as difficult to break down as the early Ford front suspension. The first order of business—after removal of the suspension from the car—is to disconnect the spring and knock the shackle bolts out of their

bosses. Old timers used to drill a 3/8-inch hole in a piece of 3/4-inch diameter soft iron rod to drive out the shackle bolts without swelling or distorting them. Even though you shouldn't reuse the shackle bolts, don't wedge them in tighter than they are. The original bolt often separates, leaving a thin sleeve in the shackle boss. If this happens, put on a pair of safety glasses and carefully chisel it out.

To save the axle bolts, carefully heat them to break the scale and rust that binds the nut in the concave boss. If all goes according to plan—don't count on it—the radius rod bolts can be driven out with ease.

Approach the job with optimism, though. Flip the assembly upside down and squirt a liberal dose of Liquid Wrench® or similar product around the bolt shanks. Let the assembly marinate overnight. Next day, replace the original castellated nuts with new standard nuts. Lubricate the threads, but don't run them down all the way. Try driving the bolts out with a 10-pound hammer.

If they won't come out in a few minutes, stop. Take the radius rod assembly to a machine shop that has a heavy-duty hydraulic press. If this doesn't work, you may have to sacrifice the original radius rod bolts, so retrieve your torch. Preheat the radius rod bolt until it's bright cherry red. Then gingerly burn them out. When two pieces of steel are rust-fused together for many years, it takes a delicate hand with a cutting torch to free them. Work very carefully to protect the part, or parts, you wish to save. If you were able to save the original axle, great. Even if you don't need it for an exchange, chances are one of your street rod buddies will.

Specialized Auto Components (SAC) Wishbone Splitting Kits for 1935–40 Fords includes a one-piece bracket, threaded spuds, and heavy-duty, easy to clean and lubricate tie-rod ends.

When the wishbone is split, the shackle bushing-to-axle angle changes. To correct this, the support must heated (The arrow pointing to the chalk mark shows where the heat must be concentrated). Preliminary heating and twisting can be done with each radius rod gripped firmly in a vise.

The boss is then twisted back to its original 90-degree relationship to the axle. Recheck your reference points at appropriate intervals.

Modifying Stock Radius Rods

The installation of a late-model engine and transmission will normally require some modification to the radius rod assembly. If, however, you are working on an original chassis and you plan on dropping in a flathead V-8 or other engine and transmission that will not interfere with the stock radius rods or their mounting, by all means leave things alone. When you've installed a new spring, shackle bushings and shock absorbers, the stock radius rod assembly with a dropped axle will work well. In short, don't fix what ain't broke!

On the other hand, if you're going to install a big engine and/or transmission, particularly an automatic, adequate clearance will be lacking. There is also the need to periodically service an automatic transmission.

Not only that, the center frame member of a less than an original car may have been modified. Therefore, there simply won't be any place to mount a stock wishbone—even if one exists. What is usually found under such a car is a split and bent radius rod assembly with welded-in tie-rod ends, bolted directly to the frame, or to crude hangers attached to the side of each frame rail. (This often seemed to be the easiest thing to do in "the old days.") Again, the problem with this modification is front suspension binding, with poor handling and overloaded mountings. If this is the case, you are in the market for an aftermarket radius rod kit. If the stock wishbone is still in good condition, however, you may simply want to split it the right way.

The key to minimal binding when splitting a cherry wishbone is to cut off the wishbone ball close to where the forging was originally welded to the tapered arms. Never cut the radius rods any shorter than necessary, you want to keep the ends as close together as possible. The logical place to mount them is on the bottom side of the forward legs of the X-member. This closely retains the stock suspension geometry and provides ample clearance for most automatic transmissions.

Several street rod components man-

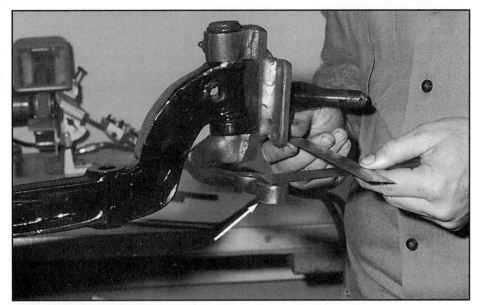

The base of a stock spindle arm (arrow) will not clear the "S" curve of a dropped axle. It must be slowly heated to a dull cherry red, but not too fast or too much. This is the first recontouring step.

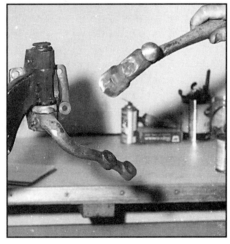

Work the softened spindle arm down and out until it can turn clear of the axle. This clearance is critical for free movement of the tie rod. A hammer and a pipe wrench are the tools of choice at this point. Exactly determining just how much twist is necessary is best done by bolting the radius rods and axle together and installing the assembly in the chassis with the axle centered.

ufacturers offer "Wishbone Splitting Kits" for 1935–40 Fords. Installation is similar in all cases. First, a threaded spud for the adjustable fitting is welded into the end of each radius rod. The favorite split-wishbone pivot is the tie-rod end. (It is easy to keep clean and lubricate.) Both rods are then assembled on the dropped axle. It's best to use new or replacement radius rod

bolts, but used ones in good condition often have a lot of service life left. The kit bracket(s) are then installed on the chassis.

In some cases, new boltholes will have to be drilled; in other applications, existing bolt or rivet holes are used. Either way, they must be positioned in a location compatible with the length of the radius rods. Some of

the brackets are small; all are substantial. Others that do double-duty, such as providing a rear transmission support plate, are fairly large.

Roll the modified radius rod and dropped axle assembly under the frame. Bolt the adjustable ends in the brackets and center the axle in the frame using the square hole in the crossmember as a reference point. You'll see that when the wishbone is split and the radius rods are moved outward, the shackle bushing-to-axle angle changes. To correct this, you must heat the arm and twist the bosses back out to their original 90 degree relationship. Although this can be approximated before the axle assembly is moved under the car, final adjustments must be made with the assembly securely bolted in the frame, front and rear. The spring with new shackle bushings installed can then be trial fitted. Recontouring spindle arms is a two-man job. It is a hot job as well, wear those welding safety goggles.

Now the problem is to regain full rotation of the spindles on the dropped axle. The unmodified steering arm will not adequately clear the bend of a dropped axle. Although some additional muscle will be needed, you should be able to make this change. You'll need a large vise, an oxyacetylene outfit with a #5 tip, a large pipe wrench, and two straight edges. A length of steel tubing or heavy pipe can be used to lever steering arms. It's possible to reshape the steering arms with the dropped axle and spring assembly mounted in the frame, but it's easier to do it on the bench. The process of heating, bending and reshaping early Ford steering arms is essentially the same for all models. Before you begin, carefully study the

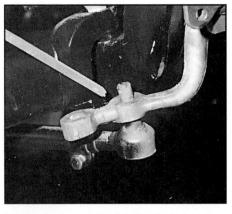

Recheck your work periodically to be sure all original relationships have been maintained even though the arm looks distorted. Everything must be square and parallel to the ground. Don't forget the tie rod must adequately clear the radius rod.

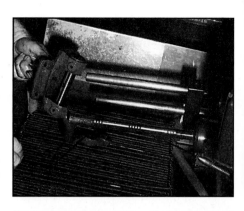

The last step is to replace the kingpins and bushings, a job best left to an automotive machine shop where both spindle bores are honed simultaneously to ensure perfect alignment and full pin-to-bushing contact.

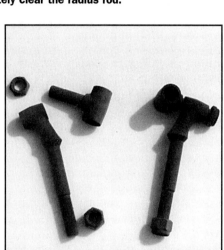

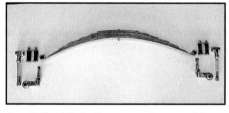

Specialized Auto Components assembles a transverse spring kit for 1935–40 Ford models.

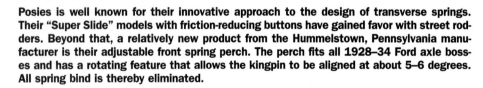

Posies is well known for their innovative approach to the design of transverse springs. Their "Super Slide" models with friction-reducing buttons have gained favor with street rodders. Beyond that, a relatively new product from the Hummelstown, Pennsylvania manufacturer is their adjustable front spring perch. The perch fits all 1928–34 Ford axle bosses and has a rotating feature that allows the kingpin to be aligned at about 5–6 degrees. All spring bind is thereby eliminated.

accompanying photos.

Rebushing the Spindles

The next step is to rebush the spindles and replace the kingpins. If you've ever driven an old Ford with a worn-out front end, you know what "shimmy and shake" means. The built-in tendency of a solid axle to cause wheel tramp can be dramatically aggravated with worn kingpin bushings. When the kingpins start to wallow around in the spindles, all semblance of driveability disappears.

Fortunately, spindle reconditioning is easy, requiring no more than a trip to an automotive machine shop. Every automotive machine shop has a honing machine, primarily used for fitting piston pins and reconditioning connecting rods. They hone both spindle bores simultaneously to ensure perfect alignment and full pin-to-bushing contact.

Spring Replacement

Now is the time to replace the original transverse leaf spring. NOS springs (when available from antique

car parts houses) come in six varieties: 1928–31 (A-5310), 1932–34 (40-5310), 1935–39 (78-5310), 1940 (O1 A-5310), 1941 (11A-5310), and 1942–48 (51A-5310).

Manufacturers of new street rod springs aren't such sticklers for detail. They usually lump 1928–34 models together and 1935–48 passenger-car models together. There's no harm done. Only a purist would find fault— and purists don't build street rods.

Although it is possible to recondition an original spring bundle by breaking it down, thoroughly cleaning it, and then reassembling it, don't do it unless you need the exercise. Old springs are just that . . . old. There's no sense in trying to make do, considering that a new spring assembly is reasonably priced and, when assembled with polypropylene liners or buttons, ride

As soon as my old friend B. F. O'Brien set up his alignment gauges, he noted that the axle in this Forty had an unusually bad bend, and that the camber was "way out of whack."

The four-link or parallel radius rod suspension, pioneered by Pete & Jake, has become standard equipment for 1928–34 street rods. They are also showing up with ever-increasing frequency on later model, full-fendered rods

In order to rectify the problem, O'Brien had to substantially secure the front suspension in his Hunter Alignment Machine. These holding devices don't just look massive, they are! That's a 20-ton jack on the left, and a 12-ton jack on the right. O'Brien advised that normally old Ford front suspensions don't have enough camber, ". . . so we hold the axle on the ends and push it in the middle to bring the ends out. I am doing just the opposite here, I am holding it in the middle and pushing it out at both ends. That decreases the camber." The procedure may take several applications before the technician is satisfied that the axle has been trued . . . and will stay true. "Usually I can bend an original axle with one 12-ton jack because most of the time I am increasing the camber. Here, I had to hold it on one end and bend it on the other. Sometimes I have to work both side until I get it just right."

improvement is significant.

REPLACING THE STOCK RADIUS RODS ALTOGETHER

It is entirely possible you don't want to go through the hassle of tearing apart the existing front suspension and modifying the stock radius rods and spindles. You don't have to; you can purchase new parts from a number of manufacturers to complete your front suspension. Everything you need is as close as your mailbox. Once again, we must thank the pioneers of the street rod parts industry.

The parallel radius rod suspension showed up on track roadsters built right after WWII, but it wasn't seen on many street rods until Pete & Jake came along. They "re-invented" and popularized it in the early 1970s.

The parallel radius rod suspension is deceptively simple. It eliminates many of the suspension problems encountered when an early Ford front suspension assembly is modified. The four-link setup eliminates binding and cast-

er angle changes. The ends of the axle can move up and down independently with virtually no twisting or binding. Ride and handling are improved considerably.

The installation of a four-link suspension is straightforward. The frame brackets are positioned on the side rails using factory holes as reference points. Once located, they are welded in place, and the remaining components bolted together.

SETTING IT STRAIGHT – HEAVY DUTY FRONT END ALIGNMENT

The old-time I-beam axle is one tough number. Even when it is subjected to the rigors of stretching and dropping, it usually bounces back with renewed vigor, ready for another forty or fifty years of road service. However, not without a little old-timey R&R.

Many times the dropped original axle is out of shape, making an alignment check a must. One simply cannot buy and install a dropped original axle

and expect to drive on down the road with no problem. Mind you now, we are not talking about new manufacture, early Ford style, early Ford axles.

135

WHEEL ALIGNMENT CHART
(Courtesy Bear Manufacturing Corp.)

Trouble	Camber	Caster	Turning Radius	Toe-in	Steering Gear	Wheels
Cuppy Tire Wear						Bent or Out-of-Balance
ExcessiveTire Wear	Incorrect		Incorrect	Incorrect		
Pulling to One Side	Unequal	Unequal				
Wander or Weave		Not Enough		Incorrect	Loose or Tight	
Hard Steering		Too Much			Tight	
Excessive Road Shock		Too Much			Loose or Worn	
Low Speed Shimmy		Too Much			Loose or Worn	Bent or Out-of-Balance
High Speed Shimmy						Bent or Out-of-Balance

The above should be considered probable causes only. Steering problems and excessive tire wear can also be cause by faulty brakes, a bent frame, improperly adjusted front wheel bearings, improper tire inflation, faulty shocks, loose spring shackles, weak springs and out-of-round tires.

STOCK EARLY FORD WHEEL ALIGNMENT DATA

Year	Model	Preferred Caster (Degrees)	Preferred Camber (Degrees)	Toe-In (Inches)	Kingpin Inclination (Degrees)
1935–36	All	+ 6 3/4	+ 5/8	3/32	8
1937–38	All	+ 6 3/4	+ 5/8	1/16	8

Note: O'Brien further refines the above for street rods. "We want about three quarters of a degree of camber on the left, and about half a degree on the right within a quarter or half a degree thereof.

These are in perfect shape and usually only a minor alignment of the front suspension is required after everything has been assembled.

Major problems only arise in true dropped axles where a stock component has been modified to obtain that highly desirable lowered look. Ninety-nine percent of them are bent one way or the other. The company that does the dropping will usually straighten out the axle so that it lies flat, but that's about all. You will not be fully aware of just how significantly it is twisted or bent until it has been placed in service and you experience squirrelly handling or premature tire wear. Either way, you are a good candidate for a first class, heavy-duty front-end alignment.

No big deal you say, you'll just head on out to the closest front end shop or tire store and let 'em have at it. Maybe yea, maybe nay.

Some type of alignment equipment with its caster, camber and toe-gauges is in all front-end shops. The major manufacturers are Hunter, Beeline, Bear, Weaver and Alemite. That doesn't mean just any shop can handle a street rodder's old car problems, however. The equipment is only half of the equation; the other half (perhaps the most important half) is the skilled operator. Most present day front-end shop personnel have only been schooled in late model independent front suspension service.

THE STEERING SYSTEM

13

The street rod builder has a number of steering boxes available to him. Many will function, but only a few are worth seriously considering.

If you chose the traditional early Ford transverse spring/parallel radius rod front suspension, your steering gear selection is more or less pre-determined by the kit manufacturer. The predominant options—early model Mustang or Cougar recirculating ball units—have been well tested and not found wanting. If you're using a Jag or Mustang II independent front suspension, the factory rack-and-pinion steering is the logical choice with a few options offered by some kit manufacturers.

If you have chosen to go it alone, your options are as many as there are different steering systems in the salvage yards. Nevertheless, the vast majority of builders still rely on a handful of manual and power-assist recirculating ball-and-nut steering gears and one or two rack-and-pinion selections. In short, the best steering gear is the one that is compatible with the type of front suspension you've selected and should come from a car that's in the same weight range as your street rod.

A wide variety of different steering setups has been used by street rod builders down through the years. These range all the way from rebuilt Model A gears to the latest power rack-and-pinion plucked from an expensive import. In the early days of street rodding, before and just after World War II, the most popular steering gear swap, believe it or not, was the 1934 Ford Gemmer. Compared to its pre-decessors, it had a very fast steering ratio. It slipped neatly down alongside the flathead V-8 in a Model A or Deuce frame. Guys who drove later model Fords rarely changed the factory steering box unless it was completely dry of grease and inoperable. Parts were available, most rods were light and easy on their feet, and few builders felt the need to look any further.

By the mid 1950s, however, the ravages of old age were beginning to be felt. The 1940–48 Ford Gemmer-3 gear and its cross-steering drag-link arrangement began to show up in 1935–36 Fords even though 1940-type spindles had to be used.

The parallel drag-link steering school of thought elected to use the then-new steering from 1954 and later Ford and Chevy pickups. The Ford F-100 gear was preferred, but the Chevy gear was easier to install. The Chevy unit only required minor frame trimming to fit; the F-100 gear required reworking or replacing the Pitman arm, and fabrication of a bracket. No matter, all of those possibilities are behind us now.

A NEW STEERING SYSTEM

Instead of using a traditional steering gear, use the best. In doing this, keep a few critical considerations in mind when choosing and installing steering components. Otherwise, you risk upsetting the already disturbed sleep of old Rudolph Ackermann, the father of modern steering geometry.

Steering geometry is not a fancy phrase. It refers to the arrangement of the steering system components in relation to the suspension components. For instance, it determines how much effort and how many spins of the steering wheel are required to make a turn. Steering geometry also determines

A side-by-side comparison of the old faithful 1940 Ford steering (left) with the mid-1960s classic Mustang box graphically shows their similarity. The hardware inside the Mustang, however, is what makes the critical difference . . . and a swap desirable.

how much each front wheel turns to negotiate a corner and how much road feedback is transmitted through to the steering wheel.

Ackermann Steering

Rudolph Ackermann devised the basic method of geometrically "correct" steering over 175 years ago. When doing this, though, he was working with low-speed, horse-drawn wagons, and such a thing as slip angle was unknown. Let's look more closely at Ackermann steering.

Ackermann steering is based on the premise that during a turning maneuver—right or left—the inside front wheel of a front-steer vehicle must turn more sharply than the outside wheel. This is sometimes referred to as "toe-out in a turn" because the inside front wheel must turn on a shorter radius than the outside wheel. However, they turn around the same point, which is on a line that is a projection of the rear-

axle centerline. As the turn tightens, turning radius decreases, and the turn-angle difference between the front wheels increases.

This steering arrangement reduces tire scrub, which would occur if both wheels turn at angles different from that of a perfect Ackermann geometry. However, because Ackermann didn't take into account slip angles—which move the center about which the vehicle turns forward—perfect Ackermann is not achieved, but is close enough.

What determines Ackermann? It's the relative locations of the inner and outer tie-rod pivots to themselves and the steering arms, and the angle of the steering arms. For instance, angle the steering arms in on a front steer setup and Ackermann increases steering angle between inside and outside wheels. On rear-steer setups, the reverse is true. Similar changes can be made to inner and outer tie-rod points, but further discussion can become overkill.

The Corvair steering box, cast-iron or aluminum cased, has been popular with T–bucket builders since it was first used in the early 1960s. It is often mounted on top of the frame, but to do so, the input shaft must be reversed in the housing.

Some Ford builders wouldn't be caught dead installing an early Chevy van steering gear in a traditional roadster. Nevertheless, the heavy-duty, and easily adaptable Saginaw box found in mid-1960s GM vans is worth considering.

Bump Steer

Bump steer is more important than Ackermann because it affects down-the-road handling. Bump steer at the front occurs when steering angle changes from nothing more than vertical wheel travel, such as from going over a bump or negotiating a turn. If steering wheel angle doesn't change, the vehicle is said to have neutral steer. Toe-out from bump steer promotes understeer, toe-in causes oversteer. It's oversteer that can be dangerous. However, an excessive amount of understeer is also undesirable.

To reduce oversteer in a front-steer vehicle (where the steering linkage is ahead of the front-wheel center line) the inner tie-rod points are raised. For a rear-steer vehicle, the inner tie-rod points are lowered. The opposite at the outer tie-rod ends achieves the same effect.

If your street rod has parallel drag-link steering, and you don't want one of the commercial cross steering kits, keep clear of trouble and stay with your current setup. Changing to cross steering on your own can get you in difficulties quickly. In fact, there's no pressing reason to use a cross steering setup on an early Ford type front end with a transverse-spring. In fact, most builders only switch to cross steering for cosmetic reasons—they don't want the steering to show.

One of the prime considerations in choosing a steering gear, or any other factory component for a street rod, is that a steering system designed for lightweight stockers should only be used in lightweight street rods. I don't know why this is often overlooked. Don't even consider a component—from steering to driveline—if the donor car weighs less than 90 percent of your street rod. In addition, if you have to guess, for safety's sake guess on the heavier side.

Speaking of safety, when it comes to modifying the hardware of a steering system, don't weld Pitman arms or other steering components unless you are a certified welder. Restrict steering modifications to machining whenever possible. If this can't be done, look for an alterative. Proceed with caution even if you are a certified welder. Have every welded component Magnafluxed at a USAC, FAA or similarly approved inspection station. These are usually found near municipal airports. Automotive machine shops are not the place to have critical suspension and steering components inspected. Go where the flyboys go. Beyond that, if you are planning to use other than a brand-new steering gear, have it checked. A good front-end alignment shop can do this. It'll never be cheaper or easier to do than right now.

Most street rods with a curb weight of 2500 pounds or less don't need power steering. Nevertheless, as you get closer to 3000 pounds, you'll appreciate a helping hand. If you have the room—and want faster steering—power units are usually about 25 percent faster than their manual counterparts are.

Before making your final decision, check out the street rod component manufacturers listed. Many installation kits are available for popular steering gears. Remember, it simply doesn't make sense to skimp where safety is involved. Professionals have already done the engineering—and found the problems you can expect if you try to reinvent a steering setup. You are buying safety when you go with one of them.

CONVENTIONAL STEERING GEARS

The first of the modern conventional steering gears used in street rods was the early 1960s Corvair, particularly the aluminum-cased version. It is a steering gear that has remained popular with the builders of lightweight

139

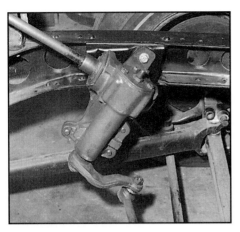

The classic Mustang steering is one nice installation in a heavy street rod such as a 1938–40 Ford sedan with stock style cross steering and a dropped axle. It is neat in appearance when viewed from above, and unobtrusive from the side once the engine is installed.

The Vega, from a relatively lightweight automobile, is best restricted to a lightweight rod. It and almost all late model steering gears are of the recirculating ball-worm and nut-gear design. The worm on the lower end of the steering shaft and the ball-nut which is mounted on the worm, have mating spiral grooves in which steel balls circulate to provide a low-friction drive.

Most popular steering boxes are well covered by the street rod components industry. This is the adapter, box, and Pitman arm offered by SAC Hot Rod Components.

street rods such as the Fad T. The Corvair gear is probably the best looking steering gear around when the aluminum case is polished and detailed.

At about the same time the Corvair steering was being accepted in street rod applications, along came the parallel drag-link steering systems from Chevy, Ford and Dodge vans. These occasionally appear on older street rods, but they are rarely installed nowadays.

It wasn't until the mid 1960s that street rodders found a manual steering gear that met most of their needs and has stood the test of time. This is the FoMoCo recirculating ball-and-nut gear used in the first Mustangs. It is a reliable manual steering gear for a 2500–2700-pound street rod. Adaptation required nothing more than simple bracketry. Two versions are currently popular with street rodders—one with a 1-inch sector, another with a 1 1/8-inch sector.

Later, the 1971–77 Chevrolet Vega steering was discovered to be very adaptable in lightweight street rods. (The Vega's curb weight was 2310

pounds.) These are available brand new, and Mullins Steering Gears has a replacement for the stocker—a 6061-T6 billet aluminum box that is a real looker.

The "big boy" in the GM line-up, however, is the large Saginaw series in both manual and power-assist ver-

sions. Pete & Jake helped popularize it when they offered an adapter plate for the manual version pirated from the 1964–65 Chevelle. This steering gear has a Pitman arm that can be re-tapered for Ford tie-rod ends. The power-assist Saginaw gear is larger than the manual, but not much. It has long been a favorite with builders of larger, heavier street rods, particularly later sedans.

These, then, are the popular conventional steering gears. This is not to infer that other gears are not as good or better for your installation. The wrecking yard is full of possibilities. The adventuresome may be tempted, but

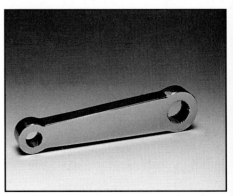

Flaming River of Ohio is a major manufacturer of over 50 critical steering components. Their colorful catalog is well worth paging through. One of the products that interested me is the performance Vega style steering box that is an all-new unit designed specifically for street rods. It is stronger than the OEM box with a smooth needle bearing design. It is further complimented by the aircraft steel alloy, double tapered Pitman arm.

If you really want heft in a heavy street rod, consider the power-assist GM 800 series. SAC Hot Rod Components has an adapter that bolts to the stock 1939–40 type steering bracket and the Saginaw box with only two minor modifications—enlargement of a hole in the stock bracket and one in the 800. Although not quite as discreet as the Mustang, the Saginaw 800 has all the authority your better half could desire.

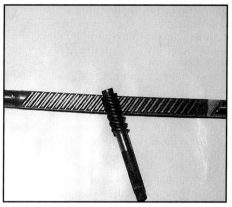

Stripped of its housing, the horizontal rack and the intersecting pinion are about as simple as a gear drive can get. Nevertheless, it steers a vast number of production cars and a good number of modern street rods!

don't forget, experimentation with steering gears can get tricky in a hurry. Use good common sense and prudence when looking over the wrecking yard crop.

By the way, if you are buying an older street rod, and you're not planning to change anything on the front end, it's always a good idea to have each component thoroughly inspected by a professional. One never knows what wrecking yard survivor went into the mix.

RACK-&-PINION STEERING

In discussing steering systems, just as with everything else, there are differences of opinion. Some builders prefer the plain and reliable engineering of the conventional recirculating ball-and-nut steering gear; others lean toward the sophistication of rack-and-pinion gears.

Germany's BMW first perfected

rack-and-pinion steering in the mid 1930s. The 1951 MG was the first rack-and-pinion equipped car to be sold in the United States. The first American car with rack-and-pinion steering, the Ford Pinto, didn't hit the road until twenty years later.

In the rack-and-pinion, turning the steering wheel transmits turning motion through a series of jointed shafts to a pinion gear. Pinion rotation is transformed into lateral sliding motion at the rack. Tie-rods attached to each end of the rack transmit this

lateral movement to the front wheels. Conventional steering drag links or Pitman arms are not required.

The ratio between turns of the steering wheel and of the front wheels is low. The result is quick, responsive steering. This quick ratio coupled with fewer parts between the steering wheel and the front wheels transmits more "feel" of the road than does conventional steering. Overall, it shouldn't be difficult to see why many builders think rack-and-pinion steering belongs in a street rod with an independent front suspension. It occupies little room in cars that most often are already crammed full of V-8 engine. In fact, of all the possible steering setups, the average rack-and-pinion gear interferes least with the engine and exhaust headers.

Unfortunately, the worst street rod steering installations I've encountered in older street rods have been poor rack-and-pinion swaps. Most of the problems involved a rack-and-pinion gear that was simply not designed for the suspension it was mated to or the loads foisted upon it. For a while, it

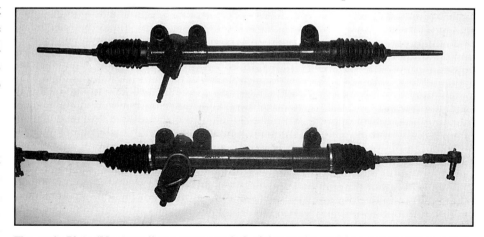

The early Pinto/Mustang II non-power rack & pinion works well in a car or pickup weighing 2500 pounds or less. The rubber mounts reduce shock loads and road noise. The steering ratio is 24:1 with four turns lock to lock. A manual rack and pinion is ideal for a responsive steering system in street rods and it eliminates the oversteer common with the power rack. If you are a little concerned with using a wrecking yard steering that has already seen 30 years of service, Flaming River Industries builds an all-new unit.

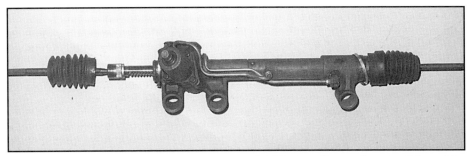

However, you may want to consider a power-assist Mustang II gear if your rod is weighs more than 2800 pounds. This backside view shows what you already know—special, dedicated plumbing and topside hardware is required. Ain't nothin' easy!

The Mustang II R&P, stock or aftermarket manufacture, manual or power-assist, is the only serious contender in any of the stock Mustang II adaptations or clones thereof.

was unjustly maligned in favor of conventional steering systems. That's behind us now.

Solid Axle Suspensions

One case that doesn't make any sense, however, is the attempt to mate a rack-and-pinion gear to a solid axle front suspension. It is possible, but not practical simply because a single tie-rod must tie both front wheels together. Moreover, the tie-rod must move with the axle. Consequently, to achieve correct steering geometry, the gear assembly has to be mounted on the axle. This, of course, increases unsprung weight. In addition, because the axle moves, splined, flexible couplings must be incorporated into the steering shaft. Rube Goldberg would be proud. So, if your car has a solid front axle, stick with conventional steering.

Independent Front Suspensions

The reverse holds true for street rods with independent front suspensions. In production cars without a rack-and-pinion, the steering linkage is divided into at least three separate components: Two tie-rods about as long as the suspension control arms and pivoting in similar arcs, and an idler arm to a relay rod—center link—across the width of the frame to an idler arm. Attempts to reproduce this hodge-podge of hardware in a street rod usually wind up with the builder pulling out his hair before he gets everything right. This is where the rack-and-pinion has a well-defined advantage. It's relatively easy to install. Just remember that the tolerable margin of error is very small with a rack-and-pinion installation.

The rack-and-pinion gear is normally bolted to brackets on the front suspension crossmember of the donor car. When installed in a street rod, the gear must be mounted on brackets that are equally flat and parallel. Anything less will warp the housing when it's bolted down, causing binding.

Furthermore, bump steer will occur when the steering geometry is incorrect. This can result if the length of the tie-rod is not equal to the length of the suspension control arms, if the tie-rod angle and the angle of the control arms are not equal, or if the centerline of the frame mounting is not in line with the tie-rod pivot. "Good road feel" can suddenly become very annoying when front wheel vibrations work their way back up to the steering wheel.

If that's not enough to scare you off, an improperly matched rack-and-pinion gear will make the car hard to park. It's because of that low steering ratio I spoke of earlier. Mechanical advantage is also low, and if the wrong rack and-pinion is installed, the effort required to steer the car at low speeds—or to park—is considerable.

It is common knowledge that the effective ratio of a conventional steering gear can be modified by shortening or lengthening the Pitman arm, but other than actually changing the size of the pinion gear in a rack-and-pinion assembly (which is hardly recommended) the only way to change the overall ratio is to shorten or lengthen the steering arms on the spindles themselves. This, of course, is possible, but it would be a touchy operation. I don't recommend it.

Finally, the location of the rack-and-pinion assembly is critical. The tie-rods should generally be placed near and parallel to the lower control arms.

The mix and match of steering components is an endless game. Just be sure all pieces are pirated from donor cars that weigh at least as much the rod you are building. In the case pictured, an Audi U-joint was used at the steering pinion, and a Jag U-joint was used at the column.

best steering system for a modern street rod with an independent front suspension. On the other hand, it's risky to design your own steering geometry without an in-depth knowledge of automotive engineering. Consequently, the rack-and-pinion installation kit offered along with independent front suspension kits is always the best route.

THE MISSING LINKAGE

The connection between a steering gear and steering column is of major importance. I am passing on to you the cardinal safety rules impressed on me by SCTA inspectors many years ago: 1) All welding on steering components should be performed by a government certified welder, not a novice with a $500 arc welder. 2) All welding on steering components must be subjected to appropriate non-destructive testing methods by a USAC or FAA certified-testing station. (Test stations can be found listed in the Yellow Pages

Likewise, the inner tie-rod pivots should be in line with the lower control-arm inner pivots. Obviously, some compromise may be required in a custom installation, but not much. You can only compromise on steering

geometry a little bit.

In no way is the foregoing meant to scare you away from a rack-and-pinion steering system. On the contrary. Rack-and-pinion steering is by far the

The steering column is often a hard choice to make. There is the original, which can often be slightly modified to work, and looks perfect in a resto-rod application. Next up is a slightly thicker column and linkages kit such as this one from Specialty Cars in Artesia, California.

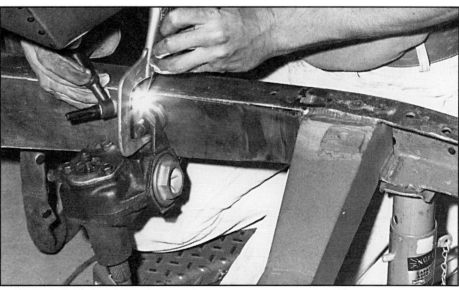

Steering adapters and brackets that are welded to the chassis require equipment and skills the beginning street rod builder is not likely to posses. Farm it out if you have any self-doubts. More importantly, all welded steering components must be welded by a certified technician. Anything less and you put your life at risk. Steering work is no place to cut costs.

The street rod builder who wants to design his own setup has to carefully consider space and mounting demands. There are three areas that call for close attention: The firewall exit, around the headers, and the front of the engine. Failure to accurately mock up the entire assembly can lead to enough problems to require a complete redo. That, you don't want!

under TESTING.)

Now, let's get on with the missing linkage—the connection between the steering column of your choice . . . and the steering gear you either selected or came with your front suspension upgrade. In most cases, you'll need one or two small aircraft-quality universal joints. In some cases, you'll also need a pillow block bearing, which has a housing that can be mounted on a flat surface or a bracket.

The amount of work that will be required to complete the installation depends largely on what steering column you are using. If the original column and steering shaft is used and installed in its original location (or at a slightly different angle to accommodate driver comfort or simply cosmetics), the shaft can be shortened a few inches. A careful analysis of the photos and captions should be sufficient for you to evaluate your own situation.

MANUFACTURERS AND SUPPLIERS

Flaming River Industries, Inc.
800 Poertner Drive
Berea, Ohio 44017
(440) 826-4488; Fax: (440) 826-0780
www.flamingriver.com

ididit, Inc.
610 S. Maumee Street
Tecumsah, Michigan 49286
(514) 424-0577; Fax: (517) 424-0577

Mullins Steering Gears
2876 Sweetwater Avenue, Suite 2
Lake Havasu City, Arizona 86406
(520) 505-3032; Fax: (520) 505-3055

SAC Hot Rod Products
633 W. Katella Blvd.
Orange, CA 92867-4627
(714) 997-3433, Fax: (714) 997-3693
www.sachotrod.com

Specialty Cars
17211 Roseton Avenue
Artesia, CA 90701
(562) 924-6904

INDEPENDENT FRONT SUSPENSION

14

The street rodder's love affair with the Jag IFS began some years ago. The genuine article is hard to come by these days, but there are some darn good replacements.

If you think that an independent front suspension swap under an early Ford hot rod was something dreamed up during street rodding's re-birth in the late 1960s, think again. In the spring of 1947, Ak Miller noticed that the coil-spring independent front suspension on a 1941 Chevy could be unbolted and, with a bit of modification, fitted under his Deuce highboy roadster. No sooner said than done, he welded it in place, boxed the frame to add torsional rigidity . . . and went out

to the El Mirage Dry Lake. In his first test run on El Mirage in July 1947, Ak clocked 106.25 mph with no problem. Later, he fondly recalls, he could "thread a needle with that thing at 120 mph! No more Ford dead axles for me."

Ak Miller, a dedicated hot rod racer and president of the Southern California Timing Association at the time, could never be called a traditionalist—his nonconformist powerplant in the same roadster was a Buick straight-eight!

WHY "NO MORE DEAD AXLES"?

There are several good reasons for using an independent front suspension under a street rod. It is better than any solid axle could ever hope to be in terms of both ride quality and handling superiority. Also, if the installation is properly done, it will enhance the market value of the street rod should a parting of the ways ever come.

There is a caveat, however: The ego

trip that owning a street rod provides leaves no room for anything that doesn't look good. Only a stranger to this hobby underestimates the street rodder's penchant for beauty and grace in things mechanical. (Such things in other folks' cars are usually covered with road grime and grease.)

That's probably why the independent front suspension didn't catch on earlier than it did. It's true, there were half-hearted attempts to popularize the mundane Corvair IFS in the early 1960s. However, it was the wrong time and the wrong place. The Corvair excited few fenderless car owners and only slightly more full-fendered rod builders.

ENTER THE JAG

I'm not sure who was the first street rod builder to consider the E-Type Jaguar independent front suspension, but one of the oldest hands at installing a Jag in an early Ford was Jerry Kugel. Kugel started building installation kits in 1969 for '32 Fords. Why they were immediately accepted is no mystery—they fit well under many early street rods . . . and they looked good.

The early 1960s E-type Jaguar coupe and roadster with wheelbases and front/rear treads of 96 and 50 inches, respectively, had overall dimensions not unlike early Ford coupes and roadsters. True, they weighed several hundred pounds more than the typical Deuce highboy did, but the weight was in the body and engine. The well-designed front and rear independent suspension could do street rodders no harm. The basic design of the E-type Jag IFS incorporates a pair of unequal-length control arms. The spindles are attached to the outer ends of each pair of control arms and tubular shock

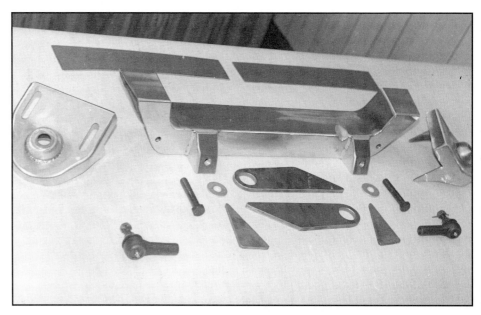

The demand for a clean installation of the wrecking yard Mustang II lead to the development of kits such as this early offering from Progressive Automotive.

Aftermarket crossmembers eventually gave way to entire (or nearly so) reproductions. This is one of the Total Cost Involved's IFS assemblies.

absorbers. Instead of coil springs, torsion bars are used. The torsion bars are attached at their forward end to the lower control arm, and at their rears to brackets on the frame. The top of each shock is mounted to a frame bracket, the bottom to the lower control arm.

Unfortunately, even though the expensive Jaguar front suspension provided the best of both worlds—engineering and aesthetics—the supply of available Jaguar suspensions has dramatically dwindled. That's the

bad news. The good news is that new products have appeared, and today, the range runs from independent front suspensions incorporating a mix of aftermarket components and inexpensive wrecking yard parts to completely new fabrications. With a little planning, one of these suspensions can be neatly tucked away out of sight under the vast expanse of sheet metal that covers the front ends of not just early Fords, but most 1935 to 1948 cars and light trucks.

CHOOSING A PRACTICAL IFS

Cost and aesthetics aside, there are three major factors you must consider when selecting an independent suspension for a given street rod frame—width, vehicle weight and suspension adaptability. Although a particular IFS may work like a charm in the donor car, it may be inappropriate for your street rod.

Minor variations in frame width can be compensated for in the design of the replacement crossmember. A hundred pounds either way in load capacity can be accommodated with spring interchanges from a heavier model, custom-wound springs or coil-over-shock suspension units.

Awkward configurations and mountings can often be dealt with by installing a custom fabricated crossmember that accepts the new suspension components and fits the old chassis. Another approach is a judicious reengineering of the original suspension hardware. That's part of trial-and-error street rod building. Nevertheless, you must start from a logical point again: width, structural stability, and overall adaptability.

The one economical independent front suspension found to be close to ideal for installing in street rods based on cars from the mid-1930s to the late 1940s is the 1974–78 Mustang II and its slightly smaller clones (the 1974–80 Ford Pinto and Mercury Bobcat) that used many of the same components. It dominates the field.

Mustang II IFS

In its original setting, the Mustang II front suspension with its stabilizer bar and compression-type struts mounts in a subframe. The coil springs are on the

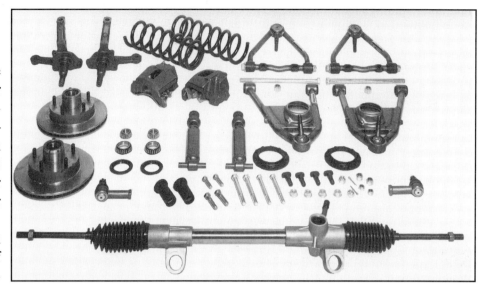

The 1974–78 Mustang II and 1974–80 Ford Pinto and Mercury Bobcat is close to ideal for mid-1930s to the late 1940s street rods. Pictured is the complete kit offered by Heidt's Hot Rod Shop. Larger-than-stock rotors are frequently optional and worth any additional cost.

Installation of a Mustang II independent front suspension requires fabrication skills. Only you know if you have them. If not, there is professional assistance all around the country. This job is being tackled by the Heinzman Street Rod Shop in Phillips, Nebraska.

lower control arms with the shock absorbers mounted in the center. The Mustang II front tread is 55.6 inches—a fraction narrower than its rear tread. The verifiable-ratio rack-and-pinion steering is available in both manual and power versions, but the power version typically proves the better choice for cars approaching the 3000-pound mark. The Mustang II's 9.3-inch disc-brake rotors, even though smallish, add a plus to the mix, making this suspension even more desirable. Best of all, the 1978 Mustang II with the V-8 option had a curb weight of about 2750 pounds—close to the typical full-fendered coupe, sedan and pickup based street rod.

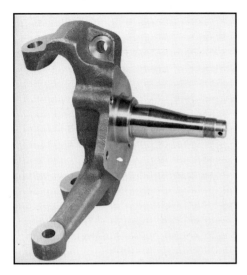

Heidt's Hot Rod Shop advises that stock Ford spindles are steel, not cast iron. Consequently, they offer 2-inch dropped Mustang II spindles made from 1045 heat-treated alloy steel. All stock rotors, bearings, calipers, etc. fit, making them easy to install.

I've got to hand it to Brent VanDevort of Fat Man Fabrications. He now offers an independent front suspension modification kit that doesn't sacrifice the classic look of the dropped axle. His Vintage IFS™ for 1928–34 Fords (even highboys) cleverly incorporates a Vega cross steering. It will work with most 2-inch tubular axles such as the SuperBell Magnum running either four bar or radius rod linkage. He reports ride height is not changed and camber angle is fully "tunable" with the supplied mini-leaf spring kit and stacking shims. All parts to be modified are unbolted from the chassis for ease and accuracy.

The late 1970s Mustang II has conventional short upper and long lower control arms. The control arms are isolated from the body structure by large rubber bushings. Because the coil springs are mounted on the lower arms, the spring towers are low. The compression struts, which extend from the lower control arms to an anchoring bracket on the frame, are also mounted in rubber. This feature allows the front wheel to deflect slightly to lessen road shock.

The Mustang II front suspension was engineered to minimize toe change from wheel travel and turning to improve handling and minimize tire wear. Finally, the control arms are angled—as are all modern front suspensions—to minimize nose-dive during braking. About the only drawback to the Mustang II front suspension is the installation. Although the control arms and excellent power rack-and-pinion steering packages with the stock crossmember readily fit under a variety of street rodable cars, the mere thought of removing, cleaning up and then welding in the factory crossmember, was enough to bring a shudder to even an experienced rod builder 20 years ago. No wonder it wasn't long before the street rod components industry took over.

Street rod builders have come a long way since Ak Miller first peeked under that '41 Chevy.

Fat's Narrowed IFS

Fat Man Fabrication's 56 1/2 inch narrowed rack-and-pinion kit uses a modified Mustang II R&P, either power or manual. The one in this installation is a manual. (The manual steering gear's slower ratio delivers more responsive handling, although parking requires a tad more shoulder in heavier cars. Manual steering also has the added advantage of being easier to hook up with no pump problems.) The kit rack is shortened and the housing is sectioned for an overall two-inch reduction, but it mounts stock-like, bolting through the crossmember. It is rigid and shimmy-free, and is aligned using stock Mustang II specs.

Why narrow a stock R&P at all? Well, Fords of the 1935–40 era with a stock width Mustang II IFS are limited to a 14x6 wheel with zero offset, or a special back spaced wheel. The narrowed kit allows up to a 15x7 wheel.

Kits come with complete instructions, but this brief photographic trail of Bud Matthews's installation in a '40 will give readers unfamiliar with the general procedure a better idea of what awaits them.

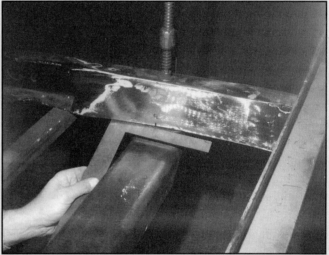

With the car securely supported by jackstands, and everything forward of the firewall removed, including the original crossmember, Bud located the axle centerline using the original rubber snubber holes, which are 11 1/8 inches behind the rear holes for the front bumper brackets. He then made a temporary brace at the forward end of the frame to maintain the original dimensions during the welding that would follow. (The outside rail-to-rail measurement should not exceed 30 1/2 inches on 1935–40 Fords.) The frame rails must be substantially boxed from where the original X-member terminates to a point 4 inches forward of the axle centerline.

Bud clamped the kit crossmember to the frame rail after carefully referencing the center marks. The outer holes, which mount the lower A-frame, must be equidistant from each frame rail. Welding takes place only after all checks are satisfied.

The shock towers/spring mounts were next clamped to a length of angle iron in the way they mount to the frame. The shock mounts are 35 1/2 inches center-to-center on the 1935–40 Ford.

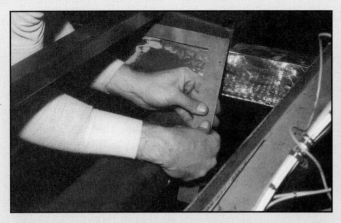

With the assembly atop the frame on the axle centerline, the point where they must be notched to clear the frame was located and cut out to a depth indicated by the inside lip of the shock tower.

Bud rechecked the center-to-center distance, the levelness across frame, and the angle with respect to the ground. The flat part of the shock tower should be level when viewed from the front with a slight downward rake at the rear to recreate the stock Mustang anti-dive geometry. When everything is perfect, Bud welded the assembly in place. The kit-supplied gussets were then welded in to support the shock tower.

Matthews mounted the lower control arm (minus the spring), bolted on the strut rod, and installed the kit-supplied bracket with the flat face aligned with the outside of the frame rail. He heated the rod to a dull red just back of the lower control, bent it outward until the brackets aligned with the frame rail and welded it in place. The strut rod is in line with the crossmember for maximum strength, and the bracket is made of quarter-inch plate, doubled to a half-inch at the bushing for extra strength.

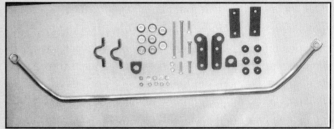

It's not exactly cutting edge technology, inasmuch as a front anti-roll bar first appeared on Fords in 1940, but it is necessary. Period. Pictured is the Total Cost Involved kit.

Installation is straightforward. The front hole of the pillow block is located at the third factory rivet back from the front of the frame rail, but of course, the rivet must be center-punched and then drilled out. The bar is bolted to the chassis using the kit-supplied pillow blocks and urethane bushings.

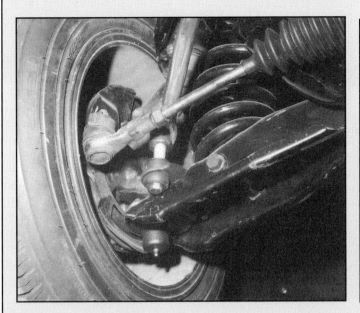

Then the lower mount is installed on the bottom of the spring perch, and the connecting link between bar and lower mount is made using the hardware and urethane bushings supplied.

Does an independent front suspension and a length of twisted spring steel bring sports car handling to a 63-year-old highboy coupe? Not really, but the net gain in handling relative to the cost and work involved is substantial.

THE INDEPENDENT FRONT SUSPENSION KIT MANUFACTURERS

Chris Alton's Chassisworks
8661 Younger Creek Dr.
Sacramento, CA 95828
(800) 722-2269
(916) 388-0288
Fax (916) 388-0295
www.cachassisworks.com

One of the first to adapt Mustang II IFS to street rods, Alton provides step-by-step photo-illustrated instructions "prepared with the home builder in mind." His all-new A-arm system boasts modern handling, braking, ride and appearance, plus correct steering geometry.

Fat Man Fabrications
8621-C Fairview Road. Hwy. 218
Charlotte, NC 28227-7619
(704) 545-0369; FAX (704) 573-0401
www.fatmanfab.com

Brent Van Derwort knows that correct steering geometry is critical, but all too often overlooked in the homebrew mix and match automobiles we call street rods. That's why he and his crew of experienced hot rodders, (led by a trained engineer, no less) go to great pains to insure every kit they sell has the correct geometry built in. Beyond that, some cars just don't look right or function properly with a more or less standard MII IFS, particularly those with Model A style fender lines. Fat Man's "Affordable IFS" is custom made for many unusual cars. No matter what you are planning to build, Fat Man can probably come up with an installation. The company's crossmembers are made with 5/16-inch wall material (the heaviest in the industry) and 3/16-inch top plates. All components are sawn or plasma cut. Brent's proudest boast, however, is his industry exclusive narrowed Mustang II kits for 1933–40 Ford models which often have tire-to-fender fit problems when a stock width Mustang II IFS is installed.

Heidt's Hot Rod Shop, Inc.
1345 N. Old Rand Road
Wauconda, IL 60084
(800) 841-8188

Long-time street rod components manufacturer Gary Heidt has the entire range of independent front suspension kits and parts in his catalog, but I always look for the hidden treasures—those items that are not offered by any other company. Heidt's one-piece dropped Mustang II spindles fit the bill. His 2-inch dropped spindle is manufactured from 1045 heat-treated alloy steel, and uses stock rotors, bearings and calipers. (It is noteworthy that stock factory geometry is retained.) In general, Heidt's kits include a TIG welded main crossmember for maximum strength, adjustable tubular arms, 11-inch vented disc brake rotors in either the Ford or Chevy lug pattern, adjustable coil-over shocks with chrome springs, front-mount rack-and-pinion steering, stainless steel adjusters with urethane bushings and factory ball joints and tie-rod ends. An additional Heidt offering that merits consideration when the rod builder has something other than the pre-WWII Ford in mind is the 60-inch tread width MII kit. It is intended for use with his 4-inch rack extension kit to keep the steering geometry in line.

Heinzman Street Rod Shop
1305 North C Road
Phillips, NE 68865
(402) 886-2275
Fax (402) 886-2998

A builder of frames with independent front suspension for 1934–57 Chevrolets and 1928–48 Fords with over 25 years of experience.

Kugel Komponents
451 Park Industrial Drive
La Habra, CA 90631
(562) 691-7006
Fax: (562) 691-5708
www.kugelkomponents.com

There's no immediate threat of a shortage of Mustang II, Pinto and Bobcat front suspensions, but the supply of available E-Type Jag front suspensions has grown smaller each year. Therefore, a handful of enterprising street rod shop owners eventually began marketing a hybrid design of Detroit and Coventry front-suspension hardware that functions similar to that of the Jag, and honestly looks better!

The Kugel IFS is in the forefront of this "new wave." The heart of Jerry's "Kugel Komponents Stainless Steel Independent Front Suspension" is a one-piece spindle and upright, and a bolt-on steering arm. Both the upright—on which the spindle has been relocated vertically for a lower ride height—and the steering arm have been investment cast of 17-4 stainless steel. Stainless-steel caliper adapters, JFZ aluminum calipers and Chevy disc-brake rotors, bearings and ball joints round off the wheel assemblies. Kugel's upper and lower A-arms are fabricated of 7/8-inch x 0.156-inch wall 304 stainless-steel tubing. The lower arms are made of 1-inch x 0. 188-inch wall 304 stainless. The Kugel IFS breaks with the Jag influence with regard to steering and springs. Coil-over shocks and Vega cross steering is used, a concept, Jerry reports, that is borrowed from Porsche. Overall, the Kugel IFS is a tidy, carefully engineered package that is found under many high-tech street rods.

Progressive Automotive
125 W. Rome Street
Baltimore, OH 43105
(800) 232-6512; (740) 862-3330
www.progressiveautomotive.com

Progressive is located in the rolling hills of south-central Ohio, but the company has spread their fame wherever street rodders congregate. It was begun in 1976 by Frank Shetrone, Keith Helwig, and Tom Artusi to develop independent front suspension kits for street rods based on the Mustang II suspension. They have come a long way. Owned and operated today by Bob Shetrone (Frank's son), Progressive manufactures complete street rod chassis, leaf spring and four-link suspension kits, and fiberglass 1947–53 Chevy truck bodies!

The Rod Factory
3131 N. 31 Avenue
Phoenix, AZ 85017
(602) 269-0031
www.rodfactory.com

Builders of "Hi-Tech IFS chassis" for 1928–32 and 1932–34 Fords, as well as a variety of Mustang II crossmember kits for 1936–54 Chevys and 1942–52 Ford pickups.

Scott's Hot Rods 'n Customs
1255 Callens Road
Ventura, CA 93003
(805) 658-7467
Fax (805) 639-3398
www.scottshotrods.com

Scott's advertises that their "SuperSlam" is the only IFS on the market with nine inches of travel while keeping correct castor and camber. A variety of hub-to-hub assemblies are offered including some with air-bag suspension.

Street Rod Engineering, Inc.
P. O. Box 1932
Lake Havasu City, AZ 86405
(928) 855-5616
Fax (928) 505-3740
www.streetrodengineering.com

Street Rod Engineering states their fully assembled kits are ready to install and feature "super strong design welds to both vertical walls of frame as well as across the bottom. Several times the weld area as competitor's kits that only weld to the bottom or insides of frame." They also point out that their "rack-and-pinion mounts are leaned back to make steering shaft hook-up much easier, requiring fewer U-joints."

Total Cost Involved Engineering, Inc.
1416 W. Brooks Street
Ontario, CA 91762
(909) 984-1773
Fax (909) 391-1526
www.totalcostinvolved.com

This company, long known for their reproduction frames and ready–to-roll chassis, also builds (on a custom basis) a complete IFS system that they advertise is the "easiest to install and align."

Total Performance, Inc.
400 South Orchard St., Rte. 5
Wallingford, CT 06492
(800) 243-6740; Fax (203) 265-7414
www.tperformance.com

Total Performance offers their own E-Jag IFS installation kit for the Model T, A, Deuce and 1933–34 Ford. The kit includes front shocks and mounting brackets of their design, which necessitates modifications to the spindles. TPI provides the instructions or will perform the machining and welding operation in-house for you. They also have a kit to mount either the Saab rack-and-pinion or Vega cross steering in place of the Jag gear.

THE STREET ROD REAREND

15

There are a great many possibilities when one is shopping for a rearend for a street rod project. Always canvas your rodding buddies first, but remember most auto dismantlers provide return privileges.

Even when flathead power was fast-disappearing, one could live with a reconditioned, but old-fashioned front suspension and steering. However, once torque production doubled, failures could be expected in an original rearend, rebuilt or not.

The worst offenders in early Ford torque tube drivelines were the axle keys, the axles proper and the drive-shaft. It didn't take much torque to break something. Surprisingly, original Ford transmissions and U-joints were reasonably reliable with mild flathead power.

155

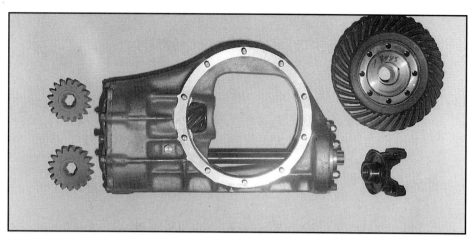

The "quick-change" gear assembly was developed during the heyday of midget and sprint car racing . . . and torque tube drivelines. Ted Halibrand's version was soon adopted as the standard for Dry Lakes and Bonneville cars, and eventually it was featured under high buck street rods. The street rodder who wants to remain as faithful to tradition as possible can have his cake and eat it too, with the much more modern (and strong) Halibrand setup for an open driveline.

The Halibrand has competition in the street rod market today as witness this handsome Dutchman Motorsports QC displayed at the 2002 L.A. Roadster Show.

Today, only restorers and die-hard traditionalist street rodders chance using early Ford rearends. Almost every owner of an original sheet metal resto-rod has relegated the torque tube rear axle assembly to a dark corner of the garage, hoping some restorer will buy it. He doesn't want to build unreliability into his new car just for the sake of tradition.

Beyond that, although you may pride yourself on being able to do most of what needs to be done on your project car, not everyone can be a renaissance man—a design engineer, machinist and prototype fabricator. We all draw on the skills of our acquaintances, automotive repair professionals, and of course, the manufacturers of street rod components.

This is demonstrated by the universal problem of safely installing a late-model rear axle assembly. Component manufacturers from the very beginning of street rodding have met the need with well-designed and economical products to hang a modern rearend. If you wanted to tie a date to the start of their efforts, my money would be on February 11, 1959. That's when Gene Scott, originator of Hot Rod Hardware, opened the doors of Performance Specialties, Inc., better known as PSI.

Until that time, nonprofessional rod builders toiled over the design of locating and anchoring devices as well as spring and shock mounts. Salvage yard steel plate was often the material for fabrication. It was great fun, though. That's why some of us stayed in the hobby for so long. Nevertheless, the product of those labors of a bygone day wasn't the best appearing piece of hardware. Gene Scott not only changed that, he single-handedly launched the entire street rod components industry. I'll continue our discussion of rearend installation in a later chapter. For now, let's examine the late model rearend itself more closely.

THE MODERN REAR AXLE ASSEMBLY

The most common rear axle assembly incorporates a one-piece housing containing the differential and axles. It is typically located in street rods by semi-elliptic leaf springs mounted longitudinally to the chassis (the Hotchkiss drive), or with coil-over-shock suspension units mounted at an angle. Vertical coil springs are less common today, and torsion bar suspensions are very rare. In all cases, however, the rearend proper is free to move and transmit cornering, braking and driving forces to the chassis.

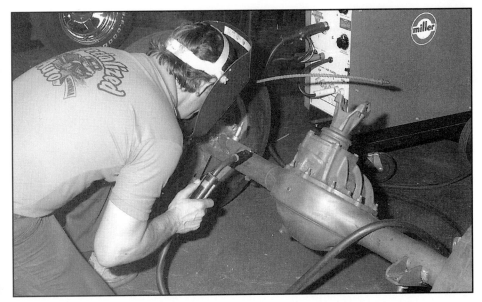

Few would argue against a late model rearend as the most practical for street rods in terms of expense and installation requirements. Its reliability is why it has been used for so long in so many cars and light trucks. Best of all, it is a snap for the homebuilder to slide under his street rod with the use of a commercial installation kit.

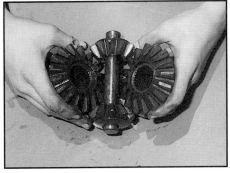

All street-driven vehicles have to make turns, and when a vehicle turns, the wheel closest to the center of the circle traverses less real estate than the wheel farthest from the center. The "spider assembly," a set of four small gears, permits differences in speed and direction of motion. The larger two, properly called side gears, are splined to the axles.

Inside the Conventional Rearend

Most rodders know rearend gears are there to multiply engine torque and propel the car. Although there are several design variations, they all incorporate a driving gear, called the drive pinion, that is linked directly to the engine by means of the flywheel and clutch (or flexplate and torque converter), the transmission proper, and the driveshaft. Within the differential housing, the pinion meshes with a driven gear called the ring. The ring gear is fitted to the axles by means of beveled side gears.

When a car negotiates a turn, the inside rear wheel covers less ground than the outside wheel. If there weren't some mechanical accommodation, the inside tire would spin, wearing off rubber in the process. Differential pinion gears (not to be confused with the drive pinion) resolve this conflict. These little gears, in sets of two or four depending on strength demands, are commonly called "spiders."

Driven by the ring gear, the differential pinion gears mesh with the side gears at the ends of the axle shafts. They transmit the power flow to either axle, but not always with the same torque or speed. For instance, if one axle offers less resistance, it gets more torque. If resistance is equal, torque is transmitted equally. This torque-splitting feature can be a mixed blessing, as you may well know if you've ever been stuck in the mud.

The open driveshaft rear axle assembly as described above has seen wide service in most American rear-wheel-drive passenger cars since the 1930s. There are two major types, however. One employs a removable gear carrier, the other an integral gear carrier. Street rodders have learned the former is far more user friendly.

Removable Carrier Rearend

The removable carrier, sometimes called the third member or drop out, contains the driveshaft yoke, drive pinion, ring gear, two side gears, two to

Almost everything you've read says that the Ford "drop out" 9-inch gear carrier is the way to go. Here it is in all its greasy glory. Like all modern rearend gears, it is of the "hypoid" design. Hypoid means the centerline of the drive pinion is below rather than on the horizontal centerline of the ring gear. There is a wiping action between the ring gear and pinion, however, and that is why a specially formulated "hypoid lubricant" must be used in a modern rearend.

four differential pinion gears, and the supporting bearings. The splined end of each axle slips into the side gears. Within the gear carrier, the drive pinion is mounted in two tapered roller bearings. It is overhung at the gear end, as opposed to being straddle mounted, as is the case with the integral carrier rear.

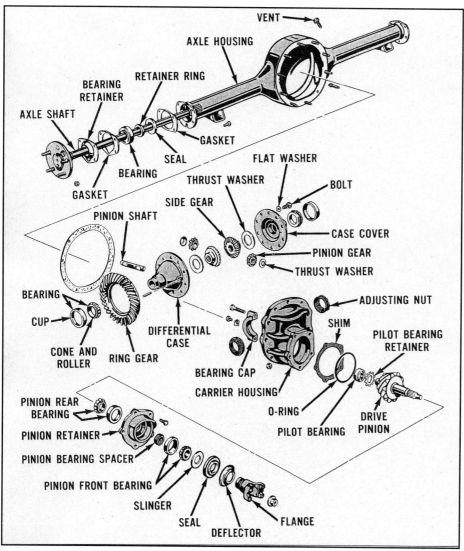

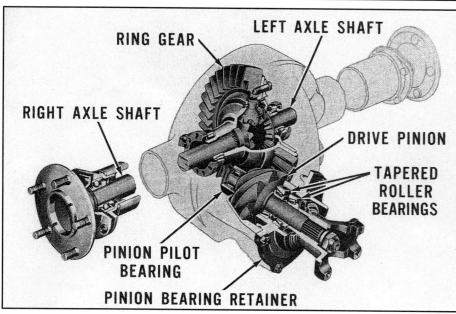

Removable carrier details.

The drive pinion is preloaded by a spacer and precisely located by a shim between it and the rear pinion bearing. The front bearing is held in place by a washer and locking nut. Ring-and-pinion backlash is regulated by the adjustment of two threaded sleeves.

The entire gear assembly is supported in the carrier by two more tapered roller bearings. Any adjustment or modification to the carrier assembly, such as the replacement of the drive pinion and ring gear, requires the skill and tools that only a professional will have. Consequently, you should farm out such work to a competent specialist.

Almost all modern conventional rearend assemblies are used in conjunction with an open driveshaft, a stout tube with an U-jointed slip yoke at the transmission end, and a companion flange and U-joint at the rear. In this configuration, it is readily adaptable to any American transmission or back axle assembly manufactured since the 1950s.

Rearends with removable carriers have been used in a number of Ford cars and light trucks from 1957 to date, as well as many from Chrysler and GM. The Ford back axle, however, is the only serious contender for use in a street rod. Its unitized axle housing and payload of massive gears and thick, non-tapered axles are so far superior in strength to early Ford counterparts as to render any comparison absurd.

Putting reliability aside for the moment, the beauty of a removable third member is the ease with which final drive ratios can be swapped. With the exception of a true quick-change rearend, no other design permits such easy gearset removal and installation.

As noted above, setting up a ring and pinion is a job for the professional.

However, once done, these assemblies have been known to live for 200,000 miles with nary a peep out of 'em! As to their versatility, street rodders who favor traditional manual transmissions for around-the-town performance keep a "taller" gear ratio on the shelf for long distance, open-road trips. (The advent of automatic and manual transmissions with built-in overdrive, however, has rendered that need obsolete.)

Integral Carrier Rearend

The other type of conventional rearend assembly is the integral carrier design, sometimes called a Salisbury, Spicer or Dana-Spicer. The most common versions are GM's 10- and 12-bolt Salisbury, and Chrysler's Spicer 60 series, which is manufactured by the Dana Corporation. These terms reflect the names of various designers and/or manufacturers and are unnecessarily confusing, so I use the simple generic designation of "integral gear carrier." Each type is encased in a similar appearing cast-iron, non-removable gear carrier with pressed-in steel axle tubes.

They are strong, rugged rears on their home turf, but every gear ratio change must be farmed out. Worst of all, the welding of radius rod brackets will easily warp the thin steel axle housing, often causing axle bearing failures. The brackets have also been known to tear off during hard acceleration when traction is good. All things being equal, the Ford back axle with its removable gear carrier is your best choice, assuming you have not decided on an independent rear suspension. However, not all Ford rears are created equal. If you plan to run a modified V-8, some are better than others.

The second of the two basic gear carrier designs is the integral type in which the drive gears are installed, piece by piece, through an access cover in the rear of the axle housing. Pictured is a 10-bolt Salisbury, so called because of the number of bolts fastening the cover to the housing. I hate to tell anybody who's contemplating one that it's a "weak sister," but I have to be honest.

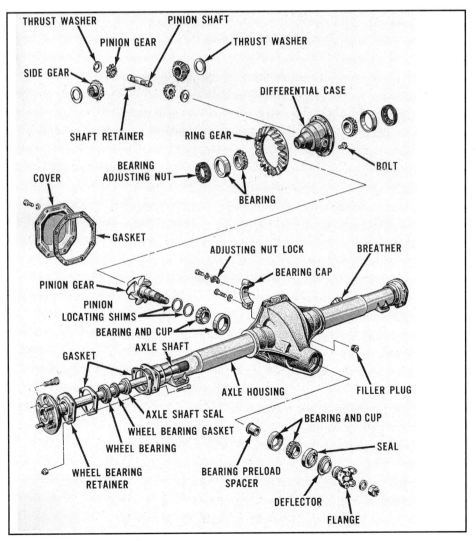

Integral gear carrier details.

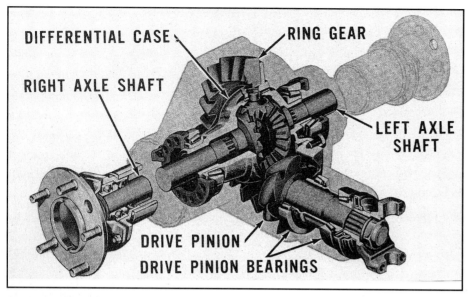

Integral carrier details.

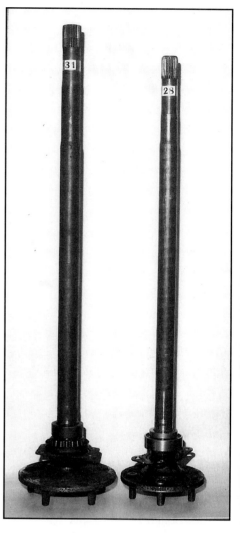

I'm not even going to try to list all the possible axle lengths in Ford rearends. Suffice it to say there's a bunch. It's not nearly so bad when it comes to 9-inch axle thickness/spline count, however. The 9-inch is commonly found with 28-spline axles. For rodding purposes, it is more than tough enough. The 31-spline axle is about 30-percent stronger, but that is overkill.

MORE THAN ONE FORD

Within the Dearborn lineup, several different ring-and-pinion assemblies have been used in passenger cars. One has an 8 3/4-inch ring gear with two differential pinions; another has a 9-inch ring gear. Beefier than both is one with a 9 3/4-inch ring gear and four differential pinions, all encased with a nodular-iron housing. The latter can be identified by a bold "N" cast on the front. All 8 3/4-inch ring gear assemblies, commonly, but erroneously called an 8-inch, and most 9-inchers have 28-spline axles. The 9 3/4-inch heavy-duty units have 31-spline axles. The latter is not interchangeable as is. No matter, they are expensive, and are overkill for most street rods.

The factory intended the 8-inch gear in intermediate-weight cars with six-cylinder or small displacement 2V carbed V-8s. It should only be used in like situations. It is easily identified by the fact that it only has four wheel lugs. The standard five-lug, 9-inch gear assembly that was used in the 1967–72 Cougars, Falcons, Fairlanes, Mustangs, Montegos and Torinos and many other models from the late 1950s until well into the 1970s, is more than able to handle all of the torque of any healthy V-8. That's why the majority of rearend installation kits sold are designed to adapt to this era Ford rear axle. Yes, it is more than 40 years old in some cases, but with a one-time rebuild at a competent shop, you can install it yourself and forget it.

I know there are some who will have questions about the "limited slip" or locking differential varieties. These are the Ford design Equi-Lok and Traction-Lok units, and the Detroit Locker that wasn't manufactured by Ford, but used in Shelbys and other exotics. Of these, the torque-sensitive Traction-Lok, which uses a multiple-disc clutch to control differential action, is the best for general high performance street use. Again, it is costly, a bit noisy and sometimes tempermental, and should be rebuilt (or at least inspected by a professional) before it is installed. I've owned them, but for the above reasons never saw the need to install one in my street coupe. I simply traded them off.

SIMPLY THE BEST REAREND

Okay, a 9-inch, 2-pinion, 5-lug, 28-spline, one-legged Ford rearend it is, but we've still barely narrowed the field. Well, I'm going to cut to the chase. In my opinion, the best rear for the practical street rod is the 1977–80 Lincoln Versailles, Ford Granada, and Mercury Monarch with disc brakes.

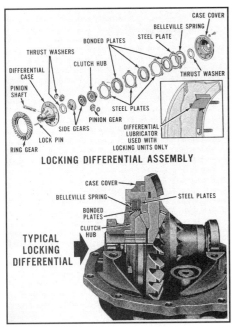

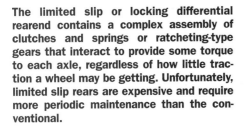

The limited slip or locking differential rearend contains a complex assembly of clutches and springs or ratcheting-type gears that interact to provide some torque to each axle, regardless of how little traction a wheel may be getting. Unfortunately, limited slip rears are expensive and require more periodic maintenance than the conventional.

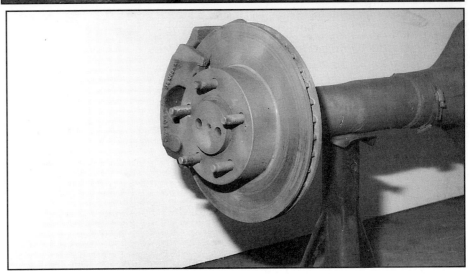

I'll stick my neck out and flatly state that the rear found under the 1977–80 Lincoln Versailles, Ford Grenada and Mercury Monarch is my first choice for a street rod. Size-wise, it is almost an exact duplicate of the stock pre-WWII Ford (and most other domestic cars from the mid-1930s to the late 1940s). The gear assembly is in the center of the axle housings, which means the 28-spline axles are the same length, and as you can see, it comes with disc brakes.

The size is perfect for the early car, measuring about 53 inches from the inside plane of the right rotor to the inside plane of the left. With tires mounted on standard steel wheels (no offset), the center-of-tire to center-of-tire distance is 57 inches. This is almost identical to the stock Ford (and Chevy) rear of the pre- and post-WWII era!

What more could you ask for when you want a tough rear with disc brakes that installs under the typical street rod with no fuss? Well, price. Let's face it, wrecking yard operators read street rod magazines and books as well as enthusiasts. They want to be up on the latest trick of the week. I've bought two Versailles rears in recent years. Both were under $400 each. However, I was quoted prices ranging up to $750 in several wrecking yards. Forget them, I just shopped around a bit more.

What's the going price in your neck of the woods? I don't know, but you're the guy with the cash, so don't be afraid to negotiate. Auto dismantlers never let a fair market offer get away.

DETERMINING GEAR RATOS

Aside from operational and mounting considerations, the rod builder must take into account the rear axle ratio when reviewing his options. Chances are the builder knows that better mileage comes with taller (numerically lower) gear ratios. Be forewarned, however, it is easy to go too tall. Lugging or overworking the engine can damage the clutch, cause excessive downshifting in some automatics, and actually decrease mileage! Efficiency and economy of operation is a question of torque output vs. weight. Furthermore, most rodders like to cruise at an rpm level that is pleasantly quiet, about 2500, give or take 100 rpm. Rarely do they exceed 3500 rpm for very long. Arriving at a satisfactory compromise requires a little math on your part. The following will help you determine a specific and appropriate gear ratio.

The formula used to determine which rearend gear ratio will produce a given engine speed with a known combination of miles per hour and tire size is: **TS x RPM/MPH x 336 = Gear Ratio (GR)**
(TS is the overall diameter of the rear tires, and 336 is a constant.)

The formula used to determine what RPM will be produced at a given road speed and a known gear ratio is: **MPH x GR/TS x 336 = RPM**

The formula used to determine what road speed will be produced with a given engine speed and a known gear ratio: **RPM x TS/GR x 336 = MPH**

After you've purchased your rearend, strip it down. Bring your third member to a competent mechanic and have him at least inspect it for excessive wear. (You don't need a mechanic to tell you the gears are bad if they are blue. That means it was run low on oil.) Have all bearings and seals replaced while you're at the shop. When you get home, you can do the dirty work yourself. Pick up a few cans of carb cleaner, and take the housing to a coin wash. Spray the solvent inside and out, then wash it down with high pressure water and soap. Bring the housing home right away and blow it out with compressed air (wear goggles!). Then coat all bearing and seal surfaces with Cosmoline. Wrap it up and store it until you're ready to put everything together.

INDEPENDENT REAR SUSPENSIONS

16

The stock 50-inch rear tread of early E-type Jag coupes and roadsters made it a natural for street rod installation. Earlier assemblies used knock-off hubs, which were modified for conventional stud/lug nut wheels.

The class act in street rod rear suspensions is the independent. Installing an IRS is not as simple or as economical as installing a suspension that incorporates a conventional axle, however. That was why only two production car IRS assemblies—the Jag and the Corvette—ever made the street rod builder's short list of preferred IFS twenty-five years ago. Let's take a closer look at the Jag unit first.

THE JAGUAR E-TYPE IRS

Without a doubt, the most common IRS that found a home under street rods from the 1970s through the 1980s came from the E-Type Jag coupe and convertible that debuted in 1963. It first gained popularity in fenderless roadsters, but before long, the larger Jag sedan independent rears began to appear in heavier rods. In fact, they've been mounted in every conceivable kind of custom car from lightweight

Fad Ts to 4000-pound Ford F-100 pickups—but not always correctly. Too many times, the ride and handling characteristics of the original suspension were ruined by incorrect radius rod geometry and unsuitable mountings that replaced the factory structure—known as the cage—which was removed from the differential assembly for cosmetic purposes.

In the mid to late 1960s Jaguar, the entire rear suspension unit is enclosed in, and supported by a structure called the crossbeam. It is mounted to the body through four rubber blocks. The fore and aft position of the suspension unit is maintained by two radius arms mounted in rubber bushings on each side of the car between the lower control link and unitized body structure.

Most rod builders, however, thought that the crossbeam hid the beauty of the Jag IRS. Maybe they were right; who can deny that the rotating axle shafts and action of the springs and shocks is a handsome sight? The practice of uncaging the Jag began with the first street rod installations, and it never lost favor.

The differential assembly in the classic Jag rearend is the Salisbury design with an integral gear carrier. A Thornton "Power-Lok" limited-slip unit is usually installed. In lieu of conventional axles, short driveshafts—sometimes called half shafts—with universal joints at each end are used. The inboard ends are mated to axle output shafts. The output shafts also provide a mounting for the inboard disc brakes. The rotor in the early E-types is approximately 10 inches in diameter. The brake-pad area is adequate for light-weight street rods. Later sedans use larger calipers on the rears than on the fronts. Overall, however, stock Jag

brake hardware is wanting.

Two coil-over-shocks support each wheel of the Jag rear installed between the frame and lower control arm. As noted earlier, this installation led the way for non-independent rear coil-over-shock suspensions, although in the latter case, only one coil-over is normally used per wheel.

The rear wheels are located laterally by two control arms. The half shafts double as the upper arms. In technical terms, this is called a stressed half shaft. The inside end of each lower control arm is attached to the differential carrier; the outside end pivots in an aluminum housing, or suspension upright. The upright supports the rotating spindle (stub shaft), bearings and wheel. As the wheel and control arms move up and down, the coil-over-shock units compress and extend. An anti-roll bar connects the right and left lower control arms. At the center, the bar is mounted to the chassis.

The removal of the crossbeam in the pursuit of visual appeal placed many a 1970s rod builder in the danger zone. The crossbeam does more than simply secure the rear suspension assembly to the body; it ties everything together. It provides inner pivot points for the lower control arms and upper mounts for the shocks. It also houses the cable operated scissors-type parking brake assembly and mounts much of the brake plumbing.

The removal of the rear-axle assembly from the crossbeam necessitates new bracketry that faithfully reproduces all original mounting points. The bracketry must also be strong enough to compensate for the loss of the original structure. Because of the Jag's popularity, street rod components manufacturers quickly came to

the rescue. Installation kits are available. More so, in fact, than complete Jag IRS units. If you are fortunate enough to have a complete Jag assembly sitting in the corner of your garage, kits are the easiest and certainly the best way of correctly installing the complicated Jaguar IRS.

Jag Installation Kits

Virtually all commercial Jag IRS installation kits are designed for the Model T through 1940 Ford frames. Of course, they come with full instructions. These rearends, however, have also been installed in nearly one of everything else. The formula for success in the non-Ford street rod is your ability to adapt all or part of the Ford-oriented hardware to your particular vehicle. Therefore, assuming you start with an adequate supply of crossmembers, radius rods, straps, struts, brackets and miscellaneous hardware (which you should have with a Jag IRS-to-Ford kit) the following general outline should get the installation job done.

Obviously, it is impractical to attempt an installation with the car's body on the frame, but before you get started on the installation proper, establish the centerline of the original rear axle on the chassis. Many frames have rubber jounce bumpers—sometimes called snubbers—to cushion suspension bottoming. These are located directly above the axle centerline. The bolt hole for the snubber is an ideal reference point.

Next, position the Jag assembly under the frame. Keep it caged if possible. If the crossbeam has been removed, however, it won't create a significant problem. Depending on the chassis in question, stock rear frame sections or crossmembers may or may not have to be removed. If in doubt, leave everything alone until you're certain.

The Jag differential is typically mounted to a thick steel plate approximately 7-inches square, which is, in turn, welded to a length of square or rectangular 1/8-inch wall tubing. Although this can be fabricated in its entirety, it's often possible—and better—to modify an existing kit piece. Either way, the Jag rear needs to be spaced one inch down from the bottom of the crossmember in order to clear the parking brake calipers. Jag bracketry must be beefy enough to secure the differential, and prevent it from winding up under torque loads.

The frame, crossmember and Jag rear should then be set in position to check fits and clearances. The original axle reference points must be duplicated on the street rod chassis and carefully verified before the crossmember is welded in place. Several street rod suppliers are equipped to handle the necessary machine work to change knock-off hubs over to studs and lug nuts.

Once the correct wheels are mounted, the suspension assembly can be uncaged and the dogbones installed. These are the fabricated links between the lower suspension arms. They provide the inner pivot points for the lower suspension-arm pivots that were lost when the cage was removed. They are available from any street rod shop that offers IRS kits.

Radius rods and strut rods can be either fabricated or pirated from a Ford installation kit. They should be long enough to clear the stock rear anti-roll bar, and strong enough to handle acceleration and braking forces. With

regard to the latter, remember that rearend wrap-up occurs under acceleration and braking. When the inboard disc brakes are applied, torque loads are transferred to the axle housing and its mountings. Also, fore and aft loads must be taken at the wheel. This is done with radius rods or struts that run from the frame to the suspension upright.

Thirty-inch long radius rods are a good compromise in most installations. Strut rods, which often mount the forward dogbone, will be about 35 inches long.

There are many opportunities to mess up the stock Jag's rear suspension geometry. The most frequent one is the angle of the coil-over shocks. A major deviation from the original angle will cause problems. Therefore, if you're fabricating a crossmember from scratch, duplicate the original upper shock mounts using the original crossbeam mounting points as a reference. This completes the high points of installing a Jag IRS, but you're not finished.

Alignment

Once installed, you must align the wheels. Unlike a solid axle, an IRS must be aligned in the same manner as a front suspension. Otherwise, handling will be unpredictable and rapid tire wear will result.

Typically, the wheels of some independent rear suspensions toe-in under acceleration, and toe-out under braking. As for the Jag setup, an eighth-inch toe-out is built in to ensure that toe will be zero while under power. When the original crossbeam is replaced with a new structure, chances are that this built-in toe setting changed. This isn't a problem because

the changes can be compensated for by adjusting the radius rods on alignment equipment.

CORVETTE INDEPENDENT REAR SUSPENSION

The Corvette IRS is every bit as popular as the early Jaguar. Although the initial cost of a Corvette rear is about that of the Jag, many rod builders have decided to "stay home" with their selection of suspension components because Corvette rebuild bits and pieces are typically less costly and more readily available than those for the Jag.

Although 1963–64 Corvette rear suspensions are essentially the same as 1965–79 rears, they are less desirable. This is because drum brakes are used and the Eaton-design Posi-Traction limited-slip differentials are not quite as strong as the Dana units first used in 1965 are.

There are also mechanical advantages to the 'Vette rear. For instance, brake-pad area is more than twice that of the Jag, and many more gear ratios are available. Another big plus is the wide assortment of aftermarket suspension hardware available for Corvettes that transfer to street rod applications.

The early three-link Corvette IRS uses a single trailing arm to locate the rear wheels fore and aft. As with the Jag, a stressed half shaft is also used as the upper control arm, and there's a separate lower control arm. The stock lower arms are rather large, bulky affairs and are usually modified or replaced in a street rod installation.

Early models of the Corvette use a seven-, nine- or ten-leaf transverse spring. Later models (in the time frame most economically practical for

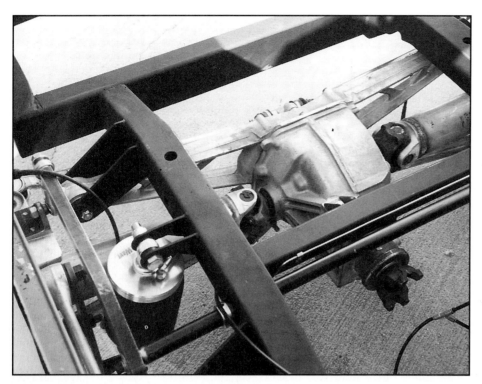

Progressive Automotive has recently introduced their all new 1984–96 Corvette IRS kit for 1936-up Chevys and 1935-up Fords. Progressive also custom builds for non-Chevrolet or Ford frames.

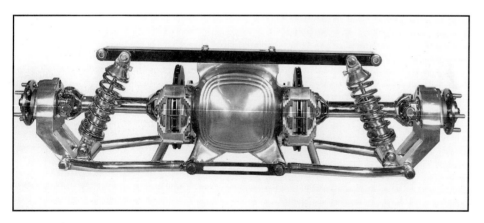

The geometry in Heidt's version of a street rod IRS is designed to be compatible with the company's Superide™ IFS as well as most other independent front suspension kits. It is a complete hub-to-hub assembly that begins with a cast aluminum alloy center housing and an aluminum Ford-style 9-inch gear carrier, both of which are available fully polished. All popular gear ratios are standard, and there is an optional Posi-Traction. Track widths of 55, 56, 58, 60 and 62 inches are inventoried, as are inboard disc brakes with Wilwood calipers and rotors, Corvette outer bearing assemblies and flanges and Aldan billet coil-overs. Half shafts include heavy duty 1350 U-joints. Lower control arms are available in steel, polished stainless steel or polished billet aluminum.

the average street rodder) use a single-leaf transverse spring. Both mount similarly.

When given the opportunity to choose from one of the older 'Vette IRS units, many budget-minded rodders favor the 1975–79 models with their disc brakes, beefy half-shafts and

strut-rod ends, and 10-leaf spring.

Next choice is the 1969 issue, which has a stronger third-member case than previous models. There is a downside to these models though. Ever follow a 'Vette with a three-link IRS down a bumpy road? Next time notice how the rear darts from side to side as it goes over the bumps.

Rodders with heftier wallets often look to the 1984-and-later Corvette five-link IRS with its numerous aluminum components, fiberglass reinforced transverse single-leaf spring, Bilstein gas shocks and other high-tech innovations. This setup is undeniably better than previous 'Vette IRS setups. The five-link setup doesn't exhibit severe bump steer (toeing in or out during wheel travel). In addition, it's more softly sprung. Sophistication of design aside, more than a few believe the aesthetics are every bit as appealing as the Jag IRS. In short, it is a great rearend.

In its natural habitat, the Corvette gear carrier is bolted to a rubber-mounted crossmember. A generation ago, it didn't find such a cushy home in street rod installations. Builders weren't fortunate enough to have the variety of commercial installation kits now available, or made-to-order frames with all the installation bracketry built it.

Early builders did realize, however, that the lower control arms and half shafts could be shortened—just like conventional driveshafts—for improved fender clearance. Knowledgeable builders were also able to modify the original control arms and design appropriate bracketry for early Ford under-chassis mountings. Some even elected to dispense with the transverse spring in favor of Jag-type coil-over-shock

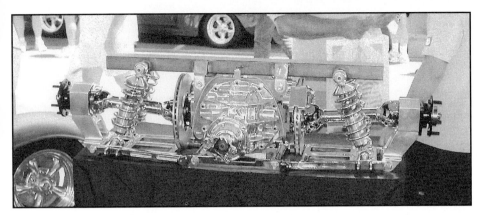

Kugel Komponents' complete, functioning independent rear suspension, with five full inches of wheel travel, is available in widths from 52 to 62 inches. In this L.A. Roadster Show exhibit, it is outfitted with the optional Strange aluminum 9-inch gear carrier. Final drive ratios from 2.50 to 4.50:1 are available. The assembly comes with Corvette or Wilwood calipers and vented 11-inch rotors. Other features include tubular steel control arms, heat-treated aluminum housings and outer hub uprights. The unit is equipped with new forged steel 28- or 31-spline axles, heavy duty U-joints and half shafts, Corvette hub flanges and bearing packs, bearings and seals. The basic unit uses a single shock and spring per side, but an additional coil-over per side for cars weighing 2800 pounds and up is recommended. Not shown are the Torque Arrest™ radius rods and pinion support kit, which are required. The suspension is fully assembled with camber and toe-in adjustments set.

wrecked performance car suspension might have, there are several alternatives. Do yourself a favor and gather up the catalogs from the listed manufacturers. They offer sheer beauty as well as sophistication in their after-market IRS assemblies specifically designed for the street rod market.

suspension units.

If you wish to forego a commercial installation kit with its attendant instructions, you'll find no less of a challenge designing your own Corvette hardware than you would with the Jaguar.

In some early Ford installations, a tuck-in mounting plate for the Corvette differential carrier can be incorporated into the stock rear crossmember. If an entirely new crossmember is fabricated, it should be made from at least 2 x 2-inch heavy-wall rectangular steel tubing. Either way, an additional crossmember serving as a carrier front support must be fabricated. One-inch minimum diameter round or square heavy-wall tubing must be used. This crossmember can also function as the top mount for the shock absorbers.

If you wish to design your own control arms, pay close attention to the configuration of the stock units. They must be at least as strong. A bracket fabricated from 3/8-inch steel plate with a bolt pattern to match the holes

in the Corvette bearing carrier can be designed to mount both the replacement radius rods and spring. High quality spherical rod ends or some of the top-notch aftermarket hardware should be used at the front pivot of each radius rod so there's free suspension movement. All in all, the Corvette rear suspension assembly is worth the installation effort if you're prepared to face up to the engineering demands of doing the job right. Nevertheless, I see no advantage, either monetarily or time-wise, for the average street rodder in trying to "reinvent the wheel" when reasonably priced kits are available. Professional builders, by virtue of their day-in, day-out exposure to all of the possible problems—and fixes— are far more likely to come up with an efficient approach to the installation of a complicated independent rear suspension. Moreover, they all have a tech "hot line.

Finally, if you don't want to haunt the auto dismantlers or to take a chance on hidden damages any

17

ENGINE INSTALLATION

We'll never know the name of the street rodder who tackled the first motor swap back in the 1920s. We don't even know who put the first small-block Chevy V-8 in a Ford in 1955. What we do know, however, is that the Chevy V-8 is the all-time swappers' favorite

The early backyard rod builder could usually do simple motor swaps. Even if his homemade mounts were somewhat crude, they were functional. In the mid-1950s, a few manufacturers began mass-producing mounts for the installation of the more popular OHV V-8s in the early Ford chassis. *Hot Rod* *Magazine* provided exposure and instructions. Swapping was off and running.

As for current motor mount availability, if you decide to break away from the crowd and use a motor and/or chassis that is limited in popularity, you are right back where it all started . . shade-tree engineering. It is simply not practical for a manufacturer to tool up to meet the needs of a handful of customers. There's a price to pay for individualism, and that is the work that goes beyond merely welding or bolting in store-bought motor and transmission mounts. With an endless list

Measuring tools are the first things the rod builder reaches for when scoping out an engine swap (or any other mix and match of components, for that matter). Record all dimensions when the window of opportunity is open.

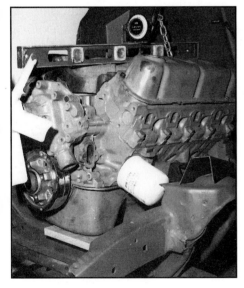

Second in popularity is the 302 cid Ford small-block. It, however, requires much more perseverance on the part of the rod builder. For starters, the full-size front oil pan sump almost always clashes with the front crossmember of an early car frame, modified or not. You won't know this for sure until the motor is suspended in place by a chain hoist and leveled with a floor jack.

of possible combinations, off-the-wall swapping again becomes a do-it-your-self operation.

By far, the most popular motor for street rod swapping is the small-block Chevrolet OHV V-8, and of that long running series, the 350 cid version takes the prize. I don't think I'm over-stating the case when I say that the Chevy swap is a piece of cake. That rearward oil pan sump is the primary reason.

PREPLANNING ON PAPER FIRST

If you are installing Brand X motor in Old Car Y, do your design work on paper before you reach for a cutting torch and wrenches. Carefully measure the engine hold and general underhood area from every direction and angle. Then, lay out your findings in three-view form on poster board. Pay close attention to the configuration of the firewall and the exact location of the front crossmember and steering gear. Cross-sectional views are necessary if your engine compartment significantly narrows from front to back.

Next, measure and sketch the motor and transmission you are going to install. Be sure the distributor, intake and exhaust manifolds, starter and

alternator are all in place. That doesn't mean that some of these won't be modified or repositioned. You simply want to eliminate as many surprises as possible before you commit yourself to anything.

This preliminary work might seem unnecessary, but don't be in a rush. An hour or two spent measuring and sketching can pay handsome dividends. It may also save you grief later on. If you do your homework, you should get a fair idea of where your motor swap problems lie, maybe even before you rush out and buy that dual overhead cammer that looks so good in its natural habitat. Who knows, you might even decide that a common-as-belly buttons carbureted small-block isn't such a bad idea after all!

Regardless of how careful you are,

169

The fix is one or another of the truncated front sump pans along with the remote oil pump pickup. Even so, a special aftermarket timing chain cover and/or a shorter water pump may also be required to avoid significant firewall modification. Again, the only way you can tell for certain is to use your floor jack to move the motor up and down, and back and forth, until a suitable position relative to the firewall is located.

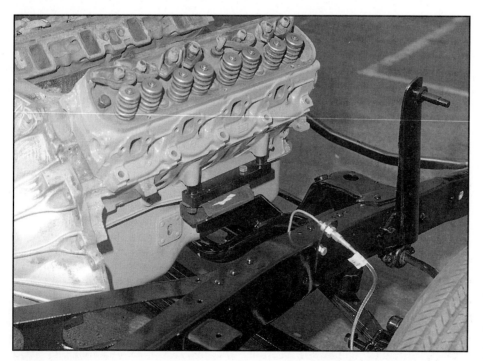

Study the layout of the motor installation. Use the bosses cast into the block for store-bought or custom mounts. Anticipate where interference problems may occur. Consider accessibility for routine maintenance such as plug removal, head-bolt torquing, oil-filter access, as well as the steering gear you plan to use, transmission shift linkage, and routing of the exhaust pipes through the chassis.

you won't find every problem until you physically drop that mill into the motor compartment. There, suspended by a chain hoist and manipulated by a floor jack, the motor and transmission can be moved up and down and back and forth until a suitable position is found. A carpenter's level on the intake manifold carb mount will be a big help in determining the desirable attitude, but perfection isn't always attainable.

Once you have the motor where you want it, sit back and study the layout. Keep in mind when designing any bracketry that the simplest design is usually the best. Note where the motor mount bosses are cast into the block. If possible, use them for bolting on your custom mounts. Anticipate what and where interference problems may occur. Consider accessibility for routine maintenance such as sparkplug removal, head-bolt torquing, oil filter access and clearance for the steering gear, exhaust system, and transmission shift linkage.

Anything can be done in a dozen different ways, so review your options before you go too far. You should never weld or cut into a frame unless and until it is necessary. Examine the situation from several angles and consider all methods of mount construction before you light the torch. Remember, even if you don't care if something is cut or crudely beaten into submission, a potential buyer sometime in the distant future will care. So, don't trash the car and ruin a future sale by not doing things carefully and neatly. Do it right the first time.

Steel is very difficult to work with. It's hard, and it takes a lot of tiresome cutting with a saw or torch. Even grinding rough edges is time-consuming. So, to speed the job along, get

Few OHV V-8s fit the pre-1949 Ford frame and body as well as the ubiquitous small-block Chevy. About the only thing that has to be eliminated is the stock fuel pump. It's difficult to say if the Stovebolt's enormous street rod popularity is due to its picture-perfect fit . . . or its vaunted performance potential. The stock "ram's horn" exhaust manifolds admittedly add to the ease of installation, but there is a downside in that exhaust efficiency is sacrificed. There are better ways to accomplish both goals.

some more poster board, a pair of scissors and a 12-inch straight edge. A roll of masking tape and a tape measure will round out your basic tools.

Following your preliminary design, cut pieces of poster board into various shapes and tape them in position. Trim or add pieces in place with masking tape until you achieve a perfect fit. Don't be unwilling to change or modify the design. Poster board is cheap. It's easier and less costly to use a pencil, paper and masking tape than it is to use a cutting torch!

Motor Mounts

Don't over-design your motor mounts. Nevertheless, keep in mind that your power package, which weighs more than 600 pounds, will try to torque right out of your car when you're on the pedal. The motor and

transmission assembly must be supported in at least three places: left and right sides of the motor and somewhere under the tranny.

The carburetor base must be approximately level and the crankshaft must align with the driveshaft. Furthermore, mounts not only position and support the motor assembly; they must also resist torque loads and prevent the frame rails from deflecting. In fact, the weakest feature of any mount is usually the method of securing it to the chassis, so design accordingly.

After you've finalized your motor mount design, transfer the designs, full scale, to a fresh piece of poster board and cut them out. Accurate bolt patterns can be obtained by holding a piece of poster board to the bosses on the block and tapping gently around the edges with a ball peen hammer. To

double-check the fit, tape the pattern pieces together and then tape the mockups in place on both sides of the motor.

A good design may not develop first time around, but it shouldn't take more than one additional attempt. Once you're satisfied with what you have, take the poster board patterns to a sheet-metal shop that has a heavy-duty shear and have two sets cut from 1/8-inch thick steel. This thickness is usually adequate unless you were too stingy with gussets. If you don't feel comfortable welding lighter gauge sheet metal, use 1/4-inch plate. It's bulkier, but certainly won't hurt anything. (Why two sets? Just in case you mess one set up! It won't be that much more expensive, and it sure could save a lot of time.)

When you return with your custom mount kit, bolt the designated parts to the block and frame and fit in the connecting pieces. Don't weld the mount together on the bench; warpage and misalignment will result. The best method of assembly is to tack weld the pieces solidly together with the motor and frame acting as a holding fixture. Take care not to burn rubber-insulated supports.

After you have an assembly and are happy with the overall fit, finish the welding job on the bench. Run a weld bead on both sides of the joints whenever possible.

Prefab Mount Kits—If you elect to install one of the mainstream motor-and-transmission combinations in an early Ford or Chevy frame, the street rod components manufacturers have already done the design and fabrication for you. Prefabricated motor mounts can greatly simplify your motor and transmission installation

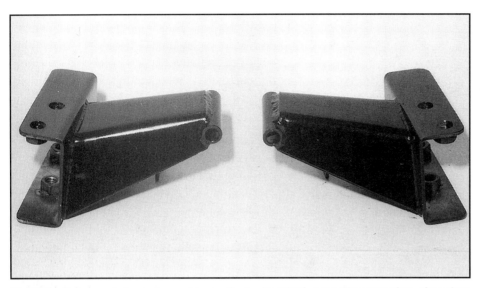

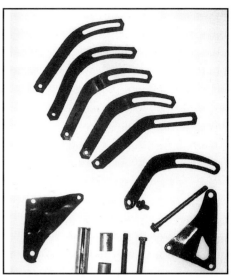

Prefabricated mounts for motor and transmission installation greatly saves time, time that can better spent solving unique, swap-related problems for which there are no commercially available products. Pictured are SAC's mounts for the small-block Chevy in a 1939–40 Ford.

By the way, don't let such things as alternator brackets, etc. that came with your motor package slow you down. There are a number of alternatives in the wrecking yard costing no more than a dollar or two.

and reduce overall cost. Not only that, you have a lot more time and energy to resolve the swap-related problems for which there are no commercially available products.

Whereas street rodders were once hell-bent on matching a powerful V-8 to every strong-looking transmission, today it is certainly more sensible to use the factory transmission and mating hardware. Installation kits reflect this and offer compatible motor and transmission mounts.

Today's commercial offerings are not significantly different from their forebears although there is much less emphasis on dual-purpose drag/street cars, and more emphasis on show quality hardware. Modern motor mounts are lighter, and often incorporate factory rubber-insulated components.

You should keep original body and firewall sheet metal intact whenever possible. Even though many rodders still prefer one or another of the stock exhaust manifolds for either quietness of operation or lower cost, the additional expense of commercial "block

Just in case you were wondering, the small-block Chevy fits equally well in the prewar Chevy passenger car and light truck. Better, in fact, if you consider that the firewall of many models incorporates a factory recess that perfectly accommodates the back-of-the-block distributor.

hugger" or downright full custom-made headers is more preferable than modifying vintage tin. Commercial prefabricated exhaust headers are available for popular motor/old-car combinations, and are usually designed with metal preservation in mind.

Indeed, if you are working with the enormously popular Chevy (and to a lesser extent, the Ford) small-block V-8 and the early Ford chassis, you will find that the world of commercial street rod components is your oyster. You can pluck from it whatever variety of pearl you wish. Your choices are not limited to motor and transmission mounts, either. A wide array of related components from radiators to supercharger installation kits are available.

Even if you have only half the popular combination—a Chevy or Ford motor and transmission—you'll find enough universal mounting hardware to bolt your power package into most any old car chassis. Commercial offerings typically include tubular-type crossmembers with longer-than-necessary length end pieces. Some trimming and fitting is all that is necessary to get the job done.

Motor installation encompasses more than just mounts. There are a number of accessories that have to be accommodated. Most beginning rod builders will wisely choose a basic four-barrel carb such as the Holley (left) or the big-block friendly Rocheste (right). I'm running an Edelbrock/Carter (not shown) as my choice for trouble-free induction. Nevertheless, that's just the beginning.

The big-block Chevy has a hard-core following among those who appreciate its brute torque. Its rear oil pan sump location allows easy installation in early cars and pickups, but suspension modifications are often required to accommodate the weight. (If that deep-dish crossmember has you wondering, it was used in 1941 Ford pickups and panel trucks with inline flatheads.)

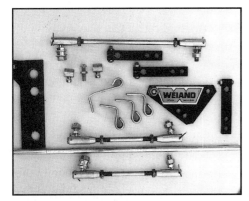

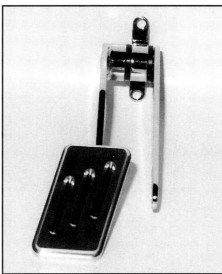

The rod builder must also contend with throttle linkage and a compatible foot pedal. Because there are so many possibilities when one considers not only carburetors, but also firewall and cockpit floor configurations, finding the right combination will require careful analysis. There are two basic approaches: "hard linkage" (upper left) and cable linkage like Gennie Shifter's throttle kit offerings (above, and at left).

Before you marry your power package to the chassis for (hopefully) the last time, it's a good idea to spin the oil pump with a (reversible) drill motor to bring up the oil pressure. You'll never have a better opportunity to look for oil leaks.

MANUFACTURERS & SUPPLIERS

Edelbrock Company
Torrance, CA 90503
(800) 416-8628
www.edelbrock.com

Ford Performance Parts
(810) 468-3673
P.O. Box 5134
Livonia, MI 4815
www.fordracing.com/performanceparts
Specialty water pumps.

SAC Hot Rod Products
633 W. Katella Blvd.
Orange, CA 92867
(714) 997-3433
Fax: (714) 997-3693
www.sachotrod.com

Universal Machining
17722 Metzler
Huntington Beach, CA 92647
(714) 842-8797
Doug Upton at Universal, has developed a CNC-machined timing chain cover and water pump that reduces overall small-block Ford length almost three inches.

DRIVELINE INSTALLATION

18

The "driveline" includes everything in the chassis back of the block that delivers the horsepower to the rear wheels. As always in street rod building, there are many options.

An automatic transmission usually fits in the typical, more-or-less original street rod chassis without difficulty. In cases where a reasonably small transmission is chosen—the TH 2004R, or Ford AOD—the primary problem is clearance in and about the area where chassis members converge at the center of the frame. All but the very early Ford frames have some

type of K-member or X-member for strength, so some interference will occur in these installations.

Back in the days when little thought was given to neat chassis modifications, the usual approach was to eliminate interferences with a cutting torch. Just get that engine and transmission bolted in. Afterwards, if the frame then seemed a little too flexy, channel-iron

sections were welded in parallel to the transmission.

In actuality, much the same thing is done today, only with more finesse. Instead of crawling under the chassis with torch in hand, you should do the job right and take your sweet time. Transmission-to-chassis interferences should be carefully chalked out, then cuts should be made with a sabre saw

If the chassis doesn't accommodate the transmission of your choice, modify it. Don't just take torch in hand, however. Street rod shops have prefabricated pieces on the shelf for such project. Pictured is the SAC "chassis widener."

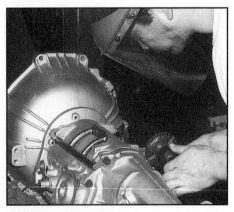

The casting flash on many automatics has to be removed before some parts of the tubular mounting can be attached.

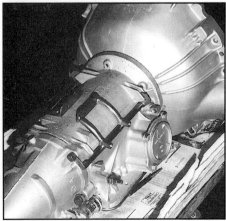

It is best to install the mounting bracketry sequentially as per the kit instructions lest some critical adjustment be overlooked.

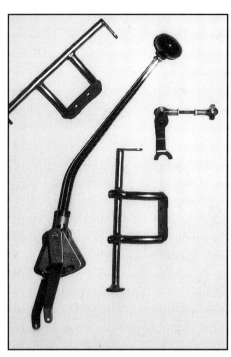

At one time, aftermarket automatic transmission shifters were built with the low-slung muscle car in mind. No heed was taken of highboys or other early cars. The Gennie Shifter, with its "stock-above-the-floorboard" cosmetics, brought positive latching and shift control to street rods built with resto-rod styling. Kits for rod-popular auto trannies use steel bracketry or tubular mounting.

or hacksaw. A cutting torch should only be used as a last resort. It is best if the body is off the frame, but if not, at least the seats and flammable upholstery should be removed.

As always, what was removed from the frame must be returned even though it may be in a different place. Parallel C-sections are still the most common approach but not just any old chunk of channel iron can be used. Several street rod components manufacturers offer bits and pieces for the more common installations. They are time-savers and attractive replacements.

Where store-bought pieces are not available, take measurements and make either a cardboard pattern or a

sketch of what you need. Perfect-fit C-sections of the right gauge and dimension are as close as the nearest sheet metal shop. Prices are so reasonable you'll wonder why the old timers even considered using a piece of channel iron.

Shifters & Gear Selectors

Although some automatic transmissions in the wrecking yard will have their original floor shifters attached, many will not. You'll either have to pay extra for a stock shifter or purchase an aftermarket unit. Fortunately, the higher cost of a top-quality aftermarket automatic shifter is easily justified when compared with the original factory units. Not only do the aftermarket shifters better lend themselves to street rod applications, they are designed for heavy-duty use. Many original floor shifters use cables and relatively weak linkages.

Better aftermarket kits incorporate positive latching and shift control. Once you are accustomed to using such a shifter, it's nearly impossible to miss a gear. What! Miss a gear with an automatic? Sure, ask the driver of any potent street rod with an automatic who has "gone through the gears" and mistakenly dumped it in reverse!

Column Shifts for Automatics

Not everybody wants a floor shifter, of course. Many family-oriented street rods, such as Model A Tudors and Fordors, need all the passenger comfort and space they can get, particularly when there's no intention of doing any weekend racing.

There are several ways to eliminate the floor shifter for an automatic transmission. You can modify the original column shift or install an aftermarket

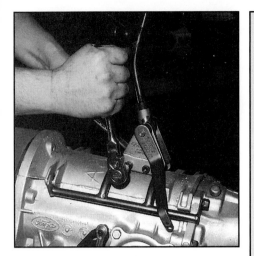

Shifter drag is adjusted by jam nuts on the cross shaft. It should be noted that a moderately heavy amount of drag is needed to avoid "self-shifting." By the way, in some installations the rod builder will find that the stick is a little too high for his driving comfort. It can be shortened by removing a section from the bend area, then welding and re-bending it. Gennie Shifter stocks several lengths, however. Check with them before modifying yours.

ididit

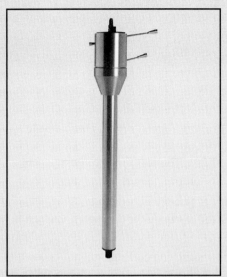
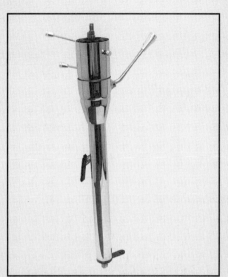
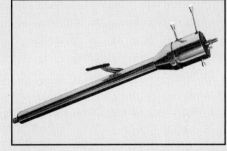
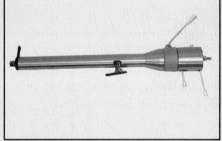

ididit is a company that specializes in steering columns and accessories for street rods with automatic transmissions. They offer a variety that includes an aluminum tilt (top left), a chromed steel non-tilt (top right), a chromed steel tilt (bottom left) and an unpainted steel non-tilt (bottom right).

street rod steering column with shifter. The relatively thin, custom-made steering columns with a built-in shifter install easily and look at home in most early cars.

Aftermarket steering columns with built-in shifters often use proprietary hardware to change gears. Backyard builders have used the housed, thick, but flexible cable that came in big Fords through most of the 1970s. It was a hefty, easily adaptable cable but the wrecking yard supply has obviously dwindled. A readily available option is the stainless-steel Morse type cable. It is classy and trouble free. Any marine-supply house can make up one to the exact length required. Marine supply houses also have a good assortment of the attaching hardware that is necessary when a Morse cable is used.

By the way, several types of transmissions have one gear-selector lever for a console (floor) shift model and another for a column-shift model.

Usually the gear-selector assembly is easily exchanged. If your transmission has the opposite of what you need, drop by a transmission rebuild shop. They often have miscellaneous parts such as these.

Tilt Steering

The adaptation of a late-model steering column with a built-in shifter was popular a few years ago. Unfortunately, many stockers are thick and look disproportionate in an early car. Nevertheless, it is difficult to get in and out of some early coupes and sedans. Again, as so many times in the

past, the innovative street rod components industry has come to the rescue. Tilt steering columns that look right are now available. Although the installation of a tilt column is easiest when a late steering gear is used, the hook-up is no different from those discussed in the chapter on steering systems.

INSTALLING A MANUAL TRANSMISSION

I've already said you'll be better off using the transmission that belongs to the engine of your choice. If, however, you decide on using some other transmission, foreign both to engine and

Aftermarket engine-to-transmission adapters came on the scene when rodders got serious about putting engines other than flatheads in early Fords. Eventually, they started putting transmissions other than early Fords behind flatheads! Pictured is Offenhauser's special adapter that permits the ease of the early Ford clutch release shaft, fork and throwout bearing, when connecting a Chevrolet transmission to the early Ford/Mercury adapter flange. Offenhauser, best known for intake manifolds, continues to lead the field in just about any kind of adapter a rodder could realistically want.

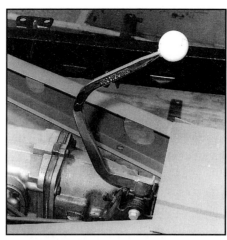

Aftermarket floor shifters for modern manual transmissions were pioneered by George Hurst. The interchangeable handles they accept are available in a wide variety of configurations and lengths. A workable combination for most any street rod—highboy or channeled—can usually be discovered.

I have used one model or another of the 1964–1973 Ford Top Loader 4-speed manual transmissions in my rods for years. The most positive gear selector didn't come from Ford, however. It is the one used in several models of Jeep CJs. Entire units require some wrecking yard research, but parts are still available. Manual transmissions aren't for everybody given the vast popularity of automatic transmissions. If this is your cup of tea, see the December 1990 issue of *Street Rodder Magazine* for conversion details.

car, you must use an adapter plate or adapter bellhousing to bolt the two together.

Before transmission adapter plates and bellhousings were commercially available, the hot rodder made his own. A word of caution, however: If you want to mate an unusual powerplant/drivetrain combination, you'd better have substantial metalworking skills or machine shop resources. Precise alignment is critical.

The multi-speed transmissions we discussed in the previous section are built with smaller front case configurations than were earlier gearboxes. Therefore, the adapter needed is a more complicated bellhousing that sandwiches between the engine and gear case.

In some cases, a pilot-bearing adapter is also required. It locates the input shaft directly in the center of the crankshaft and, although it's a relatively simple bronze component, it must be precisely dimensioned.

Caution: Even though I touched on this earlier, I'll say it again. When installing a hybrid power package, pay special attention to the engine and transmission mounting points. The engine and transmission should always be mounted at no less than three points. In addition, it is not good practice to use front mounts a la the flathead or, heaven forbid, a single mount even though Oldsmobile and a few other manufacturers have done so in the past. Powerplants supported at the front of the engine and at the rear are subjected to excess bending loads. This may cause damage to the transmission case, attaching bolts and the adapter. Aluminum housings and cases in this type of installation have fractured under high performance use.

Regardless of how neat you think it is to run through "real" gears, especially when the transmission is behind

a healthy V-8, functional installation in an early car requires careful planning if you want to do it neatly. The basic measurements are often deceiving. A transmission case is so many inches long and wide, and because most are slim, you may assume that manual transmissions install just as easily as an automatic. They don't!

It's true that a manual gearbox usually doesn't take up any more space than its automatic brethren. In fact, it often has fewer bulges. And, year for year, the four- or five-speed manual transmission frequently uses an identical spline count, the same length yoke and the same driveshaft as does the automatic. Automatics and manual transmissions often share the same mount and crossmember.

The problem lies with the shifting linkage. The stock Ford top loader shifter and linkage assembly, for instance, is about 27 inches to the rear of the flywheel and extends left of center about 6 inches. You can guess where that's going to put it in the typical street rod cockpit. Yep, almost under your right foot . . . or worse, under your seat. Even bucket seats don't help much. It's a typical problem.

Because of that, and no matter how sacrosanct you may hold the original floorboard and frame members, there's simply no way of avoiding alterations in some cases. Frame and/or floorboard modifications can be performed without leaving irreparable damage, however.

Most jobs will be done without prior knowledge of just what is required, so you must put an access hole in the floorboard. Cut out a slightly larger than necessary section of the floorboard, but please use a sabre saw! Save the cutout, part of it can be welded back in after the framework is completed. A big piece is a lot easier to modify and return than a too-conservative cut that may well require additional trimming . . . and leave you with a bunch of useless scraps.

Shifters for Manual Transmissions

The modern stock floor shifter was designed for cars that sit quite a bit lower than most street rods unless they are channeled. In 1935–48 rods, the driver must hunch over to reach the shift lever. Because he must also depress the clutch at the same time, he can quickly grow weary. The ergonomics—or mechanics of the body—just aren't there.

With the exception of the Borg-Warner T-5 described earlier, it is difficult to modify older stock shifters because the handle is often a tubular affair mounting finger levers with cables running through for reverse gear.

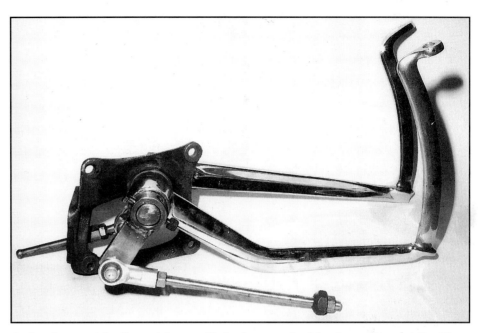

A chassis mount for the pedal assembly is always preferable when space permits. There are two traditional early Ford favorites—the 1939 and the 1940. Both (and they are different) accommodate master cylinders, but the 1939 model (pictured) can be readily modified to actuate a late model clutch. Both can be re-bushed at any automotive machine shop.

In short, they are too complex. It is far more sensible to review the catalogs of the aftermarket shifter companies. Although most are designed primarily for later model cars, the likelihood of arriving at a workable combination is much greater than with stock parts.

Pedal Problems

The further you progress in the construction of your street rod, the more you'll become convinced that the task you so willingly accepted in the beginning is more demanding than buying parts and screwing them all together. Often it's an exercise in decision-making and a test of one's problem-solving skills. Devising a suitable clutch and brake pedal assembly can be one of those tasks. Those builders who have purchased a reproduction chassis with a built-in pedal assembly, can of course, dismiss the subject entirely. Such accessories are one of the advantages.

Rather quickly, you must make another one of those pesky, but impor-tant decisions: Are you going to mount swing pedals on the cockpit side of the firewall, or in the frame below the floorboards as they were originally. Of course, you must coordinate the approach to your pedal problems with the decision you make regarding the method of clutch activation . . . hydraulic or mechanical. Decisions, decisions.

The rehabilitator of a semi-original, previously street rodded chassis may still have the factory pedal assembly, but if not, he has a wide variety of domestic and import production car and light-truck assemblies from which to choose. The wrecking yards are full of 'em. Nevertheless, the best place for you to begin your survey is the accumulation of street rod catalogs wisely ordered before starting on this journey. The reproduction chassis companies' offerings are usually two-fold, one set-up for their in-house frame, another as a replacement for popular original frames.

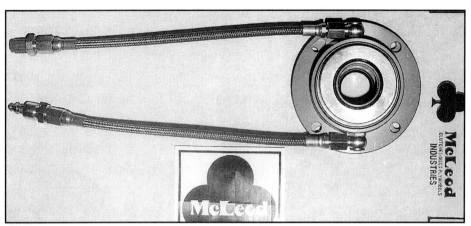

McLeod's hydraulic release bearing covers a broad range of applications and can be adapted to most any bellhousing or transmission installation. It eliminates mechanical linkage.

Like so many other rod-building problems, I believe it is best to approach the installation of pedal assemblies with pencil, paper and tape measure nearby. The size and configuration of the frame at its midsection, plus the width of the transmission, may be such that the firewall is the only practical place to mount a pedal assembly. A large transmission in a small street rod frame is a challenge if floorboard pedals are desired because there's precious little space betwixt and between. Unfortunately, you must accept the fact that the stock firewall is usually too flimsy for pedal mounting. That means you have to design in extra beef if swing pedals are to be used.

Or, structural integrity and space considerations aside, perhaps you simply don't like the aesthetics of firewall-mounted cylinders. In that case, look outside of the accepted street rod parts resources at something akin to the polished aluminum mini-wonders that dune buggy and off-road builders use.

Sometimes, when all is said and done, nothing will work "out of the box." Although there are literally hundreds of pedal assemblies to choose from, old-fashioned street rod back-

yard engineering may still be required to achieve a sanitary installation that functions safely and properly. That means coming up with a unique design incorporating bits and pieces from stock and aftermarket assemblies. Street rod building has always had that as its bottom line.

Regardless of which type of linkage you use and where you mount the pedals, pedal travel and load are two factors with which you must be concerned. For instance, limit pedal travel to 6 inches and load to about 50 pounds, 40 pounds if possible. This is done by calculating the various lever ratios and/or hydraulic-cylinder sizes you're considering for the clutch linkage.

Don't Forget the Clutch

Another thought-provoking problem is clutch activation. You have two ways to approach this problem: devise a one-off mechanical linkage or install an extra master cylinder and a hydraulic slave unit.

Mechanical Linkage—Designing a suitable mechanical linkage that fits in tight quarters and doesn't collapse or bind when you "lean into it" isn't easy. Notice that few modern cars have them. That doesn't stop the aftermarket

companies from offering suitable kits for the push-pull trade. McLeod Industries, well-known for their street and competition clutches, has universal kits for racecars. The mechanical clutch-linkage kit is based on the 1955 Chevy design, but lends itself well to street rod application.

Hydraulic Linkage—Because designing, building and mounting clevises, bell cranks and pushrods are often very difficult, many street rod builders turned to hydraulic clutch linkages years ago. The major advantage with a hydraulic linkage is that you don't have to package all those bell cranks and pushrods, just a length of hydraulic hose.

Back in the 1960s when the muscle-car four-speeds gained popularity, the hot tip was to use the 1958 Ford half-ton pickup slave cylinder for the custom installation of a "juice clutch." The unit worked well with any stock passenger car brake master cylinder when the check valve was removed. A number of full-size Chevy and International pickup truck models from the '60s and '70s used dual master cylinders and correctly sized slave cylinders that are easily adapted to the street rod. Independent auto parts stores can still get replacements for some decades-old trucks. There are also complete hydraulic clutch and brake-pedal assemblies offered by the aftermarket.

INSTALLING THE CONVENTIONAL REAREND

Before the street rod builder reaches for a wrench, he has to decide what type of spring he is going to use to hang that five-foot wide, two hundred pound conventional rearend he bought. If he is building a "Fad T," he probably will want the bell-shaped Model T

Hanging a rearend is best done in a bare frame. Sometimes, however, it just isn't practical. Safety is a prime consideration with overhead work.

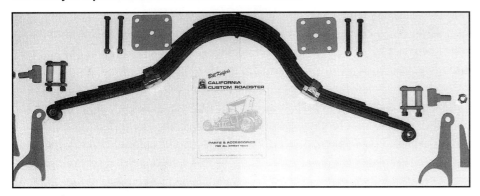

The "Fad T"(long may it haunt the burger drive-ins), requires a rear transverse spring in the general configuration of its parent, the Model T Ford. California Custom Roadster has just the right spring and all the hardware necessary to mate it to your favorite rear axle assembly. Detailed installation instructions are available.

styling. If he is building a fenderless, flathead powered Deuce roadster, he is likely to be thinking in terms of the traditional bow-shaped buggy spring or coil-over-shock suspension units. On the other hand, the fat fenders of the 1937–1948 coupe allow him great latitude, even if the suspension hardware is not particularly attractive as in the case of parallel leaf springs. As the old carnival huckster groaned, "Yer pays yer money, and yer takes yer choice." See the sidebar on page 184 for an example of a conventional parallel leaf suspension installation.

THE DRIVESHAFT AND THE UNIVERSAL JOINTS

Prior to 1949, Ford cars were built with torque tube drivelines. A universal joint was splined to a solid driveshaft, which was, in turn, attached to the differential pinion gear by means of a splined collar. The entire apparatus was enclosed in the torque tube. Stout as this arrangement may appear, it was no trick to tear up a universal joint or shear the end off of a driveshaft with a mildly hopped-up flathead. Few street rodders missed its departure.

The last hurdle in building the modern street rod drivetrain, therefore, is fitting a tubular driveshaft—the so-called open driveline.

The driveshaft—technically known as the propeller shaft—is the connecting link between the transmission and differential. In order to transfer the rotary motion of the transmission output shaft to the differential, two facts of conventional front engine/rear wheel-drive powertrain design must be taken into consideration. First, the engine and transmission are more or less rigidly attached to the frame; and secondly, the rear-axle assembly is more or less flexibly attached to the frame by springs.

Now, this may seem like a simple mechanical challenge, but engine torque must be smoothly relayed to the rear axle assembly while it is continually moving up and down, and twisting and tilting as you're driving along. The geometry is far from simple. Drive torque, braking and road irregularities are constantly changing both the angle of drive to the axle assembly, and the distance between the transmission output shaft and differential.

The U-Joint

Fortunately for us all, the English physicist Robert Hooke solved part of the problem centuries before the automobile was invented. Hooke's joint—two yokes on planes perpendicular to each other and pivotally connected by a cross-shaped piece—was the first successful means of transmitting rotary motion through two shafts that are at an angle to each other. Hence the modern universal joint or simply, U-joint.

Two separate devices are necessary to compensate for the variation in angle and length in the modern auto-

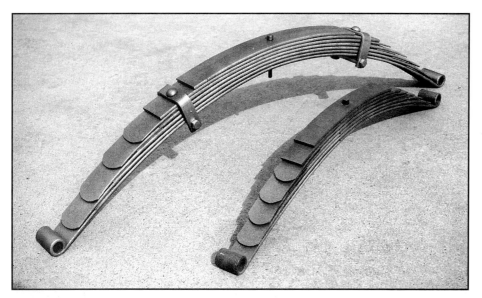

There will always be a strong contingent of street rodders who favor as much of the traditional look as practical. The time-honored rear transverse spring is about as traditional as one can get, but "practical" is the key word here. Nobody cuts up 1936 Ford axle housings for spring perches anymore. There's simply no reason to with products such as Posies rear perches and the company's Adjustable Super Slide Spring. The perch eye bolts to the bracket and can swivel. Therefore, the pinion angle can be set after the car is finished and at the correct ride height without binding the spring. Ride height can also be adjusted because the bracket has two holes for the perch bolts. Not only that, Posies' rolled and tapered transverse springs are quite attractive! Photo courtesy Posies.

motive driveline, however. Universal joints are only used to compensate for variations in the angle of drive. Additionally, a slip joint is needed to allow fore and aft movement. Such slip joints usually have outside splines on one shaft and matching internal splines on a mating hollow shaft. This arrangement causes the two shafts to rotate together while also permitting the two to move endwise in relation to each other. Changes in the distance between the transmission and rear axle are thereby accommodated.

The slip joint is on the transmission end of the driveshaft and mates to the gearbox's output shaft. Although many different slip yokes are interchangeable (meaning you should be able to match any driveshaft to any transmission) when you find one that fits, chances are it will be too long. We'll deal with this problem in a moment, but first let's take a closer look at the

basic U-joint and its limitations.

There are three different kinds of automotive universal joints, but two of them are rarely used in street rods. These are the constant-velocity joint, which consists of two U-joints linked by a ball and socket, and the ball-and-trunnion joint, which is a combination U-joint and slip joint.

The U-joint with which we are most familiar is a two-yoke combination (driving and driven) with a journal cross supported by four needle-bearing cups in the ears of the yokes. The cups are held in place with retaining rings.

Universal joint velocity fluctuates twice with every revolution of the driveline. The extent of this fluctuation depends on the angle between the driving and driven shafts. For instance, a relatively severe U-joint angle of 28 degrees can develop a high-speed variation that will lead to rapid wear.

In the typical front engine/rear-

wheel-drive street rod with a wheelbase of 100–120 inches, the irregularity in U-joint velocity can be eliminated. This is done by using one U-joint at each end of the driveshaft, providing the planes of the two joints are exactly aligned and the angle of the transmission output shaft and driveshaft is equal to the angle of the driveshaft and the differential pinion yoke. Nevertheless, it is important to plan your drive train installation so the U-joint angles are as small as possible—5-6 degrees when the car is at rest with a maximum of 18-20 degrees when the suspension is in full rebound.

Getting In Phase

Installation geometry, however, is only part of your concern. All components must mate with precision. Usually engine/transmission/differential matings from the same family are easily accomplished after the driveshaft has been shortened, but not always. There are enough variations within every manufacturer's product line to ensure a mismatch once in awhile, not to mention the hybrid driveline—Chevrolet transmission and Ford rearend, etc.

There's no insurmountable problem regardless of what transmission and differential are destined to work as a team. You simply need the skills of a competent machine shop versed in driveline service. There, you can either have your mismatched parts modified or a completely new driveshaft tailored to your car's unique requirements.

Prior to that, you should be certain that the engine, transmission and rear axle assembly are correctly located in the frame and in phase—the transmission output shaft is parallel with the axis of the pinion gear.

As long as the engine, transmission and rear axle are squarely installed in a frame that is perfectly square, the driveline will be in phase in the horizontal plane. This can be verified in your shop with nothing more than a tape measure. To check the rear axle installation, measure the distance from the left rear axle centerline to some fixed point on the left frame rail, such as a factory rivet or hole. Find the same point on the right rail and measure from there to the right axle centerline. Both measurements should be within 1/16 inch of each other.

To verify that the engine is square in the frame, measure from the center of the crankshaft snout to both sides of the frame. Then, measure from the center of the transmission output shaft to both sides of the frame. If the center of the crank nose is closer to the passenger side frame rail than it is to the driver side by 1 1/2 inches (for instance), that's OK . . . if the transmission output shaft center is equally as close to the same rail. If it isn't, now is the time to correct the problem.

With the frame positioned level, determine the angle of the pinion shaft by placing your angle finder on the flat side of the pinion yoke.

Install a slip yoke on the transmission output shaft to determine its angle because the output shaft is too far inside the housing to support the angle finder. If these two components are in phase, the sum of the positive (pointing down) angle of the transmission and the negative (pointing up) angle of the pinion shaft will equal 180 degrees. If they don't—well, as the old song says, "There'll be some changes made." Or, at least there should be.

The determination of the length of the driveshaft is a simple matter. Assuming the engine, transmission and rear-axle assembly are solidly bolted down; slide the slip-yoke onto the transmission output shaft. Push it all of the way on until it bottoms, then measure from the center of the yoke ear back to the bearing cup hole in the pinion flange. A helping hand will ensure accuracy. Subtract two inches from your measurement. This distance is the length of the driveshaft you'll need. Either you can start looking for one a few inches longer to cut down or you can have one custom made.

Measuring U-Joints

Hold on though. Before you leave for the machine shop, measure the universal joints so you'll know what you need. Street rod builders typically use American passenger car rear axles manufactured since 1957 without constant-velocity or ball-and-trunnion U-joints. The most common methods of bearing retention are either inside or outside retaining rings, with either U-bolts or straps binding the bearings and cross at the differential yoke.

About three dozen different universal joints could conceivably be used in a street rod. Getting the correct fit could be a real hassle if it weren't for the fact that only six U-joint conversion kits are made. You'll likely find a compatible pairing for your driveline regardless of its origin. Any good parts house counterman can give you exactly what you need if you can tell him exactly what you started with, or the transmission and rearend you plan to use.

INSTALLING A PARALLEL LEAF SUSPENSION

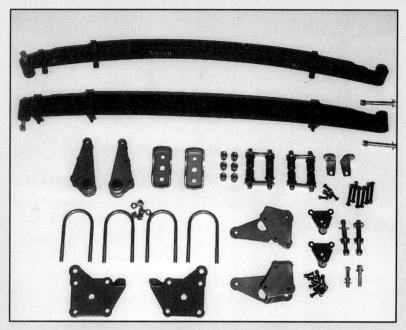

Most beginning street rodders will choose a conventional rearend with a parallel leaf spring suspension, and then select an installation kit from one of the suppliers. Here's how a Total Cost Involved kit, which includes springs, a shock installation kit, mounting brackets, and hardware, is installed.

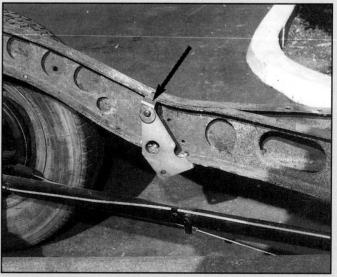

The front spring hangers mount through rivet holes in the lower lips of the rails just forward of the frame kick-up, so the rivets must be removed and the holes enlarged to 3/8-inch. The extension bracket is then bolted to the top of the rail (arrow) and the spring hanger attached. The hanger is used as a template for remaining holes.

The outside of the frame rail is then center-punched, and 3/8-inch holes drilled for the spring hanger's lower attaching bolts.

The rearmost hole in the rear spring hanger is located 2 1/2-inches forward from the center of the inboard bumper bracket bolt hole, generally in the frame from the factory, but not always. (Chalk-marked "1" in photo.) Tubular spacers are installed on the inside of the frame rail.

Center-punch points (chalk-marked "2" and "3") on the outside of the frame rail using the rear spring hanger as a template, and drill 3/8-inch holes.

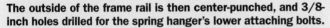

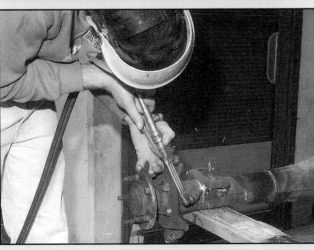

The rearend can now be readied for installation. First, however, cut off the stock spring pads, then gently smooth out the area. FoMoCo 9-inch axle housings are tough, but not impervious to heavy-handed grinding.

Installing A Parallel Leaf Suspension (continued)

The next step is to install the springs in the chassis. Attach only the front end of the springs to the hanger, however. Allow the rears of the springs to rest on the ground. Now you can roll the rearend under the chassis. Using a floor jack, attach the rear ends of the springs to the rear hangers. Put the spring pads on the springs and set the rearend in the notch of the pad.

At this point, you should verify the centering of the rearend. Measure from the rotor to the edge of the frame, side to side.

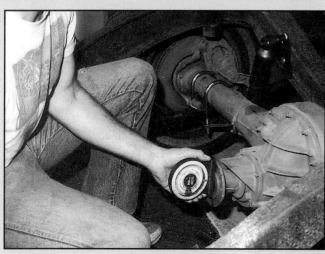 

It is always best to keep the pinion angle the same as the engine and transmission centerline. An angle finder is indispensable in this operation. Once you know that the rearend is centered and the pinion angle is correct, clamp the rearend housing to the spring with the U-bolts.

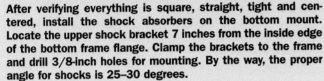

After verifying everything is square, straight, tight and centered, install the shock absorbers on the bottom mount. Locate the upper shock bracket 7 inches from the inside edge of the bottom frame flange. Clamp the brackets to the frame and drill 3/8-inch holes for mounting. By the way, the proper angle for shocks is 25–30 degrees.

Once again, double check all measurements, and make sure everything is square, straight, tight, and centered. Then tack-weld the new spring pad to the rearend housing. For a professional chassis builder like Bud Matthews, it is easy enough to leave the rearend under the frame while welding. Bud also uses a heli-arc which delivers concentrated heat. Unfortunately, that is a piece of equipment the home builder is not likely to have. Using whatever welding equipment you have, tack-weld the pads on the housing and stop. You can then remove the U-bolts, and flip the rearend over upside down and completely weld the pads to the housing. The axles and third member should be installed to keep the housing stiff. In any case, the housing should be checked by a machine shop to ensure its "straightness" after welding. It doesn't take much welding heat to cause warpage. (As in all street rod welding involving critical suspension and steering components, a high degree of welding skill is necessary. If you are unsure of your own skills, take the rearend to a professional welder.)

INSTALLING A CHASSIS ENGINEERING REAR ANTI-ROLL BAR

All street rods can benefit from an anti-roll bar at the rear. Highboy body types like 1937–48 cars and pickups need one. Unfortunately, the FoMoCo Versailles back axle does not accept the conventional anti-roll bar in the conventional location on the chassis rails behind the axle housing with the links attached to the lower parallel leaf spring bracket. The links clash with the caliper assembly. The solution is the method used by the folks at Chassis Engineering of Iowa. Here, the anti-roll bar is U-bolted to the rearend housing and the connecting links are mounted to the chassis. Their kit includes the bar, chassis mounts, housing mounts, and linkages.

The Versailles "stepped diameter" axle housing often needs to be massaged and smoothed off a bit for the kit U-bolts to slip over the tubes.

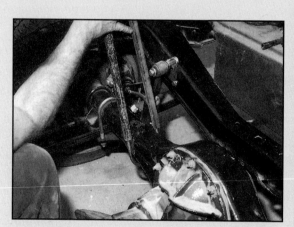

Even then, the rearend housing expanded the U-bolts a little too much for the ends to fit through the lower bracket, so they were tightened up slightly using a couple of pieces of scrap tubing as levers. (Wrap the threads with masking tape to avoid blunting the threads.)

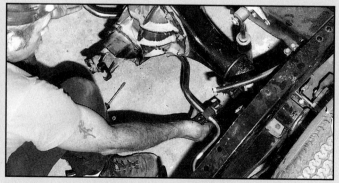

The Chassis Engineering rearend mounts for the bar are designed to fit over and around the stepped Versailles housing. The mounts are centered side-to-side and spaced 27 1/2 inches apart. The bar is then hung in the mounts. One of the advantages of this design is that the bar will fit many different frame configurations inasmuch as it attaches to the axle housing. Unusual installations, however, may require custom fabricated chassis mounts for the linkage.

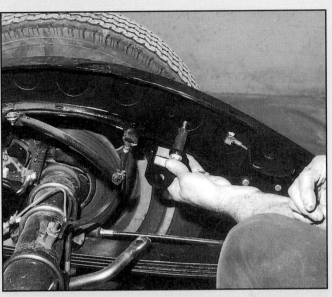

In this 1941 Ford pickup installation, however, the kit-supplied brackets fit the frame with only a minor modification. The inner chassis wall had to be notched slightly for the 2-inch spacer. Mounting holes (11/32-inch) were marked on the bottom frame lip and side rail with the mount itself serving as a template.

The installation is completed when all the hardware is securely bolted together. Obviously, the anti-roll bar is more easily installed in a rolling chassis, but after this job was finished, a running car was lifted on a hoist, and a kit was installed without much more difficulty.

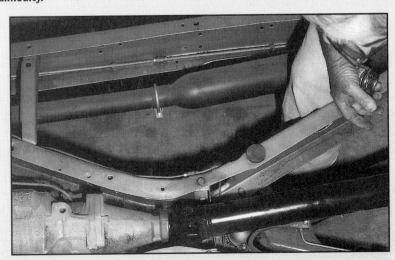

Although determining the proper length of the driveshaft seems simple enough, costly mistakes have been made many times. Dan Dohan demonstrates the correct way. First, slide the yoke onto the transmission output shaft unit it bottoms out. Next measure the distance from the centerline of that yoke's U-joint to the centerline of the U-joint on the rearend's companion flange, then subtract two inches. That's all there is to it. When the new driveshaft has been made, it must be straight with a tolerance of 0.0005-inches, and it must be balanced.

19

THE BRAKE SYSTEM

The most important street rod marriage is the mating of a modern brake system to that old car chassis. No matter how much performance and sophistication there is in the powertrain, how gleaming the paint, or plush the interior, all is lost if it won't stop on the proverbial dime!

The hot setup for brakes on early street rods was juice stoppers—hydraulic brakes—pirated from a 1940 Ford. They were a substantial improvement over the original mechanical, cable-operated brakes. The hydraulic brakes from a 1939 Ford worked equally well, but most rodders considered the required wheels far too ugly to hang on a fend-

erless roadster or coupe. The better looking 1940 drums and wheels were fitted to earlier spindles with the help of an adapter kit consisting of two bearing spacers and two rings for locating the backing plate. These kits were the earliest brake conversion components manufactured and sold to rod builders.

In the late 1940s, Ansen Automotive

Engineering began manufacturing a complete hydraulic brake conversion kit for 1928–38 Fords. It incorporated the then-new 1948 Ford master cylinder, backing plates, wheel cylinders, shoes, brackets, fittings, flexible hoses and copper tubing needed for the installation. Today, of course, copper tubing is definitely forbidden. Nothing but dedicated hydraulic tubing such as

The Ford F-100 pickup truck front brakes backing plate bolt pattern is similar to that of the 1939–48 passenger car. However, the F-100 brake assembly is a bit larger, and more importantly, self-energizing. That is, the rotation of the brake drums against the shoes helps apply the brakes, therefore reducing pedal effort considerably. Installation is simple enough, the early spindle backing plate bolt holes are enlarged slightly, and the F-100 backing plate is modified to better fit the spindle interface.

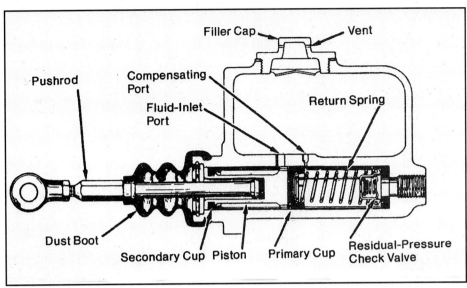

In the basic single master cylinder, the fluid reservoir is above the cylinder proper. Fluid enters the cylinder through ports and is pressurized by the pushrod-operated piston.

the tin-plated, soft steel double-wall tubing should even be considered.

The best aftermarket brakes in those postwar days were the fabled Kinmont Safe-Stop discs. In 1950, Roy Richter, of the equally fabled Bell Auto Parts, bought the manufacturing rights to the Kinmonts. He offered them to the racing and hot rod market, but their high cost—about what a basketcase roadster sold for—kept them in the wishbook category. Those old 1940–48 Ford brakes, difficult as they were to adjust, had to do for the vast majority of street rodders.

In the late 1950s some unknown street rodder was totally fed up with how much effort was required to stop his coupe with those dated Ford passenger car brakes. In all likelihood, he was a mechanic and he noticed that the F-100 pickup truck backing plate bolt pattern was similar to that of his car. Not only that, the brakes were self-energizing. The rotation of the brake

drums against the shoes helped apply the brakes, reducing pedal effort considerably. For the next 10 years or so, F-100 brakes were installed in many street rods, although the 1940–48 systems continued to be more popular.

Through the years, a few others such as the early Lincolns, with their massive lining area, and handsome finned aluminum drums from contemporary Buicks vied for the street rodder's attention. However, only when the stock rearend was replaced with a late model differential and some sort of self-energizing brakes were swapped up front, was any significant improvement in street rod "stopability" realized.

All that changed in the early 1970s when disc brakes, plundered from a variety of domestic cars, began to appear on street rods. As often as not, the adaptation was by means of relatively crude brackets. A few enterprising machine shops—usually owned and operated by street rod enthusiasts—began offering the first of many professional conversion kits. Today, it's a rare street rod that isn't equipped

with front wheel disc brakes, and at least a third of those sport rear wheel discs as well. Before we get too far along, though, let's examine the basic brake system.

HYDRAULIC PRINCIPLES

A hydraulic brake system consists of two basic components: the foot pedal-operated master cylinder, and the individual cylinders located at each wheel. In between each is the plumbing in which a special fluid is contained. When the driver steps on the foot pedal, the force is transmitted from the pedal to a pushrod, which moves a piston in the master cylinder against the fluid, pressurizing the entire system. The pressurized fluid is then converted to a force on the pistons in each wheel cylinder and, thus, the brake shoes or pads against the drums or rotors. Forces on the pistons are in direct relation to their sizes—the bigger the piston, the greater the applied force. The corresponding force of the friction material of the shoes or pads against the drums or rotors is converted to stopping torque at the wheels.

The "fruit jar" single master cylinder has only one outlet servicing both front and rear brakes. Although it doesn't have the safety features of the dual, it is a real space saver in tight frames.

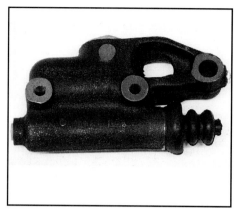

This diminutive Lockheed single master cylinder is a universal unit that requires the least amount of mounting space. It is popular for use in really tight frames such as those under a "Fad T" where every cubic inch counts. Photo courtesy California Custom Roadsters.

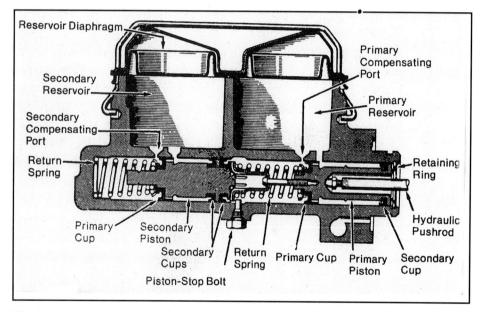

The dual master cylinder is two conventional master cylinders combined in a single cast-iron housing. Half of the cylinder body actuates the front brakes and the other half actuates the rears. The outlet for the front brakes is on the outboard side; the outlet for the rear brakes is on the bottom.

This operation, the force exerted on the brake shoes from hydraulic pressure within the system, is a practical application of Pascal's principle: "Pressure applied to an enclosed fluid is transmitted throughout the body of the fluid equally in all directions without loss."

In essence, that's about all there is to it. However, the most important consideration in the design of a street rod brake system is component compatibility. Street rod systems are often assembled from parts gathered from several sources. All of them—pedals, master cylinder, power booster, proportioning valve, wheel cylinders, shoes or pads, hydraulic lines and even the fluid must work together. That means they must be matched, or sized, one component to the other.

The Master Cylinder

Although few rod builders install the master cylinder first, it is the principle unit in the hydraulic system, and determines the remaining parameters. Its job is to pressurize the fluid. A larger master cylinder piston gives a lower system pressure and vice versa, simply because the force from the brake pedal is distributed over a larger or smaller area, respectively. This pressure is then converted to a force at the wheel cylinders.

The master cylinder also corrects for temperature changes and hydraulic fluid seepage by maintaining the required volume of fluid in the closed system. (That's why master cylinder fluid level may be low, but the system still functions.) Finally, the master cylinder charges the system with fluid upon each release of the brakes.

In a conventional master cylinder, the piston rests against a stop in its released position. A compensating or bypass port opens in this position and—if the master cylinder is designed for disc brakes—a residual pressure check valve is closed. The open port connects the cylinder with the fluid supply reservoir and compensates the system for changes in volume caused by the application or release of the friction material.

The closed check valve holds approximately 6–8 pounds per square inch (psi) residual pressure in the lines so the disc brake pads don't fully retract from the rotor surface. If this were to happen, take-up pedal travel would be excessive.

Force applied to the brake pedal is

multiplied several times at the piston by the pedal's mechanical advantage—leverage. As the pedal is depressed, moving the piston off its stop, the piston closes the compensating port and the residual check valve is overcome. Hydraulic pressure now develops and fluid moves from the reservoir into the rest of the system. A 100 pound force on the pedal with a 7.5:1 lever ratio will result in a force of 100 pounds x 7.5 or 750 pounds force at the master cylinder piston.

When the pedal is released, spring tension on the pedal arm pulls the piston pushrod away and an internal master cylinder spring retracts the piston. At the same time, the wheel cylinders retract and fluid flows into the master cylinder as the residual check valve is forced off its seat.

The returning fluid cannot flow as fast as the spring-loaded piston returns, however, and this develops a vacuum in the cylinder. The vacuum causes reserve fluid to enter through an intake port. This extra fluid flows through ports in the face of the piston, collapses the primary cup lip, and continues on around it to reduce low pressure and recharge the system. Surplus fluid returns to the master cylinder reservoir through the open bypass port.

The residual check valve also maintains a slight pressure in the system when the brakes are released, not only to prevent excess wheel cylinder retraction, but also to lessen the possibility of air leaking into the system during bleeding.

There are dozens of master cylinders available at any parts house. However, because you must maintain system compatibility, let's put the discussion of the master cylinder on hold for now. A closer look at disc brake rotors,

This Mustang II kit offers 11-inch rotors and large (non-metric) GM calipers. Although the calipers are slightly smaller than most other kits use (most other kits move wheels out), the aluminum hubs do not require wheel offset. (ECI-704)

drums and wheel cylinders, and their mountings is in order.

FRONT WHEEL BRAKES

Under hard braking, where the front brakes in the conventional front engine/rear drive car provide 70 percent of the stopability, the rodder has several options. I have no qualms advising you to scrap the stock brakes on any of the old cars in the mainstream of street rod popularity. They were adequate in their own time, and of course the restorer is honor-bound to keep his car as original as possible. We're talking street rods here, though. A prudent rod builder wants the safest braking system adaptable to his early iron.

There's simply no question that disc brakes have been the first choice of the front end of street rods for nearly forty years, and with good reason. They offer three distinct advantages over the best drum brakes. First, discs are more effective even after repeated high-speed stops and during normal driving. Unlike the interior of a brake drum, the

rotor surface is exposed directly to the outside air. Consequently, although the disc brake operates at a higher temperature, heat buildup is easily dissipated.

Because the rotor sheds water, disc brakes are immune to its deleterious effects. The third advantage of discs over drums is uniform braking—straight-line stops are assured. The street rodder who chooses a front suspension based on the traditional early Ford beam axle is well advised to update the brakes.

Although there are varieties within each manufacturer's product line, American carmakers have offered only a few basic disc brake designs over the years. Fixed calipers were introduced on many 1965 models; floating calipers were first used in 1968; and sliding calipers were introduced in the early 1970s.

Kelsey-Hayes Fixed Caliper, Opposed-Piston Disc Brakes

One of the first adaptable assemblies came from the 1965–67 Mustang. This Kelsey-Hayes design uses a fixed,

These new 5 1/2-inch bolt circle disc brake kits for 1937–48 Ford cars and pickups use 1973–93 Ford F100/F150 (2WD) rotors with 1971–76 GM big car calipers to provide vastly increased braking capability without spindle modification or machining. Kits include caliper-mounting brackets, hardware and inner bearing adapters as required plus new rotors, rebuilt caliper assemblies with pads and mounting bolts. Note: They may not fit reproduction spindles; so interested builders should call for current information. (ECI 730 CK)

four-piston caliper on a ventilated rotor. The caliper itself consists of two housings bolted together. Each half contains two cylinder pistons fitted with a seal and molded rubber boot to prevent dust contamination.

Kelsey-Hayes Floating Caliper Disc Brakes

Kelsey-Hayes' single piston, dual-pin floating calipers are found on late 1960s/early 1970s Mustangs, Cougars, and other intermediate and full-size FoMoCo models. This assembly is made up of a floating caliper mounted on an anchor plate. The anchor plate is bolted to the spindle upright. The caliper is attached to the anchor plate on pins with spring steel stabilizers. The caliper slides back and forth on two guide pins, which are also attached to the stabilizer. Instead of two pistons as in earlier models only one large piston is used to force the pads against the rotor.

Delco-Moraine Disc Brakes

Of course, not everybody wants Ford-based brakes. Many kits use Type I Delco-Moraine single piston discs with two mounting bolts. This is a sliding caliper design and incorpo-

rates a one-piece housing. The inboard side of the housing contains the piston. When the brakes are applied, fluid pressure forces the piston against the inboard pad, which is then forced against the inboard side of the disc. This action causes the caliper assembly to slide on the mounting bolts and force the outboard lining in contact with the rotor. Both linings are then forced against the rotor in direct proportion to hydraulic pressure.

Delco-Moraine Opposed Piston Disc Brakes

Four-wheel discs have been used on Corvettes since the early 1960s, and Delco-Moraine opposed piston disc brakes through the 1982 models. Those rod builders who have installed a Corvette independent rear suspension favor the compatible front discs even if they are a bit more expensive. The caliper assembly has four pistons, two on each side of the rotor. The rotor is riveted to the hub flange at the front wheel and to the spindle flange at the rear wheel. It rotates through the

ECI's Mustang II high performance disc brake conversion uses 1988–95 Corvette aluminum two-piston front calipers and Corvette rotors and the factory Corvette mounting cradle to ensure correct caliper and rotor alignment for maximum braking performance. No spindle modifications are required, but 16-inch or larger diameter wheels must be used.

Some street rodders prefer to keep rear axle drum brakes. ECI offers rebuilding kits for 1967–74 Camaro and 1967–73 Mustang rears, and come complete with new drums, new shoes (not relined), new wheel cylinders, new hardware and spring kits.

caliper assembly, which is bolted to a support attached to the steering knuckle at the front wheel and upright at the rear wheel. The parking brake system consists of a miniature set of brake shoes mounted on a flange plate and shield assembly attached to the rear wheel upright.

REAR WHEEL DRUM BRAKES

The majority of street rodders install a conventional rearend, and a good many of them are equipped with drum brakes. Rear drum brakes are acceptable, and will continue to be used because they are simple, inexpensive, and adequate. (Remember, the front brakes do most of the work.)

There are two types of drum brakes: non-servo and servo. Non-servo brake shoes are individually anchored to the backing plate. With a double-ended wheel cylinder—two pistons—acting on the upper ends of the shoes, the front shoe self-energizes. That is, the forward rotation of the drum increases the force of the shoe against the inside

of the drum. The front wheel-cylinder piston acts against the leading end of the shoe. The reverse acting shoe is de-energized because drum rotation against it unloads the shoe. The rear wheel cylinder piston acts against the trailing end of the shoe.

Some non-servo brake systems use two separate, single-piston wheel cylinders—one at the top and one at the bottom. Each acts against the leading ends of one shoe.

Because of the vast popularity of Ford rearends, the majority of rear drum brakes that rod builders use are of the servo or compound-action type manufactured by Bendix, Delco-Moraine and Wagner. In this design, the brake shoes are linked together in a single operating unit. The combined action of the primary and secondary shoes compounds the braking effect in a wedging action similar to the leading shoe.

Servo-type brakes are easily recognized by the single shoe anchor attached to the backing plate directly above the wheel cylinder between the ends of the shoes. The bottom ends are

linked together by a spring-loaded assembly that includes a star-wheel adjuster.

When the brakes are applied, the rotation of the drum assists the wheel cylinder piston in moving the forward facing shoe out against the drum. At the same time, the shoe is forced against the floating link. The link, which is also attached to the secondary shoe, forces the leading end of that shoe into contact with the drum. The braking force is compounded, thus the servo, or self-energizing action. The secondary shoe actually performs most of the work in forward movement. That's why it has more lining.

Wheel Cylinders

The conventional wheel cylinder assembly has a straight-bore, double-end cast iron housing with two small aluminum pistons. A short link is typically used between each piston and the end of one shoe. The most important specification of the rear brakes you must keep in mind is cylinder bore diameter and consequent piston area. Piston area, which determines fluid displacement of the wheel cylinders is critical to the overall efficiency of the brake system. (Piston area, expressed in square inches, is obtained by multiplying the square of the bore diameter by 0.7854.)

Although there is considerable interchangeability within every manufacturer's brake components, it is not necessary for you to go overboard with regard to using the biggest possible brakes at the rear. In terms of drum size, lining area and wheel cylinder size, the brakes found on the rearends of late 1960s/early 1970s Mustangs and Camaros are suitable for all but the very largest of street rods.

Admittedly, these rearends are getting a bit long in the tooth, but they remain popular because they are still available, relatively cheap, easy to rebuild, and easy to install under the really old cars and pickups (and reproductions thereof), that the vast majority of street rodders still seek out in this new century! So, if you plan to use one of these, measure—and record—all the specifications in your logbook.

REAR WHEEL DISC BRAKES

If you've decided to use a conventional back axle, you don't have to forego the use of four-wheel disc brakes. Not only are there several aftermarket kit suppliers, both GM and Ford have produced rearends with disc brakes that are suitable for street rod use.

Delco-Moraine Rear Disc Brakes

This is the design used on many GM four-wheel disc brake systems, except Corvettes. When the brakes are applied, an internal cone and piston move out as one part. When lining wear occurs during service, the cone and piston do not return to their original position, but rather leave a small gap equal to the lining wear between an adjusting nut and the cone. An adjusting spring rotates the nut on the high lead screw to close the gap, thereby adjusting the caliper.

When the parking brake is applied, a lever on the inboard side of each caliper turns the screw and adjusting nut to move down the screw, which clamps the lining. Upon release of the parking brake, the cone rotates on the clutch interface and readjusts the caliper. The clutch prevents the cone from turning when the parking brake is applied.

Rods running GM and Ford back axles can adapt 1980–85 Cadillac Seville/El Dorado rear calipers and 1979–81 Trans-Am rear rotors. The calipers come complete with the parking brake mechanism installed. This kit is the easiest way to get rear disc brakes with a functional OEM style parking brake. Kits are supplied complete with rebuilt rear caliper assemblies with, new rotors and pads, brackets and hardware. Minimum machining is required for rotor installation. (EC-840)

Ford Rear Wheel Disc Brakes

A hydraulically powered brake booster provides the power assist for the Ford-design four-wheel disc brake system. Except for the parking brake mechanism and a larger inner brake shoe anti-rattle spring, the rear wheel caliper is basically the same as the larger front wheel caliper. The parking brake lever, located at the rear of the caliper, is actuated by a cable system similar to that used on rear drum brake applications.

Upon application of the parking brake, the cable rotates the lever and operating shaft. Three steel balls, located in pockets between the opposing heads of the operating shaft and thrust screw, roll up ramps formed in the pockets, forcing a thrust screw away from the operating shaft. This, in turn, forces the caliper piston and brake shoe assembly against the rotor.

An automatic adjuster in the assembly compensates for lining wear. It also mains correct clearance in the parking brake mechanism.

Rotor cooling is improved by cooling passages created by curved vanes that join the inner and outer rotor surfaces. Unlike most disc-brake assemblies, the Ford rear-wheel rotors are not interchangeable because of the directional nature of the curved rotor vanes. They are identified by a right or left cast inside the hat section of each rotor. The rotor is secured to the axle flange much the same as a brake drum. A splash shield, bolted to an adapter, protects the inboard rotor surface.

MASTER CYLINDER CONSIDERATIONS

As I said earlier, there are many appropriate master cylinders for a street rod brake system. The Ford dual master cylinder, however, seems to have gained acceptance by a great many rod builders. Generally, it is two conventional master cylinders combined in a single cast-iron housing. One portion actuates the front brakes and the other the rears.

A failure of either system does not impair the operation of the other. On factory installations with disc brakes at the front and drums at the rear, the dual master cylinder has the outlet port for the rear brake system on the bottom of the master cylinder body. A bleeder screw is on the outboard side of the casting. The front brake system outlet port is also on the outboard side. This type of master cylinder also contains a pressure-differential valve assembly and a switch that activates a warning light located on the instrument panel of the donor car.

Earlier, I was emphatic with regard to system compatibility. This means that you must use a master cylinder that is compatible with the wheel brakes. Taking this further, you should use one that matches the front-wheel brakes. For instance, if you installed a late model disc brake conversion kit, the disc brake master cylinder of the type used in the donor car will work best. Fortunately, it is rare that the disc brake master cylinder and front disc brakes for which it was designed won't be compatible with almost any drum brake rear.

Although there isn't that much difference in modern rear drum brakes, there is a procedure for determining the fluid requirements of the complete system to ensure the compatibility of the master cylinders and all wheel cylinders. Apply the following procedure to be absolutely sure you're maintaining system compatibility.

The master cylinder must have the capacity to displace as much fluid as required by the combined wheel units plus 30 percent for a margin of safety. Any master cylinder used with disc brakes must be designed for use with disc brakes. Otherwise, the residual pressure check valve must be removed.

For purposes of illustration, let's see what master cylinder you need for a typical street rod with 1968 Mustang front discs and a 1969 Fairlane Ford rear with drums. Starting with the rears, a direct measurement of the piston diameter finds it is 15/16 inches. This converts to 0.9375 inches.

Next, calculate the area of the top by using the formula mentioned earlier, or 0.7854 x diameter in inches squared = piston area in square inches. Plugging in the numbers, 0.7854 x (0.9375 square inches) = 0.6899 square inches. Rounding off, we have 0.69 square inches of piston area. Multiplying that area by a convenient constant used for all drum brake strokes—0.2 inches— we get 0.69 square inches x 0.2 inches = 0.138 cubic inches, or 0.14 rounded off. But wait! There are two wheel cylinders on a Fairlane rearend, right? Therefore, total fluid volume demand of the rear drum brakes is 2 x 0.14 cubic inches = 0.28 cubic inches. (Don't forget that number.)

Going to the front, check the disc brake pistons. The 1968 Mustang has one piston per caliper. It measures 1.625 inches. Plugging into our formula, we come up with 0.7854 x (1.625 square inches) = 2.07 cubic inches rounded off. Multiply that area by the constant for all disc brake strokes— 0.07 inches—and get the following: 0.07 inches x 2.07 cubic inches = 0.14 cubic inches fluid displacement.

Although disc brakes are usually designed with one, two or four pistons per rotor, we only need to concern ourselves with how many are on one side of the rotor to calculate the fluid demand per caliper, but because there are two calipers, double the figure to obtain 0.28 cubic inches total fluid displacement for the front disc brakes.

Combined fluid requirement will require a master cylinder that can adequately displace the 0.29 cubic inch front discs plus the 0.28 cubic inch rear drums for a subtotal of 0.57 cubic inches. Add that 30 percent safety margin I mentioned earlier, or 0.17 cubic inches for a grand total of 0.74 cubic inches. That is the minimum volume requirement of the master cylinder. Any less will lead to inadequate operation. A master cylinder displacing more than that won't be a problem.

If you are building a brake system on your own without the help of street rod suppliers, the easiest way to determine the capacity of any given master cylinder is to ask the parts house counterman to look up the bore of the master cylinder that is designed for your front brakes. His catalog will list that figure, but they seldom list strokes. It's a good idea, therefore, to bring along a depth gauge so you can measure the stroke directly. Once you have that, apply the formula: Piston area squared x 0.7854 x stroke = fluid displacement. If you luck out and find that the master cylinder contains at least 30 percent more than your wheel units need, you're on your way.

Actually, unless you have some outlandish rear wheel cylinders, chances are good that the master cylinder designed for your front discs will be OK for the rear. Not always, but usually.

ECI's power brake booster/master cylinder and pedal assemblies are designed specifically for street rod applications. They are available for under-floor installation in 1928-48 Fords as well as many early GM and Chrysler cars. The small 7-inch diameter makes installation easy and provides power brake performance with dual master cylinder safety.

The compact Midland-Ross power booster, originally designed for small motor homes, can be installed in any convenient area in the frame between the master cylinder and the wheel cylinders. Shown is SAC Hot Rod Components installation in a 1940 Ford chassis.

ECI's remote booster has primarily been designed for street rods that are so low, there may not be enough room for even the smallest booster. It can be mounted in the trunk and unlike many others, works with any dual master cylinder. ECI also offers an electric vacuum pump with a low manifold vacuum sensor and switch that runs the pump only on demand. (Rods with blowers often cannot generate enough manifold vacuum to safely operate a brake booster.)

Nevertheless, measuring and calculating your brake system demands is necessary to prevent problems later on.

POWER BRAKES

Power brakes have been around since the mid 1950s, and most rodders don't consider them an option any longer. Beyond that, disc brakes require greater line pressure for proper operation—as much as 14,000 psi. (Pressures required for drum brakes are seldom above 1000 psi.) Therefore, you'll have to choose—and find a place for—a conventional power booster.

The modern passenger car power assist unit is either a vacuum-suspended type (VSPB) that operates off engine vacuum, or is hydraulically assisted, drawing its supply of pressurized fluid from the power steering pump. The power unit of either system is typically bolted directly to the back of the master cylinder. Unfortunately, they are rather large and not particularly attractive.

Try to locate as much of the hardware under the floorboard as possible. It is usually best to fit it in after you've installed the engine and transmission, but before the exhaust system is built. Installing the master cylinder below the floorboard is worthwhile for more than just cosmetic reasons; it is struc-

turally desirable. Adequately beefing up the firewall of an early car can be difficult whereas adding support bracketry to the chassis is relatively easy.

An alternative to the conventional power-boost unit is the remote unit mountable in the brake line wherever convenient as long as there is access to the air bleeder valve. The Bendix HydroVac, a derivative of the conventional vacuum-suspended booster, has been around for years. It is installed in the line after the master cylinder, but before the tee-off to the wheel cylinders. There is one catch, however, some remote power boosters cannot be used in conjunction with a dual master cylinder.

Metering, Proportioning, and Residual Pressure Valves

Three of the most misunderstood components in the brake system are metering, proportioning, and residual pressure valves. Some combination of metering and proportioning valves, however, is a must when a combination disc/drum brake system is used.

The metering or "hold-off" valve is used for the front discs in a disc/drum system to allow the rear drum brakes to actuate first, an essential function in a hybrid system.

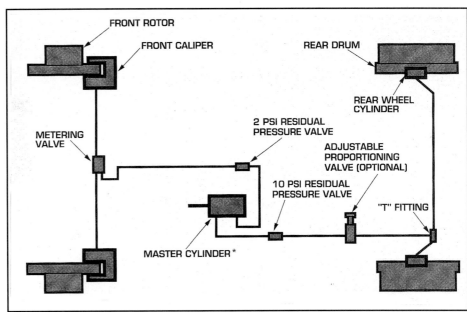

Typical Front Disc/Rear Drum Brake System Plumbing Schematic. A 10 psi residual pressure valve is used to prevent air from being sucked into the system when the brake pedal is suddenly released. Note: Always connect the master cylinder outlets the same way as in the OEM installation. Reversing the outlets does have an effect on system operation.

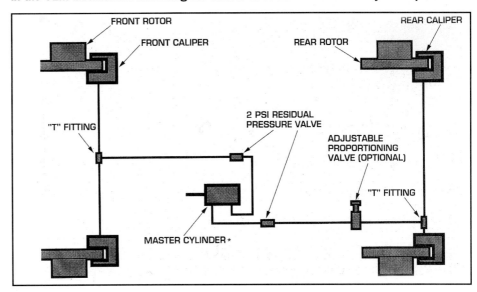

Typical Front Disc/Rear Disc Brake System Plumbing Schematic. A 2 psi pressuve valve is use when the master cylinder is below the height of the calipers. Note: Always connect the master cylinder outlets the same way as in the OEM installation. Reversing the outlets does have an effect on system operation.

The metering or "hold off" valve in a disc/drum brake system prevents the disc brakes from being applied under light braking (low line pressure) and allow the rear drum brakes to actuate first. The discs function when line pressure reaches about 135 psi. (Pressure at the drum brake wheel cylinders overcomes tension on the brake shoe return springs so the shoes contact the drums at the same time the disc brake pads make contact with the rotor.) Most factory type disc/drum combination valves have this function built in, and the rod builder must use either the factory valve or an aftermarket stand-alone valve.

On the other hand, the proportioning valve (and some are adjustable) is installed in the line to the rear brakes (disc or drum) to reduce pressure at the rear brakes when a preset line pressure is reached. This helps prevent rear wheel lock-up during heavy braking. Weight is transferred from the rear to the front wheels, reducing in proportion the braking requirement at the rear and increasing it at the front. These are built into OEM combination valves, so thoroughly understand what you have. Depending on the compatibility of your brake system components, one may not be needed.

If you've ever had to double pump your brake pedal after you've been parked on an incline for an hour or so, chances are very good you need a residual pressure valve! A 2-psi is used in disc brake systems when the master cylinder is below the height of the calipers. They act as an anti-siphon valve, preventing brake fluid from siphoning back into the master cylinder when the pedal is released. In the interest of safety, install one even if the master cylinder is slightly above the caliper.

A 10-psi residual pressure valve is used in a drum brake system to prevent air from being sucked into the

This brake pedal/master cylinder/power booster assembly for 1928–48 Ford passenger cars and pickups is engineered with correct leverage. The kit includes bronze Oilite bushings, a pushrod with a spherical rod end, pedal pad and all hardware. (ECI-520)

This ECI adapter mounts their Mustang master cylinder to the stock 1939-40 pedal assembly. It comes with all necessary hardware and uses the stock Ford pushrod and boot. If you are building a later Ford or a non-Ford based rod and there are no direct or universal replacement pedal assemblies that please you, I hope you still have the originals! If so, adapt the modern master cylinder to the stock pedal base. There are a few adapters on the market, but if these won't do, a simple 3/8-inch piece of aluminum flat stock usually gets you started. Once again, try to avoid firewall-mounted pedals where you can unless you plan to build in significant structural reinforcement.

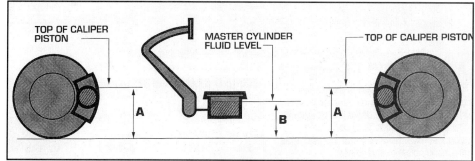

Determining the need for residual pressure valves. Residual pressure valves are needed when "A" is greater than "B."

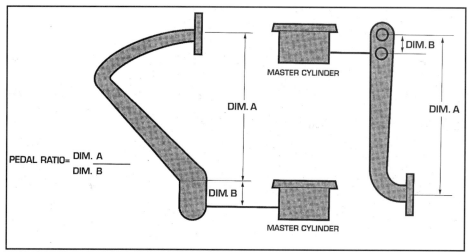

$$PEDAL\ RATIO = \frac{DIM.\ A}{DIM.\ B}$$

Force applied to the brake pedal is multiplied several times at the piston by the pedal's mechanical advantage. A typical pedal ratio for manual brakes is about 5:1, and for power brakes, about 3:1.

system when the brake pedal is suddenly released. Conventional wheel cylinder seals are only effective when there is pressure behind them. A vacuum in the system will cause them to relax and suck in air. Ten psi in the sys-tem at all times is the preventative. Although some disc/drum master cylinders have 10-psi residual pressure valves installed internally, some don't. Check this out when you buy yours. By the way, if you purchase wheel cylinders with cup extenders, you don't really need the residual pressure valve. Caution is the better part of valor, however, so if in doubt, install the valve, extra protection won't hurt. Seventy-five psi is required to overcome the return springs.

Beginning in the 1970s, most American cars equipped with front disc and rear drums came with a combination metering valve and proportioning valve. Although several different types of metering, proportioning and combination valves are available, the unit the factory installed, along with the master cylinder you select, should work in your car if the weight distribution and center-of-gravity are similar to that of the donor car. Therefore, it is best to avoid master cylinders and valve combinations originally designed for late model cars that are significantly heavier than your street rod.

The included schematics show the location of the metering valve, residual pressure valve, and the optional adjustable proportioning valve in both the front disc/rear drum and four-wheel disc brake systems.

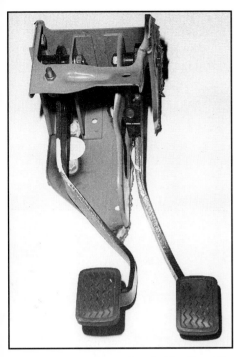

There're a number of suitable firewall-mounted pedal assemblies in every wrecking yard. Admittedly, they offer a clean floorboard for attractive upholstering as well as a convenient service area. If you choose a set, you must build in significant structural reinforcement.

THE REST OF THE SYSTEM

In addition to the major components, there are the brake lines, fluid, and pedal assembly. If you decided to install a manual transmission, chances are you have already tackled the problem of pedals. If not, and if your project car is based on a 1927–40 Ford or replica, you'll find ample reproduction chassis-mounted pedal assemblies in the catalogs of most street rod component manufacturers.

With regard to brake lines, the best

Pure Choice Motor Sports of Lake Havasu City, Arizona catalogs a line of zinc plated steel master cylinder fittings with a banjo to –3AN design. Such fittings allow a 90-degree flow out of the master cylinder where clearance is a problem, or simply if a cleaner look is desired for brake lines.

advice is to buy a number of commercial double-flared short, medium and long lengths and a fistful of connector fittings. Often, you can get return privileges if you don't bend, cut or scratch the tubing. Use them as is when you can. Shorten only one end when necessary. Several inexpensive brake line bending tools are available, and you'll need a good flaring tool and tubing cutter with a sharp blade.

As for fluid, every brand is Department of Transportation (DOT) approved. Some street rod builders, however, prefer silicone fluid. It is expensive, but it isn't something you use by the gallon. One or two quarts should supply the needs of your street rod.

Finally, use the best parts in your brake system. Brakes are not the place to skimp. Always buy new, not rebuilt

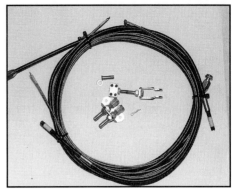

Lokar's universal parking brake kit comes in two versions, one with a basic black housing, and another with a braided housing. All the hardware needed to make those oft-ignored auxiliary brakes functional on a drummed back axle is provided. A variety of brake handles is also available.

master cylinders. Moreover, be absolutely sure wrecking yard rotors, calipers and drums are in top condition. In fact, I would only use second-hand components to mock up your system while designing it. Replace these parts with new units before you hit the bricks. Put your best effort into your brake system the first time around . . . you may not get a second shot.

However, because of the limited space in this multi-subject book, there're too few pages to cover the entire subject in the depth some may wish. Rod builders interested in designing their own brakes are advised to get Mavrigan and Carley's *Brake Systems* published by HPBooks. It deals with all aspects of practical brake theory.

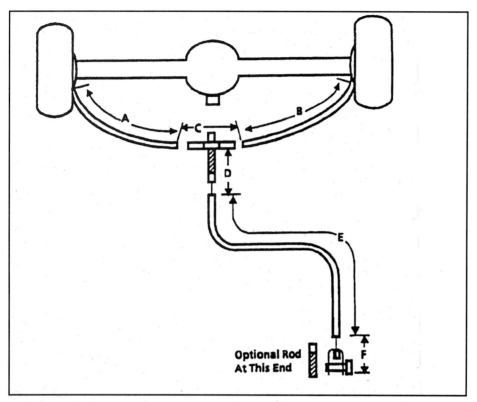

Optional Rod
At This End

FoMoCo and GM rearends with disc brakes must have functional parking brakes. Control Cables of Santa Fe Springs, California offers specialized assemblies that make life easier for street rod builders. The two most common parking brake installations are center pull and side pull. Illustrated is the layout for the center pull style and the critical dimensions needed for them to build a custom assembly:

A) Backing plate to housing bracket on the passenger side.
B) Backing plate to housing bracket on the driver's side.
C) The length of the exposed cable.
D) Mounting bracket.
E) Front cable housing, bracket to bracket.
F) Mounting bracket to clevis pin in handle.
G) Mounting bracket to end of adjusting rod/rear cables.

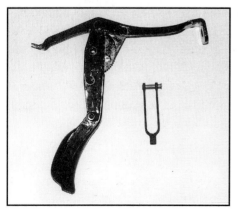

In keeping with the resto-rod look I prefer in my '40 Ford coupe and '41 Ford pickup, I used the stock parking brake handles for the muscle end of my disc brake Versailles rearends parking brake cables.

ECI's mechanically operated parking brake system for Ford rears provides a static retarding force in excess of 1800 ft-lbs. from factory or aftermarket parking brake handles. A 3:1 hand ratio requires just 35 pounds of input force. The assembly mounts to the standard Ford pinion housing mounting flange and only minor machining of yoke is required for installation.

THE COOLING & EXHAUST SYSTEMS

20

THE COOLING SYSTEM

The automotive cooling system must maintain an efficient operating temperature regardless of driving conditions and road speed. If too little heat is removed, cylinder-to-bore clearances go away, causing metal-to-metal contact as the pistons attempt to expand larger than their bores. This is quickly followed by disastrous results such as pistons seizing and galling. If the motor runs too cool, thermal efficiency—the relationship between power output and the latent fuel energy—drops off. Excess bore wear also results. Efficient operating temperatures are always precariously balanced somewhere between too hot and too cool in stockers, but few street rodders have ever had to worry about running too cool.

Since the days of the flathead V-8, and probably before, street rod builders have had to deal with overheating. Even the best home-built cars suffered from this malady. Part of the problem is that most street rods are equipped with modified motors that tend to run hotter than their stock brethren do. Beyond this, the motor usually has a larger cubic inch displacement, and often is physically larger than the original, leaving less room for airflow.

Another part of the problem arises from external modifications to the radiator, shrouds, ducting, fan location, and so on, which further reduce airflow.

The Number One problem facing running street rods is adequate cooling. Address preventative measures early in the game.

Add to this the fact that all too often street rods are equipped with inadequate radiators. Overheating is the price one pays for miscalculations.

Automotive lubricating oils have been improved with the advent of emission control regulations and the introduction of unleaded fuels. Nevertheless, the lubricating properties of most grades rapidly break down when motor temperatures climb past 600 degrees F. (Temperatures can actually reach as high as 4500 degrees F in the combustion chambers.) Much of this heat is passed out through the exhaust system, but the heads, cylinder walls and pistons absorb a significant amount. In order to keep the motor in the narrow, but efficient temperature band, the cooling system

Several companies that build custom radiators for street rods will factory install an integral condenser if the car is equipped with an air conditioner. Take advantage of this option. The installation will be much cleaner than most add-ons.

If you are thinking about having a local shop build you a custom radiator, you find a wide variety of sizes and styles from which to choose. (This is just a sample of the core inventory at Continental Radiator in Stanton, California.) Take the basic measurements of the area between the beginning of the grille and the front of the motor, and from the frame horns to the fender/hood interface. Discuss your cooling concerns with the shop owner, and he'll advise you from there.

There are two types of core designs in standard use, the tube and plate fin (left), and the tube and corrugated or serpentine fin (right). Both have a series of flat tubes extending from the top tank to the lower tank. Outside air passing between the rows of tubes absorbs some of the heat. The fins improve heat transfer. Cores manufactured with 7–20 fins per inch are standard. Higher counts are considered heavy-duty.

must remove about 35 percent of the remaining heat.

The Radiator

The conventional liquid-cooled street rod employs a system with a chassis-mounted copper/brass or aluminum radiator and a mechanical, motor-mounted cast-iron or aluminum coolant pump. Hoses connect these components.

The radiator most often used in street rods has a top and bottom tank and a ventilated core in the center. During its cycle, heat-bearing coolant is delivered to the top tank; it cools as it flows down through the core to the bottom tank, then the coolant is drawn into the pump from the radiator through a hose in the bottom tank. The radiator is designed to allow a large volume of air to move through a large volume of coolant in its core, where it transfers heat from the coolant to the air.

Radiators have been manufactured of copper for many years. Copper is strong and dissipates heat rapidly although lead soldering is a minor detriment. However, when the big push for auto weight savings came on the heels of the need for better gas mileage in the early 1970s, Detroit was quick to respond to the challenge

with aluminum. (The significant price differential between aluminum and copper didn't hurt either.) Today, the street rodder has his choice.

The radiator core has two separate components—tubes and fins. The two types of core designs in standard use

The honeycomb styled "heat sponge radiator," available exclusively from the Brassworks Company, utilizes 1800 copper tubes per square foot of frontal area to provide three times the surface area of the conventional radiator in direct contact with the coolant. They point out that copper tubing conducts heat twice as fast as aluminum, and four times faster than brass.

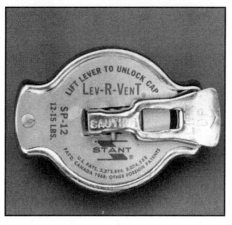
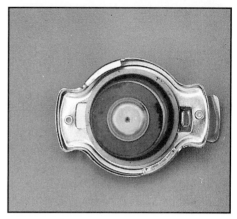

The pressure cap contains two safety devices. The blow-off valve lifts when system pressure exceeds a specified pressure. The vacuum-release valve compensates for the partial vacuum that develops when a hot motor cools. When vacuum reaches the danger point, the valve opens and admits air into the system preventing excess pressure. A 13- to 15-pound pressure cap is recommended for normally aspirated small-block powered street rods.

are the tube and plate fin, and the tube and corrugated or serpentine fin. Both have a series of flat tubes extending from the top tank to the lower tank. Outside air passing between the rows of tubes absorbs some of the heat. The fins aren't there just for decoration, either; they improve heat transfer. Cores manufactured with 7–20 fins per inch are standard. Higher counts are considered heavy-duty and are usually more expensive.

The number of tubes (arranged in rows) determines the cooling capacity of an automotive radiator. The standard tube is approximately 7/16 inch wide by 3/32 inch thick; heavy-duty tubes range up to 3/4 inch by 1/8 inch. Although special radiators can be built with as many as six rows of tubes—Ford flathead radiators had four—cooling efficiency falls off as the core increases in overall thickness due to restricted airflow.

There is another core design, the honeycomb styled "heat sponge" introduced by the Brassworks Company of San Luis Obispo, California, utilizing copper tubing (1800 tubes per square foot of frontal area) to provide three times the surface area of the conventional radiator in direct contact with the coolant.

The metals and designs in use today have a lot of good points, and a few relatively minor downsides. The auto manufacturers have essentially switched to aluminum and serpentine fins across the board. Production costs, I'm sure, weigh heavily in the corporate design. However, the street rodder, while always keeping a wary idea on cost, is most interested in maximum cooling efficiency. With that end in mind, he is willing to pay a little more for trouble-free driveability.

The Pressurized System

Radiators do not cool by virtue of tubes and fins alone. Increasing coolant pressure and preventing evaporation and surge losses dramatically improves the efficiency of the cooling system. Atmospheric pressure is near-

ly 15 psi at sea level and, at that pressure, pure water boils at 212 degrees F. By merely installing a "pressure cap" on the radiator, cooling system pressures increases. For each additional psi, the boiling point of pure water is increased 3 degrees F. Because the difference between the coolant temperature and the temperature of the air surrounding the radiator is greater, coolant temperature drop is greater.

The radiator pressure cap is more complex than you may realize, containing two separate safety devices. One is a blow-off valve, which is held against its seat by a calibrated spring. The valve lifts when system pressure exceeds a specified pressure.

The other safety feature is a vacuum-release valve. It compensates for the partial vacuum that develops when the motor is shut down and begins to cool. When vacuum reaches the danger point, the valve opens and admits air into the system. Therefore, neither excess pressure nor vacuum, both of which are potentially dangerous, can develop.

Most radiator builders recommend a 13 to 15 psi pressure cap for normally

Electric fans have become very popular with street rod builders, and with good cause. Not only do they provide location options that motor-driven fans obviously cannot offer, they are not power drains. Space considerations not withstanding, they should be mounted behind the radiator whenever possible. A draw-through fan is more efficient. In my own small-block Ford powered rods, however, I did not have that luxury. Nevertheless, the front mount I am stuck with gets the cooling job done very well.

If the fan is more than an inch from the radiator, maximum efficiency is lost. The solution is to install a fan shroud one inch larger than the fan diameter. When installed, the fan should be about half the way into the shroud at the blade tips.

aspirated small-block powered street rods.

The Water Pump

The pump contains an impeller with curved vanes or blades. As the impeller rotates, the vanes force coolant through the outlet and into the motor, where it is circulated through "water jackets." The jackets are voids cast into the block and heads that encircle the cylinders, combustion chambers, valve seats and ports. As coolant is routed through the motor, it absorbs rejected heat and carries it to the radiator where it is transferred to the air. The coolant is then recirculated to the motor. By the way, fancy machined water pump pulleys have long been popular with street rodders. No problem, but always try to use the same diameter as the stock pulley. Underdriving the water pump can aggravate a minor overheating problem.

Hoses

The best fitting radiator hoses for street rods with motor swaps are the flexible, spiral-wound types with internal wire reinforcement. The wire helps maintain a full diameter even when the hose is bent into a soft curve. This is particularly important for the bottom hose that operates under low pressure. In addition, it's a rare motor swap that doesn't have at least one or two necessary bends somewhere betwixt and between. Once you find the hoses that match the radiator and water pump (and there are literally hundreds of shapes and sizes), record the part numbers in your logbook. Remember that hoses are "consumables." Change them every two years or so, particularly the bottom one. It's more likely to fail first because the coolant is sucked through it.

Mechanical and Electric Fans

The fan draws air through the radiator to improve coolant-to-air heat transfer. Unfortunately, some rod builders give the fan the old heave-ho.

Although it is true that the fan is of relatively little value once the car is moving more than 30 mph, and a motor-driven fan does use horsepower, don't eliminate it from the equation. There are alternatives.

One way to keep a motor cool without sacrificing horsepower is to install an automatic or clutch-type fan. Most have a bi-metallic spring thermostat. The spring senses air temperature and regulates a control valve. When the valve opens, a silicone-base oil is released into the drive-plate housing and the fan speeds up. As air through the radiator cools, the fan idles and horsepower drain is reduced.

Another option is the flexible fiberglass or thin stainless steel bladed fan. These lightweight designs typically have variable-pitch blades—a kind of self-adjusting action. Blade pitch is at a high angle during low rpm operation, causing the fan to draw in plenty of air. The blades deflect and flatten out at higher rpm, resulting in less power drain at higher speeds.

Although not the most efficient, my

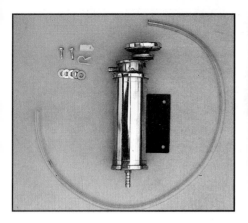

An important adjunct to the cooling system is a "catch can." No need for those unsightly plastic bottles when several street rod suppliers have handsome metal vessels. Depending on the configuration of the radiator neck and the recommendations of the coolant recovery bottle, a non-vented radiator cap can be used.

personal favorite is the heavy-duty "pusher" electrical fan built specially for street rods. They are adaptable to different radiator sizes and are relatively easy to install. Some have a built-in, adjustable thermostat, which cycles them on and off. Others are simply controlled by a manual switch under the dash and a watchful eye on the temperature gauge. With regard to overall blade diameter, always use the largest that will fit between grille and radiator. True, they can be noisy, but that's a small price to pay.

Shrouds, Thermostats, Coolant and Recovery Tanks

When a fan is mounted on the motor side of the radiator, it should pull air through the radiator core. If, however, the fan is more than an inch or so away from the radiator, or off-center, efficiency is lost. The solution is to install a fan shroud. It will improve maximum cooling dramatically. The funnel shaped design ensures that all air pulled by the fan is drawn through the radiator. Various fiberglass fan shrouds are available from new car dealers, but finding the right one can be difficult. The shroud should be about one inch larger than the fan diameter. When installed, the fan should be about half the way

into the shroud at the blade tips.

One way to find the right shroud is to sample a variety of late-model offerings at the local wrecking yard. These, though, are frequently damaged in front-end accidents. They are reasonably priced however, so you can buy two or three to see which will fit best in your street rod. That way you know for sure what model, size and shape, you need before you buy a new one from the dealer.

The thermostat, like the radiator fan, is another cooling system component that's often misused, abused or not used at all. Leaving it out, in fact, is the most common mistake novice rodders make with their cooling system. A functioning thermostat is necessary for coolant temperature control at all times. Its job is to close off the water passages between the motor and the top of the radiator to ensure quicker warm-up time and that the coolant is maintained at a minimum temperature. A thermostat that's in good operating condition does not cause a motor to overheat. The thermostat is nothing more than a spring and a valve. When the spring is cold, it keeps the valve closed. As motor temperature increases, the spring expands, opening the valve, and allowing coolant to circu-

late through the radiator and motor.

Thermostats are designed to operate within specific temperature ranges. The popular 160 degree F unit starts to open between 157 and 163 degrees F and is fully open at 183 degrees F. "Hotter" thermostats rated at 180 degrees F and 192 degrees F are popular in northern climates. Many late model cars, however, use 225 degree F thermostats to achieve lower emissions. Fortunately, motor oil improvements have kept pace with higher operating temperatures.

Coolant

Water is not the best coolant with which to fill the radiator. It won't lubricate the water pump seal or control corrosion and electrolysis. Also, pure water boils at a lower temperature than a mixture of water and antifreeze/antiboil. I live in an area with notoriously hard tap water full of minerals. I use a 50/50 mix of distilled water and antifreeze/antiboil. I've found that all major brands of ethylene glycol antifreeze/antiboil concentrate are adequate.

They're all expensive, too. So, use one of the closed system coolant recovery tanks on the market. They not only pay for themselves in short time; they eliminate air from the system.

The Temperature Gauge

The final cooling system component to consider is the temp gauge. It alerts the driver to abnormally high motor temperatures. Two types of temp gauges are available: electrical and mechanical.

An electrical gauge consists of a pair of coils and an armature to which a needle is attached. As motor temperature rises, resistance of the sending unit drops and additional current is passed through the coils. The greater magnetic field attracts the armature, and the needle moves correspondingly. Unfortunately, I have found some electrical gauges off by several degrees. At best, the run-of-the mill, uncalibrated electrical gauge is useful merely as a point of reference.

In my experience, top quality mechanical gauges are more accurate. The fact that they are more expensive than electrical units doesn't bother me a bit. The conventional mechanical or vapor pressure gauge uses a sensing bulb containing a liquid that evaporates at low temperatures. The sensing bulb—sending unit—is inserted into the water jacket in the intake manifold or cylinder head where it comes in direct contact with motor coolant.

The bulb is linked to the gauge by means of a transmission line. The gauge contains a small curved Bourdon tube, which in turn, is linked to the indicator needle. The liquid in the bulb reacts to a rise in temperature by expanding and creating a pressure that is relayed through the transmission line to the gauge. As pressure increases, the Bourdon tube changes shape and the gauge needle indicates the temperature rise. Although they are

Healthy motors need an equally healthy exhaust system. The pursuit of performance, however, often incurs installation problems. Sometimes it is a real "Hobson's choice." Should you modify the body sheet metal, or compromise the ideal exhaust system?

admittedly more unwieldy and more difficult to install than a simple wire, I much prefer mechanical temperature gauges. By the way, for those of you who just like to keep accurate tabs on what's going on under the hood, as a rule, coolant temperature in the motor is about 10 degrees F hotter than in the radiator.

Paying the Price

Regardless of how well individual components work, and how they interrelate, eventually you must make some hard economic choices. My experience tells me to choose new water pumps over rebuilt ones, electric fans over belt-driven fans, and as stated above, mechanical temperature gauges over electrical gauges. Moreover, when it comes to the most important component of them all, the radiator, I believe in the best. Today, most any radiator shop can build a custom fitted radiator for those one-off street rod creations. If you are going the resto-rod route and want some-

thing that closely approaches the look of the original, several companies stand ready to offer you their wares.

THE EXHAUST SYSTEM
Factory Exhaust Manifolds

What goes in must come out. That's why you must eventually deal with your street rod's exhaust system. Of course, there is the penurious approach. If the stock exhaust manifolds do not interfere with the steering gear or any other major components, just tow the car over to the nearest muffler shop and have the man weld up a brace of header pipes. The installation of two mufflers, a pair of exhaust pipes no more complicated than they absolutely have to be, and a couple of chrome tips finishes off the job with a minimum of capital outlay.

Ah, but if you want the best bargain in the high performance field, consider a truly efficient exhaust system. Nowhere else in all of street rodding can you get a picture-perfect motor swap, an honest increase in net horse-

John Athan's '29 roadster, which he built in 1939, is still running 60-plus years later. It demonstrates that perceptive early street rodders were aware of the need for a low-restriction exhaust. This is even more amazing because so many contemporary rod builders still use restrictive small-block Chevy and Ford stock cast-iron exhaust manifolds. I'll admit that their use is economical and facilitates the motor swap, but a significant loss of performance is the inevitable downside.

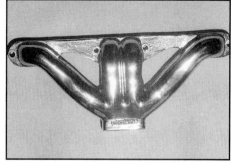

Sanderson's cast iron headers for the small-block Chevy equal the backpressure reduction of shorty tubular headers, but without the problems of leaks, rust and burnouts.

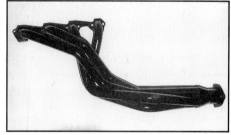

High performance exhaust systems have equal length primaries. Unfortunately, it's not always practical or even possible to install the perfect exhaust system in a street rod chassis.

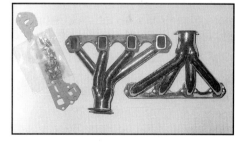

Sanderson stainless steel small-block headers may not be fully appreciated until you realize they were mail ordered and fit without modifications! They are made from 304 stainless steel and heli-arc welded for uniform strength.

power, and a simultaneous increase in fuel economy. It will cost a few bucks up front, but first-class exhaust plumbing is guaranteed to please.

I discussed motor swaps early on in this book, because that's where the story of hands-on street rodding begins. Installing a popular V-8 in any early automobile is surprisingly easy in most cases. If it weren't, there wouldn't be so many rods with motor swaps on the road. With few exceptions, however, the most difficult part of the swap for the novice builder is finding appropriate exhaust manifolds. Aside from providing reasonable exhaust flow, the manifolds must be able to bolt up flush to the cylinder heads, miss exiting into the steering gear, new motor mounts, chassis or firewall. They must also allow you to change sparkplugs with ease.

There are a few motor swaps with stock exhaust manifolds that meet all of these criteria. The first to come to

mind is the ubiquitous 1960s era small-block Chevy V-8 "ram's horns" cast iron manifolds. Rare indeed is the early Ford car—and to a lesser extent, the early Chevy—that doesn't accommodate this combo. On the other hand, the small-block Ford with the standard passenger side manifold and the late 1960s "high performance" driver's side manifold also fits popular street rod choices fairly well once all the other headaches are resolved. Nevertheless, the years have a habit of slipping away, and the availability of such parts commonly found in wrecking yards three decades ago are now limited to the swap meet offerings by gray-bearded street rodders (a group righteously known for hoarding "surplus inventory").

Better Than Stock

The rod builder who doesn't install a V-8 that is a close approximation of the size and configuration of the motor

it replaces can expect problems in the exhaust department. The most practical solution is the aftermarket "block hugger" or "shortie" header designed for the popular late motor/early car combinations followed by custom bent exhaust tubing and compatible mufflers. This is a very satisfactory solution in almost all cases. In a word,

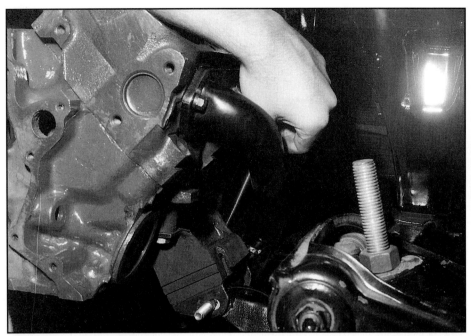

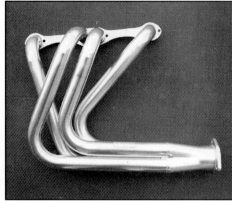

Rewarder Custom Headers of Camarillo, California uses 3/8-inch flanges, and heavy gauge, mandrel-bent tubing. Then the assembly is TIG-welded for a clean look. After the header is built, they apply a ceramic coating in-house.

Before mail ordering headers, carefully measure and photograph several critical areas, particularly around steering gear. If you can borrow a buddy's header, by all means, mock up the assembly. Pass information on to the header company to help them make a reasonable judgment as to whether or not there will be any clearance problem with their headers.

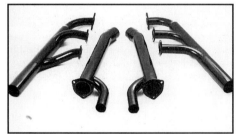

Speedway Motors offers original styled headers for flathead Fords just like the hot shoes used at the lakes in the '50s. They incorporate a separate, capable outlet for easy opening when the traditionalist wants straight-through exhaust.

block huggers are more efficient than the finest factory cast-iron manifold.

The ultimate, of course, is the exhaust system truly custom built from the heads to the rear bumper. Custom headers go wherever necessary to circumvent the steering gear and motor mounts, and the best part is, no matter how circuitous they become, they always look good.

That's the upside. The downside is that custom headers are a bit "tinny" sounding, require premium gaskets to prevent minor leaks, and demand special ceramic coatings for durability unless they are made out of stainless steel tubing. Not only that, they are extremely difficult for the amateur to build although "U-Fab" kits are available for rod builders with an eye for spatial perception, handy with tin snips and can weld light-gauge tubing. They also have to be patient and willing to accept some waste before a tight, presentable package is achieved,

a tall order to say the least.

I have seen passable headers built by non-pros who took the trial-and-error, approach. For most of us, however, farming the job out to a professional (when one can be found) is the most desirable in terms of exhaust system efficiency and beauty. However, even if you accept that premise, you may still need a little more convincing that the cost of a custom exhaust system is justified.

The honest horsepower any normally aspirated internal combustion motor is capable of producing depends largely on the quantity of air/fuel mixture drawn into its cylinders and the evacuation of the burned gases after combustion. Most production car motors fall short of their potential volumetric efficiency in the high rpm ranges. After all, that's why hot rodding was invented in the first place!

The most significant aspect of the exhaust problem is back pressure—the

resistance to exhaust flow through the stock cast-iron manifolds. Oh sure, Motown took a giant step forward in reducing back pressure when dual exhausts were first installed on Cadillacs in the 1950s. With rare exception, however, that's about where they stopped. Detroit seldom strayed far from the practice of installing cast-iron log-type exhaust manifolds except on muscle and special interest cars.

Admittedly, cast-iron manifolds have some redeeming qualities, at least for a mass-produced passenger car. They are inexpensive, quiet, easily installed and last nearly forever. What more could the manufacturer and the

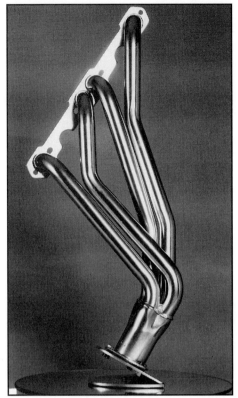

Low underhood temperatures are always a plus in a full-fendered rod. Therefore, you could think of ceramic coating on headers as insulation, reducing heat transfer to the motor compartment. Jet-Hot applies their coating to the exterior surfaces of stripped headers in a crosshatched pattern. The interiors of the headers are flow coated twice, to assure complete protection of the substrate. The coatings are then cured at 650 degrees for 50 minutes to produce a corrosion resistant shell.

buying public want? The performance-minded street rodder, however, wants volumetric efficiency, and conventional exhaust manifolds simply won't do. Not only that, excessive backpressure isn't the whole story.

On a normally aspirated motor outfitted with typical log-type manifolds, when one exhaust valve opens, high exhaust pressures from that cylinder force burned gases into the adjacent low-pressure cylinder as the second cylinder's exhaust valve is about to close. This mixing of hot exhaust gas with the fresh, cool, incoming fuel/air

mixture is known as charge dilution. It tends to increase with camshaft overlap. Charge dilution and the fact that some exhaust gases remain in the combustion chamber after the piston reaches top dead center (TDC), downgrades performance.

There's another problem indirectly related to exhaust gas flow—cast-iron manifolds exaggerate underhood temperatures. Manifolds not only retain a lot of heat; they store it right up alongside the cylinder head. Think about it. We've just finished discussing the best way to get rid of some of that heat, and yet with stock manifolds, a lot of heat is stored where the cooling system can't do much good beyond what air flows through the motor compartment. Tubular headers, on the other hand, dissipate heat rapidly.

Tubular headers do not make up the entire exhaust system, however. All of the plumbing from the exhaust valve to the chrome tip must provide a reasonably straightforward exit for the gases. True, there is a helping hand in the form of combustion pressures. For, unlike the fuel/air mixture that enters the combustion chamber under atmospheric pressure in a normally aspirated motor, high combustion pressures hurry along exhaust gases.

As soon as the exhaust valve lifts from its seat, the work of the exhaust system begins. The burned gases rush past the valve into the port, where they immediately collide with the air that fills the port and its extension. This sets off a pressure wave that travels down the header and exhaust pipe faster than the actual speed of the gases. When the pressure wave reaches the end of the tailpipe, it expands and sends a negative pressure wave back up the pipe to the still-unseated

exhaust valve. This assists in extracting the exhaust gases from that exhaust port.

Many long hours have been spent developing and enhancing the extractor effect in racing motors. For ordinary street rod purposes, however, we need not go into any exotic design formulas. The most basic set of headers with primary pipes (those that are welded to the flange and bolted to the cylinder head) of equal length is good enough for the boulevard cruiser.

The high performance street rod header design in common use today is the four-into-one system. In both "block hugger" and longer primary pipe layouts, the primary pipes are separate until, after a reasonable approximation of equal length, they are joined together at a collector. This is a practical design for both the commercial manufacturer with a production line and the small shop that builds one-off custom headers for the street rod market.

Although some low-end torque is lost, the headers install easily and are attractive. In fact, even with its shortcomings, the design is so far superior to factory cast-iron exhaust manifolds that no one seriously compares the two. They have been universally accepted by street rodders with the exception of the hard-core racer.

The Custom Exhaust System

In all honesty, custom header building is fast becoming a lost art. There are still several tubing artisans set up where there is enough racecar business to sustain them, but street rodding stretches across the country. Nevertheless, if you decide to go this route, and are willing to trailer your car to the mountain, here's why you'll find the

The ultimate in exhaust systems is the custom-built header. Yes, they are more expensive than store-boughts. The informed street rod builder is best advised to consider the racer's adage: Speed costs money; how fast do you want to go?

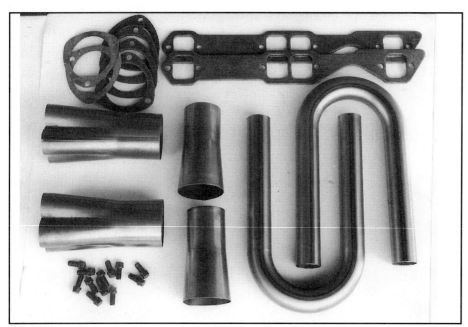

Several street rod components companies catalog kits contain just about everything a rod builder needs to fabricate his own custom headers. Even so, unless you have done this several times before, find a local supplier of exhaust tubing to replace the pieces you mess up.

price tag is so high upon your arrival.

The biggest problem the custom header builder must contend with is preserving the car's sheet metal or fiberglass. He is well aware that the owner will be upset if he takes a ball-peen hammer to the firewall or burns a hole in a fenderwell. The second biggest headache is achieving equal lengths for all primary pipes. That small-block Chevy or Ford street rod motor will generally require longer primary pipe lengths than a racing motor because it should develop peak usable horsepower at a much lower rpm.

Equal length primary pipes are important to performance. The ideal is no more than a half-inch variation. A one inch variation is no problem for general street use, but plus or minus more than two inches will reduce performance. Achieving perfection building equal-length primaries in tight situations is easier said than done.

Determining the correct primary pipe diameter is simple. It should equal the inner diameter of the exhaust valve seat. If it is a little large, no problem, but it should not be smaller. Also, the inside diameter of the pipe should approximate the diameter of the exhaust port.

One of the more critical aspects of header design is collector length. It is there to gradually reduce the pressure of the exhaust pulse shock wave before it reaches the atmosphere. By doing so, it improves mid-range performance, arguably the only performance band that counts for most street rods. The rule of thumb states that the collector should be approximately twice the volume of one cylinder, and at least 5 1/2 inches long. Some commercially available headers fall short here. If you have a pair that otherwise fits, you can retrieve some mid-range performance by taking the headers to a muffler shop and asking them to lengthen the collector until it equals the volume of two cylinders.

After The Headers, What?

It is not always practical, but if your chassis and transmission configuration permits, you should build a balance tube into the exhaust system. This is a short connecting tube running perpendicular between the header pipes. It should be at least 2 1/4 inches OD. The balance tube reduces back pressure even more and enhances the resonance and tone of straight-through mufflers. In effect, it nearly doubles the volume of the exhaust system.

With regard to the exhaust pipe, it too should be at least 2 1/4 inches OD for best performance. If you want to build the best system, install a 1 1/2-inch "Y-bend" behind each collector, and run two exhaust pipes per bank toward the rear bumper. Then, trim them in enough to install a pair of Corvair-type "turbo" mufflers or Mopar "reverse-flow" mufflers per side. Four mufflers can be costly, but you'll get usable performance.

I dislike quoting figures that can't be verified, but if you discard the stock cast-iron manifolds, install a set of custom or semi-custom headers with only two high performance mufflers on any strong small-block Chevy or Ford, you can recoup 10–20 horsepower that would otherwise be lost to back pressure. In short, you'll never spend a better performance dollar than what you spend on a first class exhaust system.

COOLING SYSTEM MANUFACTURERS

Brassworks
289 Prado Road
San Luis Obispo, CA
(805) 544-8841
Fax: (805) 544-5615
www.thebrassworks.net

Flex-A-Lite Automotive Products
(800) 851-1510
www.flex-a-lite.com

Cooling Components, Inc.
3968 I-40
Proctor, AZ 72736
(901) 336-6194

Mattson Radiator (Fan Man)
10529 Beach Blvd.
Stanton, CA 90680
(866) 432-6626
www.the-fan-man.com

Walker Radiator Works, Inc.
(800) 821-1970
Fax: (901) 529-0397

U.S. Radiator
4423 District Blvd.
Vernon, CA 90058
(323) 826-0969
Fax: (323) 826-0970

EXHAUST SYSTEM MANUFACTURERS

Rewarder Headers
590-E Constitution Ave.
Camarillo, CA 93012
(800) 878-6968
Tech line (805) 445-1015
www.rewarderheaders.com

Speedway Motors, Inc.
300 Van Dorn
P.O. Box 81906
Lincoln, NE 68501
(800) 736-FREE

Stainless Specialties
P.O. Box 781035
Sebastian, FL 32978
(561) 589-4190

Sanderson Headers, Inc.
517 Railroad Avenue South
San Francisco, CA 94080
(800) 669-2430
Fax: (650) 583-8475

Jet Hot
Tech Line (610) 277-5646
Order Line (800) 432-3379

Power Effects
1800 "H" Industrial Park Drive
Grand Haven, MI 49417
(616) 847-4200

Never-Rust
4279 Ohio River Blvd.
Pittsburgh, PA 15202
(800) 487-7775
(412) 766-7775

Powerpac Mufflers
(800) 942-1455
www.powerpacmufflers.com

Spin Tech Performance Mufflers
(888) 550-7746

21

RESTORING VINTAGE TIN

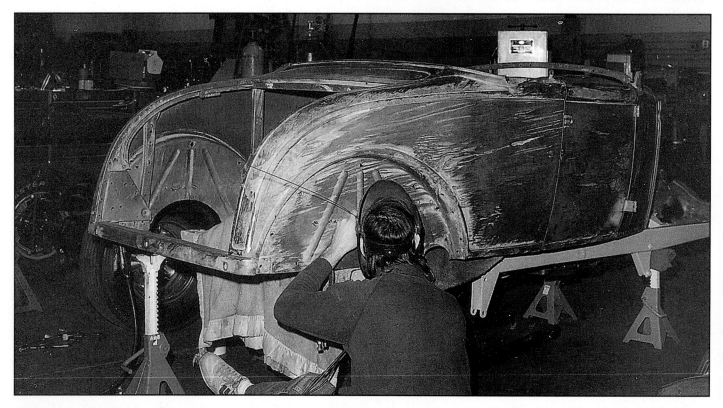

There are few old cars suitable for street rodding that won't need major body work before that goal is reached. The rod builder has to decide whether he will farm the job out to professionals, or tackle the task himself.

It's no surprise that available vintage tin for new or even updated street rods is scarce. The quality of what is left is often so marginal as to be discouraging. Yet, unless you are determined to own a genuine 1932 Ford phaeton or some other rarity, metal-bodied cars can still be found. Nevertheless, even with the best of luck, automobiles surviving six to seven decades haven't done so without suffering battle scars, metal fatigue and rust. And those are the good ones. The bad ones sometimes defy description, but committed

rod builders will attempt to restore their bodies.

BUST THAT RUST

Repairing and restoring a metal-bodied old car isn't the same as repairing a modern automobile body. Not only is the past performance of tin benders long gone to their reward obfuscated by lead, putty and paint, there is often a significant amount of rust that must be removed before any corrective bodywork can begin.

The traditional home builder meth-

ods for removing rust, in ascending order of their effectiveness and safety, include wire brushes, disc grinders and diluted hydrochloric (muriatic) acid. Wire brushing is usually minimally effective. Disc grinding is hazardous to sheet metal gauge and texture. Muriatic acid, even when diluted, is an extremely dangerous product requiring great care when handling. Not only that, sometimes it doesn't know when to stop . . . and that is hazardous to the remaining "good" metal. Prudently used, however, these methods are fine for small work pieces. Forget 'em for anything larger and less accessible than fenders. Look for a commercial service for the big stuff.

The Fast Blast Methods

Commercial outfits offer a range of blasting means. True sandblasting (defined as pneumatically conveyed silica sand) is no stranger to street rod builders with even minimal experience. It is great for tough frames and suspension components encrusted with equally tough rust and "road accumulations" such as asphalt, petrified grease and undercoating overspray. Unfortunately, it is destructive to tender vintage tin. You might think of it as the Dirty Harry of rust removal. All too often, it blows everything away.

Unwanted coatings can be removed from sheet metal in more efficient and less destructive ways using powdered walnut shells or soft plastic particles rather than hard abrasives. The walnut powder is very similar to that used by firearm cartridge reloaders in case tumblers. It and specially manufactured recyclable, soft plastic bits are also pneumatically conveyed. Each, however, is applied at low pressures of 20 to 40 psi, and as the literature says "quickly remove surface coatings and accumulations without causing any damage to the underlying substrate." Well, "surface coatings" common in the rod-building world includes enamel, lacquer, polyurethanes, and even baked-on powder paint. The "substrates" that can be stripped not only include tender tin, but also stainless steel, aluminum, brass, copper and even fiberglass!

The advantages to the rod builder are significant. There is no pitting, stretch-

There are two Redi-Strip processes. One removes paint and similar coatings, and another eradicates rust. A part can be derusted without damaging desired surface coatings. Or, one that isn't rusty need not enter the derusting tank if removing paint is all that's necessary. The combined processes will remove just about anything that is brushed, glued, splattered, sprayed, forming or growing on metal except chrome plating. When your pride and joy is lifted from the Redi-Strip tanks, it is as close to new metal as it can be. (Photo by Terry Smith)

ing, warping or metal loss to the surface of the body or part, and the process results in a superior surface that facilitates the bonding of lead, plastic filler, primer and all types of paint.

The Slow Immersion Methods

A full body dip in a commercial acid or caustic tank takes much longer, but liquid media goes where no solid can. Unlike painting muriatic acid on your fender in the backyard all gussied up in a rubberized rain coat and a face mask, a mild acid strip in a huge vat far removed from operating personnel is perfectly safe and a perfectly satisfactory way to remove rust. The companies that perform this service are well acquainted with the do's and don'ts.

An alternative to an acid skinny dip is the alkaline electrolytic immersion method. This has long been my personal favorite, and since it so often misunderstood, I want to spend a few

paragraphs discussing it. The Redi-Strip Company, exclusive owners of the process, was originally concerned with chemically removing paint. During their research and development, they subsequently discovered an alkaline method of eradicating rust.

Their process was only available to Southern California street rodders in the early 1970s, but today, this outstanding service is available to rod builders in other areas because Redi-Strip has a number of franchised branches.

The process is often confused with acid bathing. (At one time drag racers would dip stock bodies in hydrochloric acid to thin the metal and save weight.) Dipping a car body in hydrochloric acid for too long can cause hydrogen embrittlement. This is a condition in which free hydrogen molecules work their way into the metal and eventually cause brittleness, which leads to fractures. Old car metal has its share of fatigue to start with.

The Redi-Strip method only removes rust and non-metallic coatings such as paint or rubberized undercoatings, no metal. When your pride and joy is lifted from the Redi-Strip tank, excluding preexisting metal fatigue, it is as close to new metal as it can be.

The chemical solution in the dipping tanks is charged with direct current. The part being derusted is the cathode or negative electrode. Rust molecules are released from its surface and every crack and crevice in the body or component. Rust and paint settle to the tank's bottom; lighter coatings disperse and float above the solution.

There are two Redi-Strip processes: one for removing paint and similar coatings, and another that strips surface oxidation. So, a part can be derusted without damaging desired surface coatings. Or, one that isn't rusty need not enter the derusting tank if removing paint is all that's necessary.

The combined process will remove just about anything that is brushed, glued, splattered, sprayed, forming or growing on metal except chrome plating. It will remove acrylics, asphalt, chromate, enamel, epoxy, lacquer, latex, plastic body filler, resins, synthetic rubberized compounds, shellac, tar, urethane, varnish and even zinc!

Redi-Strip's first step for cleaning an automobile body is usually paint stripping. Although the body need not be completely disassembled, efficiency is improved if doors, fenders and so forth are removed. The window glass should be removed, not only to protect it, but also to ensure that the stripping solution can get into all those little crevasses. The paint stripper is chemically similar to hot-tank caustics, so be careful what you leave on the car. Some of the wood supports will swell

and plywood glues will dissolve.

Complete stripping of tough original paint and all interior undercoating used on old car bodies takes from two to three days. Fenders and smaller components require less time. When the body or part is removed from the stripping tank, it is placed on a concrete pad. Here, the soft paint goop still clinging is hosed off with high-pressure hot water. After this cleaning, the still rusty, but paint-free body is ready for the second step.

Some precautions are required before the body or component goes into the derusting tanks. Because the rust removal solution is compounded to remove oxidation from steel, it adversely affects most die-cast soft-metal alloys, aluminum, brass, copper and lead. All components made of these materials should be removed from the body, or they will be damaged. In fact, some die-cast "pot metals" will completely dissolve. You are responsible for detaching these parts before taking the body to Redi-Strip. No need to worry about stainless steel, though.

The rod builder unfamiliar with or skeptical of this method should submit a sample to evaluate their capabilities. Every square inch of metal will be returned totally bare—showing only the die-forming marks induced when the piece was originally stamped in the 1930s or '40s.

After the body is removed from the tanks and is drying, a white residue forms on its surface. This is a solution byproduct that is a short term preservative. It is water-soluble. If wetted or washed off, the metal begins to oxidize faster than ever because there is no paint or other protective coating. As long as the metal is kept absolutely

dry, no rust will form. When it's time to paint, meticulously scrub off the white coating. Otherwise, nothing will stick.

Therefore, it is strongly recommended that you ask Redi-Strip to phosphate the body or component right after derusting. Phosphating is similar to metal-prep solutions painters use before they apply primer. Then as soon as you get home, spray it with a quality primer/sealer. It can then be tucked away in dry storage until the bodywork begins in earnest.

Today, when every old car is a potential street rod, safe rust removal has the highest priority. After that has been done, the rodder, be he new to the game or an old hand, must confront an always troubling question . . .

SHOULD YOU ATTEMPT METALWORK?

The dilemma of whether to attempt major undertakings in the home garage or farm them out to a professional is most often a choice between competence and cost. Sometimes the answer is apparent—the equipment required to do the job is expensive, sophisticated and substantial. The casual engine builder, for instance, is hardly well advised to fill his home garage with the tools and equipment of the automotive machinist's trade even though each and every one is required to do the job right. In such a case the rod builder can "split the difference." He can farm out the precision machine work and learn how to assemble the components at home.

Although some tasks do not require a major investment in equipment, they do demand a modicum of talent and a great deal of tenacity. Obviously, the writer of a how-to book can never

The original floorboards in open cars, i.e., roadsters and convertibles, suffer the ravages of weather more frequently and extensively than closed cars. Often the entire floorboard has to be replaced. The upside is that several companies make exact replacements.

The downside is that their installation is quite tricky. The cowl and rear body section has to be securely and accurately cross braced in order to maintain critical dimensions before the chassis is removed. Then, under the best of circumstances, all components must be securely and accurately welded together so that the rehabilitated body again fits the chassis, and the doors open and close smoothly. In short, this is one job the prudent rod builder is best advised to farm out to a competent professional.

know all of his readers personally, so he cannot counsel with credibility. My purpose in this book is certainly not to impede your do-it-yourself desires, but I'm not going mislead you about metalworking skills that take years to master. Since I can reasonably assume you're not a professional metal smith, I am honor-bound to point out the undeniable—you run the risk of further damaging a costly piece of early iron by doing your own metalwork. That's the downside. The upside is, that unless you are a real dunderhead, chances are better than even that you won't ruin the component.

The bottom line is this—metalworking tools are not cost-prohibitive. Many used tools can even be purchased without fear at swap meets. So, if you want to try your hand (literally) at some of the less daunting tasks, and you're not afraid of trial-and-error learning, have at it.

Metalworking Fundamentals & Basic Tools

Basic auto metalworking techniques are the same for both early and late

model cars, stockers and custom jobs. Still, there are specific considerations to remember about converting an early automobile into a street rod. The sheet metal used in manufacturing pre-WWII auto bodies is low-carbon steel, typically in the 20-gauge range. This relatively soft steel lends itself to factory stamping. It's also easier to repair than the tougher steels used in modern cars.

Some metals are more elastic than others, that is, they return to their original size and shape when deforming external forces are removed. Although a metal is elastic for a range of stress or force, if that limit is exceeded, the metal becomes plastic—it permanently deforms. When the force is removed, it does not return to its original shape.

Plasticity is what makes the manufacture of sheet metal products possible. Plastic deformation without heat occurs when flat sheet metal is turned

into a body panel, hood or fender in a metal-stamping press. Plasticity allows these large machines to turn flat stock into fenders and the like without applying significant heat or causing the work piece to break or crack. It's called cold forming. Body and fender repair shops, however, often have to use heat to efficiently repair major damage. That's why recognizing heat ranges by color is so important when working sheet metal.

When steel is heated beyond 400 degrees F, its color goes from pale to dark yellow, then brown, purple, and into shades of blue. It grows darker until the temperature reaches 600 degrees F. After that, the dark blue fades to gray or green. It begins turning red at about 900 degrees F, and stays dull red until 1550 degrees F, when the brightness increases to what is commonly called cherry red. As the temperature rises further, the color changes to orange, then yellow and finally white. At that point, approximately 2600 degrees F, most common steel alloys begin to melt.

Finally, heat causes several reactions in auto sheet metal, including scale that forms on the back-side of body panels when a heated area is exposed to oxygen. Other reactions are changes in grain structure and expansion. These affect hardness and cause warping, respectively. The novice must keep this in mind at all times. If it doesn't put a crimp in your plans, keep reading.

Hammers—Body hammers come in a variety of styles and weights. Most are two-headed combination hammers. One head typically has a large, flat face designed to distribute the force of the blow over a panel's surface. The head has a flat spot in its cen-

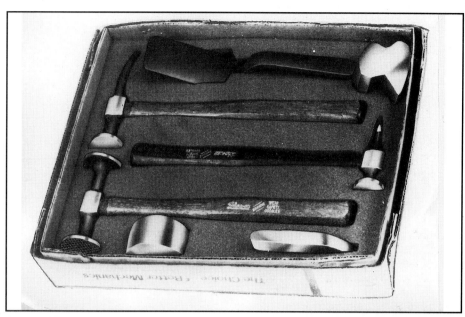

Seven of the most common tools necessary for bodywork are included in this Snap-on set: a 10-inch Light Dinging Spoon that smoothes and levels ridges; a picking and dinging hammer for panel bumping; a shrinking hammer for large area shrinking and finishing; a cross peen shrinking hammer; a toe dolly for dinging flat surfaces; a heel dolly for use in sharp corners and wide radii; and a general purpose dolly for deep-skirted fenders and shrinking when using heat. Courtesy Snap-on Tools Corporation.

ter that blends into a slightly curved edge. This shape is designed to avoid putting sharp edges in the panel. The combination hammer's other head is usually pointed and is called the picking end. It is designed to raise small low spots in the panel.

The Dolly Block—Hammers are seldom used by themselves to work metal. They are often used with a companion tool called the dolly block that backs up the metal. There are general-purpose dollies for deep-skirted fenders and shrinking. Heel dollies are used for sharp corners and wide radii. Toe dollies are for dinging flat surfaces. Loaf dollies are suitable for roughing-out metal. Fender dollies are for working angles, creases and curves in body panels and fenders.

A dolly is not merely an anvil though; its working face is used to raise a panel whether it's struck directly by the hammer or hit nearby.

Dollies usually weigh several times as much as hammers, and are sometimes even used as hammers.

Spoons—Bodyworking spoons look something like thick, bent butter knives with one relatively flat end. Spoons are used for hammering, slapping and surface metal finishing when it's necessary to spread a blow's force over a larger area. They are also used as pry bars in tight places.

Shears—Sometimes an old car body can't be repaired without trimming out badly damaged or rusty sections of sheet metal. A welding torch's cutting attachment is one way of doing so, but special body-panel cutters do a neater and better job. Shears leave the clean-cut edges replacement "patch panels" need when they are butted against older sections. At least three types are required: straight cut, right cut and left cut. Beyond these, tinner's snips and other small metal snips are useful.

Files—Some of the most important metalworking tools are flexible body files. The file holder has a large handle and turnbuckle for a range of concave and convex adjustments. A permanently attached strap accepts 14-inch blades of various shapes and cutting grades.

Files only cut in one direction, and they must be moved in the direction of the flattest section of the panel being straightened. This way, the cutting edge of the teeth will rake across the high spots, and untouched low spots can be easily seen. It is good practice during filing to turn the file a little to one side to get the maximum cut with its curved teeth. High and low spots that show up during filing can be reworked or filled in.

Disc Sander/Grinders—These tools are useful for removing excess weldment, paint and rust, as well as shaping lead and plastic filler. Although air-drive sanders are fine in many light-duty applications, electric disc sander/grinders are best for medium and heavy-duty jobs. These are available in ranges from 3/8 to 1 1/2 horsepower.

The disc pad usually has a 3-, 6- or 9-inch diameter, and a wide variety of flexible sanding discs is available. Discs have a stiff fiberboard backing with aluminum oxide or another abrasive coating. Grit coarseness is indexed numerically and by the designations open-coat and closed-coat. Open-coated discs are designed to reduce clogging, and are used for removing paint and other soft materials. Closed-coat discs are used for most steel cutting.

Gas-Welding Torch—A basic gas-welding set is essential for bodywork, and includes an oxygen regulator with

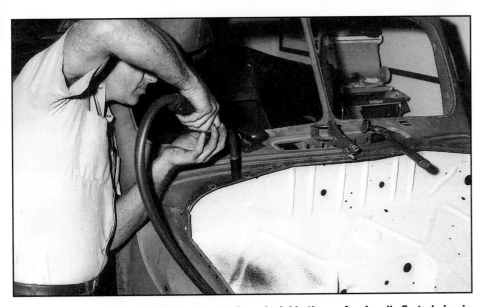

Commercial grade spot welding equipment is undeniably the professional's first choice in major panel replacement (and a firewall salvaged from a parts car is a major panel). When one is dealing with a stable structure securely bolted to the frame, however, the installation can be accomplished with gas or electric welding equipment. Obviously, much practice on scrap is necessary before you approach your car. The heat control skills required to fuse sheet metal must be acquired first.

Welding supply houses will work out an arrangement where the home builder can keep a pair of gas cylinders for as long as necessary. The empties are exchanged for a fresh pair with no delay. Unless space is a significant problem, one should get full-size cylinders. (The oxygen bottle is larger because it will always be depleted first. Its consumption rate is 1.1 times that of acetylene when a neutral flame is used.) Both gas cylinders must be chained upright to something stable: a sturdy cart, workbench or a stout wall hook. If a high-pressure oxygen bottle falls over and the valve breaks, it will blast off like a misguided missile!

No Sunglasses Allowed!

High quality safety goggles with gas and arc welding tinted lens and flexible welding gloves are absolutely required. And although working with gloves may take some practice, you only have to burn your fingers or singe the hair on your arms once to know how useful they are. You don't want to know how painful "sunburned" eyes are!

Basic Metalwork Techniques

Hammers and dollies are used at the start of bodywork for bumping—bringing the panel into rough shape. It may seem more an art than a science, but it's within your capability if you practice. Begin practicing on a fender—but not a good one. Don't saddle yourself with the stress of making a practice job perfect. If need be, buy an extra fender for your car. It needs to be reasonably solid and bolted to the body. Few professionals would chase a loose fender around with a hammer, so why should you? Consider the fender's price an investment in developing your metalworking skills. Besides,

low- and high-pressure gauges; an acetylene regulator with low- and high-pressure gauges; 20 feet of hose; and a torch and cutting attachment with a selection of tips. Beyond these staples, the metalworker needs a torch lighter, safety goggles, tip cleaners, leather welding gloves, a soapstone for marking metal, and a good selection of welding rod and flux-coated brazing rod.

High-pressure gauges indicate supply pressure in the cylinders; low-pressure gauges indicate delivery pressure at the torch. Pressure-reduction regulators are delicate devices designed to reduce the pressurized gas in the bottles to working-line pressures.

There are two types of regulators. The single-stage regulator will compensate for slight delivery pressure changes. Two-stage regulators are best for most bodywork and other tasks requiring a constant delivery pressure over varying inlet pressures.

For safety, all oxygen and compressed air hoses are green and right-hand threaded. Acetylene hoses are red and left-hand threaded.

An equal-pressure welding torch allows oxygen and acetylene to flow together in equal amounts. Oxygen flows through an inner tube in the torch handle and is directed through the center hole at the tip. Acetylene flows through orifices that surround the oxygen port, but exits at the center hole in the tip. Knobs attached to the handle adjust the oxygen and acetylene mixture. Welding tips are selected according to the gauge of the metal being welded, but relatively small tips are used for bodywork.

Besides oxygen- and acetylene-adjustment valves, the torch has a third valve that releases a jet of high-pressure oxygen through the tip. The tip has an orifice in its center for oxygen flow and several others surrounding it for the preheat flame. Although not normally used in bodywork, the cutting attachment is invaluable around any home-based shop.

219

Repairing your old car doesn't always require professional tools and sophisticated skills. Money can be saved by doing many small jobs yourself. Point in question, a good soldering iron, sharp tin snips and a drill motor. Small holes (and what old dash doesn't have a bunch?) can be cleaned, tinned and patched as adequately in the home garage as in a body shop. A little plastic filler finishes the job. Voila! Thirty bucks still in your pocket for the really tough tasks.

you can always sell it to a novice after you've mastered the skill!

The basic technique of hammer-and-dolly work is learning to swing the hammer accurately and with just the right amount of force so it bounces back after the blow. The dolly must not bounce away from the panel, however. It should remain in contact with the panel at the time of impact.

Hammer-On—In this hammer-and-dolly operation, the hammer strikes the high spot of the damaged area and the dolly backs up the blow. The usual sequence is to start in the middle, but to move quickly to, and concentrate around, the circumference of the damaged area.

Hammer-Off—This is another bodyworking method. The dolly is not exactly opposite the hammer blow, but rather off to one side and under the low spot. The hammer blow pushes the high spot down while the dolly forces the low spot up. Yes, plenty of practice is necessary before you can do this well. Nevertheless, an old fender and the in   depth discussion of the correct technique in HPBooks' *Paint & Bodywork Handbook* by Don Taylor and Larry Hofer, will prove invaluable.

Hole Filling With Solder—Holes and punctures up to 1/8-inch diameter can be filled with solder. Holes bigger than that will usually require a metal patch. Pieces cut from a food tin are ideal because they are lightweight and don't require too much heat for solid bonding.

Of course, such imperfections can be welded, brazed or leaded-in. Simple soldering has an advantage over conventional metalworking, however. The panel isn't heated excessively and distortion can be minimized. The melting point of most lead-tin solders is 361–437 degrees F, which is far less than the heat required for the other approaches.

Soldering is straightforward. First, thoroughly clean and tin the surface to get the solder to adhere. When filling a hole with solder alone, bevel the edge of the metal slightly with a small rat-tail file for a better bond. Acid-core solder melted onto the preheated work area works quite well for tinning. The soldering gun tip must be tinned, too, so oxidation won't interfere with the bond during soldering.

After tinning, the work area will be bright and shiny. Then, more solder can be melted in to fill the hole. Flux is necessary when soldering to chemically clean and to remove any oil or oxides that might accumulate. A rosin-core solder will do this.

In soldering, only enough heat is applied to keep the solder plastic. The

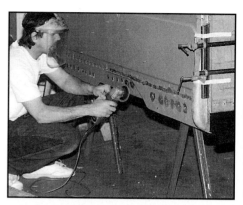

Sander/grinders are indispensable when paint and rust or excess weldment must be removed. A gentle touch must be developed, however. Practice with a small unit first. Air drive sanders work well for roughing out lead and plastic filler and other light-duty tasks, but go electric for medium and heavy-duty jobs. Always wear full-face protection.

broad tip of the soldering iron or gun is used to spread the solder. Work slowly around the edge of the hole to fill it in.

A thin metal patch is necessary for quarter-inch or larger holes. Outline the hole on a piece of scrap, then slightly taper and tin the edges. Bond and blend in the patch with solder. Spread more solder over the face of the patch after the joint has cooled. After soldering is complete, clean off excess resin with lacquer thinner. The filled patch can then be ground down with a #36 or finer open-coat disc.

PARTS CARS OUT, AUTHENTIC REPROS IN

My own 1940 Ford coupe was rear ended in 1969. Although far from totaled, the damage was severe enough to buckle the frame and tear the engine and transmission off their mounts. The deck lid was badly dented and warped, and the panel below it was mangled. This repair was going to be expensive.

Fortunately, I had the room (and cooperative neighbors) to stash a couple of spare coupe bodies in my backyard. One of them had a decent deck

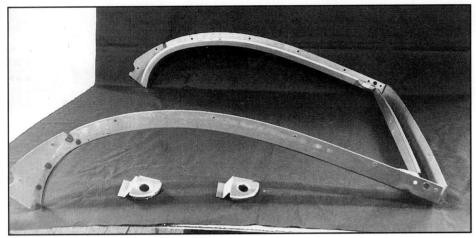

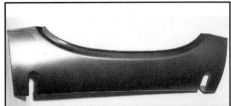

Over thirty years ago, I cannibalized what today would be a very salable 1940 coupe body to get a so-so rear deck panel. Oh well, I couldn't wait for the reproduction parts industry to tool up. Fortunately, the 21st century rod builder can take his pick of perfect, brand new replacements from the catalogs of several manufacturers.

Rain gutters are among the most difficult areas of an old car to repair. Thankfully, those inside the trunk of the 1928–31 Model A coupe and roadster are being reproduced by Howell's Sheetmetal Company of Nome, Texas.

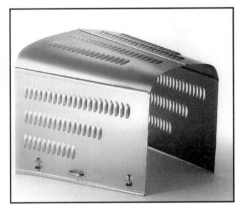

When it comes to reproduction hoods for early cars, no one holds a candle to Rootlieb of Turlock, California. Not only do they make hoods for Fords from the Model T through the 1937 passenger cars and pickups, they also belt out "bonnets" for 1931–38 Chevies, and several models of early Plymouths and Dodges.

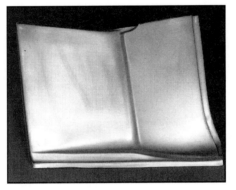

Engineering & Mfg. Services of Cleveland (EMS), has made a concerted effort to provide Bowtie rodders with nearly every needed reproduction panel. Pictured is the EMS 1939 Chevy lower front cowl panel at left, and their 1935–36 Ford lower front cowl patch panel, at right. Courtesy EMS.

lid, and the other a salvageable deck panel. Out came the torch for the sections I needed.

The result of my vintage-tin hording was a well-repaired rear end at a moderate price. Today, both "parts cars" and moderate repair bills are memories. Now, your best resource is the first-class reproduction sheet metal industry for everything other than major components.

This industry isn't a newcomer. It's been active since the 1950s. Many of the early pieces were manufactured in Argentina and primarily aimed at the Model T and A restorer. Even though the panels weren't perfect replacements, they were better than none at all. In the mid-1970s, the quality of sheet metal replacement panels improved. Nowadays, a number of catalogs list nearly every panel you may need for early Fords and a few other popular marquees.

Installing Reproduction Patch Panels

Discretion is the better part of economic valor when it comes to major metalwork on a valuable vintage body.

Don't learn a skilled trade on a $20,000 early Ford coupe. Nevertheless, if you've done gas-welding on light-gauge sheet metal, and know how body metal responds to heat, installing a reproduction panel is within your skills.

Know Your Crowns—Veteran body repairers often speak of crowns, a term that refers to the curvature of a panel. There are four classifications of crowns in automotive sheet metal panels: low curvature, high curvature, a combination of both, and reverse curvature.

Panels with low crown have very little curvature, and very little load-car-

Sometimes you just can't find the reproduction of a piece you need. When that is the case, turn to your local sheet metal shop. Although most are not in the automotive business per se, if you bring them a dimensionally accurate sketch, chances are they can knock it out.

rying ability. The full metal roof first used on the mid-1930s Fords is an example of a low-crown panel. A high-crown panel curves rapidly in all directions. Think of a 1940 Ford front fender; that's one high-crown panel! It is strong and resists deformation.

Combination high- and low-crown panels are used in several places on early cars, most notably in the doors. These, too, are quite strong and require little reinforcement. Reverse crowns are rare in the simple designs of pre-WWII cars. They are found in the cars of the 1950s and later. An example is the flaring out of a fender's section to accept a taillight assembly. Duplicating this effect is called frenching by customizers.

Most flat patch panels are large enough to replace more than the rusted-out area. For example, the expected rust-out in a 1934 lower cowl panel is perhaps 2 x 6 inches. The replacement panel will be 6 x 12 inches. You'll have to judge how much of it is necessary for the repair. It's usually better to keep weld beads—and heat—to a minimum, so the smaller the patch, the better.

Mark the area to be removed with a heavy black line. Then trim the patch panel to fit. Don't cut out any body section until you've carefully matched the patch to the pattern.

Don't end up with a patch that is an eighth-inch smaller than the cut-out it's filling!

Remove the section of original metal with "cold tools," a rotary pneumatic or electric cutter, or appropriate metal snips. Avoid using heat. Don't cause any more warpage than absolutely necessary. Also, don't forget there are structures behind the panel that must be preserved.

Damage behind a rusted panel can be more extensive than you assumed. If so, internal repair will be needed. Rusted-out sheet metal should be cut away and new pieces welded in. An interior, out-of-sight repair doesn't require the same cosmetic attention as an exterior one, but don't get sloppy, either.

Next, hold the patch panel to the body with C-clamps and tack it in using low heat and mild steel rod. Readjust and fit it as you proceed. Once it absorbs heat, the panel will seem to have a mind of its own. Place the tacks 2 to 3 inches apart and let each cool a bit before starting the next. Bodyworkers differ in their approach, but many recommend tacking one full-length seam at a time. If the panel

seems to absorb too much heat, apply a damp rag to help it cool.

The tedious part of this job is the final welding. A bead must be run all the way around the patch with precision and patience or the panel will warp.

After the replacement panel is fully welded, grind off the excess bead. The seam need not be any thicker than the gauge for strength. A disc sander/grinder is the best tool for this job, but a small air-driven sander and drill motor are adequate as long as the proper grit disc is used. Avoid grinding with too much pressure or you'll gouge the surrounding metal. Carelessness here could spoil an otherwise good job.

Hammer-Welding—I've assumed that if you use the previous method of installing a panel, you'll use lead or plastic filler to cover the weld. The next step up in quality is hammer-welding and metal shrinking. They require more experience and skill than simply welding sheet metal.

Hammer-welding involves working a hot weld with hammer and dolly. The bead is worked into the base metal and only a thin, discolored line reveals the touching edges of original metal and patch panel.

The first step in hammer-welding is to precisely fit the patch panel to the cut-out in the body or fender. If there is much of a gap, the job simply won't turn out well. The patch is tack-welded in as before, with a tack every 2 to 3 inches. Work quickly and carefully to minimize heat distortion.

Once the panel is tacked in place, select a broad, flat-faced body hammer and a dolly that matches the contour of the work area. Hammer-welding requires alternating torch heat with hammer-and-dolly work. Switch from torch to hammer and dolly every few minutes, and prepare a safe, handy place to store each when using the other.

The technique works best when short sections of the seam—two inches at the most—are welded in and then followed by hammer-and-dolly work while the joint is still hot. To work the weld bead down into the surrounding metal, move rapidly from torch to hammer before cooling sets in.

Add a minimum of filler rod. It's that much more metal to be worked. The key to successful hammer-welding is in the ability to weld and follow up with hammer work before the weld cools. Admittedly, that's easier said than done.

Metal-Shrinking—Depending upon how well you master patch-panel installation and hammer-welding, there will be some lumpiness in the end product. The artful way of smoothing it out is by metal shrinking.

Metal shrinking is just what its name implies: reducing raised or stretched places in worked sheet metal by heating, gentle hammering and rapid cooling. Depressed areas are leveled similarly. It is a painstaking process. Small sections of panel are worked a little at a time. Hammer force is concentrated on the heated area and, as the metal cools, it draws slowly inward. With lots of practice, the desired shrinking can be achieved with minimal hammer-and-dolly work. Overworking the metal with a hammer and dolly can cause excess shrinking when it cools, which adds to the overall distortion. Shrinkage can be controlled by using a wet cloth to speed cooling.

A dolly can be used as a hammer

It would take at least a dozen photos to graphically describe the steps taken to bring just one of the fenders on my '41 pickup to the point where the filler can be applied. Note, however, that a holding fixture was built first. Chasing a fender around the floor is no fun, and neither is attempting to reach in and around a mounted fender to heat, hammer, and file the resisting metal.

from the underside to raise the metal. Then shrinking is used to flatten and reform the metal to the desired shape. Different metals require different amounts of heat. Learning how much to apply, and for how long, requires practice.

One indicator of the temperature of the metal is the size of the blue ring that develops around the torch flame. The metal is soft inside this ring, and it is the area that can be worked with effectiveness.

Like so much metalworking, panel shrinking is one that requires considerable practice before perfection can be achieved. If you aspire to a satisfactory level of work, you can look forward to long hours on a practice fender. That's better than ruining a good fender, however.

FILLER

In general, the better the metalworking job, the less the filler. Even so, it's not practical to pound and grind away

at a panel until it's ready to paint. Filler is the material used to smooth a repaired section after welding, hammering and shrinking. There are two types of body filler: lead, and what is commonly called "plastic." Lead was used exclusively for many years, and is generally preferred over plastic by many traditional rod builders. Often, I think, just because it is traditional. I don't want to rekindle the debate about which is best. Either material properly used will result in a satisfactory job. It is true, however, that more experience and skill are required in lead work. It has developed a certain mystique and desirability over the years. Let's talk about it first

Leading

It is tempting to think of lead work as a lost art, but it isn't. Like hammer welding and metal shrinking, it is simply not economical for the professional body shop geared for maximum profit in the least time. If you want first-class lead work, you must find someone with ability and time to do a correct job. This service will not come cheap.

A word of caution before you light your torch, however. Lead fumes are highly toxic. Do not, under any circumstance, work in a confined area without adequate ventilation.

Lead must be applied with heat. Its melting point is low enough to keep body-metal distortion to a minimum. Moreover, its expansion rate is closer to that of the 20-gauge sheet metal used in early car bodies. If a lead job is done well, it will not crack or peel away from a repaired surface. All in all, lead actually makes the repair job easier, but it does require more talent and time.

The alloy typically used in quality metalwork is a mixture of 70 percent lead and 30 percent tin. The major tool required is an oxyacetylene welding outfit with a leading tip that fits over the conventional tip and passes only acetylene. Holes in the leading tip draw in air to support the acetylene combustion and produce a flared, gentle flame for melting the lead without warping the sheet metal.

You'll need a flat, stubby hardwood paddle to move the soft metal around, and a tray of beeswax to coat the paddle so that hot lead doesn't stick to it. Get some tinning compound specifically designed for body leading, and coarse steel wool to apply it.

Some of the lead will have to be removed. For that, use a flat and a curved vixen file. These files have well-spaced, curved cutting edges that won't load up while the lead is being planed. A sanding block and a supply of #80-grit sandpaper are needed for finishing work.

Before beginning the lead work, grind all paint, primer and old lead off the panel. The area to be leaded must be exceptionally clean or the lead won't adhere. If a panel that was once leaded is being refinished, check for pits or holes that may leach old tinning residue. These show up as small dark spots in the metal. If not worked out, the residue can prevent the new lead from sticking.

Once the work area is clean, heat it and brush on the tinning compound with steel wool held in a pair of old pliers. The acid-based tinning compound cleans the work surface. The small amount of lead in the compound remains as a thin coating of lead on the sheet metal. This helps to bond the body lead to the surface.

Spreading the tinning compound over a larger area of the sheet metal than needed will ensure an adequately clean and prepared work surface. Let the area cool after it is tinned. Then wash the surface with tap water to rinse away remaining acid.

Next, apply lead to the area. Best results are achieved with a thin coating. Don't build up more than a quarter-inch. If more lead is needed to fill the low spot, more hammer-and-dolly work is probably needed.

The key to successfully applying lead is mastering the paddle. Heat the beeswax until it starts to melt and forms a slick surface on the paddle's bottom. Then melt enough lead onto the tinned surface to complete the job. The molten lead shouldn't stick to the waxed paddle.

First, practice leading on a horizontal panel. Move to a vertical panel after you've mastered horizontal application. Avoid overheating the metal when melting and flowing the lead. As

soon as there is sufficient lead melted on the work area, start shaping it to the desired contour with the waxed paddle. Keep the torch moving all the time.

Work the lead as smooth as possible to reduce the filing and shaping yet to come. Excess lead can be spread onto the untinned metal and discarded, it will not stick to metal that hasn't been tinned.

When the lead has cooled, it can be shaped with vixen files, and then finished with #80 sandpaper on a sanding block. If any depressed areas are noted during filing, a picking hammer can be used to raise them from the back. Then file the high spot smooth.

Plastic Body Fillers

A new word entered the street rodder's vocabulary during the mid-1950s: Bondo®. This is another registered trademark that has become a generic term. Dynatron/Bondo Corporation's product, Bondo Plastic Filler, Bondo, for short, has become synonymous with plastic fillers.

Bondo, and most of the plastic fillers that followed it, are compounded from a putty-like resin base and a syrupy hardener. As long as the two remain separate, they stay pliable. Once hardener is mixed into the resin, the compound hardens in a few minutes.

Plastic fillers, in their characteristic pink, green, gray or black colors, were looked down upon by most custom and street rod builders when they first appeared—and for some time afterward. Their quality has improved since the 1950s. Today's plastic filler will easily last as long as lead.

When properly applied, high-quality modern plastic filler will produce a hard finish. It will not crack, shrink or lift off the base metal even under extreme operating conditions and temperatures.

Avoid "economy" fillers. Major companies have paid their dues over the years, so take advantage of this and use their superior product, even though the price may be higher.

Also, avoid the many economy fiberglass repair kits. Although major brand names are of good quality, they are primarily designed to repair damage in fiberglass bodies. They will work reasonably well on metal bodies for repairing a small rust spot. However, there usually isn't enough material for the type of repair job we're discussing.

Plastic fillers won't last if they are used in body areas subjected to stress and flexing. We can't overlook that the bolt-together pre-World War II auto body, under the best of circumstances, is a "flexy flier." Those billowy fenders flop around in the wind! Don't use plastic fillers in an exposed edge because they will chip away. Repair edges with lead.

Applying Plastic Filler—As in all bodywork, the surface of the repair area must be clean and dry. All paint and rust must be removed, and the surface cleaned with lacquer thinner. Plastic filler won't adhere to a super-smooth surface as well as it will to one with a bit of roughness. So, scuff it with a sander/grinder using a #24-grit open-coat disc.

Next, follow the manufacturer's directions for mixing resin and hardener. Usually a few drops of hardener are mixed into a wad of resin the size of a golf ball. The mixture takes about thirty minutes to harden at room temperature. The resin and hardener can be mixed on plastic palettes and applied with plastic applicators. Both are available at auto paint supply stores. Nevertheless, bodyworkers have used everything from cardboard to coffee can lids for applicators.

Apply the filler as soon as the hardener is worked in. Use an applicator flexible enough to follow the contours of the fender or panel. Remember, you must work within the drying time limit of the filler.

Don't apply more than a quarter-inch thick coating of filler during any one application. Apply it in the shallowest part of the repair area first. Work out any bubbles. Small applications are best, with adequate drying time between coats. Take care that no filler gets on surrounding painted areas. Aside from being a sloppy job, the filler won't adhere properly and will start to lift from the panel.

The most popular tool used for shaping plastic filler is commonly known as a cheese grater. It is more properly called the Surform®, and is manufactured by the Stanley Tool Company. There are several styles of blade holders. They use replaceable steel blades with a non-clogging design that passes the shavings through the teeth openings. Flat, half-round, and round blades are available.

It's not necessary or even desirable for the completed filling to be rock hard before beginning to shape it. Work can start as soon as it is firm, and long shavings will pass through the teeth of the cheese grater. Use a light touch with a fresh blade. When shaping is almost completed, let the filler harden completely. Finishing touches are made with a regular body file, then #180 and progressively finer grits of sandpaper.

22

'GLASSWORK

They start out in perfect condition from the manufacturer, but there's up to 3000 miles of highway travel before that reproduction body gets to your house! Check it out immediately upon its arrival.

The day the freight truck pulls up to your house with a crated fiberglass reproduction body will be a memorable one if you're a first-time street rod builder. Let's hope it will be a happy one, as well. The joy of taking delivery of your brand new 'glass body fuels the fire of resolve to build a street rod. Not, however, if shipping damage is discovered.

I dislike beginning this chapter on a negative note, but having been on the receiving end of damaged goods a few times, I have found that the time to inspect a new shipment is right now; the time to report damage is immediately after it is found.

Fiberglass bodies are big and unwieldy, and occasionally they get smacked about. Not always, but enough to warrant a careful inspection of every square inch of exterior and the interior. If damage is found, photograph it and contact the manufacturer. He will advise you of the steps to take. These words to the wise should be sufficient to cover the bases insofar as shipping problems go.

Now, let's jump right into the main thrust of this chapter—getting a 'glass body ready for its more-or-less permanent installation on your rolling chassis.

SUPPLEMENTAL WORK ON A NEW BODY

For our purposes, supplemental work is that work necessary to ready a fiberglass body for permanent installation. Painting prep is covered in the next chapter.

The amount of supplemental work required on contemporary 'glass bod-

Once the body is uncrated, things like doorjambs and deck lid openings are subject to distortion. Therefore . . .

. . . a new fiberglass body should be fitted and bolted to its intended frame as soon as possible.

Minor supplemental work includes fitting the body to the frame, hanging the doors and deck lid, and fitting fenders. It also includes installing dashboards, seat risers, insulation and accessories such as windshield frames. Much of the latter is in the instructions that come with the body assembly. Major supplemental work involves the installation of a plywood floorboard and reinforcing the body in modified areas. Before any of that can begin, however, you must be certain your repro body is bolted to the frame and properly aligned.

Initial Body Bolt-Up

The builder of a vintage tin street rod is (or should be) aware that once the body is uncrated, doorjambs are subject to distortion. The problem is far worse in open cars than in coupes or sedans. Steel bodies that have been properly reinforced as per the last chapter bolt back on their frames easily. To be sure, there will be some shimming here and there, and the doors and deck lid may have to be adjusted to re-align them, but that's a straightforward operation.

A new fiberglass body should be placed on its betrothed frame, reproduction or original, as soon as it is uncrated. Of course, your frame (reproduction or original) may or may not be as perfect as a factory-fresh original. No one I know is bold enough to expect perfect interchangeability between the products of a dozen different body manufacturers on one hand and an equal number of chassis builders on the other. And "close" isn't good enough in quality street rod building. In short, it will take time to properly fit a repro body to a frame even if you have done your part

ies is well within the skill range of the average street rodder. Even if you make mistakes, you can correct them. That alone makes the fiberglass reproduction street rod body an attractive alternative to high-dollar vintage tin.

There are several grades of fiberglass bodies and they are easily categorized by their prices: The most expensive require a minimum of supplemental work prior to painting, and the least expensive require the most.

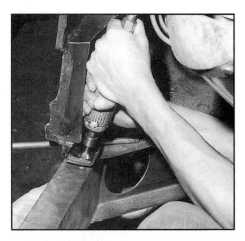

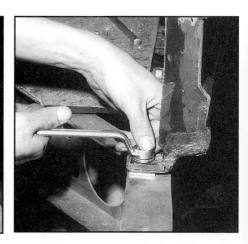

To pinpoint "blind" body mounting holes, grind points on a set of bolts and fasten them to the frame, points up. Carefully position the body on the frame and center punch each mounting spot on the body. Then lift it from the frame and place it on sawhorses with the center-punch marks exposed. Drill them out with a slightly undersize bit, and replace the body on the frame. Open the holes just enough to drop bolts through. When you satisfied with the fit, shim and bolt the body down. "Fine tuning" is likely to be needed later, but this will prevent any body warpage as your project progresses.

to keep things on the straight and narrow.

I have long recommended that the rod builder defer his purchase of a fiberglass body until his chassis is at least on wheels. Even top-quality bodies that are well cured will eventually warp if they aren't supported in perfect alignment. They simply must have the all-points support of a frame. In short, the day that delivery truck arrives with your repro body is the day it should be bolted to the frame. Of course, it may have to be removed a half dozen times or more, but that's all right. The point is, even a temporary shoring up is better than none at all. While you're at it, trim off any excess material along the lower edge and floorboard area, and lightly sand all edges with #220-grit paper. Even the best bodies will occasionally have a few sharp edges and burrs.

Some fiberglass bodies with integral floorboards aren't pre-drilled at the frame mounting points. Instead, these are marked by indentations. Manufacturers have designed their bodies to fit on a stock frame, and most reproduction frames have the body mounting holes in the same location as stock. Your first task is to confirm this, and if such is not the case, to precisely position the body on the frame.

Sometimes that's easy. Occasionally, however, the contours of both body and frame are such that you can't get the body exactly in position, and a miss is as good as a mile. Pinpoint the mounting holes with as much precision as you can muster. One way of doing this is to grind points on a set of bolts and fasten them to the frame, points up. With the assistance of at least three friends, carefully lower the body on the frame and position it. Center punch each mounting spot on the body just hard enough to leave an impression in the 'glass. The body is then lifted from the frame and turned upside down or placed on sawhorses to expose the center-punch marks. All that's left to do is drill 'em out. Nothing to it.

Once this is done, the body can be securely bolted to the frame until you wish to resume work on the project. In the meantime, it can leisurely cure. A fresh fiberglass body requires from four to six weeks to completely cure, depending on temperatures and weather conditions. However, inasmuch as you can't know for sure when the body you have was originally laid up, it's best to begin the supplemental work as soon as possible.

To verify the alignment of the body, you'll need 50 feet of nylon cord, two or three heavy flat washers for "plumb bobs," and a 25-foot tape measure. Assuming the frame is straight and true, its longitudinal centerline will be the baseline. With the body off, and motor and transmission removed, this critical point of reference is easily determined with a tape measure. The frame should be level and squarely supported on four jack stands. (If the suspension has been installed, the wheels should be off the ground.) Record a series of frame width measurements from front crossmember to rear.

Bolt the body back on the frame, and locate its longitudinal centerline along the floorboard using a tape measure. It should exactly correspond with the longitudinal centerline of the frame.

It's a little more difficult to find the

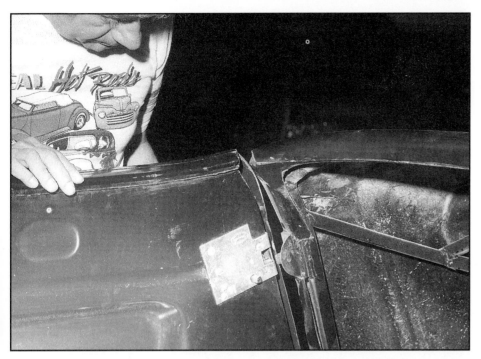

It doesn't take much cowl tilt in a roadster to result in poor door alignment. Install the hinge and handle hardware as soon as the body is securely bolted to the frame.

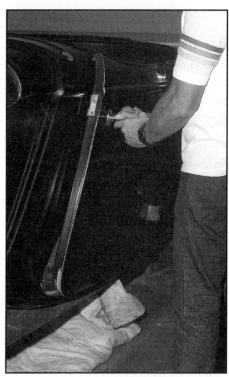

Open and close the doors, watching closely for binding and interference.

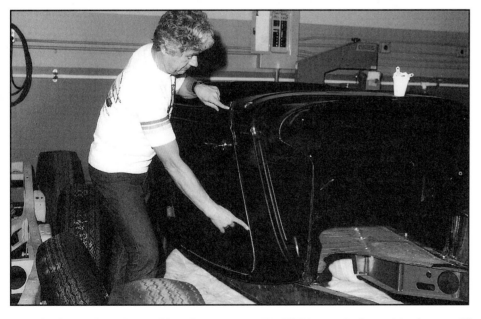

Function is not the only consideration, however. The "fit" has to look good to the eye. All interface gaps should be parallel, and just wide enough so that the paint doesn't chip.

topside centerline of the body. The center of the cowl vent opening is a good front-of-the-body midpoint. Use the center of the deck lid opening for the rear midpoint. Drop your makeshift plumb bobs down to the centerline of the floorboard at the lead-ing edge of the deck opening, and to the frame somewhere around the transmission access port at the front. Anything more than a quarter-inch off-center could be the first indication of trouble. Fear not, however, today's high quality steel-reinforced fiberglass and composite reproduction bodies will rarely be off significantly.

WOODING THE 'GLASS BODY

At one time, "wooding" was necessary with most bodies. Those of us who faced that task are thankful that almost all modern reproduction bodies are substantially reinforced at the factory. Several manufacturers also offer channeled models. Still, there are a few manufacturers of economy bodies, and I'll never fault a rod builder on a severe budget. Been there, done that!

Even so, unless you are planning to build something unusual, your best bet is to order a body with an integral fire-wall and floorboard, as well as latched and hinged doors and deck lid. The additional cost of this, relative to the time and effort you would otherwise have to expend, is negligible if you plan to stay with a conventional or

229

Not too many years ago, builders had to "wood" a 'glass body and construct a floorboard. Lots of work to be sure, but part of the game. That is behind us, now unless you plan to channel, or significantly modify the body.

resto-rod look. However, the history of street rodding tells us that is not everybody's piece of cake.

If the body you have selected to customize requires some additional reinforcing, wood is adequate if you're short on equipment and experience. Not only that, your tool collection should already include what's needed—drills, saws, chisels, scissors, razor blades, putty knives and old paint brushes. The fiberglass supplies required are inexpensive and readily available at paint or hardware stores.

If the body is without floorboards or you want to channel it to your own dimensions, you'll need a piece of 3/4-inch exterior or marine plywood. (Make sure it wasn't stored outdoors at the lumberyard where it could absorb moisture. Moisture adversely affects the curing of resins.) You'll also need

several 1 x 2-inch and 2 x 2-inch hardwood strips. It is best to buy a little more than you need.

In the earlier discussion of fiberglass products, I mentioned the thick, heavy sheet of non-directional spun glass fibers called mat, and lighter weight bi-directional cloth. Both can be used for supplemental reinforcement of repro bodies, but there's another type of fiberglass material—a paste-like substance called adhesive filler. It's designed for bonding and filling fiberglass panels on Corvettes and the like. This non-flowing filler makes duck soup of otherwise difficult fiberglass-reinforcement jobs.

The quantity of fiberglass materials needed depends upon the degree of reinforcement necessary. When using mat or cloth, use about three times the surface area of the plywood panel to

be bonded to the body. Also, use the heaviest mat and cloth available. Two gallons of resin will be adequate for a full-length floorboard.

Closely follow the directions for mixing catalyst with resin. Recommendations vary from one manufacturer to another, and the exact percentage of hardener is important. If too much catalyst (hardener) is added, the mixture will kick off too quickly, possibly causing cracking. If too little is used, the result will be a sticky mess that may never harden. As in all 'glass-work, experiment until you find the exact amount of catalyst required for the weather conditions of the day you are working.

Those inexpensive cardboard paint containers sold by hardware stores are excellent for mixing resin, but only mix small quantities. Fiberglass workers favor pie tins as secondary containers for spreading resin.

On mild or warm days, it normally takes about 30 minutes for well-saturated mat and cloth to set-up. This provides the time needed to work out air bubbles and excess resin. It also allows you to shift the mat or cloth around if necessary.

Don't forget that the batch of catalyzed resin in the can is kicking, too. It only takes one oversight for you to forever remember that you must apply catalyzed resin as soon as possible. As you gain experience, you'll quickly learn how much you can handle before disaster strikes in the form of a batch of hardened resin.

Get a gallon of acetone for clean-up. Acetone is both toxic and flammable, however, so use it with utmost care. Some folks simply cannot work with gloves, but if sensitive skin is even a minor problem, wear rubber gloves when working with fiberglass.

The key to maximum strength when reinforcing a fiberglass body with wood is not how much or how thick the plywood is, but how well the mat and cloth is saturated with resin and the number of bonding layers used. In short, the more substantial the fiberglass lamination, the greater the strength.

INSTALLING FENDERS

If I had my way, all early model street rods would be fenderless just like the original dry lakes jobs of the 1930s and '40s. I admit, though, that some street rods benefit from the full-fendered "look." In fact, many feel that 1933–34 Fords don't look right without fenders unless they are channeled. Beyond cosmetics, of course, is the Motor Vehicle Code. Few states permit anything but 1500-pound flyweights to run around fenderless.

Therefore, in the interests of keeping your car street legal, let's look at installing fenders. This is not much of a problem for "real steel" guys, but sometimes a real headache for the 'glass bunch.

Fiberglass rear fenders fit nicely on most early bodies because there's enough supporting structure for attachment. In addition, the fenders are relatively light. On the other hand, front fenders sometimes flex too much and split on early model cars. The front fenders are heavy on many early models, and all that weight is flopping around in the wind, largely unsupported. Although the quality of modern fiberglass fenders is quite good, stress cracks can still appear.

Unfortunately, there is no cure-all for the cracking problem. About all you can do is ensure the fender-attach-

Installing fiberglass fenders often presents problems. For a sound, as well as an attractive fit, the home builder must occasionally provide a little extra reinforcement.

ing points are beefy. Some builders add a few layers of cloth on the inside of the body and the underside of the fender in attaching areas. Oversize nut plates or fender washers should always be used to distribute the load at the fender well. Of course, substantial stock-type fender braces—where originally used—are critical. Again, some home builders add a second or third brace. Such braces are easily fabricated and can be designed so they follow the inside contours of the fenders. In short, anything that can be discreetly done to stabilize and support the front fenders will be worth the effort.

Just as with the body and doors, trim off any excess material and lightly sand the edges of the fenders and splash aprons with #220-grit paper.

If the fenders, splash aprons and similar bolt-on components are not pre-drilled, they ordinarily have impressions or other bolt-hole indexes. No matter, it is up to you to take considerable care in first locating and then

securing components to the body proper. Precision requires additional effort.

The first pieces to mount on a full-fendered 1927–34 Ford-based reproduction body are the running boards and splash aprons when used. These components are the least likely to be misaligned and they determine the exact location of both rear and front fenders. Before they are installed however, be certain the metal support brackets are not kinked or bent.

It's almost impossible to properly install fenders and the like without some help, so don't try it alone. Depending on the mounting arrangements for your car and the as-delivered readiness of the components, several small C-clamps may also be needed to temporarily attach the running boards to the frame or brackets. When clamping or bolting fiberglass, however, remember that it is brittle. If you apply too much pressure, it may crack.

Once the running boards are

clamped or bolted in place, and repeated checking confirms that their location is correct, the rear fenders can be installed. Most rear fenders tuck up into the fender well. Because fiberglass is much thicker than sheet metal, however, interferences may be encountered. Match the fender as best as possible with the running board and the rear of the body or rear deck panel. It may be necessary to grind or sand down the fender material to get a neat fit. Many manufacturers deliberately leave excess material just to make close-tolerance fitting simpler. It's easier to remove material than add it when fitting a body panel!

Once you're satisfied that the fender fits, and all seams match, gently clamp the fender to the body and running board in as many places as possible. Again, be very careful not to overtighten and fracture the 'glass.

Drill the first holes in the topmost mounting points using a sharp bit for a clean cut. Some rod builders drill two or three small holes just big enough to secure the fenders with machine screws so they can back off and check fender alignment with the wheels and tires in place. (Yes, you should have your wheels and tires about this time.) At any rate, if something doesn't look right, new holes can be drilled and the extra small holes filled.

Another method is to drill one oversize hole so you can wiggle the fender a little. Either way, once the fender is aligned to your satisfaction, the remaining boltholes can be drilled. Before doing so, however, make sure the fender is secure to the body along its full circumference before drilling. Drill through both the body and fender at the same time. It is also much easier to drill from the inside of the body wherever practical. By the way, the final boltholes should be somewhat larger than the attaching bolts. Fenders should never be bound in so tightly that there is no room for some shifting or installation of bead welting.

As just mentioned, the largest fender washers possible should be used behind the bolts. As for nuts, the best to use are the aircraft type with nylon locks. They won't back off even when they are not fully tightened. Don't forget bolts in fiberglass should not be torqued as much as if they were in sheet metal. Otherwise, you'll crush the fiberglass.

When the running boards and rear fenders are securely mounted, install the front fenders. Mounting is essentially the same as with the rears, but using the wheels and tires as reference is doubly important, particularly if additional bracketry will be used. Not only should the wheels be centered in the fender opening, there must be no interference from steering or suspension movement.

PAINT WORK

23

Paint is the most visible product of a rod builder's labors. Whether it's a critical job by a professional in a spray booth, or a firewall redo in the driveway, it must be perfect.

If you are going to paint your car, look forward to three things: lots of hard work, learning based on trial-and-error, and personal satisfaction that no other rod building endeavor offers. The paint job, more than any other aspect of your street rod, is on public display. The casual audience may never get a glimpse of the motor, and they may never get more than a peak at the interior. Few will ride in the car, so how are they to be impressed with its

power or handling? Even fewer will appreciate the quality of the metal or 'glasswork because they didn't see what you began with.

Ah, but day or night, rain or shine, those whom you pass on the road will have the opportunity to marvel at the perfection of your street rod's paint work. It is not much thicker than the paper these words are printed on, but it brings out the classic styling of a refurbished old car. It is the final touch of

beauty for all who behold it. That's why most street rodders have no trouble farming the job out to a professional painter using professional equipment in a professional setting.

Nevertheless, some rod builders still consider doing the job themselves, knowing full well that as air pollution regulations slowly spread to all areas of the country, fewer and fewer will be able to do so without full professional facilities. For now however, if such is in your plans, plan to do it right.

THE WORK AREA

Unquestionably, the most significant detriment to a do-it-yourself automotive paint job is the work area. True, more than one street rod has been sprayed on the concrete pad in front of the home garage. A number have also been painted right in the middle of the garage. Most communities, however, have local ordinances concerning such activities. Check with your local fire department before a neighbor complains or you have to face an irate judge. Beyond the legalities, overlooking safety hazards can be tragic.

Such hazards are easily identified. The hot water heater is often located in the garage. Attached garages have entryways into the house. Clothes washing and drying appliances are often in the garage, plus the boxes of stored items a family accumulates over the years.

Rendering the home garage safe for spray painting requires your full attention. First off, since there can be no open combustion in the work area, the flame in the pilot light of any gas appliance such as the water heater or clothes dryer, and the gas feeds, must be turned off.

Next, other items in the work area that might be damaged by the unavoidable overspray must be removed. Items that can't be moved easily, such as a washer and dryer, must be completely covered.

Following that, all entrances to the living quarters must be sealed. That means taping off doorways from the garage to the house.

Finally, fresh air is not only essential to your health, a lack of ventilation can easily result in problems such as poor drying, dulling and wrinkling. The trick is to make sure there's plenty of ventilation and adequate exhaust of overspray while at the same time preventing dust contamination on fresh paint. That's why paint booths were invented in the first place!

If you were able to primer, blocksand, and finish coat your car in one straight-through operation, the above precautions could possibly be managed. They can't however. Everything you've just done to your garage has to be undone, and redone several times. That's why I don't recommend extensive spray-painting at home. Spray booths can be rented in larger metropolitan areas. Do yourself a favor and locate a facility away from home.

If you can't swing this, however, and you still want to paint your own car piece by piece at home, please follow the above precautions.

BASIC EQUIPMENT

The paint spray equipment you buy for your home shop is, as always, dependent on what you can afford. Although you only need an air compressor, an adequate length of 3/8-inch ID hose, an air-pressure regulator and filter, and a decent spray gun, there's a wide variety from which to choose. Not only that, there are several other pieces of related equipment such as buffing and polishing tools that makes the jobs easier and better.

This doesn't mean you have to purchase the most expensive professional equipment, but it does mean you have to acquire good equipment. In fact, with the exception of the most modern spray guns, moderately priced air compressors, air filter/regulators, air hose, and many supplies are available from large auto parts stores such as your local NAPA dealer.

The Compressor

The first piece to consider is also the most expensive—the air compressor. It was discussed at length in the chapter on tools, but remember that air compressors are rated according to their volume delivery in standard cubic feet per minute (CFM). A 220-volt unit on wheels, suitable for painting should be capable of at least ten cubic feet per minute (cfm). This often requires as much as five horsepower to prevent having to stop periodically during painting to wait for pressure to build up. (This is not only aggravating; it adversely affects the quality of the paint job.)

In any case, it must put out more cfm than the gun you chose requires. Air storage tanks of about 30-gallon capacity are OK for uninterrupted spraying, but don't go smaller. If you elect to use a conventional siphon-feed spray gun, a combination air pressure regulator and oil and moisture extractor unit is often the most practical.

Spray Guns

The next major factor in producing a good paint job is the spray gun. There are two basic types used in automotive work—siphon-feed and gravity-feed. The one you are most likely to have seen over the years is the conventional "non-bleeder" with a one-quart screw-on cup hanging down. It uses air pressure to siphon-feed the paint. The gravity-fed gun looks upside down with its angled cup atop the gun, but most professional painters prefer it. These are just the configurations, however.

HVLP Guns—The most important changes in modern spray gunology is what the trade refers to as the "HVLP"

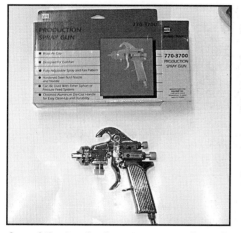

One of the two basic spray gun configurations types used in automotive refinishing is the conventional siphon-feed equipped with an under-slung, screw-on cup. The one on the left is for big jobs, but that little touch-up gun will come in handy more times than you might imagine.

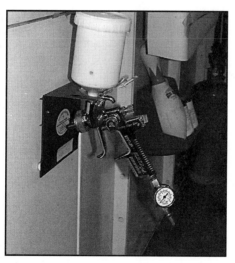

Spray guns have changed over the years. These are SATA Jet 2000 HVLP gravity-feed guns. The one on the left has a digital air pressure readout in the gun handle. The other has the air micrometer below the handle. Pressure control is extremely important. If it is too low, it results in an under-atomized (orange peel) surface. If the pressure is too high, it leaves a rough, dry finish. These guns weigh only 24 ounces and have an operating pressure of 29 psi and an air consumption of 15 cfm at 29 psi. Modern paint guns can still use standard shop air compressors, however. High pressure shop air is converted to low pressure at the gun itself. Most new guns are of the non-bleeder type and therefore trigger the same as older, conventional guns.

design—High Volume/Low Pressure—and that has nothing to do with the used car business. The HVLP gun was developed to reduce the amount of paint overspray that releases toxic chemicals into the atmosphere. The design (and nomenclature) of the HVLP gun refers to how much and at what pressure atomized paint leaves the gun. Low pressure is defined as less than 10 psi as opposed to 45–70 psi for traditional equipment. Although some HVLP guns use a siphon-feed, most models are gravity-feed.

Most of the HVLP guns built today require an air compressor that can deliver 10–11 cfm at 80–100 psi into the gun in order to have 8–10 psi at the air cap, where the paint is atomized.

Consequently, the manufacturers recommend a compressor with a minimum of five hp.

High volume boils down to a parameter known as transfer efficiency—the quantity of paint that actually adheres to the surface being sprayed. A traditional gun with an outlet pressure of 40–50 psi only leaves 25 to 30 percent of the sprayed paint on the sheet metal. The remainder is lost in overspray. From 65 to 75 percent of the paint leaving the HVLP gun lands on the car. That's a heck of a lot of savings when you see what a gallon of the latest SuperShine paint costs!

The trade-off is cost. HVLP spray guns are in the pricey neighborhood of $600, and even with high dollar paint, one has to question the economics if it will only see periodic use. Conventional guns are readily available and much less expensive, often under $300.

Whether or not the HVLP gun came about because of governmental "encouragement," or simply the advance of technology is moot. It's here, it works, and it's environmentally sound. The environmental regulations concerning spray guns in communities with air pollution problems are quite clear, and the more severe the problem, the more severe the regulation. The HVLP gun is a major improvement over older models, and has become mandatory in some areas. Explore the regulations in your town with your local automotive paint dealer.

MODERN AUTOMOTIVE PAINTS

All paints are alike in at least one way: They are composed of pigments, binders and solvents. Pigments are the dry powders that give paints their colors. (There are as many as 15,000 possible automotive color variations.) Pigments also add to the durability of the paint.

The binder, a clear, syrup-like liquid, is the constituent of paint that allows it to adhere to a surface. Pigment is evenly distributed throughout the binder during the manufacture of the paint.

The final component of paint is the solvent, or thinner. It gives fluidity to the pigment/ binder mixture. Without some kind of thinning agent, the paint could not be applied with a spray gun—or even a brush. The solvent, however, is a fugitive agent. It begins to evaporate the instant the paint is sprayed on the surface. Depending on the type of paint used, complete evaporation takes from a few minutes to several hours. Only the pigmented binder remains and that, of course, is the hardened paint film.

The casual painter will rarely be involved with formulating the pigments and binders, but not so with solvents. Although all solvents are similar in appearance, viscosity and smell, each has a dramatically different effect on the way the paint sprays, adheres, flows out and finally looks when dried. It also affects paint durability.

That is why it is imperative to stay within a brand line when dealing with automotive paints, and as always, follow the manufacturer's directions. The best way to know exactly what they are is to pick up a Material Safety Data Sheet (MSDS) for each specific product.

Today's most common automotive paints are acrylic lacquers, acrylic enamels, and acrylic urethanes. Most are designed for two-stage application. That is, a pigmented basecoat is followed by a clear topcoat. All must be thinned or reduced enough to pass through the gun and be atomized. Let's take a look at them.

Undercoats

Although different manufacturers have pet names for their undercoat and topcoat products, and the never-ending evolution of synthetic variations, the old standby definitions are still needed to adequately outline what each is designed to accomplish.

Undercoats include the primers, primer/surfacers, sealers, primer/sealers and putties that provide the base for the color coats. There are many different varieties, but only a basic understanding of these concern us. The details are in the specific MSDS.

Primers are designed to grip the bare body surface and establish a secure foundation for all that comes later. They are typically applied in thin coats and are not meant to be sanded or to fill in scratches or other imperfections.

Primer/surfacers, on the other hand, contain about twice as much pigment as do straight primers. They are designed to offer the good adhesive qualities of a straight primer—preparing bare surfaces for painting—but they also fill in minor imperfections and scratches. Primer/surfacers can be sanded when dry, and the smoother their final coats, the more glossy the finished color coat.

Sealer is yet another type of undercoat. It is applied over a previous paint coat to improve the uniformity and gloss of the final color coat. A few, but not all, sealers are designed to stop color bleed-through from a previous paint job. This latter-type sealer should not be used unless bleed-through protection is specifically required.

Primer/sealers not only seal off old finishes and prevent lifting, they also prime bare surfaces. They are not designed for filling, however.

Putty undercoats are the final type. They are available in tubes and fill deep scratches and imperfections. Essentially, they are thick primer/surfacer pastes with a minimum amount of solvent. They are not sprayed on, but rather applied with a flexible plastic paddle.

Topcoats

There was a time when the fledgling rod builder only had to learn the differences between automotive enamels and lacquers. Enamels were paints that dried slowly, but when dry were about as glossy as they would ever be. Buffing was not needed. Lacquers, on the other hand, had a component called nitrocellulose that caused them to dry very quickly. Moreover, everyone knew that lacquers needed to be rubbed out to achieve a glossy finish. In the days when magazine-feature cars boasted the inevitable "20 coats of hand-rubbed, show-quality lacquer," no serious street rodder doubted what finish he wanted on his car. Enamel was for taxicabs and Uncle Mert's stocker. Solvent-based lacquer had its shortcomings, though. It would shrink over time and eventually crack.

Finishes of 40 years ago hardly exist in their traditional form today; this is the age of synthetics and plastics. In fact, when my coupe was treated to its one and only candy apple red paint job over 25 years ago—see *Street Rodder Magazine*, August, 1976—the already legendary Stan Betz provided the paint. Stan, a long-time supplier of custom paints to the West Coast trade, told me then that he wouldn't be surprised if the true nitrocellulose lacquer

The Sherwin-Williams Ultra 7000 line is a two-stage Acrylic Urethane System with excellent durability. The premium quality, high solids, Ultra Speed-Plus Performance Clearcoat is designed for air dry or force dry environments. It provides a "buff the same day" finish. That is something practicing street rodders who are always changing things can appreciate. The scratch-resistant clear is great for abuse-prone metal running boards such as those on my '41 pickup as well as firewalls and inner fender panels. The system must be applied by a professional in a professional setting, however.

and toners he dug up and mixed for me were some of the last in Southern California—I had better enjoy them while I could. Although fun, a scavenger hunt for paint is hardly what I recommend.

Before we look at paints you can buy at any auto paint supply today, you should be aware of the demands of OSHA, EPA and VOC. You probably know something about OSHA and the EPA. They are the governmental regulatory agencies that oversee the health and welfare of workers and the general environment. If you're not in the painting trade, however, VOC may be a new one for you. Nevertheless, once you put your finger on the nozzle of a rattle can, you are in the mix.

VOC stands for Volatile Organic Compound or Content. It covers a class of materials that include most of the solvents used in automotive refinish products. It is the amounts of evaporative solvent contained in refinish materials. Solvent is a major component of not only thinner, but also of the unthinned color and the catalyst/hardener used in automotive acrylics.

The reason the regulatory agencies care about VOCs is that they react

chemically with sunlight. When mixed and sprayed, the VOCs evaporate out of the paint film and into the atmosphere. There, in combination with auto emissions and dust, they create pollutants known as photochemical smog.

Well, even though driveway paint jobs are street rodder war stories of the past, that doesn't mean a guy can't refinish 10 square feet of classic sheet metal without an $80,000 professional spray booth. It simply means that he should check with his local and state organizations regarding the air quality regulations in force.

Acrylic Lacquer

True lacquer was made from the resinous secretions of the lac bug and cellulose acetate, a resin derived from plant tissues. Some years ago, however, paint manufacturers began to use acrylic resins (thermoplastic polymers) in lieu of the ancient ingredients. The result is a fast-drying, amateur-friendly automotive finish. Acrylic lacquer is relatively easy to apply in the home shop environment with modest protection. It only needs a thinner to reduce its viscosity, and it air-dries. It is easy to repair runs and sags during

application, and to spot-repair minor damage later on down the road.

It does require several days to apply. A typical job requires as many as 18 coats with overnight drying after six or eight coats. It must then be wet-sanded with 600-grit paper to remove orange peel and dust. The final coats are thinned with a slower-drying thinner to increase the gloss.

When correctly thinned and sprayed, acrylic lacquers flow out nicely, hold up well when color-sanded—still necessary to achieve high gloss—and, in general, are much more durable than the old-time nitrocellulose lacquers. Lacquers, both true and acrylic, dry from the inside out. Consequently, early color sanding shortens the drying time. Although acrylic lacquers haven't quite duplicated the depth—that ethereal, mirror-like dimension—of nitrocellulose lacquers, the trade-off has been a sound one.

Unfortunately, automotive lacquers have been banned in some areas of the country by the local air pollution authorities. A recent quick check of the Sherwin-Williams Automotive Finishes web page did find black acrylic lacquer listed along with a range of clears, thinners, and retarders.

The Enamels

Originally, enamels were made from the milky juice of the varnish tree. It was first used in Libya of all places. Modern enamel manufacture has also been revolutionized by thermoplastics.

Synthetic Enamels—Synthetic enamels are undeniably better than "true" automotive enamels used until the 1960s. Today, these very slow-drying finishes are the darlings of well-equipped commercial paint shops because of their low cost, excellent durability and high gloss—not to be confused with depth—when applied in a spray booth and baked in an infrared heat lamp oven. Without the latter, as much as 24 hours are required for complete drying.

Acrylic Enamels—Acrylic enamels are somewhat less troublesome to spray than the old stuff or straight synthetics. They dry much more quickly, but often not quickly enough to avoid problems. In short, they require a completely dust-free environment for a superior job. Consequently, they are not practical for home-shop use. However, they are well suited for the hurry-up work of a commercial shop.

Apart from drying time, the benefits of acrylic enamels are numerous. For instance, there's no need to rub out the last color coat; the finished product has a reasonably high gloss, and the durability of acrylic enamel is outstanding. Sherwin-Williams' web delineates what they call the "Acrylyd Acrylic Enamel Refinishing System." The finish is resistant to rock chips and scratches. Best of all, it can be touched up or recoated at any time. That's a boon to the street rodder who drives his car daily.

Catalyzed acrylic enamels are available off the shelf in many colors, including a variety of candy colors, metallics (polychromatics), pearls and iridescents.

The Acrylic Urethanes

They're called the "Plastic System" by some manufacturers, and they have, or will soon dominate the automotive finishes market. The pros tell me they are the best, and the fact that they are legal to spray even in such hypersensitive pollution-control areas such as Southern California sure doesn't hurt.

Both catalyzed acrylic enamel and urethanes are quite durable, and inasmuch as a greater quantity of paint is applied with each coat, fewer coats are needed.

All that is well and good, and certainly a significant reason to be happy to accept them in a professional setting. The practical home-working rod builder is going to have to pass on them, however. Urethanes contain poisonous cyanide compounds, which means their fumes are highly toxic. Expensive full-body suits with hoods and high-quality respirators and other safety gear must be worn, and they must be applied in a booth that is a properly filtered and ventilated. Even when urethanes are drying (outgassing) they can attack exposed skin and tear ducts!

REDUCERS, THINNERS & SOLVENTS

The number and types of reducers, thinners and solvents can boggle the mind . . . and would, except for the cardinal rule: Always use the exact thinner or reducer recommended by the paint manufacturer.

Technically, reducers are the sol-

vents used in acrylics, synthetic and urethane enamels. Thinners are the solvents for lacquers. The major differences between thinners are their evaporation rates—from seconds to days—and their ability to dissolve the binder. Some thinners won't dissolve certain binders at all. Not only that, you may not find this out until the paint is actually sprayed on the car. So, read the instructions on the cans before you start, not after you're trying to figure out what went wrong!

Retarder, another type of solvent, is an agent that slows drying. There are two types, one for lacquers and enam-

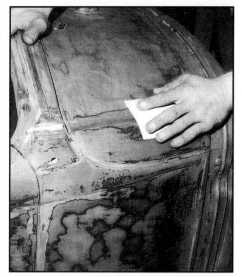

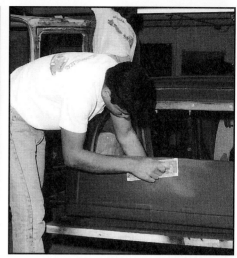

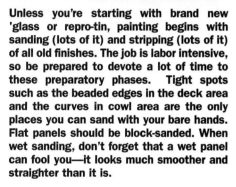

To obtain a measure of perfection in your paint job, spot primer and block-sand dozens of times until you're satisfied with the surface of the body. Be certain any spray painting outside of a booth is legal in your community. With acrylic lacquer, weather is no problem as long as the ambient temperature is above 60 degrees F. Regardless, always allow ample time for thorough drying. Moreover, please, do as I say, not as this fellow is doing. Inside or out, wear a good respirator when shooting acrylic lacquer. (Don't even think about shooting urethanes at home!)

Unless you're starting with brand new 'glass or repro-tin, painting begins with sanding (lots of it) and stripping (lots of it) of all old finishes. The job is labor intensive, so be prepared to devote a lot of time to these preparatory phases. Tight spots such as the beaded edges in the deck area and the curves in cowl area are the only places you can sand with your bare hands. Flat panels should be block-sanded. When wet sanding, don't forget that a wet panel can fool you—it looks much smoother and straighter than it is.

els called a universal retarder; the other is for urethane-based paints.

Although most of what you need to know about paint is in the MSDS, chances are you won't get very far without a question or two popping up. That's why you should develop a good working relationship with the fellows at the paint supply store. You'll be spending several hundred dollars at their establishment before you finish the job. Along with the paint can come a lot of good, solid advice . . . if you ask for it. Don't hesitate. They are more than willing to pass on the vast array of printed information provided by paint manufacturers, and other pertinent information as well. Painters who squirt cars in year-round rainy climates do things a little different from those who paint in desert regions, so this "custom" information can be very

important to you and your street rod.

SURFACE PREPARATION

There can never be too much effort expended if you expect to achieve a lasting and successful paint job. Therefore, if you haven't stripped your car, start by removing the old finish. Don't try to get by with merely sanding the surface. Older rods that have seen any appreciable street duty invariably have been refinished, and there's simply no telling what lies under the existing paint. All too often, checks or cracks invisible or hidden to the eye exist. That's doubly true when "custom" paint jobs have been previously applied. Often, "to the metal" is the only direction to take.

Paint Stripping

If the car doesn't need or hasn't been treated to one of the rust and paint-removing processes described in an earlier chapter, prepare the previously painted surface as follows: All exterior trim such as mirrors, radio antenna,

accessories, chrome or stainless-steel ornaments, bumpers and brackets, grille, headlight and taillight buckets and running boards must be removed. Remove all window glass and securely tape in sections of cardboard to prevent overspray from entering the passenger compartment.

Solvent-type paint remover is probably the fastest way to remove old finishes from non-metal cars. Rarely do the best of them get it all off, but most will lift the bulk of the paint film. Eye protection is necessary, as are gloves. Protective garments will prove their worth the first time a glob of the remover lands on tender skin.

Power Sanding

Unless your car is very small, the application of remover is at least a two- or three-day job. Often, there are stubborn areas that resist multiple applications of remover. At any rate, power sanding is next on the agenda. A favorite power sander for this type of work is a small hand-held pneumatic random orbit-finish sander that uses sandpaper strips or discs. First passes over the body should be made with relatively coarse paper, about #60 grit. Follow this with successively finer #80- and #100-grit paper to finish the metal and smooth scratches. The more you sand, and the finer you "grit down," the smoother the metal. Fanatics use steel wool for the very last go 'round.

Degreaser

As soon as possible following the last sanding, wash the entire car with a degreaser, and if the paint you plan to use permits it, "fisheye" remover. (Fisheyes are small blemishes in the paint caused by surface contaminants.) This will remove all wax, grease and dirt residues left over from the stripping and sanding. This is most important when solvent-wax type removers have been used. Don't be afraid to apply the cleaning solvent liberally, use plenty of paper towels.

Blow out all the cracks, crevices and moldings to remove hidden dust or paint sludge. Caution: Always wear eye protection when using compressed air.

Next, wash down any recently soldered or leaded-in areas with ammonia, then thoroughly rinse with water.

Metal Prep

The last step in preparing a metal body is applying phosphate-type metal conditioner. Sometimes called metal prep, this mild acid not only removes all oil, surface rust and silicones, it slightly roughens or etches the metal surface. This ensures improved paint adhesion and greatly lessens rust renewal later. Reduce and apply the metal conditioner according to the instructions on the container. Leave it

Following the last sanding before the basecoat is shot, the car must be washed with a wax and grease cleaner to remove all residues remaining from stripping and sanding. Use paper towels, and apply liberally. If there has been a significant delay since the last sanding, the body should again be lightly sanded with 400-grit wet to ready the primer for best adhesion. Base coats like a freshly sanded surface. All nooks and crannies should be blown out with compressed air, dried and wiped with a tack cloth.

on for a minute or so. Wipe the conditioner off carefully with clean, dry paper towels. Finally, blow out the cracks and crevices again.

By the way, clean air is critical. All too often poorly maintained compressors lead to pinholes, fisheyes and other adhesion problems. Moisture condenses in the tank and hose.

Masking

Unlike late models, complete disassembly of an old car body is the rule rather than the exception. Nonetheless, careful masking avoids the sloppy appearance of painted edges on glass or trim.

Paint supply houses carry rolls of inexpensive Kraft paper for masking purposes. The few square yards you'll need won't cost much. Don't use newspaper for masking—the ink may dissolve in paint solvents and cause staining. Also, spend a little more and get

When the modified firewall in my coupe was repainted a few years ago, my son Angelo masked around edges where the tape-line wouldn't be seen. The rest of the car was covered in lightweight Kraft paper (a paint store item) to prevent overspray. Easy-to-remove tin foil was used to wrap wiring and hoses, and other awkward areas. It is important to cover everything that isn't to be painted. Paint dust will settle everywhere. After sanding the firewall and fender panels with 220-grit, it was given a thin coat of plastic filler. After final sanding, it was washed with soap and water, and then cleaned with a wax and grease remover. One area at a time was cleaned and wiped thoroughly dry with fresh paper towels. This is very important, because if the panel is not wiped down when it is wet, the grime that the cleaner released will still be there. That's where the amateur gets in trouble; pinholes develop and the paint does not adhere properly. The panel should not be touched after cleaning.

good quality masking tape rather than trying to scrimp by with cheap, second-rate stuff that tears where and when you don't want it to.

Start by masking curved areas with quarter-inch tape. It's more flexible than wider tapes. Use one or two inch tape to extend the masking where necessary.

Prepare the Paint

Don't get careless when preparing primer or paint. The most frequent error of all is the failure to simply stir the paint sufficiently before pouring it into the spray cup. Many primer/surfacer problems are from insufficient stirring.

Thorough stirring ensures a uniform mixture of pigment, binder and thinners. Undercoats, because of the heavier pigment content, require especially conscientious stirring. Slowly add the correct type and percentage of thinner while continuing to stir. The percentage of thinner should be monitored carefully.

Strain the thinned paint though a fine-mesh metal or cloth strainer. Undercoats are poured through a 50-mesh screen, topcoats through a finer 100-mesh. Most of the better spray guns have replaceable metal strainers, but strain all paints before pouring them into the cup.

Using the Spray Gun

It looks so simple, the easy back-and-forth movement of the spray gun—in the hands of an experienced painter. Then you pick it up for the first time. It's heavier than you thought. Dry practice a few left and right passes. So far so good. Then you notice that you somehow dribbled a few drops on your hands and you know if that paint had fallen on the surface of the car it might have burned right through to the metal. Yeah, unsprayed primer and paint is "hot"—it acts as its own solvent.

Practice is what makes perfect, but it shouldn't take years to develop the eye/hand coordination that will allow you to do a good paint job on your own car provided you take the time to correct your mistakes and learn your on-the-job lessons.

Paint spray guns are delicate, precision tools. Every one that leaves the factory has been tested for general operation and adjustment, for atomiza-

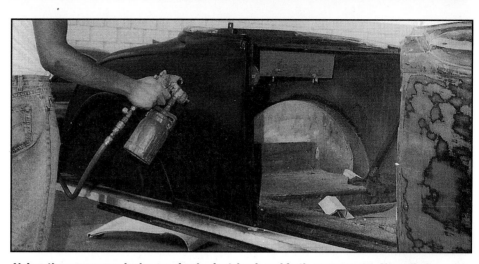

Using the spray gun looks so simple, just back-and-forth movements. Nevertheless, it's heavier than you think. The beginner should dry practice a number of left and right dry passes, then a number of wet passes. Don't practice on ready-to-paint sheet metal with hours of prep time invested, however! Use an old piece of plywood or some such mock-up, in both a vertical and horizontal position. When you realize that paint dribbled out of the gun and landed on the surface, you'll understand unsprayed primer and paint acts as its own solvent. When you feel confident with a piece of wood, move on to primer. It's much more forgiving and expendable than paint!

tion, and for spray-pattern size and uniformity. It's neglect and carelessness that subsequent owners subject a spray gun to that causes the majority of spraying problems. Moreover, 90 percent of the neglect is related to improper cleaning of the gun.

There are two knobs on the backside of the spray-gun body. The top one is for air pressure adjustment; the lower one is for fluid-flow adjustment. You know where the off/on trigger is. The rod that goes from the trigger into the body of the gun is the air-valve stem. The "business end" of the gun is the only part besides the cup that disassembles. The air cap unscrews to reveal a fluid tip. The tip slips off to further reveal the fluid needle. When replacing the fluid tip and air cap, make certain the cap is tightened securely in position.

Unless your spray gun is brand new, make sure it is clean. Several paint companies make gun-cleaning solvents that work best to keep the aluminum alloy parts in tip-top shape.

Never immerse your spray gun in thinner because it will destroy the lubricant in the packings around the fluid needle. A few ounces of clean solvent placed in the cup and sprayed through the gun is fine, but the gun and cup should be wiped clean and dried immediately afterward.

Once you've familiarized yourself with the gun and its parts, mix some primer and thinner in the recommended percentages. Strain this mixture into the cup and make sure the regulator is set at the recommended pressure.

Obtaining the proper width and shape of the spray requires nothing more than trial-and-error manipulation of the air and fluid adjustment screws. The airscrew governs the shape of the spray. Turning it clockwise produces a round or conical spray; turning it counterclockwise produces a fan shape. The fluid-adjustment screw governs the amount of primer or paint going through the gun. It must be regulated according to the type of material being sprayed. As the width of the spray is increased, more material must be passed through the gun to get the same coverage.

When you are ready to practice spraying, shoot a test pattern on a piece of plywood. Check it and adjust the gun accordingly. Initial adjustments are made by backing off the fluid screw two or three turns from the fully closed position. Make pattern corrections with the air-adjustment screw. Anything less than a perfectly uniform pattern—an elongated ellipse—with good atomization is cause for further adjustment.

If the fan-spray pattern is heavy in the middle or has a splatter effect, raise the atomizing pressure at the regulator. If you see a split spray—heavy on each end and weak in the middle in the shape of a peanut—atomizing air pressure is probably too high. Reduce it at the regulator. The split, however, may be due to the material being too thin for the width of the spray. This can be corrected by turning the fluid-adjustment counter-clockwise, while at the same time turning the air-adjustment clockwise. This reduces spray width, but eliminates the peanut shape.

A tear-drop spray pattern—heavy and wider at either the top or bottom—usually means that the material has dried around the outside of the fluid tip and is restricting the passage of the atomizing air. A loose air cap is sometimes the culprit. If not, remove the air cap and fluid tip and clean them with thinner. Do not use a wire or anything hard to clean the air passage.

Spraying Technique—The temperature at which paint is sprayed and dries is critical to the smoothness of the finish. Painting at home rather than in the controlled conditions of a spray booth has its drawbacks. For instance, you'll have to pick a day when there is no hint of rain or high humidity. Both the shop temperature and the temperature of the sheet metal must be at least 75 to 80 degrees. Fiberglass bodies are usually at room temperature. If a metal component is sitting outside before you shoot it, remember that direct sunlight will raise its surface temperature significantly. If you spray outdoors, you may have to use retarder to slow drying. Specifics such as these are best discussed with your paint-supply dealer.

Spray guns deliver their best performance with acrylic lacquer at 6 to 8 inches from the work surface. (The rod-building amateur will not be shooting enamels and urethanes, but they are normally sprayed from 8 to 10 inches away.) Get too close and the velocity of the spraying air will ripple the wet paint film. Get too far away and too much thinner will evaporate and you will get a good dose of dreaded orange peel.

Next, you must master the strokes and overlaps. If the gun is not square to the surface, the fan pattern will not be uniform. If it is swung in an arc, and the distance from the nozzle to the work varies, the paint will go on wetter where the spray is closer to the surface and drier where it is farther away. The gun must always be held square to the work and kept at the same distance, so watch your wrist motion. Work to a wet edge by using approximately 50 percent overlap. Control this by directing the center of the spray fan to the lower or nearest edge of the previous stroke.

Primer/Surfacer Application

Applying primer isn't difficult, but don't take it lightly. First off, don't forget that there are primers, primer/surfacers and primer/sealers.

Chances are, you'll need a primer/surfacer. Use a light-colored primer/surfacer when a light color coat will be applied, and vice versa. It's best to spray thin, wet coats of primer/surfacer and permit short, solvent flash-offs between coats. Applying heavy coats in one pass can lead to problems such as hard sand-ing, pinholes or poor hold-out—where the topcoat is sucked in or absorbed. Beyond that, it is almost impossible to be much more specific because reduction and application vary considerably, depending on brand and type.

Putty Application

As mentioned earlier, putty is a paste undercoat used to fill deep scratches and rough spots—problem areas too big for a primer/surfacer to fill. It is not a substitute for further metal work or plastic body filler, however.

When applying putty, you must work as fast as possible to ensure a smooth, uniform film. Putties contain solvents that evaporate rapidly. Therefore, balling up will occur if the putty isn't worked fast enough. Putties should be applied only to surfaces at room temperatures, and in thicknesses no greater than needed to smooth out the rough spots. Two or three thin applications with adequate drying time in between, is better than one heavy application.

For lows that are broad, a paint stick makes a handy bridge for leveling putty. A paddle or scraper that is too small will drop into the area and remove as much putty as it will put in. Careful downward stroking is the recommended method of applying filler.

Thoroughly dried putty can be sanded with #320-grit paper or finer. If there is a cut-through to bare metal, re-

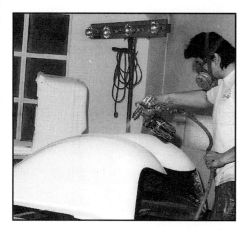

With few exceptions, the same spray techniques used for the primer/surfacer hold true for applying color coats. Just remember: Don't let the paint dry between coats, and don't apply too many coats. Always follow the manufacturer's instruction sheet.

Even a new fiberglass body will need some sanding and filling. Start by sanding out imperfections such as mold marks. When the primer/surfacer has dried, block-sand with #220-grit in long, straight strokes. (Three or four coats of surfacer are generally adequate, but follow recommended drying time between coats.) Often a dark "guidecoat" misted over the primer is necessary. It easily identifies low or high areas.

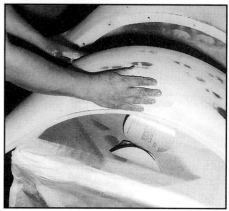

Whether in sheet metal or fiberglass, imperfections cannot always be seen. More often than not, they must be detected using an educated hand. Sanding with finer grits–#400 or #600—can be done wet or dry, but some painters like the dry method because it minimizes the mess.

spray the area with primer/surfacer.

After the filler has hardened, block-sand the repaired areas once again. Continue to look for surface imperfections. When found, mark them. A small supply of fiberglass adhesive or filler kept handy on a paint stick can then be applied to the marked spots with a small plastic paddle.

PREPPING 'GLASS BODIES

Most fiberglass bodies available today easily justify their higher prices by the quality of their exterior. Budget body shells, however, often have wavy surfaces, and considerable time and patience must be expended before they are ready for color. Regardless, if block sanding starts to get wearisome, remind yourself that the finished product will reflect your efforts in many ways.

The preparation of a fiberglass body isn't very different from a rod based on vintage tin. However, there are a few variations from what we have previously discussed.

Begin your preparation of a fiberglass body by carefully washing the entire body with a naphtha-base degreaser to remove any remaining

mold wax. If there is any left, the paint won't adhere. Next, lightly sand the body with dry #220-grit paper to break the glaze and give the surface a "tooth" for the primer to adhere. Take pains not to sand off the gel coat. It separates the 'glass fibers from the surface. The best bodies will need little sanding. However, even with the best surface, block-sanding is required for a perfect paint job.

Spray the first coat of primer/surfacer on wet. Although you shouldn't be careless, don't worry about runs. After a day or so drying time, spray on another, but not so heavy, coat of primer/surfacer. When that has adequately dried, start block-sanding with #220-grit paper in long, straight strokes. Dry sanding at this stage is better than wet sanding, but it does require more paper.

In general, three or four coats of primer/surfacer will do. However, remember to allow sufficient drying time between coats. One day drying time is minimal because primer that

shrinks can ruin any paint job.

You will get to know your street rod body intimately after all of this contact. Consequently, you should find most imperfections. One way to speed things up, however, is to apply a guide coat. Spray on a coat of dark primer/surfacer followed by a lighter shade. When dry, block-sand again. Dark spots that remain after most of the light primer/surfacer has been sanded off are slight depressions in the surface. They need more attention.

Fill the low spots with a thin coat of glazing putty, but don't try to cover anything too deeply. If in doubt, plan to re-resin it.

When you think your fiberglass body is ready for color, wash it down completely with a commercial pre-wash solution such as Fin-L-Wash. It's sold in NAPA stores. This solution will evaporate in still air, but high-pressure air from your air hose will speed drying.

COLOR-COAT APPLICATION

Wipe the car down with a tack-rag before spraying it with the color coat.

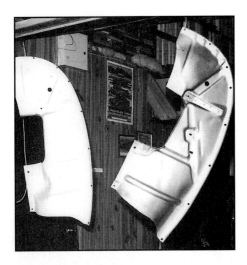

Before painting a full-fendered car, take one timely precaution. The inside of all four fenders and exposed motor compartment fender panels will never be easier (or neater) to heavily undercoat with good old 3M Rubberized Undercoating (PN 08883) than when everything is disassembled. This will protect them from starbursts—dents from the underside—caused by small rocks thrown up by the tires. A protective breathing mask should be used here as well.

Trick paint jobs require special skills. A well-equipped paint supplier is where you find them. At Betz Speed & Color in Orange, California, the man to see is Robert Zuniga, the Color Verification Specialist.

Stan Betz, famed owner and operator of Betz Speed and Color is my primary resource on automotive paints as well as Southern California Air Quality regulations. With regard to the latter, however, nothing is chiseled in stone. Regs change constantly, and it always behooves the end-user to be up to speed when he cracks open a can of primer, paint or reducer! By the way, that V-8 60-powered midget racer is Stan's latest hobby-project. It was originally built in 1941 by Johnny Parsons, the winner of the 1950 Indy 500.

You can get these at your local paint supply store. The varnish in the tack-rag cloth picks up dust and small bits of paper towel lint.

The same spray techniques used for the primer/surfacer hold true for applying color coats. Don't let the paint dry between coats, and don't apply too many coats. Again, follow the manufacturer's instruction sheet. Paint that's too thick will tend to crack. In fact, if you live in cold country, talk with some of the pros in your area to see what they do. Metal shrinks more than paint, so extreme temperature drops can damage paint.

Don't try to paint your way 360 degrees around the car. Doing so is likely to allow drying, which will make blending difficult when you return to your starting point. This is particularly true if this is your first try at painting a car. Novices tend to work slowly.

When spraying the body shell, overspray on drying adjacent panels must be minimized. One approach is to start at the passenger side of the cowl and work around the cowl to the driver's side, then to the driver's rear quarter. Spray the driver's side of the top, then the deck, the passenger side of the top, and finally the passenger side of the rear quarter. Spraying into semi-dry areas again results in orange peel.

Although it is not my intention to encourage you to attempt any exotic work first time 'round, I will mention the possibilities of applying pearls, candies and all the other "trick" (for tricky to apply) topcoats are dealt with at length in HPBooks' *Automotive Paint Handbook* by John Pfanstiehl. These paints contain suspended reflective and pearlescent flakes and need to be maintained at a consistent concentration otherwise the application turns out to be an expensive disaster. Some of these must be applied while the color coat is still wet; others are applied after drying. Depending on your level of painting skills, you may

want to go "all out." If so, do your homework first.

REMEDYING OR BETTER STILL, AVOIDING PAINT PROBLEMS

Runs, sags, and dust deposits can be remedied after the paint dries. Use a rubber sanding-block with 600-grit wet–or–dry sandpaper to gently work the high spots down. To avoid runs and sags, the painter must develop an eye for how much paint is being applied. It is a matter of experience.

The ideal temperature for spraying is 75 to 85 degrees F with very low humidity. Humidity is of special concern when shooting acrylic lacquer. Moisture trapped in drying paint causes a whitish blemish that cannot be

The final art in the application of a custom paint job is a custom rubout. One careless slip with the buffer will cut through to the primer. Don't practice on your street rod's new finish.

Not all paint comes in liquid form! I was tired of having to touch up road chips on the old coupe (currently black). Therefore, I had the louvered sheet metal grille surround and "chin" powder painted. Talk about durable! It'll survive anything short of a hammer blow.

rubbed out. Faster thinners are used in colder temperatures. Slower thinners are used in hotter temperatures.

If the paint has a dry or rough surface appearance, the first suspicion is that the spray gun was held too far from the surface. However, it is equally likely to have been caused by paint that is too thick or excessive air pressure. Which in turn has been caused by using a thinner that dries too fast.

Color Sanding

You will be sanding your car after every step from the time you strip it until you apply the last color coat. Power sanders are useful in the beginning, but eventually you must abandon them in favor of hand sanding. Surfaces sanded by hand require plenty of water, so a dribbling garden hose stationed nearby is a messy necessity. Great care must be exercised. More than one chip in fresh paint can be blamed on careless handling of a garden hose with its brass fitting still in place. Prevent this from happening to you, clip the fitting off the old hose, and buy a new one for garden use.

Custom painters usually start with #320-grit paper for color sanding, changing to #400, and finally to #600. Whatever paper you're using, remember to use a sanding pad, and to sand with light, uniform strokes. It is best to use parallel strokes in one direction only. Although it is not a hard and fast rule, you should avoid dry sanding. Using moisture eliminates dust and leaves a smoother finish. Sanding scratches that show up after the first coats of primer/surfacer are from using paper that's too coarse, pressing too hard, or not using a sanding pad. Sometimes it's simply from sanding the finish before it has dried adequately.

RUBBING COMPOUNDS, POLISHES & WAXES

Rubbing compound is designed to remove minor orange peel and produce a bright smooth finish. It consists of abrasive powder that is dispersed in water, solvent or oils. Acrylic enamel compound is usually finer than that for use on acrylic lacquers.

Although manufacturer's recom-

mendations take precedence over anything else, sprayed acrylic lacquers can be rubbed and polished within a day or so depending on the type of thinner used, the number of coats, and weather. Hand-rubbing compounds should be applied sparingly with a clean, soft cloth, never directly. Gentle back-and-forth strokes are better than hard aggressive strokes, even though it takes more time. If you are using a power buffer, the compound can be applied to the work surface with a soft bristle paintbrush. As the buffing wheel moves across the work, it spreads the compound evenly to rapidly produce a bright, dry finish.

There is an inherent danger that goes with using compounds, particularly when applied with a power buffer—cut-throughs. Cut-throughs can bring a lot of grief in the form of difficult touch-ups. Always be gentle.

Waxes and polishes are also designed to produce a glossy finish. Unlike compounds that abrade the surface, these supposedly leave a protective film of wax, oil or silicone. The controversy of whether or not this is true rages on, but I must tell you, polishes and waxes sometimes can have harmful effects on custom paint jobs, such as moisture spotting, yellowing, dulling and even checking. At any rate, don't use a polish or wax on new acrylics—lacquer or enamel—until the paint has cured at least a month. In fact, many paint manufacturers, as well as professional painters, advise that the best paint care is frequent washing with plain, warm water.

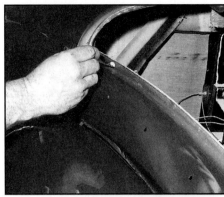

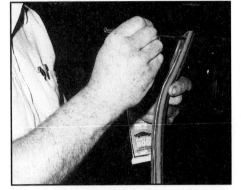
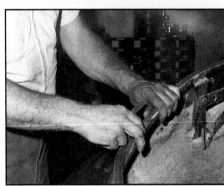

Scratching fresh paint is not a paranoid fear—it is justified! Since the firewall can't be painted with a motor in place, use old Army blankets or the like to cushion the inevitable misstep when it is reinstalled.

An entire chapter of helpful hints could be written when it comes to putting freshly painted sheet metal and fiberglass back together. The installation of rubber molding on doors and deck lids can be a sticky mess if you are not careful. Every street rodder is familiar with the 3M line of adhesive products, but that doesn't stop them from ruining good rubber. Putting the glue on the rubber and in the channel requires a delicate touch. In other words, you can't just squeeze it out of the tube like toothpaste. If you want to be neat, apply it with a little metal handle brush. After gently installing it, a series of spring-pinch clothespins encircling the circumference holds it in place until the glue fully dries.

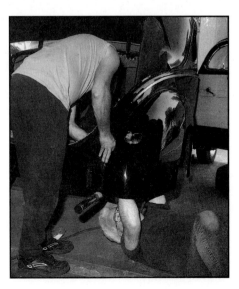

Fender installation (always a two-man job) can be a bear when it comes to neatly fitting the welting in before and after final bolt-up. Try this—measure and mark the boltholes, then knock them out with a 3/8-inch hole punch. With the bolts in place finger-tight, coordinated adjustment and final tightening is a breeze.

THE ELECTRICAL SYSTEM

24

From street rods to classic pickups, the challenge of wiring the electrical system ultimately faces the builder. The key to success is to understand the individual circuits, and then to assemble and test them one at a time.

Few rod-building tasks come with as much uneasiness as the electrical system and laying out the wiring circuits. There are more complex assignments, such as rebuilding the automatic transmission, but you know a job of that nature shouldn't be attempted without a great deal of experience, so there is no ego involvement or anxiety. When it comes to the electrical system, however, you've probably read numerous magazine articles that said wiring a street rod is relatively easy. Yet, chances are, you're not at ease looking at all those mysterious posts and tabs sticking out of the alternator, starter, distributor and the backs of all those gauges.

Of course, you've probably installed a tachometer, a CD player or an extra light. Although a fuse or two might have bitten the dust before everything was "kosher," you got the job done. Surely that doesn't qualify you to do an entire car. Or does it?

Wiring the entire car is done one component at a time, just as with gauges. And, just as you wouldn't have tried to complete high school in one sitting, neither should you try to wire an entire car in a weekend. Even if you got everything to work, chances are it would look chaotic. In street rod building, the wiring not only must be correct, it should be neat and attractive.

This chapter will attempt to simplify

12-VOLT FUSE DATA	
Circuit	Amps
Turn Signals	10
Cigarette Lighter	15
Radio, Stereo, CB	15
Heater, A/C Controls	10
Headlights	15
Brake Lights	10
Taillights	10
Parking Lights	10
Electric Fan	15
Fuel Pump	10
Horn	10
Electric Wipers	10

the technical complexities as much as possible. I can't include a detailed schematic for every possible ignition and charging circuit or trace the installation of every possible accessory. No matter which component or gadget you choose, you simply must have the appropriate instruction sheets, not only for the wiring specifics, but also for everything else you will eventually need to know about it. This chapter is merely an introduction. If your appetite is whetted, however, get a copy of HPBooks' *Automotive Electrical Handbook* by Jim Horner. It is devoted exclusively to this subject.

AUTOMOTIVE ELECTRICAL CIRCUITS

In most cases, the street rod electrical system and its wiring is no different from standard American production cars in the simpler days before the on-board computer and confusing array of pollution controls. The only exception is the fiberglass reproduction body, but even that doesn't significantly alter the wiring.

An understanding of the basic automotive electrical system begins with

the electrical circuit—a closed path through which electric current can flow. Most automotive circuits consist of low-resistance wiring that conducts current to electric appliances and accessories with a minimal voltage drop.

Each appliance or accessory should have enough resistance to make the electromotive force drop 12 volts (in a 12-volt system) when the required amperage is passed through the circuit. If it doesn't, there will be overheating.

Almost all automotive circuits are of the one-wire (common-ground) type, so-called because the metal body or chassis completes the circuit. The battery, the source of electromotive force in the car, is grounded to the motor block through a heavy woven-copper strap. Its live, or hot, post completes the current path through a heavy, insulated copper cable to the starter solenoid.

If the hot lead or conductor touches any other part of the car, resistance is insufficient for circuit balance, and a short circuit occurs, followed by arcing, burning or similar fireworks. Another, not-so-easily detected, but more benign source of trouble arises from improper grounding. Electricity will always seek the path of least resistance to ground. If the normal path is blocked or has high resistance, current will seek an alternate route. For example, if a sparkplug lead is broken internally, the 40,000-volt current will arc to the motor block, exhaust manifold or any other convenient metal object that provides the best ground. Or, if the motor is improperly grounded, current may travel down the throttle linkage, shift linkage or driveshaft. Depending on the amperage involved, this can cause the linkage to be arc-

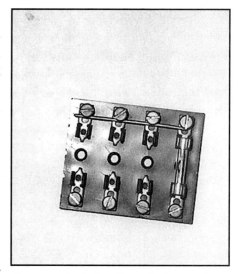

Fuses protect circuits against current overloads caused by an unwanted ground or excessive voltage. Therefore, they are critical, and should be in a readily accessible area.

welded in position or cause metal transfer from the driveshaft to output bearing or vice versa. If the ground is insufficient, it may also show up as dim or flickering headlights . . . or no lights at all!

AUXILIARY CIRCUITS

Sometimes it is necessary for automotive components to have auxiliary circuits. For instance, it takes relatively high current to operate the headlamps, far too much to be handled by a simple, low-capacity instrument panel switch. The options are to replace the low-capacity switch with a high-capacity one and heavy-gauge wiring, or bring the current directly to a relay near the headlamps. This allows you to use the low-capacity instrument panel switch to operate the circuit to the relay, which in turn kicks on the headlights. An auxiliary circuit that controls another circuit by means of auxiliary switches is known as a relay circuit.

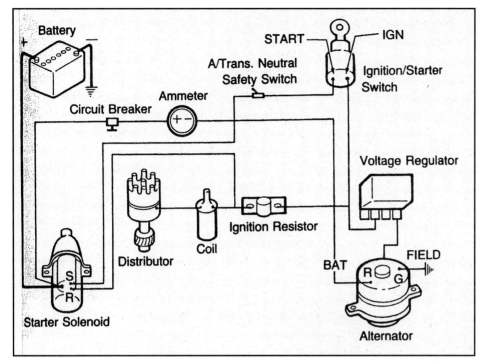

If your rod is powered by a Chevy engine, you'll want to follow the GM diagram for the ignition and charging circuits. Remember, however, we're talking about a basic non-computerized system here.

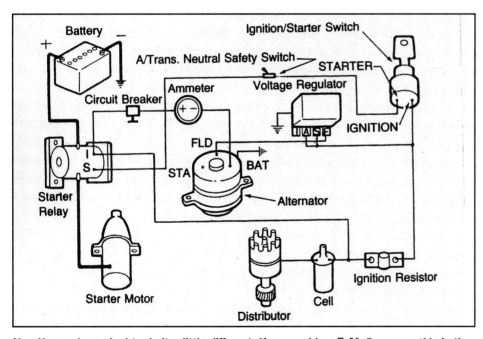

Yes, Henry always had to do it a little different. If your rod has FoMoCo power, this is the ignition and charging circuit you must follow.

Fuses & Breakers

All circuits should be protected against current overloads caused by an unwanted ground or excessive voltage. The conventional way of providing this protection is with fuses and circuit breakers. These should be in readily accessible areas. Fuses, it seems, tend to burn out at night, and if you can't find the fuse panel or see the burned fuse in the panel, you are only going to add to your frustration. Of course, merely replacing the fuse or resetting the circuit breaker doesn't solve the problem. The blown fuse or tripped breaker is only a symptom of the problem. Find the cause and correct it. Never install a higher capacity fuse as a temporary "fix." This may overload the circuit and cause more serious problems at another weak link in the wiring.

The Starting Circuit

The starting circuit consists of the battery, cranking motor, starter switch, and the cables and wires. Although it is straightforward in its basic wiring, this circuit has the all-important task of spinning the flywheel and crankshaft so the motor can fire and operate under its own power. Electrical load is high and these components draw the most current.

The Ignition Circuit

The ignition circuit consists of the key switch, coil, distributor, sparkplugs, low-tension wiring, high-tension wiring and battery. In reality, however, there are two separate circuits. The primary, or low-tension, circuit is one. It includes the ignition switch, coil primary winding, distributor breaker points and condenser, and the battery. The frame or body serves as the conductor to complete the primary current path from the battery, through the components and wiring in the circuit, and then back to the battery. Most 12-volt ignition systems also incorporate a ballast resistor—a special circuit to bypass it—within the primary circuit. The ballast resistor reduces total voltage going to the distributor once the motor starts. The bypass circuit allows full battery voltage to flow to the starter when cranking power is needed.

The other main ignition circuit is the secondary or high-tension circuit. It includes the secondary coil winding, distributor cap and rotor, sparkplugs and their wires, and the grounded portion of the entire circuit.

The Charging Circuit

The charging circuit is the complete generating and energy-storage system. It furnishes electric current for motor cranking, ignition, lights and all accessories. It consists of a generator or alternator, voltage regulator, the wiring, appropriate gauges or lights to indicate state of charge or voltage and, of course, the battery.

When the motor is in operation, the generating circuit—exclusive of the battery—supplies current for the electrical load, and keeps the battery charged. The amount of current diverted to the battery depends upon battery condition and the electrical load.

Alternators & Regulators

The modern automotive "dynamo," of course, is the alternator that supplies rectified alternating direct (ac) current to the system. The alternator became standard equipment on production cars over 40 years ago because it provides substantial current at idle speed as well as increased maximum output. It is also more durable than the old-fashioned three-brush, direct-current (dc) generator. Alternators come in a wide variety of sizes and shapes, and there are many internal differences.

Although alternators do not require current limiters, as did the old-style generator, they still need some kind of controlling device. These typically consist of a magnetic switch with

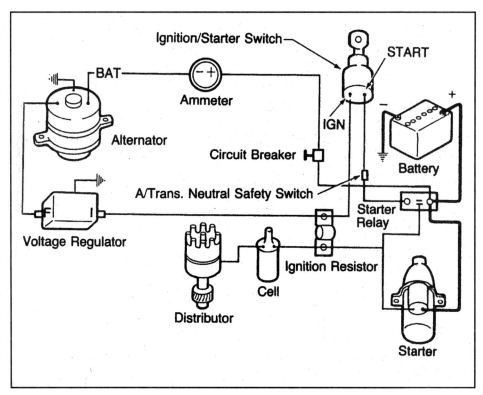

I have to be honest with you; Chrysler power is not as popular as it once was. Nevertheless, this is the Mopar ignition and charging circuit.

adjustable contact points, resistors and voltage windings. Most rod builders prefer alternators that incorporate voltage controls within the alternator itself.

The Lighting Circuit

The automotive lighting system includes—besides the battery, frame and wiring—all the lights and the various switches that control their use. There are a number of individual circuits, each having one or more lights, switches and the required conductors. In each separate circuit, the lights are connected in parallel—components are connected from one side of the circuit to the other. Each light has its own hot lead and ground to the chassis. The switches, though, are connected in series between the battery and the group of lamps they control. In series circuits, current flows from one unit to the next, and resistance is added

together to determine total circuit resistance.

Usually, one switch is used to control the individual circuit, regardless of how many units are on that circuit. An example is the parking light circuit, where one switch controls at least four lamps connected in parallel. In some cases, though, one switch controls the connection to the battery, while a selector switch determines which circuit will be placed in operation. The high-beam and low-beam headlight circuits are a good example of this. Yet another variation is the panel lighting circuit in which the main lighting switch controls the connection to the battery, and a panel-light rheostat controls the brightness of the panel lamps.

As already mentioned, relays are often used in circuits with a high current requirement. Besides reducing voltage loss, headlight-circuit relays are also used to increase the normal

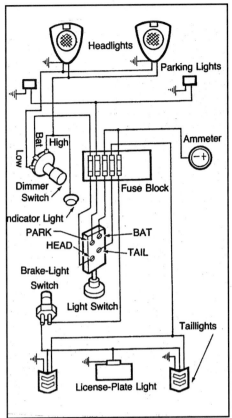

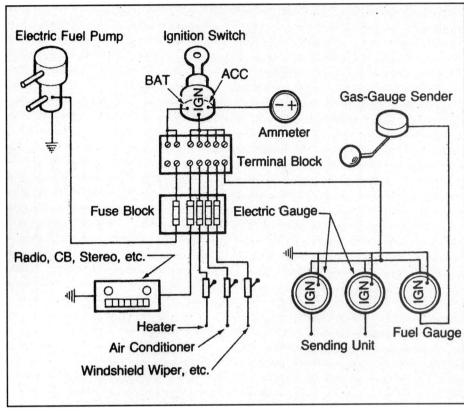

Maybe the Forty Ford headlight "doors" look a little hokey, but the lighting circuit is right on for the straightforward street rod.

Wiring gets a bit more generic when it comes to accessory and gauge circuits.

brilliance of the light. Those used in the lighting circuit are designed for continuous duty.

The Horn Circuit

There are two ways of laying out the horn circuit: One is in series with the battery, with the horn button going to ground. Another way is to insert a relay between the battery and horn. This latter method is better. When a relay is used in the circuit, the horn button acts only as a grounding switch and handles the relay-control current alone, resulting in less current through the switch.

By the way, the relay used in the horn circuit is not intended for heavy-duty use. It is designed for short, intermittent service and will overheat if

used continuously. Several variations in horn/relay circuits are possible depending upon the components used. I've included a general schematic suitable for most street rods. Some aftermarket horn kits include a specific diagram and indicate the appropriate relay.

Accessories & Gauge Circuits

All other electrical items fall into this general category. Typically, the circuits are traced from the battery to the switch (es) where they may divide and go to the individual accessory. Each accessory must be grounded to a steel body or the frame. It is usually best to actually use a ground wire rather than rely on the metal-to-metal contact of the component to the body or metal instrument panel.

Occasionally, rod builders use a two-wire system with a ground wire going

all the way to the battery rather than coming through the frame, but normally this isn't necessary. This is called a floating ground. Most accessories require a fuse, and many incorporate it within the hot lead. One or two fuses discreetly hidden out of sight—but always readily available—are fine, but too many bundled together is unsightly. Nothing beats a neat fuse panel.

WIRING DIAGRAMS

To the novice, the typical modern automotive wiring diagram is a puzzling crisscrossing of lines. All too often, every light bulb, appliance and accessory in the car is represented symbolically in a single, bewildering maze of circuitry. Therefore, pictorial representations of the starting, charging and ignition components are used to help the rodder develop the self-

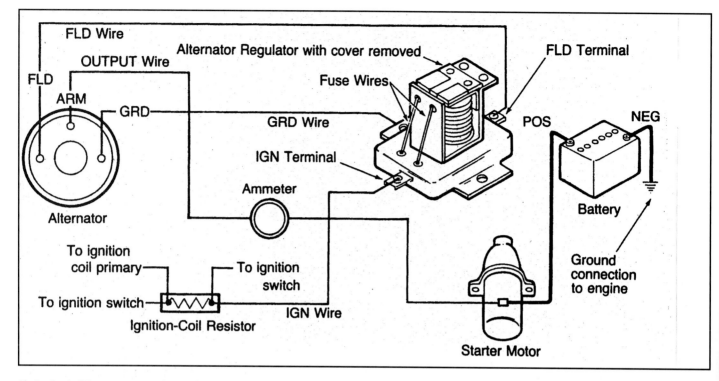

FLD Wire
OUTPUT Wire
Alternator Regulator with cover removed
FLD Terminal
FLD
ARM
GRD
Fuse Wires
GRD Wire
POS
NEG
IGN Terminal
Ammeter
Alternator
Battery
To ignition coil primary
To ignition switch
To ignition switch
Ground connection to engine
Ignition-Coil Resistor
IGN Wire
Starter Motor

If stock stuff is your game, the easiest voltage regulator to install for basic street rod wiring is the late 1970s Chrysler unit. Don't try to polarize the alternator, but make certain the negative post to the battery and regulator are well grounded, and take care not to ground the field circuit between the alternator and regulator.

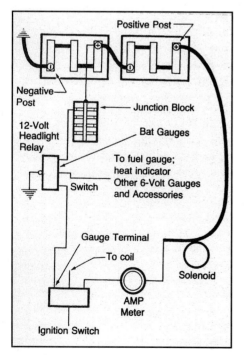

Positive Post
Negative Post
Junction Block
12-Volt Headlight Relay
Bat Gauges
To fuel gauge; heat indicator Other 6-Volt Gauges and Accessories
Switch
Gauge Terminal
To coil
Solenoid
AMP Meter
Ignition Switch

I considered dropping this diagram for the current edition, but I know there will always be a few street rodders who will want to keep original and still functional gauges. The best way is with two 6-volt batteries.

confidence necessary to take the job on. In addition, many of the circuits have been separated in the interest of clarity. (Of course, if you are installing new electronic gadgets, it's always best to use the wiring diagram supplied by the manufacturer.)

The First Step In Wiring A Street Rod

Before you jump into wiring your car, list all of the electrical components you plan to install, including the gauges and switches. Then, after studying the schematics, draw your own individual schematic. Try to lay out the system to scale, so you have some idea of how much wire you'll need. You can also get an idea of which wires will group together neatly.

The cost of the wire alone may be substantial, but don't cut corners—be generous estimating lengths. The

fewer splices you make the better.

Color-coding your system will aid any subsequent troubleshooting efforts. In addition, you will invariably want to add or change something down the road, and color-coding helps. Although all yellow wiring may look neat against a glossy black firewall, some day you'll pull your hair out—or maybe the wiring—trying to determine which wire goes to what.

Although most automotive parts houses carry five or six different wire colors, it's best to use a different color for every component. That could easily mean dozens of different color schemes. To obtain these, try a distributor that services professional wiring shops.

As you actually begin wiring, immediately record everything you do. Later draw a clean, permanent, color-coded diagram of the entire electrical

12-VOLT WIRE SIZE

Gauge	Safe Amperage
20-22	3 amps
18-19	5 amps
16-17	7 amps
14-15	15 amps
12-13	20 amps
10-11	25 amps

Gauge	Service
16	Headlights
16	Taillights
16	Parking Lights
16	Turn Signals
16	Electric Fan
16	Heater
16	A/C Switches
16	Electric Fuel Pump
16	Dash Instruments
16	Radio/Stereo/CB
16	Ignition
14	Alternator Field
10	Alternator "Bat"
10	Ammeter
10	Starter

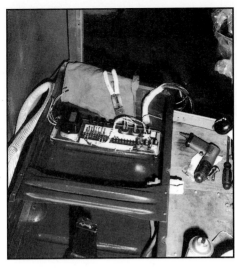

Smaller cockpits make it difficult to route wires and place components such as junction blocks or a stand-alone voltage regulator. Under the seat cushion is one location to consider, just make certain everything is well insulated. (You never know when you'll have an overweight passenger!)

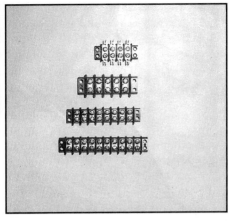

Junction blocks and quick disconnects allow the removal of electrical components without the need to cut or significantly uproot more than a foot or so of wiring.

system and carry it in your spec book. Take this precaution, and you'll never be out on a limb when minor problems arise.

Keep It Neat

Visually impressive wiring jobs require a certain artistic flair. Of course, that doesn't mean ordinary planning and patience won't be rewarded. Aside from the fact that those qualities are indispensable for correctness, they are exactly what will convert the mundane terminals and wire of your electrical system into something in which you can take pride.

Beyond that, much of the attractive-ness of automotive wiring is largely due to the varied and relatively inexpensive hardware available in most RV/trailer-supply houses. There are dozens of pieces that with a little ingenuity can be turned into shining examples of street rod detailing.

Special Tools

You don't need much in the way of tools and equipment to get on with the wiring; a pair of crimping and stripping pliers, a test light, a drill motor, and a couple of screwdrivers are essential. Nevertheless, there are some professional tools that you may want. The best place to buy these tools is, in most cases, specialty electronics parts houses. They have a wide selection of quality tools. Too many auto-parts stores carry inexpensive imported tools that are a waste of money.

ORGANIZING THE ELECTRICAL SYSTEM

The best way to organize the wiring is to run those for each system as an independent harness. For instance, all wiring for the headlight circuit should be in one harness, the wiring for the taillights in another, and so on. Moreover, although wiring is obviously a permanent part of the car, harnesses should be designed with junction blocks and quick disconnects to allow removal of electrical and mechanical units without the need to cut or significantly uproot the wiring.

Ready access in front of the firewall is of particular importance. You should always allow for the removal of the front sheet metal, motor and transmission. Rear placement of disconnects is a good idea, too; back fenders and deck lids may have to be removed for some reason later on.

In the interest of neatness and safety, pull the wires taut, and smooth out any kinks. The harness should be kept as straight as possible, and when bends are required, they should be graceful. Keep the harness away from sharp edges, places where it could be pinched, and by all means, the exhaust system. (A fire in my street rod years ago was caused by the installation of a new exhaust pipe too close to the elec-

This alternator is mounted on the differential housing—great for a clean-looking motor, but it is in a very hostile environment. Unless you only drive the car on dry Sundays. Beyond that, I wonder if there is enough exhaust heat to be detrimental to the diodes.

Solderless terminals have all but replaced those requiring solder for automotive use. Can't find what you want in this selection? Don't worry; this is only a small sampling of what is available.

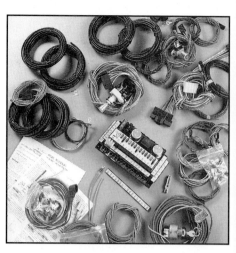

Ron Francis' Wire Works is the pioneer of street rod wiring kits. A copy of his multi-page catalog should be perused before you buy anything! Call (610) 485-1937 to inquire about a copy.

Finally there is the location of the battery. Through the years I put it just about everywhere except on the roof. My favorite location is in the trunk. I was least satisfied with an under-the-front fender location because it is a pain to service or disconnect unless you use a remote battery on/off switch. In my '41 pickup, it sits where Henry put it, and so far, so good. The reason for that choice is that a pickup doesn't have a trunk. By the way, the best cable for a remote location is the fine, multi-strand electric welder cable. Check it out at your local welding supply store.

tric fuel pump wiring.)

There are two schools of thought with regard to routing wiring—those who prefer to hide the wires so they can suddenly appear out of nowhere and shoot up to the component, and those who prefer neat, but visible wires. Of the two, my preference is the latter. Murphy's Law will get you if you hide too much wiring; ease of maintenance is a factor to consider. All you have to do to make the wiring blend into the background is to follow body and panel lines. Keep the harness off broad expanses of sheet metal where it stands out like a sore thumb.

The alternator and voltage regulator should be mounted on the starter side of the car whenever practical. This allows you to keep the charging and ignition circuit wire on one side of the motor.

Use the smallest tie wraps and clamps you can find to bundle your wiring. Don't try to get away with too few or go ape with too many. Space the ties out about every six inches, and the clamps every eight inches or so. Sheet-metal screws often look crude. My preference is for 8/32-inch machine screws. They are neater looking and more easily removed and replaced. Most early car sheet metal is thick enough for 8/32-inch threads.

If you really want to be neat, use loom tape—not electrical tape—to wrap the wires. Loom tape sticks to itself without adhesive; consequently, it's easy to unwrap.

Wiring Kits & Other Goodies

Just as with every other aspect of modern street rod building, enterprising manufacturers have dreamed up a number of wiring items that range from handy to indispensable. The most significant one in this field is the complete wiring kit. Other electrical system components are more mechanical in nature. Items such as alternator brackets that many manufacturers offer take some of the perplexity out of the finish-up. Others, like billet aluminum pulleys, are largely cosmetic, but every street rodder loves cosmetics.

If it's your first time, the task of wiring an entire car is undeniably a challenge. However, the complexity of that task doesn't justify the negative reputation all too often associated with it. Planning and patience will net you all the desired results.

THE INTERIOR & COSMETICS

25

In the natural order of street rod building, you should get serous about upholstery somewhere between wiring the car and painting it. Nevertheless, the work should begin after the car has been painted.

Start thinking about whether or not you will do your own upholstery work. Don't scoff at the idea without at least giving it some thought. It could be financially beneficial, if done properly. Upholstering your own car, especially in a conservative pattern, can save you as much as $5000 in labor charges. Assuming you purchase moderately priced materials at retail prices, rent an industrial sewing machine, and buy a few hand tools, total cost should be about half of the labor charges. Moreover, you end up with some tools and experience in the process.

If machine rental drags on for a year while you practice, the cost will increase accordingly. You don't have to make a decision just yet, just keep the thought in the back of your mind.

CLASSIC UPHOLSTERY MATERIALS

First and foremost, consider the type and quality of materials for your street rod interior. Pre-war Ford buyers had a limited number of materials from which to choose. Quoting from a 1940 Ford sales brochure: "Choice of striped mohair or broadcloth upholstery. Antique finish genuine leather for seat cushions and seat backs of Convertible Club Coupe."

In a small shop, the man behind the sewing machine—in this case, John Alduenda—is who you talk with when choosing designs and materials for your rod's interior. Study his fabric book carefully. Shops specializing in street rod work have seen it all, and are your best source of advice.

Real mohair, striped or otherwise, is made from the hair of the Angora goat. Such luxury was hardly deemed appropriate for Henry Ford's lowest priced production cars, however. What Henry called mohair, was a wool-based cloth in a pile weave with about 1/16-inch nap (fuzz). It may have been an economical material sixty-odd years ago, but it certainly was long-lasting. It was still serviceable in 1955

when I got my first '40, and I saw some decent original mohair in a well-preserved '40 in 2001. As might be expected, however, imitation or real, mohair is not cheap today.

Broadcloth, on the other hand, is a thick, closely woven wool-based fabric that is similar to mohair, but with a shorter nap. It is also stronger and more durable. For purposes of comparison, modern automotive-quality

255

Genuine leather, an upholstery material for centuries, always spells class, especially when it's draped over an equally classy Glide Engineering frame. Scientific methods of tanning have done little to reduce its cost, and leather is relatively difficult to work, but it remains very popular with street rodders.

There are many modern automotive upholstery materials, but one of the classics is velour, a closely napped, velvetlike fabric.

broadcloth is more expensive than the popular polyvinyl, but less costly than imitation mohair.

Leather, of course, needs no introduction. Imitations, synthetics, Poly, Esther and all their sisters may come and go as modern technology expands its scope. Nevertheless, genuine leather, a garment and upholstery material that reaches back to antiquity, always has and always will spell real class. Although there is hardly any shortage of leather—there are a million surplus dairy cattle in this country—scientific methods of tanning have done little to reduce its cost. Beyond that, leather is relatively difficult to work with, even for the professional upholsterer.

The omission of any mention of carpet and headliner in the early Ford brochure is not an oversight. The buyer of a brand-new 1940 Ford didn't have any choice. Only prestige cars of the day had carpeting, and this was expensive cut-pile wool. The front floorboards of the low-priced three were covered in wall-to-wall rubber mats, much like economy pickups of today. Rear-seat passengers were treated to a little more class. They rested their feet on a rubberized pile horsehair mat.

The doors were usually upholstered in a special sidewall material, a cotton/wool blend similar to, but lighter than broadcloth. Headliner material in the low-priced prewar car was a cotton/wool combination. Inasmuch as it suffered the least occupant abuse, it was a little lighter weight than sidewall material.

MODERN UPHOLSTERY MATERIALS

Leather, wool, and other time-honored organic materials began to price themselves out of the automotive market by the 1930s, paving the way for synthetics, which today dominate the upholstery field.

"Leatherette" was the popular name for a material technically known as pyroxylin, a coarse cloth coated with a nitrocellulose compound. It was developed in the 1920s and lays claim to being the first synthetic automobile upholstery material. Even so, it didn't appear in many production automobiles until the 1940s. Its use was primarily confined to door panels and the like because it did not stretch easily. (A certain amount of elasticity is an indispensable characteristic of upholstery materials used on seats.)

Another significant addition to the roster of synthetic textiles arrived with DuPont's invention of nylon. Introduced in the mid 1930s, it immediately found great favor everywhere in the industrial world except for automotive fabrics. It seemingly had everything going for it—it could be manufactured economically, dyed, stretched, and would last forever. However, it wouldn't retain heat or absorb moisture and was unpleasant to sit on for long periods. In time, however, a combination of nylon, cotton and acetate—still another synthetic fiber—overcame many of the shortcomings. As a result, blends began to be accepted for a variety of automotive upholstery applications.

The big news in upholstery fabrics, however, was the discovery of polyvinyl. This synthetic material, manufactured by a chemical process (polymerization) that links natural and synthetic compounds (thermoplastic resins) together, made its automotive debut in the late 1940s. However, it wasn't until the flexible plastic was backed up with a twill cloth that its utility was fully recognized. Polyvinyl, or simply vinyl, can truly be said to have revolutionized custom

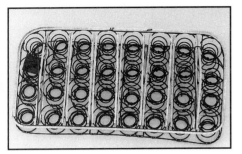

The most significant problem when upholstering an original or mild custom interior is usable seat cushions. The restoration components folks have a variety authentic reproductions, and street rod companies such as Glide Engineering scratch-build a wide array of frames and seats for popular rod models, factory fresh and ready for the trimmer.

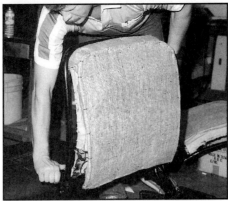

If they aren't too far gone, the trimmer can repair the original frame and spring cushion and install new padding and foam rubber.

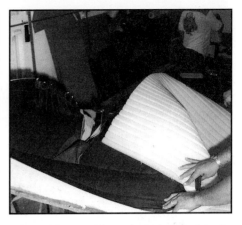

Pleated foam rubber—under several trade names—is a staple of the custom upholstery shop. The sewn covering is then fitted to the foam.

automotive interiors.

It is the first material you probably thought of when you began to ponder your street rod interior. No wonder, fully 90 percent of all street rods completed since the 1950s have had vinyl interiors. The most common brand, of course, is Uniroyal's Naugahyde®, a registered trademark. Other brands of similar synthetics include Goodrich's Koroseal® and General Tire's Bolta®. Like nylon, fiberglass, and other trademarks that have lost their capitalization and become part of our language, "naugahyde" simply stands for any kind of polyvinyl automotive upholstery to most of us.

There are several grades of automotive polyvinyl. One with only a twill or knit backing has relatively little elasticity. Better grades have a thin layer of foam rubber between the vinyl and cloth backing. Commonly called expanded vinyl, it is preferred for most custom interiors. Expanded vinyl has a pleasant, soft feel that adds a leather-like luxury to a seat. Quality vinyl is stain resistant and colorfast (fade proof) in almost all cases. Even when casually maintained, it will last for many years.

If you are not aware of the hundreds of vinyl colors and surface textures available, you will be when the upholsterer opens his samples book. Choosing one is not an easy task. It is far more difficult, in fact, than choosing a paint color. Nevertheless, it is, and will probably remain, the fabric of choice for street rods.

There are a number of upholstery materials other than thermoplastics. You can see a fair representation in any new car showroom. Those that are used in both production cars as well as show cars include all the aforementioned woven fabrics and their look-alike imitations. There's also a wide variety of wool, cotton and synthetic blends such as crushed velvet, velour, corduroy and even blue denim.

The primary advantage of these fabrics is that they better conform to irregular seat and cushion shapes than does polyvinyl, but most are not nearly as wear-resistant or stain-resistant as vinyl. Nevertheless, cloth, with its vast pattern, texture and color variety, has a special luxury all its own. In addition, the better grades are specially treated to resist permanent staining.

PATTERNS & POLYFOAMS

There was a time when every street rod simply had to have a pleat-and-roll interior. Even today, the traditional look is still considered somewhat in style. An equal, if not a greater number of interior designs, however, owe their origins to the multitude of patterns found in new cars. After all, both foreign and domestic manufacturers spend fortunes on the best artistic talent available in an effort to achieve a competitive edge. You could do worse than to draw a few ideas from their offerings.

A lot of the labor in building a complicated custom interior has been avoided with polyurethane "foam rubber." It is available in several molded designs as well as a number of thicknesses and densities. In fact, Polyfoam—a trademark of General Tire—is the mainstay of most auto upholstery shops. It is used for both structural and padding purposes. There's even an extremely dense variety that can be used in seat cushions without springs; more than one builder of a channeled roadster or rumble-seated car has found it useful and reasonably comfortable. Thanks to Polyfoam, horsehair and cotton, once the major automotive seat-padding materials, are seldom used.

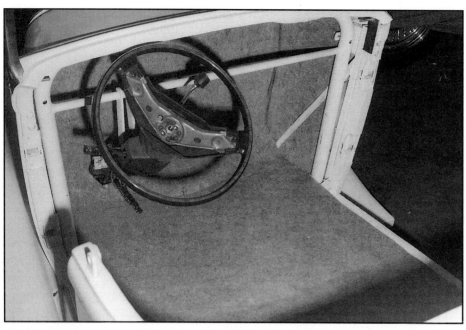

Street rod upholstery involves much more than seats. What you can't see is the sound deadening provided by jute and felt padding under the carpeting, door panels, trunk area, and headliner.

The most important step is getting good chrome—and saving difficult to replace pieces—is to discuss what you have with the shop owner. Point out the Ford logo (arrow) and that you want it to stay as crisp as possible. Full service shops can even do a bit of metal repair before the part goes into the tanks.

Another type of sound deadener—3M's Body Schutz—is easily applied with a spray gun in the home workshop, and goes where nothing else can.

the case of upholstery design, the ultimate choice is yours.

DO-IT-YOURSELF UPHOLSTERY?

What we put off before must now be dealt with—should you attempt doing your own upholstery? I can only give a thumbnail sketch with a few photographs and text on the pros and cons of the materials. The technique of machine sewing is something I'll have to defer to HPBooks' *Auto Upholstery & Interiors* by Bruce Caldwell. The need for skill and experience will become apparent the first time you try to pass a scrap of cloth through the sewing machine. Just like automotive bodywork and painting, automotive upholstery is a skilled trade. A botched job in these areas will not only reek of amateurism, material cost will be the same as for a top-quality job.

CHROME PLATING

Every experienced rod builder can sing at least one sad song when it comes to chrome plating. For instance,

CARPETING

The final major material used in custom upholstery is that for carpeting. Quality street rod interiors require "100 percent nylon." Although that percentage may be questionable, it is best for both beauty and long life. Two designs are typically available: loop pile, which has the edge with regard to durability, and cut pile, which many agree is the best looking. Both are available in various pile lengths. As in

The man at the chrome shop's buffing wheel is responsible for the health of your parts. His skill must be the best. From there the work piece goes into a series of chemical baths. Upon its removal, it is inspected for flaws before delivery to the customer.

years ago my original die-cast hood ornament was misplaced; a second was dissolved in de-chroming bath. Still another fellow's coveted embossed grille guard had FORD buffed right out of the steel! Make no mistake about it, chrome work is tricky. Not just the electrochemistry of the plating process, mind you, but the handling and storage of small parts and, most importantly, what takes place at the buffing and polishing wheels.

It should be obvious, therefore, that you should learn the in-and-outs of chrome plating services in order to avail yourself of all of the benefits, and to forestall problems,

If you want top-notch service rather than the lowest price, it's usually best to deal with a small, owner-operated shop. The man who has his pride invested in the product being turned out is most likely to give you the best work consistently. When you get the bill, you can feel confident you're getting the value for which you're about to pay.

This is not to say that you can't get good service from big plating shops. It is true, however, that the day-to-day demands of a volume production facility invariably put them at odds with the off-the-street, one-time customer who brings in a couple of bumpers and a box full of old car parts.

As always, ask questions and get opinions from street rodders in your area. Good will and word-of-mouth recommendations are what keep high-quality, low-volume shops in business.

Before metal can be plated, it must be thoroughly cleaned. Grease is removed from the work piece by soaking it in a hot alkaline solution, then vigorously hand scrubbing it when removed. If the piece was previously chromed, it must be de-plated. It is placed in a special tank containing sulfuric acid that removes the old plating by drawing it off to a lead cathode when direct current is introduced. If the part to be plated is rusty, another process is typically used—"pickling." The part is immersed for a short time in hydrochloric acid.

The use of acids brings several non-human concerns to mind, however. One is obvious—acids break down the molecular structure of most metals. Die-cast parts are particularly vulnerable. Although die-cast parts aren't pickled, no chrome shop can positively guarantee that an ancient grille or hood ornament will survive the basic plating process unscathed. So, when you bring in your die-cast jewels, be sure to impress the proprietor with the fact that they are near irreplaceable.

Hydrogen Embrittlement

Another problem (not quite so obvious as a complete disappearing act) is the dreaded hydrogen embrittlement. Part of the hydrogen released during the plating process is absorbed into the steel, which causes brittleness in certain alloys. Spring steels are particularly susceptible. Other than short pickling times, most remedies—which consist primarily of oven baking—are not easily resolved with regard to decorative electroplating.

Decorative chrome is a fact of life for all street rod builders, however, so a certain amount of risk must be assumed. Nevertheless, based on some rather extensive aircraft research done many years ago, I will repeat my oft given advice against chroming critical suspension and steering components such as springs and load-bearing shafts, arms and critical bracketry. In a word, don't.

The Perils of Buffing

The greatest cosmetic hazard in chrome work is buffing a part prior to plating. Buffing metal to a glass-smooth, bright sheen is necessary for beautiful plating. The problem is that proper buffing of metal, steel as well as die-cast, is a tender, gentle operation that simply requires a lot of experience—and an operator who cares.

When checking out a plating shop, start by asking about the tenure and intelligence of the employee who will buff your parts. Does that sound pompous? Too bad! Putting it bluntly, some shops are not cautious about the brainpower of workers assigned to the polishing and buffing room. In such a place, take great pains to explain just how important that hood ornament is to you, and that its exact shape and design be faithfully retained. If your little speech doesn't filter through, however, you're wasting your time. Don't risk your part. If you're in doubt as to the savvy of the buffer, leave. If you don't, you may be sorry.

The Plating Process

Technically, electroplating is adhering a metallic coating to the surface of another metal using direct electric current (DC). The basic process in use today differs little from the one George and Henry Elkington patented in England in 1840. The Elkington system was designed for silver plate, but except for the different chemicals used in various plating baths, all electroplating processes are the same.

Top-quality automotive chrome is a three-step process, thus the term triple plating. The piece is first copper plated, then nickel plated, then finally chromium plated.

Problems You May Face

As mentioned above, die-cast parts are the most delicate items you are likely to bring to the plating shop. If you are street rodding vintage tin, and if quality reproduction parts are not available, you and the plater must take great care with them.

If the old chrome is badly pitted, expensive reclamation may be required. The trouble is, once started, pitting is extremely difficult to stop. Die-castings poured before World War II were made with low melting-temperature alloys of zinc, tin and lead. Moisture that was unavoidably absorbed over the decades resulted in more pitting than meets the eye—it is

Aluminum polishing has been called the "tender art." The metal is soft and buffs away easily. Aside from that, the parts street rodders bring to polishing shops are extra challenging. They are full of tight curves and crevasses.

also under the chrome plating. So, after stripping off the old plating, the part should be carefully inspected. If the pitting is not so extensive as to render it worthless, heavy copper plating and very careful buffing may save marginal items. Heavy-handed buffing of the pitted area before copper plating only results in dips and low spots.

Often, previously chromed steel parts such as bumpers will require repairs. Careless welding of plated parts invariably captures some chrome in the basis metal. This will create problems during subsequent chroming. In short, repairs to steel parts scheduled for rechroming must be made after de-plating. That may mean two trips to the plating shop, but that's part of the price for quality work.

Finally, some fellows never get the message. Chrome plating is thin. A lot

of good chrome has been ruined at home by polishing it with rubbing compounds, scouring cleansers and even mildly abrasive polish. Even some of the so-called chrome cleaners are abrasive. Most good chrome will easily clean up with ammoniated liquid window cleaners such as Windex, etc. Given gentle cleaning and the protection of non-abrasive carnauba wax, the luster and sparkle of quality chrome should last for years.

METAL POLISHING

Although part of the chrome-plating process, polishing is a decorative process in and of itself. This is particularly true with regard to aluminum and stainless steel components typically used on a street rod.

If you need a reason to justify metal polishing beyond just good looks, you need to look no further than the ease with which a once handsome intake manifold quickly takes on an unpleasant scuzzy appearance. Fresh cast aluminum is porous, and inevitably shows gasoline, oil and crankcase vapor stains. And, regardless of how diligently you apply the elbow grease and all the many scouring agents available at the supermarket, a manifold just never seems to come clean.

Polishing a new or recently sand-blasted item such as an intake manifold may be too much to handle at home. Several specialized tools and a box full of supplies are required plus a fair amount of experience. After all, aluminum is soft, and mistakes are commonly made even by those who are considered experts. In short, first-time polishing should be left to a professional who cares.

This is not to say that once your parts have been professionally polished, that you shouldn't repolish them after a year or so of street duty. Many hardware chains sell metal-polishing kits and supplies. Therefore, if you have a quarter-horse electric motor and a flexible shaft with a chuck, you can easily bring back the good looks of that aluminum intake manifold. It just takes time and patience.

Another workshop task to take on is periodic machine buffing of the stainless steel exterior trim with which early Fords are lavishly adorned. Just because they are "stainless" doesn't mean they won't lose some of their gleam over the years. However, their luster comes back after only an hour or two are invested in removing and polishing them.

Anodizing is an electrochemical process designed to obtain a controlled surface oxidation. Once anodized, the sur-face can absorb a special dye. Anodizing in and of itself provides an excellent barrier against corrosion. Unfortunately, only aluminum alloys can be anodized. Anodizing shops can also spray the dyed part with a clear enamel coat- and then oven-bake it for durability.

ALTERNATIVES TO CHROME

What's that you say? You're tired of everyday, belly-button, chrome-plated ornamentation, and you want your street rod to wear something different? No problem. There are a number of other decorative treatments. Some are quite inexpensive as well.

Almost all of the options, however, require metal polishing. There's just no way to bring luster to a rough surface. Admittedly, polishing is a labor-intensive operation, which means it's expensive to farm out, or time consuming at home.

Copper & Nickel Plating

As mentioned above, the rich, reddish gold color of copper plating offers an alternative to chrome in a dry, protected environment such as the cockpit. I wouldn't recommend it for engine or exterior work, however. The same is true of nickel-plating, with or without the copper underplate. Nickel will also tarnish, but it can be polished from time to time just like silver. Its silver-like luster can be an interesting addition to any interior.

Anodizing

Anodizing is a common term in street rod parlance, although many rod builders don't quite understand exactly what it is. Technically, anodizing is an invisible electrochemical process designed to obtain a controlled surface oxidation with a depth of a few thousandths of an inch. By itself, it is not decorative per se, but once anodized, the surface can absorb a special dye. Beyond that, anodizing provides an excellent barrier against corrosion. The confusion stems from the often-overlooked fact that only aluminum alloys can be anodized.

261

Dyes for anodized aluminum are available in a wide variety of colors: black, blue, navy blue, bluish green, bronze, brown, olive brown, red brown, yellow brown, gold, orange, golden orange, red, fiery red, violet, red violet, blue violet, turquoise, yellow and brass yellow. Moreover, if that's not quite enough choice, anodizing is a perfect "primer," in that it adds excellent paint-gripping characteristics to normally hard-to-paint aluminum.

Anodizing and color impregnation is a relatively inexpensive basic process. That, of course, does not include the cost of polishing. (For color with a gleam, the part should be professionally polished. The "as-shipped" sandblasted finish of most sand-cast aluminum parts such as intake manifolds, will have a kind of dull, dark appearance after dyeing.) Unfortunately, diecast aluminum parts such as valve covers sometimes do not accept the dye well. Talk it over with the shop foreman or merely have them polished.

Incidentally, first-class anodizing shops can spray the dyed part with a clear enamel coat and then oven-bake it. The extra cost is worthwhile if you want long-lasting good looks.

Perhaps you are contemplating one of the more exotic colors. Tastefully applied, these can be striking. You should be aware that they are more expensive, and that it normally takes longer to get them back. The process is not different, but no shop can mix an unusual dye bath just for your one part. If you do decide to get something exotic, bring the part in long before you need it. When the shop schedules a commercial run of that particular color, your part can be more economically dyed.

Brass Plating

Speaking of luster, what about that old favorite of the Roaring Twenties—brass plate? You don't see much of it anywhere except on Fad T rods. That's a pity. Brass, an alloy of copper and zinc, is less costly than chrome, but requires more maintenance. In tasteful application, it just might be what sets your car apart from the rest.

Cadmium Plating

Cad plating has a number of adherents among the more frugal street-rod builders. No wonder, a polished and silver-white cad-plated part costs only a fraction of what it would cost if it were chrome plated. Cad plating is available in two major varieties: silver-white (Type 1), and iridescent gold (Type 2). Cad iridite, (Type 2), has the edge with regard to corrosion resistance. For long plating life, ask for a clear bright dip.

Cad plating has an added advantage in that parts such as hood springs, which can be severely weakened by hydrogen embrittlement if chrome-plated, can be oven-baked to significantly reduce the problem. My admonition against any kind of electroplating on suspension springs still stands, however. They should only be painted.

Metal Spraying

This process consists of passing a metal wire through a special torch where it is melted and sprayed under high pressure onto the surface of a metal component. The types of wire usually sprayed include aluminum (the most popular), brass, bronze, copper, lead, Monel and stainless steel. Note that sprayed stainless steel doesn't look as attractive as what you may be accustomed to seeing. It turns gray-

black under the heat and pressure of the application process.

The only preparation required prior to metal spraying is sandblasting. This gets the part clean. Before you take your parts to the shop, however, grind off any casting or welding imperfections.

Most metal spraying is reasonably priced. If applied thickly enough, aluminum coatings can be polished. As is, aluminum will have a tendency to absorb oil and discolor, but sealers can be used to reduce this problem.

Porcelainizing

This process unquestionably has the look of classic quality. Many classic cars of the 1920s had porcelainized exhaust and intake manifolds for long lasting, easily maintained beauty. Porcelain is a translucent ceramic made of pure clay and is available in various colored fusible materials.

Not every locality will have a porcelain shop interested in street rod work, but if you have access to one, it offers—at a cost roughly comparable to quality chrome—a handsome decorative coating simply not found on every rod that shows up at the drive-in on Cruise Night. The best parts for porcelainizing are made of steel or cast iron. The process is not recommended for stainless-steel alloys, nor will porcelainizing endure on aluminum, brass or bronze. High thermal-shock porcelain compounds in dark colors are recommended for most automotive components.

A part slated for porcelainizing is first oven-baked for several hours to drive out as much grease and carbon as possible. It is then sandblasted to eliminate the scale. When spotlessly clean, both inside and out, a thick porcelain

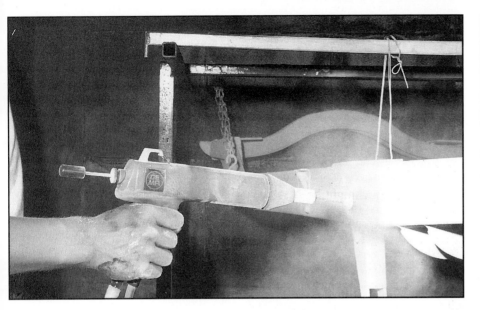

Old-time street rodders painted their Model A frames with a 10¢ can of Woolworth's best enamel. If you want durability today, have your chassis treated to baked-on epoxy powder paint. It'll outlast you.

Ron Cole's coupe is a great example of contemporary street rod interiors.

coating is sprayed on. The part is then dried over a low gas flame before being subjected to oven-baking at 1400 degrees F for several more hours. When the part has cooled, it will exhibit a smooth, glossy finish.

Powder Coating

Most decorative finishes so far described, in varying degrees, must be treated with respect. Some, such as porcelain, are downright delicate. However, if you require maximum rough-and-tumble durability, baked-on epoxy finishes, often called powder paints or powder coatings, are for you.

The materials used in this process—special epoxy powders—are fine, free floating "dusts" that are sprayed on with a special gun. The fancy name for this operation is electrostatic deposition. It is similar to the phenomenon that permits a comb to attract a piece of paper. The powder adheres to the part after it's baked in an oven at 300 degrees F for approximately 30 minutes. During baking, it melts and flows out with almost as much gloss as porcelain.

Powdered epoxy coatings offer excellent resistance to routine abrasive mishaps and most solvents except ordinary brake fluid. The powders are available in a number of standard industrial high-gloss colors, including red, green, yellow, orange, black, white and exotic hues as candy apple.

The range of uses for powder coatings is nearly limitless with the obvious exception of nonmetal components or any assemblies that cannot be baked. Powder coatings have been successfully used on wheels, suspension components, entire street rod frames, window moldings, engine blocks, bumper brackets, and all manner of accessory items. It, too, is surprisingly inexpensive compared to chrome or even conventional painting.

ADD WARMTH TO YOUR STREET ROD

Before I close this section, I think you should be aware that sometimes the decorative processes I've discussed are just a bit . . . well, for want of a better word, cold, sometimes even austere.

Chrome, in particular has a way of giving this feeling to those who don't have a true appreciation of engineering that goes beyond strict utilitarianism. This is not to say that chrome and the like, tastefully assigned here and there, doesn't add great beauty to any street rod. We all know better. These embellishments are, for the most part, best restricted to the engine compartment. Even though ours is obviously a mechanical hobby, the car doesn't have to be all nuts and bolts.

Yet, how are we to put some warmth in the cockpit or add a splash of light-hearted zest to the exterior? Furry dice dangling from the rearview mirror or fuzzy dogs brainlessly bobbing their heads back and forth sure won't do it. It has to be a little more subtle and much less campy than that.

Well, one of the time-honored methods of adding warmth to the interior is through what is called wood tones. Wood tones can be classic wood-grained paint schemes or simply brown and tan colors on metal or plastic components. On the other hand, if you want to return to a grander era than this, the age of synthetics—try real wood!

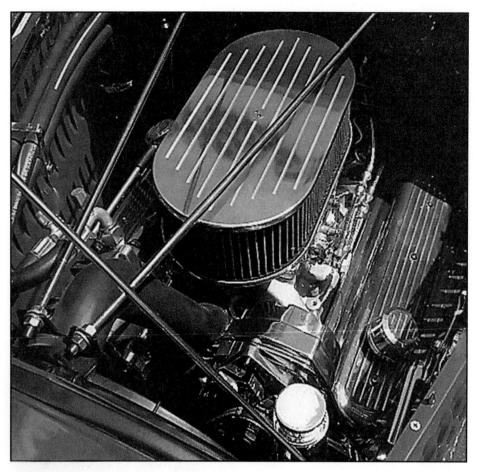

When it comes to chrome, polished aluminum, stainless steel and all the other cosmetic possibilities, as always, the key is to keep it simple!

Your choice of interior colors is naturally one of personal taste and preference. Nevertheless, I sincerely hope that holdouts for the early 1950s imitation zebra and leopard skin or checkered-flag patterns have long since abandoned street rods for mountain climbing or some other equally hazardous sport. Wood tones, however, do fit in with most modern street rod interior schemes.

Walnut and mahogany are the favored furniture woods for automotive interiors.

The best areas for that bit of wood tone warmth are dashboards, custom consoles, and of course, steering wheels. There is also an abundance of aftermarket and reproduction door handle and window crank hardware, that when sparingly used, eases the task of attractive interior decorating. Moderation, however, is always the byword.

Softening & Highlighting the Exterior

Only slightly less important than the interior, when it comes to deburring the mechanical excesses of a street rod, is a touch of softness in exterior paint scheme and graphics. The best all around approach to that end is pin striping. Your car shouldn't look like some automotive rendition of the tattooed man in the circus, but gentle accenting of the bodylines and particular styling features can make even a candy apple brick look good. If you've found a local pin striper talented enough to adorn your car, chances are his artistic judgment is astute enough to tell him when to quit. To determine this, have a look at some of his work. He should be able to show you photos of several examples.

Frank Oddo is a veteran street rodder. He fell in love with street rodding when he took his first ride in a hopped-up Ford coupe in 1951 at the age of 14. He published his first street rod article in *Rod & Custom Magazine* in 1968. During the intervening years, he has publicly revealed his fascination with high-performance "old cars" in hundreds of articles and columns on the subject. Just one example of such prolific endeavor is the phrase "fat fendered" that is today commonly used in reference to 1938–40 Fords. Oddo coined it in a series of articles published in *Street Rodder Magazine* beginning in 1972. Oddo was the first, if not the only, freelance photographer ever to gain permission to photograph street rods and custom trucks at Disneyland. Moreover, he did it three times.

Oddo not only writes about street rods, he's a hot rodder/street rodder through and through. He has built and raced roadsters at the National Speed Trials on the Bonneville Salt Flats and on El Mirage, the Southern California dry lake that has hosted hot rod time trials since the end of World War II. For a while, Oddo held a Street Roadster record in the late '70s, and a Blown Gas Lakester record in the late 1990s. He still campaigns his 225-mph, Ford Boss 302 belly tank lakester at El Mirage and Bonneville.

Nevertheless, it is as "Mister Forty Ford" as *Hot Rod Magazine* once called him, that he is best known to his readership. A title such as that doesn't come easily. It certainly begins with the long-term ownership of a 1940 Ford. Oddo reports that he has not been without a 1940 DeLuxe Coupe since acquiring his first in 1955. His current example includes parts from that coupe, and every other he's owned since then, and more photos of it have appeared in magazine tech and how-to articles than any other Forty in existence.

Oddo, as one of the charter members of Forties Limited, a Southern California street rod club organized in 1968, associate editor and technical editor of *Street Rodder Magazine* in the 1970s, and a freelancer since, has been in postwar street rodding almost from its beginning.

In this enviable position he has not only been there when things happened, he has been able to record them for posterity!

HANDBOOKS
Auto Electrical Handbook: 0-89586-238-7/HP1238
Auto Upholstery & Interiors: 1-55788-265-7/HP1265
Car Builder's Handbook: 1-55788-278-9/HP1278
Cooling Systems: 1-55788-425-0/HP1425
The Lowrider's Handbook: 1-55788-383-1/HP1383
Powerglide Transmission Handbook:1-55788-355-6/HP1355
Street Rodder's Handbook, Rev.: 1-55788-409-9/HP1409
Torqueflite A-727 Transmission Handbook:1-55788-399-8/HP1399
Turbo Hydramatic 350 Handbook: 0-89586-051-1/HP1051
Welder's Handbook: 1-55788-264-9/HP1264

BODYWORK & PAINTING
Automotive Detailing: 1-55788-288-6/HP1288
Automotive Paint Handbook: 1-55788-291-6/HP1291
Fiberglass & Composite Materials: 1-55788-239-8/HP1239
Metal Fabricator's Handbook: 0-89586-870-9/HP1870
Paint & Body Handbook: 1-55788-082-4/HP1082
Pro Paint & Body: 1-55788-394-7/HP1394
Sheet Metal Handbook: 0-89586-757-5/HP1757

INDUCTION
Bosch Fuel Injection Systems: 1-55788-365-3/HP1365
Holley 4150: 0-89586-047-3/HP1047
Holley Carbs, Manifolds & F.I.: 1-55788-052-2/HP1052
Rochester Carburetors: 0-89586-301-4/HP1301
Turbochargers: 0-89586-135-6/HP1135
Weber Carburetors: 0-89586-377-4/HP1377

PERFORMANCE
Baja Bugs & Buggies: 0-89586-186-0/HP1186
Big-Block Chevy Performance: 1-55788-216-9/HP1216
Big-Block Mopar Performance: 1-55788-302-5/HP1302
Bracket Racing: 1-55788-266-5/HP1266
Brake Systems: 1-55788-281-9/HP1281
Camaro Performance: 1-55788-057-3/HP1057
Chassis Engineering: 1-55788-055-7/HP1055
Chevy Trucks: 1-55788-340-8/HP1340
Ford Windsor Small-Block Performance: 1-55788-323-8/HP1323
4Wheel&Off-Road's Chassis & Suspension: 1-55788-406-4/HP1406
Honda/Acura Engine Performance: 1-55788-384-X/HP1384
High Performance Hardware: 1-55788-304-1/HP1304
How to Hot Rod Big-Block Chevys: 0-912656-04-2/HP104
How to Hot Rod Small-Block Chevys: 0-912656-06-9/HP106
How to Hot Rod Small-Block Mopar Engine Revised: 1-55788-405-6
How to Hot Rod VW Engines: 0-912656-03-4/HP103
How to Make Your Car Handle: 0-912656-46-8/HP146
How to Modify Your Jeep Chassis/Suspension for
Offroad: 1-55788-424
John Lingenfelter: Modify Small-Block Chevy: 1-55788-238-X/HP1238
LS1/LS6 Small-Block Chevy Performance: 1-55788-407-2/HP1407
Mustang 5.0 Projects: 1-55788-275-4/HP1275
Mustang Performance (Engines): 1-55788-193-6/HP1193
Mustang Performance 2 (Chassis): 1-55788-202-9/HP1202
Mustang Perf. Chassis, Suspension, Driveline Tuning: 1-55788-387-4
Mustang Performance Engine Tuning: 1-55788-387-4/HP1387
1001 High Performance Tech Tips: 1-55788-199-5/HP1199
Performance Ignition Systems: 1-55788-306-8/HP1306
Small-Block Chevy Performance: 1-55788-253-3/HP1253
Small-Block Chevy Engine Buildups: 1-55788-400-5/HP1400
Stock Car Setup Secrets: 1-55788-401-3/HP1401
Tuning Accel/DFI 6.0 Programmable F.I.: 1-55788-413-7/HP1413

ENGINE REBUILDING
Engine Builder's Handbook: 1-55788-245-2/HP1245
How to Rebuild Small-Block Chevy LT-1/LT-4: 1-55788-393-9/HP1393
Rebuild Aircooled VW Engines: 0-89586-225-5/HP1225
Rebuild Big-Block Chevy Engines: 0-89586-175-5/HP1175
Rebuild Big-Block Ford Engines: 0-89586-070-8/HP1070
Rebuild Big-Block Mopar Engines: 1-55788-190-1/HP1190
Rebuild Ford V-8 Engines: 0-89586-036-8/HP1036
Rebuild GenV/Gen VI Big-Block Chevy: 1-55788-357-2/HP1357
Rebuild Small-Block Chevy Engines: 1-55788-029-8/HP1029
Rebuild Small-Block Ford Engines: 0-912656-89-1/HP189
Rebuild Small-Block Mopar Engines: 0-89586-128-3/HP1128

RESTORATION, MAINTENANCE, REPAIR
Camaro Owner's Handbook ('67–'81): 1-55788-301-7/HP1301
Camaro Restoration Handbook ('67–'81): 0-89586-375-8/HP1375
Classic Car Restorer's Handbook: 1-55788-194-4/HP1194
How to Maintain & Repair Your Jeep: 1-55788-371-8/HP1371
Mustang Restoration Handbook ('64–'70): 0-89586-402-9/HP1402
Tri-Five Chevy Owner's Handbook ('55–'57): 1-55788-285-1/HP1285

GENERAL REFERENCE
Auto Math Handbook: 1-55788-020-4 /HP1020
Corvette Tech Q&A: 1-55788-376-9/HP1376
Ford Total Performance, 1962–1970: 1-55788-327-0/HP1327
Guide to GM Muscle Cars: 1-55788-003-4/HP1003
The VW Beetle: 1-55788-421-8/HP1421

MARINE
Big-Block Chevy Marine Performance: 1-55788-297-5/HP1297
Small Block Chevy Marine Performance: 1-55788-317-3/HP1317

ORDER YOUR COPY TODAY!
All books can be purchased at your favorite retail or online bookstore (use ISBN number), or auto parts store (Use HP part number). You can also order direct from HPBooks by calling toll-free at 800-788-6262, ext. 1.